The Global Advertising Regulation Handbook

The Global Advertising Regulation Handbook

MARY ALICE SHAVER and SOONTAE AN, Editors
Foreword by JEAN J. BODDEWYN

M.E.Sharpe
Armonk, New York
London, England

To my family, Hyun Seung and Frances Jin
—Soontae An

To Dan and our family, who wouldn't let me give up
—Mary Alice Shaver

Library of Congress Cataloging-in-Publication Data

The global advertising regulation handbook / Edited by Mary Alice Shaver and
Soontae An.
    pages cm
  Includes index.
  ISBN 978-0-7656-2968-5 (hardcover : alk. paper)—ISBN 978-0-7656-2969-2
(pbk. : alk. paper) 1. Advertising laws. I. Shaver, Mary Alice, editor.
II. An, Soontae, 1968- editor.
  K3844.G56 2013
  343.08'2–dc23   2013004787

Printed in the United States of America

The paper used in this publication meets the minimum requirements of
American National Standard for Information Sciences
Permanence of Paper for Printed Library Materials,
ANSI Z 39.48-1984.

~

IBT (c)   10   9   8   7   6   5   4   3   2   1
SP (p)   10   9   8   7   6   5   4   3   2   1

CONTENTS

FOREWORD

Jean J. Boddewyn

Laws and regulations pertaining to advertising go back hundreds of years, but the French claim that their 1935 self-regulatory body was the first one in the world. Shortly thereafter, in 1937, the International Chamber of Commerce (ICC; Paris) issued its first advertising guidelines, which started with the principle: "All advertising should be legal, decent, honest and truthful" (ICC 1937/2011). I cite these dates because they reveal a paradox in the study of self-regulation—namely, that it has long been in operation in the field of advertising, but students of the currently hot topic of codes of conduct and other forms of voluntary industry self-regulation are barely aware of its nearly 80-year history. Therefore, this volume of country analyses of obligatory laws and regulations as well as of voluntary self-regulatory guidelines bearing on advertising practice is much needed and most welcome as a necessary addition to the current global searches for a balance between public and private controls of business behaviors.

This book—a result of the laudable initiative of Professor Mary Alice Shaver—is also most welcome because there has been a dearth of analyses of advertising self-regulation since the 1980s and early 1990s, when researchers (mainly from the United States) conducted many national and international studies of this practice (Boddewyn 1988, 1992; Neelankavil and Stridsberg 1980). To be sure, there have been many more recent articles referring to voluntary codes of conduct in the advertising of particular products—liquor, for instance—in various countries (Wolburg and Venger 2009) and to the effectiveness of advertising self-regulation in general (Rotfeld 2003); however, these studies have not provided the kind of systematic analyses of national control systems in advertising that is provided in this volume.

Additionally, this compendium not only provides valuable snapshots of advertising controls as of 2012 but also gives us some notion of their changes and evolutions. For example, 20 to 35 years ago, tobacco advertising was only beginning to be restricted; today, it is largely banned in most countries. Similarly, the control of taste and decency in advertising in the late 1980s focused particularly on unmentionables such as feminine hygiene products, while in the twenty-first century practically everything can be mentioned in advertisements. The dilemma lies in the appropriateness of hypersexual ads involving frontal nudity, intercourse, and other sexual practices deemed by many to be too private for ad space.

The chapters in this book also demonstrate that laws, regulations, and guidelines are multiplying in reaction to: (1) newer media requiring novel rules (e.g., the Internet, which allows domestic and foreign ads to reach us at all times and places; (2) changing mores and behaviors such as using social networks (e.g., Facebook) to retransmit funny, sexy, and irreverent ads—even those that have been banned somewhere else; (3) new techniques such as behavioral targeting that allows advertisers to target ads to individuals identified through their observable behavior, interests, and previous purchases on the Internet; (4) the examples of neighboring countries and supranational regulations such as those emanating from the European Union Commission's Director General for Health and Consumer Affairs (DG SANCO 2006), which help spread controls to other member countries, and (5) pressure groups such as religious organizations and consumer associations seeking greater consumer protection—be it against misleading ads or those that offend particular segments of the population (for instance, women or Muslims).

For researchers interested in the interfaces between public and private controls, this collection amply illustrates how self-regulation tries to preempt public regulation or sometimes complement it with more precise guidelines. In most places, the two systems work in parallel; nevertheless, as revealed in the British and French chapters, for example, a trend toward *coregulation* exists in some countries. In such cases, the government sets basic goals but leaves it to the advertising associations to translate these goals into specific guidelines of their own volition, and to report regularly to the public authorities on the progress achieved toward fulfilling the agreed-upon objectives.

Moreover, the chapters reveal both commonalities and singularities in the control of advertising around the world. Some rules and guidelines are found everywhere; others reflect old or new concerns specific to a particular country. For example, the French chapter recounts that nation's singular attempts to control the use of hypersexual ads reflecting the popularity of pornochic themes after 2000. In this regard, some countries constitute the vanguard of new controls or control systems, which other nations then emulate. Thus, the British have been among the first to develop a coregulatory system, while the French self-regulatory system is presently pioneering the in-depth involvement of stakeholders—not only to adjudicate complaints but also to anticipate the need for, and content of, new voluntary rules.

Furthermore, this volume confirms how little we know about the effectiveness of public and private controls, even though new controls continue to surface. Hundreds of millions of new local, national, and international ads are produced each year, a small fraction of which may be in violation of some law, regulation, or guideline. Controversial ads are usually withdrawn when too many people and organizations complain. Better Business Bureaus (where they exist) settle quite a few local disputes, but relatively few cases end up in court or before the adjudicating juries of self-regulatory bodies.

This enforcement gap can be ascribed to several sources, most notably the fact that an effective advertising control system—whether public or private—is an expensive proposition vulnerable to changes in economic conditions and political zeal. Only the United Kingdom and the Netherlands have seen their advertising industry agree to an automatic levy on ad expenditures. Few governments proportionately increase the budgets of their agencies charged with the enforcement of an increasing number of regulations. One interpretation of this gap is that advertising control can be effective even when just "the tips of icebergs and the bottoms of barrels" are the foci of investigations and the butt of penalties. In other words, regulations send messages designed to highlight new and/or frequent infractions—the aim being to help practitioners internalize basic principles as well as new rules rather than to detect and punish every single infraction.

These are the major discoveries and confirmations that I have derived from reading the chapters in this volume, but I trust that its readers will gain additional insights from these competent and fascinating analyses of where advertising control stands today.

BIBLIOGRAPHY

Boddewyn, J.J. 1988. *Advertising Self-Regulation and Outside Participation: A Multinational Comparison.* Westport, CT: Quorum Books.
———. 1992. *Global Perspectives on Advertising Self-Regulation: Principles and Practices in Thirty-Eight Countries.* Westport, CT: Quorum Books.
Director General for Health and Consumer Affairs (DG SANCO). 2006. *Self-Regulation in the EU Advertising Sector: A Report of Some Discussion Among Interested Parties.* July. Brussels, Belgium: European Commission. http://www.asa.co.nz/pdfs/Madelin%20Report.pdf.

International Chamber of Commerce (ICC). 1937/2011. *Consolidated ICC Code of Advertising and Marketing Communication Practice.* Rev., January 8, 2011. Paris, France: ICC. http://www.iccwbo.org/Data/Policies/2011/ICC-Consolidated-Code-of-Advertising-and-Marketing-2011-English.

Neelankavil, J.P., and A.B. Stridsberg. 1980. *Advertising Self-Regulation: A Global Perspective.* New York: Communication Arts Books.

Rotfeld, H.J. 2003. "Desires Versus the Reality of Self-Regulation." *Journal of Consumer Affairs* 37(2), 424–427.

Wolburg, J.M., and O. Venger. 2009. "Regulating Sin Across Cultures: A Comparison of Alcohol Ads in Ukrainian and American Magazines." *Journal of Advertising* 38(4), 15–37.

INTRODUCTION

Advertising is a key component in launching, marketing, and establishing the brand share position of many products and ideas in the competitive global business environment. Advertisements can be used in many ways to address the particular needs of a company, including forging relationships with its intended consumers or furthering an ideological agenda for a target audience. Advertising may be used to advance a business's competitive position, to inform, to persuade, or to sell. It also may be used to illustrate company values or to showcase a particular product or brand.

Advertising is and always has been a controversial field, garnering much praise and much criticism. In a free market, questions arise as to whether and how advertising should be regulated. There are several types of ad regulation: (1) governmental regulation that takes various forms, (2) self-regulation, (3) consumerism or organized market forces, (4) media forces, and (5) natural market forces. Each of these operates in a different manner and under different circumstances. Ostensibly, regulation protects consumers from buying unfit, dangerous, or worthless goods. It may be argued that advertising regulation makes certain assumptions concerning the ability of the individual and the public to correctly assess the attributes of a product or service in relation to their needs and to understand and assume responsibility for any risks inherent in the goods offered.

Rotzoll, Haefner, and Sandage (1976) asked if these are "mutually exclusive approaches or synergistic when operating simultaneously?" One might also ask if the individual nature of a society (assuming it is a democracy or quasi-democracy) persuades it to welcome or at least tolerate regulation as a way of sorting out product attributes and protecting the consumer from investing in and using a dangerous or ineffective product. Ideally, advertising provides the prospective consumer with the information needed to make an informed discussion. The nature of consumer response has, at least in the United States, led to several distinct consumer movements during the past century. These U.S.–based movements, in turn, have led to various court decisions and were important in establishing the Federal Trade Commission. Other countries, because of the nature of their marketing processes and the role of government, have set up other types of regulation, which—as we shall see—may be more lax or more rigid.

Regulation can have many effects that may be broken down further, but these effects are derived primarily from social and economic factors in individual countries. To a large extent, the form and types of advertising regulation offer insight into the norms and beliefs of individual nations. This can also be a way of assessing the strength of a country's government and industry in controlling the means of competition and the allowance of free market practices. In considering regulation, this book recognizes that there are natural market forces, self-regulatory forces, and government forces—all of which may be at work in any given society at any time. This volume also recognizes the impact of movements such as consumerism. The media, too, may impose certain restrictions on advertising because of problems with legal issues or perceived problems with taste.

PURPOSE OF THE BOOK

The purpose of this book is (1) to examine, in a comprehensive volume, the formal and informal advertising regulations and the structure of the regulatory function for a number of countries; (2) to look at those regulations in the context of their own society and norms; and (3) to make relevant comparisons among them. With the growing importance of multinational advertising and marketing, understanding both the culture and the regulatory processes of different countries is more and more important for business.

This book should be a useful guide both for practitioners and for students. It serves to explain regulations within the context of individual countries. It also answers Rotzoll, Haefner, and Sandage's question (1976) as to whether or not the regulations are mutually exclusive or synergistic when the differing approaches are operating simultaneously.

Both governmental and self-regulatory systems are part of the report on each country, as are the relatively new European Union regulations.

There are many different forms of regulations to consider. The countries studied are placed in the category or hybrid category where they fit best. Some salient categories are strict governmental regulation; laws; governmental and industry observers/watchdogs (the latter may be appointed as outside members of an association); hybrid models in which there is some form of governmental presence as well as self-regulation; pure self-regulation; and the general public or consumer acting to stop unfair or false claims and comparisons. These actions may occur at the local level and be solved quickly, or they may be addressed by industry organizations or governmental bodies. Resolution may take place there. A refusal to comply may push the case to a higher, often governmental, forum. The media may exercise its own oversight and refuse certain types of advertising. In the United States, for example, agencies and other advertisers must be certain that the advertising produced does not conflict with established norms or laws. Accountability is a prime condition of advertising creation and placement.

Discovering and outlining the various forces at play in differing countries is another important component of the book. A major goal of this volume is to contribute to an understanding of what led to the differing types of regulation (governmental and self-regulation) and to view the regulation from the perspective of the country that enacted it.

While the authors examine several countries closely, the main task of the country evaluation is to give examples of the varying approaches to regulation and to explain them in terms of country facts, variance, and special attributes. This work seeks to provide an understanding of why and how different countries rely on differing approaches to regulation. It also provides a template for comparison.

DEFINITIONS OF REGULATORY SYSTEMS

There are several differing types of advertising regulation. Boddewyn (1992) has provided a very useful way of separating the differences among the types of self-regulation. Some of his definitions are incorporated into the following explanation of terms. *Self-regulation* can refer to many models that range from pure self-regulation by a given company to regulation ordered and enforced by a government.

- *Self-regulation.* The most informal type of self-regulation is exemplified by a firm where the participants have goals and standards and where those participants may provide in-house oversight of their own business. Norms and values are developed internally, and members must comply with them.
- *Self-regulation that involves an entire industry.* The values and norms are developed and agreed upon by the industry, and member firms are judged by their peers. Compliance may be enforced by the industry itself. This type of self-regulation may include both industry and public members (outside members) on an examining or hearing board. Complaints about

certain advertising may be brought to the attention of the board either by industry members or by the general public.

- *Associations that monitor industry advertising.* The power of this type of association lies in its ability to monitor cases brought forward by individuals or industry while simultaneously monitoring advertising and initiating cases when a firm fails to comply with laws or industry codes.
- *Associations that monitor specific types of cases.* Examples of these would be associations mandated to examine food products or drugs or another salient industry.
- *Governmental regulation.* The scope of this regulation is conducted above industry investigations. Governmental oversight and practice would bring offending industry members to mediation or to court. This type of regulation usually follows failure to resolve an issue at a lower level.

ORGANIZATION OF THE BOOK

Each of the contributors to this collection has evaluated and written about a number of issues as they relate to a particular country. If a certain type of regulation does not exist in a country studied, that is noted. The issues covered include:

- Form of government in the country
- History of advertising regulation in the country, along with current operating regulation systems
- If self-regulation, the role of public members in regulation
- Number of cases brought forward from 2000 to 2009
- Route/manner in which cases are brought forward to regulating bodies
- Advertising codes, if any, and how they work
- Amount of money spent on advertising by year
- Industry position and role
- Consumerism and its role in advertising
- Specific regulation of advertising to children, health advertising, and tobacco advertising
- Consideration of taste and culture
- Status of advertising within each country
- Sanctions and control of advertising found inadmissible
- Position of commercial speech in the country—if any

CONTRIBUTORS

Our contributors come from many parts of the world. They write on their own country and also on others that are known to them in terms of language and business culture. Each contributor is an established scholar in advertising. Having authors who are familiar with the language and countries chosen is a major and distinctive strength of this book.

COUNTRIES

The countries covered in this book were chosen because, as a group, they reflect the various types of ad regulations and business climates that exist globally. Some readers might wish to see another country included, but the editors of this book were required to adhere to page constraints. We chose to include countries that represent some variance in gross national product (GNP) and a healthy advertising community of both local and international countries. It would take several volumes to include all the countries around the world that engage in advertising. The selected group covers the range of regulation that exists globally.

Countries included are Argentina, Australia, Brazil, Canada, Chile, Colombia, Denmark, France, Germany, Hong Kong,* Japan, Korea, Mexico, the People's Republic of China, Peru, Portugal, Spain, Sweden, the United Kingdom, and the United States. The recent International Chamber of Commerce and European Union regulations are also considered.

This book should be relevant for classroom use in areas such as international communication, advertising law and regulation, and comparative systems. It has utility as a reference volume as well. The charts and footnotes are of value to those interested in and considering a study of international business.

ACKNOWLEDGMENTS

The editors wish to thank all of the chapter authors in this book. Without their individual backgrounds, experience, and thorough work, its compilation would not have been possible.

Thank you to the Media Management and Transformation Centre, Jönköping International Business School, Sweden, for the financial support for this work.

Thanks also to M.E. Sharpe's executive editor, Harry Briggs, for believing in this idea and for his patience.

PUBLISHER'S NOTE

The Publisher notes with regret the passing of Dr. Mary Alice Shaver after the completion of the manuscript, and would like to acknowledge and thank Dan Shaver and Patricia Rose for their invaluable assistance in the book's final completion.

BIBLIOGRAPHY

Boddewyn, J.J. 1992. *Global Perspectives on Advertising Self-Regulation: Principles and Practice in Thirty-Eight Countries*. Westport, CT: Quorum Books.
Rotzoll, K.B., J.E. Haefner, and C.H. Sandage. 1976. *Advertising in Contemporary Society: Perspectives Toward Understanding*. Columbus, OH: Grid.

---

*Hong Kong and the People's Republic of China still have differing systems that will continue for another 30 years.

PART I

NORTH AMERICA

CHAPTER I

CANADA

SOONTAE AN

Canada is both a constitutional monarchy and a parliamentary democracy, with a federation of national, provincial, and territorial governments. Its administrative divisions consist of 10 provinces and three territories (CIA 2012). In most provinces, the legal system is based on English common law, while the French civil law system prevails in the eastern province of Quebec. The gross domestic product (GDP; purchasing power parity) is $1.279 trillion (2009 est.), the fifteenth in the world (CIA 2012). The population of Canada was estimated at 34,670,352 in 2012 (Statistics Canada 2012).

Canada is one of the most diverse countries in the world, with a rich ethnic composition that mirrors a multiplicity of origins: British Isles (28 percent); French (23 percent); other European (15 percent); Amerindian (2 percent); other mostly Asian, African, Arab (6 percent); and mixed background (26 percent). In terms of first language spoken, 58.2 percent are English speakers, 21.7 percent are French speakers, and 19 percent use nonofficial languages (Statistics Canada 2006). Reflecting its diversity, the Canadian Broadcasting Corporation/Société Radio-Canada, the national public broadcaster, airs in both official languages and in eight aboriginal languages.

With two public television broadcasting networks, Canada has about 150 television stations, multichannel satellite and cable systems, and roughly 2,000 licensed radio stations (CIA 2012). Total advertising expenditures were $15.8 billion in 2004, $18.9 billion in 2007, and an estimated $23.3 billion in 2011. In 2007, telemarketing (23 percent) and television (18 percent) were the largest channels for advertising spending, while the Internet represented 7 percent (CMA 2007); four years later, the latter had doubled its spending, indicating its rising visibility (Martin 2012). Among Canada's leading advertisers are Procter & Gamble, Bell Canada, Government of Canada, Provincial Government Lotteries, Rogers, Johnson & Johnson, General Motors, L'Oreal, Telus, and Ford (GroupM 2009).

The government of Canada has been one of the nation's leading advertisers. In 2009–2010, the Government of Canada spent $136.3 million, $53.2 million of which went toward eight campaigns on initiatives for the Economic Action Plan and $24 million of which was spent on informational advertising pertaining to the H1N1 influenza pandemic. Specifically, Public Works and Government Services Canada (PWGSC) is contracting advertising services on behalf of various government institutions and maintains the Advertising Management Information System (AdMIS) to document government advertising activities (PWGSC 2012).

HISTORY OF ADVERTISING REGULATION

In 1957, the Canadian Advertising Advisory Board (CAAB) was founded by industry members to promote the ethical practice of advertising. *The Canadian Code of Advertising Standards,* the

Canadian advertising industry's principal instrument of self-regulation, was first published in 1963. It has been updated and now contains 14 clauses that set the criteria for acceptable advertising.

Given the two Canadian cultures, English and French, CAAB adopted its bilingual name—Bureau consultative de la publicité au Canada—in 1967. That same year, the Advertising Standards Council/Le Conseil des normes de la publicité was created to adjudicate consumers' complaints. In 1972, CAAB started reviewing broadcast advertising aimed at children, and two years later, the Trade Dispute Procedure was launched.

In 1982, CAAB merged with the Advertising Standards Council and became the Canadian Advertising Foundation/La Fondation canadienne de la publicité (CAF/FCP). In 1997, CAF changed its name to Advertising Standards Canada/Les Normes canadiennes de la publicité (ASC/NCP). ASC works closely with its strategic partners, among them the Association of Canadian Advertisers, Canadian Association of Broadcasters, Concerned Children's Advertisers, and Canadian Broadcast Standards Council. As Canada's self-regulatory body for advertising practices, ASC administers the *Canadian Code of Advertising Standards,* the consumer complaint process, and preclearance services for five advertising categories: children's, food/nonalcoholic beverages, alcoholic beverages, consumer drugs, and cosmetics.

Advertising in Canada is highly regulated, with the federal Competition Act as its principal statute. The act prohibits false and misleading advertising and is implemented by the Competition Bureau of Canada. In addition, each province has its own consumer protection statutes to regulate false and misleading advertising. The Competition Act covers both criminal and civil offenses concerning advertising practices. Section 52 specifically describes criminal misleading advertising, and section 74.01 addresses civil misleading advertising.

COMMERCIAL SPEECH

The Canadian Bill of Rights was enacted in 1960. The Charter of Rights and Freedoms, which constitutionalized the freedom of expression, was adopted in 1982. Section 2(b) of the Charter states that "everyone has the following fundamental freedoms: . . . (b) freedom of thought, belief, opinion, and expression, including freedom of the press and other media of communication (Government of Canada, Canadian Charter of Rights and Freedoms, Constitution Act of 1982).

Section 1 of the Charter gives Canadian courts the power to balance guaranteed rights against other interests without necessarily restricting the substantive scope of the Charter provisions, thereby allowing the freedom of expression to remain broad (Gower 2005). That is, the expression under section 2(b) of the Charter embraces all content irrespective of meaning or message to be conveyed and includes conduct as long as the conduct conveys or attempts to convey a meaning (Alderson 1993). The Charter allows the Canadian courts to take a liberal approach in defining freedom of expression (Cameron 1990), compared to that of the United States, where the courts must first categorize the speech. For example, the Supreme Court of Canada has recognized picketing as a form of expression and at the same time did uphold an injunction against secondary picketing on the basis that it was a reasonable limit on the expression. In comparison, the U.S. Supreme Court upheld similar picketing regulations by distinguishing between speech and conduct (Gower 2005).

Specifically, in *R. v. Oakes* (1986), the Canadian Supreme Court set out guidelines regarding limitations on speech rights and freedoms. First, courts should determine whether the objective for restrictions is sufficiently important and the measures for the objective are proportional to the objective. To determine proportionality, the following criteria are considered: "whether the measures are rationally connected to the objective; the measures impair the guaranteed right as little as possible; and there is proportionality between the deleterious effects of the measures and their salutary effects" (Gower 2005, 38).

Following the 1982 adoption of the Canadian Charter of Rights and Freedoms, the first commercial speech case was *Ford v. Quebec (Attorney General)* in 1988, concerning a French-only Quebec language law. While the official languages of Canada are French and English, Quebec enacted a law requiring all public signs, posters, and commercial advertising to appear in French only. In *Ford*, the Court held that protecting the French language and culture was indeed a substantial interest for Quebec, but the province failed to show that requiring French-only signs addressed the interest. There was no evidence showing that banning all English words would further the objective of protecting the French heritage. The regulation was declared unconstitutional.

The Canadian approach, with its built-in balancing, allows the Court to deal with each case in its own context (Gower 2005). For example, the Court upheld a complete ban on tobacco advertising toward children while striking down a complete ban on tobacco advertising for adults. That is, the Supreme Court of Canada invalidated a comprehensive ban on cigarette advertising in *RJR-MacDonald Inc. v. Canada (Attorney General)* (1995). Although the Supreme Court of Canada upheld the Tobacco Products Control Act as legal, it struck down the requirement that the health warnings be unattributed, stating such a requirement violated the right to free speech.

GOVERNMENT REGULATION

Competition Bureau

The Competition Bureau is a Canadian government agency promoting competitive markets and informed consumer choice. The bureau regulates misleading and deceptive advertising via the Competition Act, the Consumer Packaging and Labeling Act, the Precious Metals Marketing Act, and the Textile Labeling Act. As an example, the Competition Act specifically addresses: (a) deceptive notices of winning a prize; (b) false or misleading representations; (c) multilevel marketing and pyramid selling; (d) performance representations not based on adequate and proper tests; (e) price-related representations; (f) promotional contests; (g) misleading warranties and guaranties; and (h) untrue, misleading, or unauthorized use of tests and testimonials.

The Competition Bureau conducts its own investigations and receives and processes complaints. Consumers can submit a complaint against a company whose advertising practices may be in violation of any of the four aforementioned acts. If the bureau determines that a complaint warrants further investigation, its remedies include (a) public education, written opinions, information contacts, voluntary codes of conduct, written undertakings, and prohibition orders; (b) the legal authority with court authorization to search for and seize documents and other forms of evidence, to take sworn oral evidence, and to demand the production of documents and records; (c) the ability to refer criminal matters to the Attorney General of Canada, who then decides whether to prosecute before the courts; (d) the power to bring civil matters before the Competition Tribunal or other courts, depending on the issue; (e) the authority to make presentations and intervene on matters of competition policy before federal and provincial boards, tribunals, and commissions such as the Canadian Radio-Television and Telecommunications Commission and the National Transportation Agency.

Canadian Radio-Television Commission

The Canadian Radio-Television and Telecommunications Commission/Le Conseil de la radio-diffusion et des télécommunications canadiennes (CRTC) is in charge of regulating Canadian broadcasters and telecommunication companies. The CRTC was established in 1976 and evolved from the Canadian Radio-Television Commission (CRTC; founded in 1968) and the Canadian Radio Broadcasting Commission (CRBC; created in 1932). The commission is composed of up to 13 full-time and six part-time commissioners appointed by the government. Its key role involves broadcasting licenses and ownership regulations.

The CRTC does not directly regulate broadcast advertising contents, except for alcohol ads and advertising to children. Regarding the former, the CRTC regulates broadcast advertisements for alcohol through the Code for Broadcast Advertising of Alcoholic Beverages. It states various restrictions on the advertisement of alcoholic beverages, most of them related to the erroneous depiction of alcohol as a necessary factor in the attainment of status and social acceptance.

Also, broadcasters in Canada, except for Quebec, have agreed to adhere to the Broadcast Code for Advertising to Children as a CRTC condition of license. ASC's Children's Clearance Committee reviews and approves children's broadcast advertising messages in accordance with the Broadcast Code for Advertising to Children. All children's commercials must be approved by the Children's Committee and carry a valid ASC approval number prior to being broadcast on Canadian television. The committee, which includes industry and public representatives, meets every other week to review and approve finished commercials. It has nine members: the chairperson, three public representatives, and one member each nominated by the CRTC, private broadcasters, the CBC, the advertiser, and advertising agency associations.

Health Canada

Health Canada is the federal agency responsible for regulating the advertisement of health products and enforcing the Food and Drugs Act and related regulations. Health Canada may intervene when the advertising of health products poses a significant safety concern to Canadians. The agency sets the standards for health product advertising material, stipulating that it cannot be false, misleading, or deceptive. Preclearance for health products is not mandatory; however, a voluntary preclearance review is highly encouraged by Health Canada and supported by many industry organizations such as Canada's Research-Based Pharmaceutical Companies (Rx&D).

Advertising for nonprescription drugs and natural health products directed to consumers is reviewed and precleared by independent agencies, while advertising for all health products directed to health professionals is reviewed and precleared by the Pharmaceutical Advertising Advisory Board (PAAB), an independent agency recognized by Health Canada. Issues on direct-to-consumer advertising of prescription drugs are handled by the Regulatory Advertising and Risk Communications Section.

SELF-REGULATION

One of the oldest self-regulatory bodies in the world, the Canadian Advertising Advisory Board (CAAB) was founded in 1957. As mentioned earlier, it went through a few incarnations over the course of 40 years and eventually became Advertising Standards Canada/Les Normes canadiennes de la publicité (ASC/NCP). The main goal of this not-for-profit advertising body is "creating and maintaining community confidence in advertising" (ASC 2012b). ASC promotes and administers the *Canadian Code of Advertising Standards*, the rulebook of advertising self-regulation for all media in Canada, including the Internet. ASC's board members include representatives from leading advertisers, advertising agencies, and media organizations. The term *advertising,* according to the ASC, is defined as "any message (the content of which is controlled directly or indirectly by the advertiser) expressed in any language and communicated in any medium . . . to Canadians with the intent to influence their choice, opinion, or behavior" (ASC 2012a). Consumer complaints about advertising are funneled through ASC.

The Canadian Code of Advertising Standards was first published in 1963 (ASC 1963/2012), setting the criteria for acceptable advertising and providing the basis upon which complaints from consumer, trade, or special interest groups can be evaluated. It contains 14 clauses promoting standards of honesty, truth, accuracy, fairness, and propriety in advertising. One of the distinctive features of the code is clause 14 (unacceptable depictions and portrayals). It specifically prohibits advertisements that (a) condone any form of personal discrimination, including that based upon race, national origin, religion, sex, or age; (b) appear in a realistic manner to exploit, condone, or incite violence; appear to condone, or directly encourage, bullying; or directly encourage, or exhibit obvious indifference to, unlawful behavior; (c) demean, denigrate, or disparage any identifiable person, group of persons, firm, organization, industrial or commercial activity, profession, product, or service or attempt to bring it or them into public contempt or ridicule; (d) undermine human dignity; or display obvious indifference to, or encourage, gratuitously and without merit, conduct or attitudes that offend the standards of public decency prevailing among a significant segment of the population (ASC 2007).

ASC accepts written complaints by letter, fax, or through its online submission system. Each complaint is reviewed according to the *Canadian Code of Advertising Standards*. If a preliminary review by the ASC does not raise a code issue, the agency sends a letter of explanation to the person who submitted the complaint. If the preliminary review does raise a code issue, one of two routes will be taken: First, complaints under clause 10 (safety) or clause 14 (unacceptable depictions and portrayals) are forwarded to each advertiser. Advertisers have an opportunity to respond directly to the consumer. If the consumer is not satisfied with the advertiser's response, the consumer can request a review by a Consumer Response Council.

Consumer Response Councils consist of independent volunteer bodies. There are five Canadian national and regional councils: the National Consumer Response Council, French Canada Consumer Response Council, Alberta Consumer Response Council, Atlantic Canada Consumer Response Council, and B.C. Consumer Response Council. Those autonomous bodies are supported by, but independent from, the ASC.

If complaints involve code clauses other than 10 and 14, advertisers are asked to comment in writing to ASC about the issues raised by consumers. Should a concern remain, the case is forwarded by ASC to a Consumer Response Council for review. If the council decides that the ad violates one or more clauses of the code, the advertiser is asked to amend or withdraw the ad. ASC publishes council findings as well as online ad complaint reports.

If the consumer or advertiser disagrees with a council's decision, an appeal can be filed within seven days of receiving the decision. The appeal board is a five-person panel with two public representatives and one representative each from the advertising, ad agency, and media sectors. Decisions on appeals are binding and final. If an advertiser does not comply with the council decision, ASC will request the media's support and may publicly acknowledge the problem with the advertising in question.

Table 1.1

Complaints Summary, 2006–2010

	2006	2007	2008	2009	2010
Complaints received by ASC	1,040	1,445	1,119	1,228	1,200
	(723 ads)	(980 ads)	(778 ads)	(760 ads)	(743 ads)
Complaints that met Code acceptance criteria	696	1,069	801	1,034	1,059
	(448 ads)	(669 ads)	(554 ads)	(624 ads)	(642 ads)
Complaints that raised potential Code issues and were forwarded to council	115	241	194	133	180
	(57 ads)	(83 ads)	(88 ads)	(89 ads)	(122 ads)
Complaints upheld by council	95	193	126	80	84
	(40 ads)	(56 ads)	(66 ads)	(56 ads)	(58 ads)

Source: Advertising Standards Canada.

Table 1.1 shows a complaints summary from 2006 to 2010. The total number of cases received by the ASC ranged from 1,040 in 2006 to 1,200 in 2010, with the largest number of complaints (1,445) logged in 2007. According to the table, a closer look at 2008 statistics reveals that of the 1,119 complaints, 801 met the criteria for acceptance under the *Canadian Code of Advertising Standards,* while the remaining 318 could not be pursued because they did not meet the criteria. Specifically, the 801 complaints concerned the following clauses: 423 cases related to clause 14 (unacceptable depictions and portrayals); 343 cases related to both clause 1 (accuracy and clarity) and clause 3 (price claims); and 23 cases related to clause 10 (safety). Those pursued cases were forwarded to ASC's independent, volunteer national and regional Consumer Response Councils for adjudication. Consumer Response Councils reviewed 194 cases and upheld a total of 126 complaints about 66 advertisements in 2008.

When it comes to types of products or services, Table 1.2 breaks down the complaints by category of advertising from 2006 to 2010. For example, in 2008, the highest number of complaints came from retail advertising (154), followed by automotive advertising (108), food advertising (108), service (99), government/not-for-profit (82), personal and proprietary (68), recreation and entertainment (49), finance (29), and travel and accommodation (27). As shown in Table 1.2, although categories vary from year to year, advertising for retail, food, automotive, and service are the most frequently addressed across the years.

In terms of media type, television advertising generated the highest number of cases in the five-year span depicted in Table 1.3. Complaints about television ads represented about 50 percent of all complaints each year. One of the most frequently raised issues was misleading and inaccurate advertising. For example, in 2008, 43 percent of all pursued complaints cited concerns about allegedly misleading or inaccurate advertising, an increase from both 2006 (29 percent) and 2007

Table 1.2

Complaints by Category of Advertising, 2006–2010

	2006	2007	2008	2009	2010
Retail	137 (15)	196 (36)	154 (34)	156 (20)	256 (30)
Service	67 (7)	77 (22)	99 (11)	93 (19)	134 (18)
Personal/Proprietary	49 (10)	67 (0)	68 (3)	107 (6)	119 (8)
Food/Supermarkets	96 (4)	177 (35)	108 (7)		118 (8)
Recreation and Entertainment	54 (5)	60 (6)	49 (3)	63 (5)	91 (0)
Finance		49 (3)	29 (3)	66 (2)	69 (2)
Automotive	104 (44)	173 (86)	108 (38)	84 (9)	63 (7)
Government/Not-for-profit	75 (5)	117 (1)	82 (7)	73 (1)	58 (7)
Media	29 (0)			115 (2)	49 (1)
Alcoholic Beverages	25 (2)				32 (1)
Travel and Accommodation			27 (3)		

Source: Advertising Standards Canada.
Note: Numbers *not* in parenthesis indicate complaints pursued; numbers in parentheses indicate complaints upheld.

Table 1.3

Complaints by Type of Media, 2006–2010

	2006	2007	2008	2009	2010
Television	527	857	528	546	526
	(51%)	(59%)	(47%)	(44%)	(44%)
Newspapers	102	85	74	72	77
	(10%)	(6%)	(7%)	(6%)	(6%)
Out-of-Home	99	94	99	182	199
	(10%)	(7%)	(9%)	(15%)	(17%)
Internet	77	119	155	172	153
	(7%)	(8%)	(14%)	(14%)	(13%)
Radio	73	52	56	64	67
	(7%)	(4%)	(5%)	(5%)	(5%)
Flyers	51	80	77	68	68
	(5%)	(6%)	(7%)	(6%)	(5%)
Brochures/Other miscellaneous print	51	78	41	20	19
	(5%)	(5%)	(4%)	(2%)	(2%)
Point-of-Sale	23	28	28	51	48
	(2%)	(2%)	(2%)	(4%)	(4%)
Direct Marketing	20	16	34	23	19
	(2%)	(1%)	(3%)	(2%)	(2%)
Magazines	17	29	27	30	24
	(2%)	(2%)	(2%)	(2%)	(2%)

Source: Advertising Standards Canada.

(31 percent). In 2008, television advertising yielded 528 complaints, followed by Internet (155), out-of-home (99), flyers (77), newspapers (74), radio (56), other (41), direct marketing (34), point-of-sale (28), and magazines (27).

ASC also provides advertising preclearance services, and the preclearance is mandatory for children's advertising. Advertising preclearance is the review of advertising to verify compliance with specific legislation, codes, or guidelines. Since the federal government disbanded its various advertising preclearance services in the 1990s, ASC Clearance Services is Canada's leading not-for-profit preclearance body on a fee-for-service basis. The mandatory preclearance for children's advertising ensures compliance with the provisions of the Broadcast Code for Advertising to Children. In 2007, ASC's service expanded to include nonbroadcast child-directed advertising. However, unlike broadcast child-directed advertising, this clearance is voluntary. In Quebec, advertising directed to children under age 13 is prohibited by the Quebec Consumer Protection Act.

Along with consumer complaints, since 1976, ASC has offered a procedure to resolve disputes between advertisers. As a fee-based service, the Trade Dispute Procedure handles competitive disputes. The procedure deals with voluntary standards and guidelines, not matters of law. Trade disputes must be submitted in writing to ASC with the burden of proof on the complainant. The complaint should convince ASC that there are reasons to proceed with an investigation based on violations of the code.

In advertiser-based disputes, ASC first assists the affected parties to reach a mutually acceptable resolution. If resolution is not possible, a five-member Trade Dispute Panel will be formed from advertisers, agencies, media, legal professionals, and members of the public. Decisions by the Trade Dispute Panel can be challenged. The review panel consists of three members, and if it determines that there is cause for appeal, an appeal panel of five persons who were not previously involved in the matter will be selected. The decision of the appeal panel is final and binding. Complaints about advertising from special interest groups are administered under ASC's Special Interest Group Complaint Procedure. A special interest group is defined as an identifiable group, representing more than one individual and/or organization, expressing a unified viewpoint.

Other self-regulatory bodies include the Canadian Broadcast Standards Council (CBSC), an independent, nongovernmental organization created by the Canadian Association of Broadcasters (CAB) to deal with complaints from the public. Its members include over 730 private radio and television stations, specialty services, and networks. Broadcasters refer to the CAB Violence Code with respect to the rules on promotional material or advertisements containing scenes of violent behavior. Broadcasters also adhere to the *Canadian Code of Advertising Standards*, the Gender Portrayal Guidelines, the Broadcast Code for Advertising to Children, and the Code for Broadcast Advertising of Alcoholic Beverages, all of which are administered by Advertising Standards Canada.

SPECIAL TYPES OF ADVERTISING

Children's Advertising

In Canada, the issue of advertising to children has received considerable attention and, consequently, prompted many restrictions. Along with the mandatory preclearance and complaint-based system, interest groups such as Concerned Children's Advertisers actively participate in education programs covering issues from bullying to healthful eating. Children in this context are defined as persons under 12 years of age. One of the clauses discusses avoiding undue pressure:

(a) Children's advertising must not directly urge children to purchase or urge them to ask their parents to make inquiries or purchases; (b) Direct response techniques that invite the audience to purchase products or services by mail or telephone are prohibited in children's advertising; (c) In children's advertising that promotes premiums or contests, the product must receive at least equal emphasis. Promotion of the premium or contest must not exceed one-half of the commercial time. In promoting contests that have an age restriction that excludes children, this must be made clear orally or visually.

The Broadcast Code for Advertising to Children also strictly regulates promotion by characters: (a) Puppets, persons, and characters (including cartoon characters) well known to children and/or featured on children's programs must not be used to endorse or personally promote products, premiums, or services. However, the mere presence of such well-known puppets, persons, or characters in a commercial message does not necessarily constitute endorsement or personal promotion. (For example, film clips or animation are acceptable as a mood- or theme-setting short introduction to commercial messages before presenting the subject of the commercial message itself.) These puppets, persons, and characters may not handle, consume, mention, or endorse in any other way the product being advertised. (b) This prohibition does not apply to puppets, persons, and characters created by an advertiser that may be used by advertisers to sell the products they were designed to sell, as well as other products produced by the same advertiser or by other advertisers licensed to use these characters for promotional purposes. (c) Professional actors, actresses, or announcers who are not identified with characters in programs appealing to children may be used as spokespersons in advertising directed to children. (d) Puppets, persons, and characters well known to children may present factual and relevant generic statements about nutrition, safety, education, etc. in children's advertising.

Another notable clause is about social values, stated as: (a) Children's advertising must not encourage or portray a range of values that are inconsistent with the moral, ethical, or legal standards of contemporary Canadian society. (b) Children's advertising must not imply that possession or use of a product makes the owner superior or that without it the child will be open to ridicule or contempt. This prohibition does not apply to true statements regarding educational or health benefits.

Tobacco Advertising

There were no legal restrictions on tobacco advertising in Canada until 1988, when the Tobacco Products Control Act was passed. It banned all tobacco advertising and required explicit health warnings on tobacco product packages. After the passage of the legislation, RJR-MacDonald filed suit, arguing that the act was a violation of the right to freedom of expression. In 1995, the Supreme Court of Canada upheld the Tobacco Products Control Act as legal, forcing tobacco companies operating in Canada to print hazard warnings on all cigarette packs (Gower 2005). However, the Court struck down the requirement that the health warnings be unattributed, as this requirement violated the right to free speech. The "unattributed" nature of the health warnings were viewed as compelled expression imposed on the tobacco companies. Another issue was that the ban included both "lifestyle" and purely informational advertising. The Court reasoned that less severe laws such as a ban on only "lifestyle" advertising, on advertising targeting young people, or mandatory health warnings attributed to the government might have served the purpose. The Court therefore concluded that the act was overly restrictive.

In 1997, the Tobacco Act was introduced to regulate tobacco labeling and tobacco product promotion, including tobacco advertising. Section 22 states that tobacco companies may only promote their products in the following ways: in publications delivered directly to an identified adult through the mail, or that have a known adult readership of not less than 85 percent; by highlighting actual brand characteristics, rather than by "lifestyle" advertising that attempts to portray the product to consumers in a flattering light; and by providing factual information about the characteristics, availability, or price of the product. Tobacco companies may not attempt to convince young people of the desirability of their product by associating it with glamour, recreation, excitement, vitality, risk, daring, or sexuality. Nor may they depict (in whole or in part) any tobacco product, or its package or brand—or even any imagery that might evoke a product or brand; or sponsor youth-oriented activities or events; or include the name of a tobacco product or manufacturer as part of the name of a permanent sports or cultural facility.

The Tobacco Act placed restrictions on tobacco sponsorship and promotion, stating that events supported by the tobacco industry before 1997 could continue receiving such support for the five-year transition period; tobacco companies could still feature promotional materials for sponsored events at the site of the event for its duration; limitations on off-site sponsorship promotion would be implemented gradually. Tobacco brand names or elements would be confined to the bottom 10 percent of any promotional display surface; and distribution of those materials would be limited to direct mailings to identified adults and in advertisements in adult publications, taverns and bars, and at the site of the event itself.

Tobacco companies again challenged the Tobacco Act. In 2007, in *Canada (Attorney General) v. JTI-MacDonald Corp. (JTI)*, the Supreme Court of Canada upheld the 1997 Tobacco Act unanimously, in favor of the government's efforts to regulate the advertising of tobacco products.

CONCLUSION

Canada demonstrates an aggressive and intricate system of advertising regulation. Self-regulation by Advertising Standards Canada not only provides detailed guidelines for specific subjects but also collaborates closely with various interest groups in society. For example, Canada mandates preclearance of all children's advertising and such enforcement is effectively supported by interest groups such as Concerned Children's Advertisers, who actively participate in monitoring advertising and providing various intervention programs to educate children. Accordingly, the Broadcast Code for Advertising to Children is effectively enforced on all broadcast advertising for children.

Most of all, Canada's rigorous application of the issue of stereotyping and multiculturalism, along with the mandatory preclearance of children's advertising, sets its advertising regulation apart from the United States and many other countries. Reflecting the diverse and multicultural complexion of Canadian society, Canada has shown special attention to the issue of labeling. The Gender Portrayal Guidelines concerning the representation of women and men in advertisements showcases such an emphasis. For instance, the Gender Portrayal Guidelines specifically state that advertising should describe both women and men in the full spectrum of diversity and as equally competent in a variety of activities, not attempting to perpetuate images of certain roles.

While providing constitutional protection toward commercial speech, the Canadian government has shown rigorous legislative attempts to address a wide range of advertising issues. In particular, its attempt to handle such subtle issues as the matter of taste and public decency is noteworthy. Such an approach has been made possible by the Canadian court's flexible interpretation of commercial speech, dealing with each case in its own context. As such, its advertising regulation system can be characterized as elaborate, rigorous, and flexible, offering many exemplary features for other societies.

BIBLIOGRAPHY

Advertising Standards Canada (ASC). 1963/2012. *The Canadian Code of Advertising Standards.* Toronto, Ontario, Canada: ASC. http://www.adstandards.com/en/standards/canCodeOfAdStandards.aspx.

———. 2007. "2007 ASC Ad Complaints Report." http://www.adstandards.com/en/standards/previousReports.asp.

———. 2012a. "ASC Ad Complaints Report—2011: Year in Review." http://www.adstandards.com/en/Standards/report.asp.

———. 2012b. *Standards Matter: 2011–2012 Annual Report.* http://www.adstandards.com/en/AboutASC/2012AnnualReport.pdf.

Alderson, D.A. 1993. "The Constitutionalization of Defamation: American and Canadian Approaches to the Constitutional Regulation of Speech." *Advocates' Quarterly* 15, 385–408.

Broadcasting Code for Advertising for Children. 2010. http://www.adstandards.com/en/clearance/childrens/broadcastCodeForAdvertisingToChildren.pdf.

Cameron, J. 1990. "Cross Cultural Reflection: Teaching the Charter to Americans." *Osgoode Hall Law Journal* 28, 613–629.

Canada (Attorney General) v. JTI-MacDonald Corp. (JTI), 2007 2 S.C.R. 610.

Canada Post. 2011. *The Implications of Marketing Trends.* Edmonton, Alberta, Canada: Canada Post. http://www.canadapost.ca/cpo/mr/assets/pdf/business/marketingtrendsimplications_en.pdf.

Canadian Association of Broadcasters (CAB). 2012. "About the CAB." http://www.cab-acr.ca/english/about/default.shtm.

Canadian Marketing Association (CMA). 2007. *Marketing's Contribution to the Canadian Economy.* Prepared by Global Insights for the Canadian Marketing Association. Don Mills, Ontario, Canada: CMA.

Central Intelligence Agency (CIA). 2012. *The World Factbook.* Washington, DC: CIA. https://www.cia.gov/library/publications/the-world-factbook/geos/ca.html.

Code for Broadcast Advertising of Alcoholic Beverages. 2012. http://www.crtc.gc.ca/eng/general/codes/alcohol.htm.

Competition Bureau. 2012. http://www.competitionbureau.gc.ca/eic/site/cb-bc.nsf/eng/home.

Ford v. Quebec (Attorney General), 1988 2 S.C.R. 712.

Government of Canada. 1982. Canadian Charter of Rights and Freedoms: Constitution Act of 1982, Section 2(b). Ottawa, Ontario, Canada: Canadian Department of Justice. Available on Justice Laws website at http://laws-lois.justice.gc.ca/eng/Const/page-15.html.

Gower, K.K. 2005. "Looking Northward: Canada's Approach to Commercial Expression." *Communication Law and Policy* 10(1): 29–62.

GroupM. 2009. "GroupM Forecasts Global Ad Spending Recovery to Begin in 2010." Press release, December 8. http://www.groupm.com/pressandnews/details/308.

Martin, Russ. 2012. "Online Ad Revenues Top 2.6 Billion: IAB Canada." *Marketing Magazine,* September 14. http://www.marketingmag.ca/news/media-news/online-ad-revenues-top-2-6-billion-iab-canada-62002 .

Public Works and Government Services Canada (PWGSC). 2012. "Government of Canada Advertising." http://www.tpsgc-pwgsc.gc.ca/pub-adv/index-eng.html#a1.

R. v. Oakes, 1986 1 S.C.R. 103.

RJR-MacDonald Inc. v. Canada (Attorney General), 1995 3 S.C.R. 199.

Statistics Canada. 2006. "2006 Census of Population." http://www12.statcan.gc.ca/census-recensement/2006/index-eng.cfm.

———. 2012. "Population and Demography (Preliminary)." http://www.statcan.gc.ca/pub/11–402-x/2011000/chap/pop/pop-eng.htm.

CHAPTER 2

MEXICO

MERCEDES MEDINA

Mexico has an area of almost 2 million km² (more than 761,000 square miles), putting it in fifteenth position in the list of countries ranked by area (LOC 2008). As of July 2012, it had close to 115 million people, so it is the most populous nation in the Spanish-speaking world (CIA 2013). Politically speaking, Mexico is a federal, democratic, and representative republic; its government is based on a presidential system according to the 1917 constitution. It is composed of 31 states and one federal district. The constitution establishes three levels of government: the federal union, the state governments, and the municipal governments. Until 2000, the only political party in the government for 71 years was the Institutional Revolutionary Party (PRI). Since then, presidential candidates from other parties have taken power in the general elections, but in 2012, a PRI candidate, Enrique Peña Nieto, once again became president. Prior to 2000, the government centralized the control of the country and had in Televisa, one of the largest media groups, an efficient communication channel to public opinion.

MEDIA MARKET AND REGULATION

The media industry in Mexico functioned for years as a practical monopoly (Gutierrez-Rentería 2007). Grupo Televisa, a multimedia company integrated both vertically and horizontally, functioned as a private monopoly from 1973 to 1993. In Mexico, industry liberalization came around 1990, with the privatization of Teléfonos de México (Telmex), which had been the only provider of telecommunication services in the country since 1947 (Serrano Santoyo 2000). Competition for open commercial television arose at roughly the same time that Telmex was privatized. In 1993, during the presidential term of Carlos Salinas de Gortari, Imevisión, the public television company, was also privatized. This became TV Azteca, owned by Grupo Salinas (Gutierrez-Rentería 2010).

An attempt to reform media regulation and the media market occurred in Mexico in the early 2000s. More than 600 social and civil organizations contributed to a document called "Civil Power" (Commission Reform 2002), with specific proposals to improve the media market. They tried to separate the regulatory body from the political interests. One of the proposals focused on the amount of allowable commercial time. The reformists wanted to increase advertising time from 18 percent to 20 percent for television and up to 40 percent for radio, including sponsorship, product placement, and teleshopping (Esteinou Madrid 2002–2003). Another proposal had to do with political advertising, which is very much concentrated in a few groups and earns huge revenues for private media groups. The political advertising fee is far higher than the commercial one and prompted calls for reform (Esteinou Madrid and de la Selva 2011). However, the government did not follow any of these proposals, and the media monopoly and power of the large media groups continued.

Table 2.1

Media Advertising Investment (million MXN), 2005–2009

Media	2005	2006	2007	2008	2009
TV	22,150	25,955	29,956	31,394	28,882
	(58%)	(58%)	(60%)	(58%)	(58%)
Radio	3,055	3,883	4,505	4,820	4,507
	(8%)	(9%)	(9%)	(9%)	(9%)
Outdoors	4,200	4,177	4,332	4,592	4,086
	(11%)	(9%)	(9%)	(8%)	(8%)
Newspapers	3,055	4,206	4,335	4,552	4,074
	(8%)	(9%)	(9%)	(8%)	(8%)
Pay TV	1,910	2,314	2,859	3,181	2,831
	(5%)	(5%)	(6%)	(6%)	(6%)
Magazines	1,910	1,984	2,066	2,252	1,801
	(5%)	(4%)	(4%)	(4%)	(4%)
Internet	222	514	1,008	1,885	2,451
	(1%)	(1%)	(2%)	(3%)	(5%)
Others	1,688	1,309	980	1,311	1,391
	(4%)	(5%)	(1%)	(4%)	(2%)
Total MXN, million	38,191	44,342	50,041	53,986	50,023
Total USD, million	3,171	3,681	4,153	4,481	4,152

Source: CICOM 2005–2009.

As of 2012, the main media groups in Mexico were Grupo Televisa, TV Azteca, and Radio Centro. Grupo Televisa belongs to the Azcarraga clan, whose mass media empire produces and distributes content, radio, mobile telephony, broadband Internet, fixed telephony, and open and satellite television. This allows it to compete in the same national market as other Mexican telecommunication companies such as Telmex, Telcel, and Axtel, as well as with Spanish Telefónica.

TV Azteca formed in 1993, and at present, it has three national television channels: Azteca 13, Azteca 7, and Proyecto 40, directed to the middle- and upper-economic sectors; it competes directly with Grupo Televisa (García Calderón 2009).

Radio Centro is owned mainly by the Aguirre family, whose ties to Mexico's commercial radio broadcasting sector span more than six decades. The company produces and distributes content for the national market, and it is a market leader through its Organización Impulsora de Radio (OIR). Members of the Aguirre family are some of the principal shareholders of Maxcom Telecomunicaciones, which offers triple and quadruple play.

The current economic and financial recession has affected America and Europe at different levels. In most Latin American countries, the advertising revenue has not decreased as much as in Europe; Mexico is a good example of this trend, as shown in Table 2.1. Mexico's advertising investment is one of the largest of all Latin American countries.

Advertising investment in Mexico grew every year until 2009, when the economic recession took its toll. The amount of media advertising revenue in 2009 was similar to that in 2007, except for small gains in "other" and Internet advertising that grew every year. Free TV was the medium with the largest amount of investment, representing almost 60 percent of the total amount.

In 2005, Televisa took 71 percent and TV Azteca took 28 percent of television's advertising investment. Only Grupo Televisa got more than 41 percent of the total amount of media advertising (Esteinou Madrid and de la Selva 2011, 288). Advertising is a very concentrated market in Mexico, dominated by large advertisers and advertising agencies and few media. It is also a very influential industry (García Calderón 2000). The main advertisers are Procter & Gamble, Unilever, Grupo Bimbo, Nestlé, Coca Cola, Colgate Palmolive, and Radiomovil Dipsa.

Nowadays, media companies have to develop strategies to attract young audiences. The new market is characterized by a high level of fragmentation and consumers who simultaneously use and produce content. Studies show that younger generations don't like advertising invading their territory; advertisers and media will have to be more innovative and creative when presenting their products and exploring online advertising aimed at younger generations.

HISTORY OF ADVERTISING REGULATION

Liberalization of the media market started in Mexico in the 1990s, though advertising has always been the primary income for television companies. The Federal Commission of Telecommunications (COFETEL) was created in 1995, charged with regulating, promoting, and supervising the efficient development of social coverage of telecommunications and radio broadcasting throughout the nation. According to Esteinou Madrid and de la Selva (2011), this regulatory body is very much united to the political one, with no open or transparent criteria related to media and advertising contents.

Among the government institutions that regulate the telecommunications industries to some degree are the Ministry of Communications and Transport (SCT), the Ministry of Public Education (SEP), the aforementioned COFETEL, and the Federal Commission on Competition (CFC). Government-sponsored regulations typically focus on content and quality, with an eye toward ensuring diversity and pluralism.

The Mexican system of regulation is big on laws but has few efficient mechanisms to enforce them. Regulation of advertising and the mass media is governed primarily by federal law, following the tradition of the civil law from Spain.

Health care is an important issue in the realm of Mexican advertising regulation. The first health care–related ad regulations came in 1950; later, a sanitary code was published and some reforms were made in 1955 and 1973; in 1960, the regulation of beauty products advertising went into effect; and finally, in 1984, the General Law of Health was published.

The Federal Law on Radio and Television originated in 1960, and the latest revision went into effect in 2009. The first regulation of consumer protection dates back to 1976, but the Federal Law on Consumer Protection was not passed until 1992. That same year, the Regulation of Promotions and Sales went into force; it was reformed in 2004.

During the 1990s, competition increased and the era of comparative advertising arrived, bringing with it a new need for regulation. In 1991, Carlos Salinas de Gortari called for the legal system to move from "less regulation to better regulation" (Dorantes 1994). So he reformed Mexico's health law in an attempt to simplify administrative obligations and control mechanisms associated with the advertising of beauty products, food, and nonalcoholic drinks.

The government regulates these requirements as they relate to advertising activity, without violating the guarantee of freedom of the press established by Article 7 of Mexico's constitution.

GOVERNMENT REGULATION

The main advertising regulations in Mexico include: the Federal Law on Radio and Television (1960; revised in 2005–2006 and 2009); the Federal Law on Telecommunications; the General Health Law (1984–1993), along with the Federal Health Code (most recent revisions were made in 2000 and 2006); and finally, the Federal Consumer Protection Law (1992; last updated in 2011).

The government bodies primarily responsible for the regulation of advertising in Mexico are the Ministry of the Interior, the Attorney General for Consumer Protection, the Ministry of Health, the Mexican Institute of Industrial Property, and the National Banking Commission. Moreover, many federal administrative agencies have jurisdiction over advertising. These agencies have broad authority to issue fines and orders. Criminal prosecution is rare but may occur if a party repeatedly refuses to comply with administrative orders, promotes criminal acts or violence, or seriously offends public morals or national symbols.

In 2011, the Interior Ministry, along with the National Development Program and the National Institute of Women, published two documents on "advertising with equity" (UN Programme for Development 2011).These documents aim to raise awareness and establish a set of criteria and assessment tools to incorporate gender perspective in federal campaigns. Recommendations concern the elimination of all forms of violence against women, men, girls, and boys (verbal, physical, psychological, economic, and sexual, implicitly or explicitly) in advertising; the overall promotion of balance (men and women share family responsibilities, home-related responsibilities, and work responsibilities); the removal of women from situations or conditions that would not be represented by men or that would portray a pejorative role of ignorance or intellectual limitations (low intelligence, emotional and irrational actions, etc.); the avoidance of images of men showing superiority of any kind over women; and the elimination of discriminatory practices and stereotypes that create inequality. The language used when writing advertising messages should be simple and focus on a benefit that makes a product relevant. Furthermore, ads should have a broad and equal gender appeal and should rely on hard data rather than stereotypical assumptions. The key to "advertising with equity" is always to establish that men and women are equal in rights and deserve the same opportunities.

ADVERTISING SELF-REGULATION

The National Council for Self-Regulation and Advertising Ethics (CONAR) was established in 1994. It is part of the CONARED, which includes nine other countries, among them Brazil, Argentina, Peru, Chile, and Colombia. This independent, industry-created initiative is endorsed by the Communications Council, the Mexican Association for Advertising Agencies, and the Legal Marketing Communication Industry Confederation. Its members include more than 40 big advertisers, approximately 20 advertising agencies, the biggest seven media companies in Mexico (Televisa, TV Azteca, Radio Centro, Ventor, Acir, ARVM, and Impresiones Aéreas), and 25 other associations and institutions.

The Code of Advertising Standards created by CONAR does not have the force of law, but it is widely acknowledged that those who violate the code violate "good practices and morality." The principles that inspire CONAR's standards are legality, honesty, decency, veracity, dignity, respect, fair competition, welfare and health, and child protection. The importance of CONAR is shown in more flexible and limited controls coming from the industry itself rather than from the national government. Furthermore, CONAR has largely replaced the Radio and Television Commission in the control of advertising content. According to its web page, CONAR (2011) successfully resolved 98 percent of all ad complaint cases through its board of directors' regular monthly sessions.

Mexico's Self-Regulation Advertising Code of Food and Drinks for Children went into effect in 2009, in line with the European Advertising Standards Alliance (EASA). According to Ferrero (2008), while the Spanish experience of self-regulation of advertising aimed at children has achieved some success—albeit limited when compared to government regulation—the Mexican self-regulation system has been less successful. These less impressive results may stem from the fact that Mexico's system lacks both financial penalties and an impartial and independent commission made up of professionals with no conflict of interest.

PARTICULAR TYPES OF ADVERTISING

The main regulated areas of advertising in Mexico concern consumer health, consumer protection against misleading advertising, advertising time, general content, the number of allowable interruptions on radio and TV, and the use of promotions, sales, and raffles in ads.

Mexico's Federal Health Code includes regulations related to labeling. Though this is not advertising in its strictest sense, it is worthy of mention. Technical information must be verifiable, and the content of consumable products must include some sort of educational material. Moreover, low nutritional food must include caution labels, and free samples of medication may not be distributed to underage consumers.

The Decree of the General Law of Advertising and Health (2006) states that in the advertising of beauty products, there must be messages promoting health and hygiene (art. 60). Commercials must not encourage conduct, practices, or habits that might pose a health risk. Pharmaceutical products of any kind may not use cartoons in their advertising because this practice might encourage consumption by children. Violations of these norms may be penalized with fines ranging from 40,000 to 400,000 MXN (Mexican pesos; approximately US$4,000 to 40,000).

Mexico's Federal Law on Radio and Television says that advertisers will be penalized for using the following types of statements in their promotional materials: those that promote racial discrimination, or that denigrate or offend national heroes or religious beliefs; statements that promote criminal acts, violence, or vice; and discriminatory, offensive, or inappropriate language (1960/2009).

Furthermore, advertisements that clash with public morality or values; statements or images that promote the consumption of alcohol, tobacco, or illegal drugs for enhanced performance in sports activities; and statements that may cause public alarm or panic will be punished (Federal Law on Radio and Television 1960/2009).

The political control of advertising in Mexico is quite restrictive. For example, the advertisement of lotteries, raffles, and other types of drawings requires authorization from the Interior Ministry. Propaganda of Credit Institutions and Auxiliary Organizations and their operations must have the authorization of the Ministry of Finance (Federal Law on Radio and Television 1960/2009).

With respect to time restrictions, advertising must never exceed 18 percent of the total time of television transmission. Commercial slots will have a minimum of two minutes and may be made every half hour, except in cases where an interruption would be inconvenient (e.g., films, telenovelas). Teleshopping is allowed from midnight until 5:59 A.M., but it cannot exceed 40 percent of the total television transmission time. The Interior Ministry may impose fines ranging from 5,000 to 50,000 MXN (about US$500 to 5,000) for violations of this statute. Typically, the ministry imposes heavier fines in cases involving children's advertising. Advertisers must pay special attention when selecting material intended for children, to avoid taking advantage of their gullibility or lack of experience (Arochi, Tessmann, and Galindo 2005).

The Federal Consumer Protection Law states that advertising must be truthful, verifiable, and free from any ambiguity that might lead to confusion among members of the intended audience. There are specific provisions relating to publicity, special offers, and customer databases (since 2004, some rules have been introduced to protect users' personal data). Infractions are punishable by fines ranging from 300 to 960,000 MXN (approximately US$30 to 96,000) in particular cases when harm to a group of consumers such as children is likely (Arochi, Tessmann, and Galindo 2005). Consumers can take their cases to the Federal Attorney's Office of the Consumer.

Alcohol and Tobacco

Alcohol and tobacco may never be advertised on television or radio programs during time periods reserved for broadcasting suitable for all audiences (from 5:00 A.M. to 10:00 P.M.); alcohol and tobacco advertisements may not be broadcast before 10:00 P.M. Alcohol and tobacco advertising may not use models under the age of 25 in their ads and must never show actual consumption of the product (Decree of the General Law of Advertising and Health 2006, art. 29–39; Federal Law on Radio and Television 1960/2009, art. 68).

Children

As mentioned earlier, children require the most protection from targeted advertising. Children's advertising must not offend national or family values, or encourage hazardous or harmful activities. Advertisements for alcoholic beverages may not include actors or models under the age of 25; tobacco ads may not include actors or models under the age of 18.

Some guidelines have been published to strengthen the protection of children against inappropriate advertising. If there is any risk that an advertisement may be mistaken for informational material, it must be clearly marked with the word "ADVERTISEMENT"; advertisements must never promote violence or illicit or antisocial activities. Furthermore, it must never be suggested that the possession or use of a certain product would provide a physical, social, or psychological advantage or disadvantage to the user; finally, advertisements must not undermine parental authority, judgment, or preferences (Arochi, Tessmann, and Galindo 2005).

In September 2010, the Mexican Senate began a long debate about how to regulate sexual services ads in the press and other media. Similar discussions took place in other countries. The political party in office (PRI) expressed an interest in investigating these ads, but no action was taken (Informador.com.mx 2010; Peralta 2010).

CONCLUSION

In Mexico, the government has more influence on advertising than does the industry itself. Initiatives and regulation do not come primarily from the ad industry but from the political arena. According to Dorantes (1994) in matters of advertising regulation, "the State should be the guarantor, rather than the keeper." Some media groups—especially Grupo Televisa—have incredible influence. In fact, the last reform of the Federal Law on Radio and Television in 2009 was called the Law of

Televisa because it was created to facilitate Televisa's activities, both in advertising and political campaigns, and return the control of the market to the group.

The media market in Mexico is extremely concentrated and dominated by large media groups. These groups establish fixed fees, and advertisers have no choice but to accept them. Ad regulation in Mexico should be improved going forward, with efficient control tools to discourage risky advertising. It should also establish a body of rulemakers and identify disparities in advertising regulation.

BIBLIOGRAPHY

Almada, M. Hugo. 2002. "¿Qué cambia con los decretos del Presidente?" *Etcétera* 25 (November): 7.

Arochi, Roberto, Karl H. Tessmann, and Oliver Galindo. 2005. "Advertising to Children in Mexico." *Young Consumers* 3: 82–85.

Basáñez, Miguel. 1990. *El pulso de los sexenios. 20 años de crisis en México.* México: Siglo XXI.

Bernal Sahagún, Víctor M. 1993. *Anatomía de la publicidad en México. Monopolios, enajenación y desperdicio.* México: Nuestro Tiempo.

Central Intelligence Agency. 2013. "Mexico." *The World Factbook Online.* Washington, DC: CIA. https://www.cia.gov/library/publications/the-world-factbook/geos/mx.html.

Comisión Federal de Telecomunicaciones (COFETEL). 2011. Federal Commission of Telecommunications. http://www.cft.gob.mx/.

Commission Reform, Senate, Mexico. 2002. Exposición de motivos, Propuesta ciudadana de reforma a la Ley Federal de Radio y Televisión, Comisión de Reforma del Estado, Senado de la República, México, 5 de diciembre de 2002, pp. 1–3.

Confederación de la Industria de Comunicación Mercadotécnica (CICOM). 2005–2009. *Estudio valor del mercado de la comunicación comercial en México* [Yearly studies on the market value of commercial communication in Mexico]. http://cicom.org.mx/ (accessed February 8, 2011).

Consejo de Autorregulación y Ética Publicitaria (CONAR). 2011. National Council for Self-Regulation and Advertising Ethics. http://www.conar.org.mx.

Decree of the General Law of Advertising and Health. 2006. http://www.salud.gob.mx/unidades/cdi/nom/compi/rlgsmp.html.

Dorantes, Gerardo. 1994. "Evolución del régimen jurídico de la publicidad en México" [Evolution of the legal system in Mexico's advertising]. http://www.eca.usp.br/associa/alaic/Livro%20GTP/evolucion.htm (accessed January 28, 2013).

Esteinou Madrid, Javier. 2002–2003. "Hacia otro modelo normativo de medios de comunicación electrónicos en México" [Toward another normative model of the media: Electronics in Mexico]. *Razón y Palabra* 30 (December-January). http://www.razonypalabra.org.mx/anteriores/n30/jesteinou.html#7a (accessed February 10, 2011).

Esteinou Madrid, Javier, Alma Rosa Alva de la Selva, and Beatriz Solis Leree. 2009. *La Ley Televisa y la lucha por el poder en México* [Televisa Law and the struggle for power in Mexico]. México: Universidad Autónoma Metropolitana Xochimilco.

Esteinou Madrid, Javier, and Alma Rosa Alva de la Selva. 2011. "La reforma jurídica de la comunicación social y el estado fallido en México" [Legal reform of social communication and the failed state in Mexico]. *Derecho a comunicar* [Right to communicate] 1 (January-April): 99–152.

Federal Law on Radio and Television. 1960/2009. World Intellectual Property Organization: Mexico. http://www.wipo.int/wipolex/en/text.jsp?file_id=220861.

Ferrero, Federico. 2008. "Autorregulación publicitaria en México." Andinia.com, September 19. http://www.andinia.com/b2evolution/.

García Calderón, Carola. 2000. *El poder de la publicidad en México.* México: Media comunicación.

———. 2009. "Las redes del mercado. La publicidad y la "ley Televisa." In Esteinou, J.; de la Selva, A.R. (coord.). La Ley Televisa y la lucha por el poder en México. Colección Teoría y Análisis. México, 281–296.

García Sais, Fernando. 2007. *Derecho de los consumidores a la información. Una aproximación a la publicidad engañosa en México.* México: Porrúa.

General Health Law 1984 [Ley General de Salud Diario Oficial de la Federación el 7 de febrero de 1984]. http://www.diputados.gob.mx/LeyesBiblio/pdf/142.pdf.

Guinsberg, Enrique. 1984. *Publicidad: Manipulación para la reproducción.* México: Universidad Autónoma Metropolitana.

Gutierrez-Rentería, María Elena. 2007. "Media Concentration in the Hispanic Market: A Case Study of TV Azteca vs. Televisa." *The International Journal of Media Management* 9(2): 70–76.

———. 2009. "The Media Industry in Mexico." In *The Handbook of Spanish Language Media,* ed. A.B. Albarran, 34–46. New York: Routledge.

———. 2010. "Estrategia de negocio e impacto económico de grupo televisa ante la convergencia de medios (2003–2009)." *Revista de Comunicación* [Journal of Communication] 9: 23–41.

Informador.com.mx. 2010. "Pide PRI investigar anuncios de servicios sexuales." *Informador.com* [The reporter]. September 10. http://www.informador.com.mx/mexico/2010/232548/6/pide-pri-investigar-anuncios-de-servicios-sexuales.htm (accessed February 7, 2011).

Islas Luna, Susana. 1995. "Legislación mexicana en publicidad: Radio y televisión." Thesis. México: National Autonomous University of Mexico.

Library of Congress. 2008. *Country Profile: Mexico.* July. Washington, DC: Federal Research Division of the Library of Congress. http://lcweb2.loc.gov/frd/cs/profiles/Mexico.pdf.

Lorenzano, Luis. 1986. *La publicidad en México.* México: Quinto Sol.

Peralta, L. 2010. "Publicidad sexual deja poco a periódicos." CNN.expansion.com, October 14. http://www.cnnexpansion.com/expansion/2010/10/11/anuncios-sexuales-cnnexpansion-ley (accessed February 7, 2011).

Secretaría de Comunicaciones y Transportes (SCT). 2011. Ministry of Communications and Transport. http://www.sct.gob.mx/.

Serrano Santoyo, A. 2000. *Las Telecomunicaciones en Latinoamérica: Retos y perspectivas* [Telecommunications in Latin America: Challenges and Prospects]. México: Prentice Hall.

United Nations Development Programme. 2011. *Publicidad con equidad* [Advertising with equity]. The Step-by-Step Brief, April. México: Programa de las Naciones Unidas para el Desarrollo. http://www.undp.org.mx/IMG/pdf/PUBLICIDAD_EQUIDAD.pdf.

United Nations Programme for Development. 2011. http://www.conavim.gob.mx/work/models/CONAVIM/Resource/309/1/images/Manualparaelusonosexistadellenguaje%20completo%281%29.pdf.

CHAPTER 3

THE UNITED STATES

SOONTAE AN

The United States of America is a constitution-based federal republic with a population of about 315 million (Statistica 2012). It consists of 50 states, each with its own court system. The federal court system is made up of 94 district courts, 12 courts of appeals, and the U.S. Supreme Court, the latter being the nation's highest judicial body. The U.S. Constitution is the supreme law of the land, and any federal or state law that conflicts with the Constitution is invalid. In general, federal courts are limited to types of cases specified in the Constitution and federal statutes. Federal courts defer to state courts in their interpretation of state laws. When a party exhausts all remedies from the state's highest appellate court, the U.S. Supreme Court may review the final decision of state courts. The law of the United States is largely derived from the common law system of English law, except in the state of Louisiana, where the basis is the French Napoleonic Code. Consumers are protected from false and unfair advertising practices by various local, state, and federal laws, as well as by self-regulating forces within the advertising and media industry.

The United States is the world's largest advertising market and showed a 5.6 percent growth rate in 2010, while global advertising rebounded 10.6 percent to $503 billion that same year (Nielsen 2011). Regarding the media environment, there are four broadcast television networks with affiliate stations, plus cable networks, satellite networks, and a public broadcasting sector primarily supported by private grants. In 2010, the total advertising expenditure was $131.1 billion and television advertising spending remained robust, with an increase of 10.3 percent overall. Among television media, spot TV advertising rose 24.2 percent, compared to a 5.3 percent increase in network TV advertising. Spending on magazine advertising increased 2.9 percent, but newspaper advertising decreased by 3.5 percent. In contrast, Internet display ads rose 9.9 percent (Kantar Media 2011). The change in measured ad spending between 2010 and 2011 was just 0.8 percent, with total ad expenditures reaching $144.0 billion in 2011 (Kantar Media 2012).

Ad shares in English-language print media in the United States trended downward, as advertisers moved to Internet, interactive TV, and mobile phones. For example, newspapers occupied 23 percent of advertising spending in 2009 and 21 percent in 2010. Ad spending in newspapers is estimated to be 18 percent by 2013 (Bachman et al. 2010). Online ad spending totaled $32 billion in 2011—an amount that market observers predicted would nearly double by 2016 (eMarketer 2012).

In 2010, the top 10 advertisers in the United States were Procter & Gamble Co. ($3,123.9 million), General Motors Corp. ($2,130.7 million), AT&T Inc. ($2,092.8 million), Verizon Communications Inc. ($1,823.2 million), News Corp. ($1,368.4 million), Pfizer Inc. ($1,228.7 million), Time Warner Inc. ($1,193.6 million), Johnson & Johnson ($1,139.7 million), Ford Motor Co. ($1,132.2 million), and L'Oreal Sa. ($1,112.4 million). Automotive was the leading category ($13,026 million), followed by telecommunications ($8,751.5 million), and local services ($7,991.7 million).

Of note, pharmaceutical expenditures dropped 8.2 percent to $4,327.8 million, the lowest for this category since 2003 (Kantar Media 2011).

In 2011, spending by the top 10 advertisers decreased markedly in some sectors—AT&T and Verizon, for instance, spent nearly 12 percent less on ads—and rose in others—with L'Oreal's ad buys up 18 percent and Chrysler's up by a healthy 36 percent (Kantar Media 2012).

HISTORICAL OVERVIEW OF ADVERTISING REGULATION AND COMMERCIAL SPEECH

In the United States, state and local governments, along with the federal government, regulate advertising practices. The First Amendment to the U.S. Constitution prohibits the creation of governmental laws infringing on the freedom of speech. Any laws concerning advertising regulation must be consistent with the principles of the First Amendment. However, constitutional protection toward advertising as a type of speech didn't come automatically. Until the 1970s, state laws evolved without raising the issue of First Amendment protection of advertising as a form of free speech. In fact, for a long time, advertising was considered to be outside the realm of freedom of expression.

When the U.S. Supreme Court first considered the issue in *Valentine v. Chrestensen* (1942), it firmly discounted the notion that advertising deserved First Amendment consideration. Without providing much legal reasoning, the Court decided unanimously that purely commercial advertising was not the type of speech protected by the First Amendment. For more than 30 years, the *Valentine* decision was regarded as the prevailing judicial precedent concerning commercial speech.

In 1976, in the landmark case of *Virginia State Board of Pharmacy v. Virginia Citizens Consumer Council,* the Supreme Court explicitly overruled the *Valentine* decision. Emphasizing consumer interests, the Court declared that a Virginia state law banning the advertisement of prescription drug prices was unconstitutional. It reasoned that such advertisements conveyed vital information to the public and that a free enterprise economy depended upon a free flow of commercial information.

The U.S. Supreme Court outlined more specific guidelines for the protection of "purely commercial advertising" in *Central Hudson Gas and Electric Corp. v. Public Service Commission of New York* (1980). In overturning a statute banning certain advertising by utilities, the Court developed a four-part test for determining the constitutionality of advertising regulation. The four key questions are: (1) whether the advertising at issue is lawful and truthful; (2) whether the asserted governmental interest is substantial; (3) whether the regulation directly advances the governmental interest; and (4) whether the restriction is no more extensive than necessary to further the governmental interest.

Any state or federal regulation of advertising should pass the four-pronged *Central Hudson* test to survive a First Amendment challenge. For example, the U.S. Supreme Court invalidated a provision in the FDA Modernization Act (FDAMA) that banned advertising of compounded products (i.e., drugs mixed to meet specific patient needs). In *Thompson v. Western States Medical Center* (122 S. Ct. 1497, 2002), applying the *Central Hudson* test, the Court viewed the speech as not unlawful or misleading and recognized the existence of substantial government interest. However, the Court stated that the ban on all advertising for compounded products was too restrictive, failing to pass the *Central Hudson* test. The Court indicated that the FDA had other nonspeech-related means to achieve its goal.

In fact, there has been a trend toward strict scrutiny and review involving advertising regulation (Mulligan 2011). Beginning in the 1990s, the U.S. Supreme Court has rendered a number of decisions invalidating state statutes restricting advertising of controversial products or services. In *44 Liquormart, Inc. v. Rhode Island* (517 U.S. 484, 1996), the Court struck down a law prohibiting retailers from advertising prices of alcoholic beverages. In *Greater New Orleans Broadcasting Ass'n v. United States* (527 U.S. 173, 1999), the ban on advertising for legally owned and operated casinos was invalidated by stating that the connection between advertising and increases in gambling was too tenuous, although the state's interests in reducing casino gambling is substantial. Similarly, in the case of tobacco advertising, a comprehensive ban was invalidated by the U.S. Supreme Court. In *Lorillard Tobacco Co. v. Reilly* (533 U.S., 2001), the issue was a Massachusetts law banning outdoor ads and point-of-sale ads for tobacco products within 1,000 feet of public playgrounds and schools. The Court agreed that the state had a substantial interest in protecting young children but declared the rule much more extensive than necessary.

Despite the constitutional status of advertising as a type of speech, commercial speech is not protected to the same extent as other forms of protected speech in the United States. That is, while false political speech generally cannot be punished by the government, false commercial speech can be prosecuted. The Supreme Court has long held the position that "the States and the Federal Government are free to prevent the dissemination of commercial speech that is false, deceptive, or misleading" (*Zauderer v. Office of Disciplinary Counsel*, 471 U.S. 626, 638, 1985). Unlike more absolute constitutional protection afforded to political expression, for commercial speech to come within First Amendment protection, it "must . . . not be misleading" (*Central Hudson Gas*, 447 U.S. 557, 566, 1980).

Given the limited scope of First Amendment protection for commercial speech, determining whether an expression is commercial or noncommercial becomes a key issue. In the 2002 California Supreme Court case *Kasky v. Nike, Inc.*, the public relations campaigns Nike used to defend its controversial overseas labor practices were at issue. The lower court dismissed the suit by holding that the First Amendment protected Nike's speech—even if it was false and misleading. The California Supreme Court reversed that ruling, stating that the public relations materials were commercial speech, making them subject to California's consumer protection statutes prohibiting false and misleading advertising. The U.S. Supreme Court agreed to hear the appeal, but it dismissed the case later without shedding further light on the definition and status of commercial speech.

Due to the aforementioned stands on the constitutional status of commercial speech, regulation of advertising in the United States has focused primarily on truth and accuracy of advertising contents rather than more subtle taste and decency issues (Rotfeld 1992). In addition, due to the strong tradition of antitrust laws, government regulatory bodies are prohibited from entering into industrywide agreements so that any attempts at "collaborative" advertising self-regulation have been thwarted (Boddewyn 1992a).

GOVERNMENT REGULATIONS

Federal agencies such as the Federal Trade Commission (FTC), the Food and Drug Administration (FDA), the Federal Communications Commission (FCC), the Bureau of Alcohol, Tobacco, and Firearms (BATF), the U.S. Postal Service, and the Securities and Exchange Commission (SEC) have jurisdiction to regulate specific types of advertising. In addition, state and local governmental agencies are involved in regulation of advertising practices in the United States. Because advertising is protected under the First Amendment to some extent, government entities must manage a balance between liberty and public interests, such as health.

Federal Trade Commission

The Federal Trade Commission (FTC; 2012) is the principal regulatory agency for advertising. It was created in 1914 by the Federal Trade Commission Act to enforce antitrust laws. The basis of the FTC's current regulation of advertising is a series of 1938 amendments to the 1914 FTC Act. Section 5 of the FTC Act (1914/2012; 15 U.S.C. §45) prohibits "unfair or deceptive acts or practices in or affecting commerce." Section 13(b) of the FTC Act (15 U.S.C. §53) authorizes the FTC to file suit in United States District Court to enjoin an act or practice violating any laws enforced by the FTC. The FTC's requirement that advertisers substantiate their advertising claims is a powerful force regulating unfair and deceptive advertising practices. The commission's activity can be categorized into consumer protection and managing competition (FTC 2012). In 2010, it spent $165,144,000 for consumer protection, while $122,056,000 was used for maintaining competition. Under consumer protection, the largest portion ($26,038,000) was allocated for identifying fraud, deception, and unfair practices, followed by use of law enforcement to stop fraud, deception, and unfair practices ($14,191,000), prevention of consumer injury through education ($13,779,000), and research activity to enhance consumer welfare ($11,136,000) (FTC 2011).

The FTC views an advertisement as deceptive if it contains a material statement or omission likely to mislead consumers who are acting reasonably. A material statement is defined as any statement, including expressed claims and implied claims, likely to affect a consumer's purchase decision. Although only material statements are actionable, the FTC need not prove actual injury to consumers. The FTC also regulates unfair advertising that can cause substantial consumer injury, which is not reasonably avoidable and "not outweighed by countervailing benefits to consumers or competition" (1914/2012; 15 U.S.C. §45)

Remedies for violation of laws enforced by the FTC include consent decrees, in which the advertiser agrees to discontinue the problematic ad without admitting any wrongdoing; cease-and-desist orders, when the advertiser does not sign a consent decree; and corrective advertising, when the ad is found to have perpetuated long-lasting false beliefs. If the prohibition of a problematic ad is not found to dispel misperceptions conveyed by misrepresentations in the ad, the FTC may order corrective advertising. In *Warner-Lambert Co. v. FTC* (562 F. 2d 749 [D.C. Cir. 1977]), the FTC required the Listerine brand of antiseptic mouthwash to state in future advertising: "Listerine will not help prevent colds or sore throats or lessen their severity." Sometimes, the FTC requires advertisers to make accurate information available through disclosures, direct notification, or consumer education. Consumer redress and other financial remedies have been used to require advertisers to pay redress or disgorge profits. For example, in *FTC v. International Product Design*, No. 1:97-CV-01114-GBL-TCB (E.D. Va. Sept. 6. 2007), the FTC ordered a $60 million redress for customers of a purported invention promotion company. Section 5(1) of the FTC Act also authorizes the commission to seek civil penalties for violations of cease and desist orders. If the advertiser does not agree with the FTC's ruling, it can appeal the decision to the Federal Court of Appeals. The FTC's rulings are not only legally binding but also exert great influence on setting standards for state and industry regulatory bodies.

Federal Communications Commission

The Federal Communications Commission (FCC), established in 1934, regulates radio and television stations by overseeing license issues. The FCC monitors the proper use of broadcast media, including advertising content. While the FCC works closely with the FTC to regulate false and deceptive advertising by taking actions against the media, the FTC handles issues with advertisers and agencies. For instance, given its jurisdiction on broadcast ads, the FCC has dealt with tobacco advertising on TV and radio. In the 1950s and 1960s, tobacco advertisers were frequent sponsors of television programs; by the late 1960s, however, the FCC was beginning to restrict tobacco advertising on broadcast media, citing public health concerns. The Federal Cigarette Labeling and

Advertising Act of 1969 made it unlawful to advertise cigarettes and other smoking accessories, cigars, and pipes on "any medium of electronic communication subject to the jurisdiction of the FCC." The ban on TV and radio left magazines, newspapers, and billboards as the major outlets for tobacco advertising.

The FTC has primary responsibility for determining whether a particular advertising is false or misleading; the FCC accepts consumer complaints about an advertisement concerning the matter of it being obscene, indecent, or profane. (Consumers can file an online complaint at support. fcc.gov/complaints.htm.) Obscene materials are prohibited at all times and indecent or profane broadcasts are prohibited during certain times. Those who violate such regulations are subject to punishment via civil penalties, criminal fines, license revocation, and imprisonment of not more than two years (FCC 2011).

Food and Drug Administration

The Food and Drug Administration (FDA) is concerned with advertising for food and drugs. In particular, the controversial area of direct-to-consumer advertising (DTCA) for prescription drugs is under the jurisdiction of the FDA. Within the FDA, the Division of Drug Marketing, Advertising, and Communications (DDMAC), under the Center for Drug Evaluation and Research (CDER), regulates DTCA. Drug companies must submit final DTC ad materials to DDMAC at the time of initial publication of the advertisement (21 C.F.R. § 314.81(b)(3)(i)). However, the FDA does not currently mandate a pre-market review of DTC ads unless the drug in question was approved on an accelerated basis. Drug companies may voluntarily submit draft versions of DTCA materials for advisory comments.

If DDMAC finds a disseminated DTC advertisement that does not comply with FDA guidelines, DDMAC may issue two types of letters: (1) a Notice of Violation (NOV) or "untitled letter" for minor violations, and (2) a warning letter for more serious violations. The letter asks drug companies to submit a written response within 14 days and to take specific actions—among them discontinuation of the ad at issue or corrective advertising, depending on the nature and degree of the violations (Palumbo and Mullins 2002). More recently, the Food and Drug Administration Amendments Act of 2007 (FDAAA) authorized the FDA to impose civil penalties for false and misleading ads (FDA 2007).

SELF-REGULATION

In 1971, the advertising industry created the National Advertising Review Council (NARC) as a strategic alliance with four major trade organizations: the American Association of Advertising Agencies (AAAA), the Association of National Advertisers (ANA), the American Advertising Federation (AAF), and the Council of Better Business Bureaus, Inc. In 2008, the Direct Marketing Association (DMA), Electronic Retailing Association (ERA), and Interactive Advertising Bureau (IAB) joined the strategic alliance as partners of the self-regulatory system.

NARC operates four self-regulatory bodies: the National Advertising Division (NAD); the National Advertising Review Board (NARB), which is the appellate body of NAD; the Electronic Retailing Self-Regulation Program (ERSP); and the Children's Advertising Review Unit (CARU). Other major components of self-regulation in the United States include media and trade associations' codes.

National Advertising Division (NAD)

NAD has jurisdiction over national advertising, defined as: "any paid commercial messages, in any medium (including labeling), if it has the purpose of inducing a sale or other commercial transaction or persuading the audience of the value or usefulness of a company, product, or service; if it is disseminated nationally or to a substantial portion of the United States, or is test market advertising prepared for national campaigns; and if the content is controlled by the advertiser" (FTC/NARC 1998, § 2.1[A]).

Individuals, organizations, or competitors who are concerned with the truth or accuracy of an advertisement can make complaints. Upon receipt of a complaint, NAD/CARU can close the case administratively when the advertising claims at issue (1) are not national in character; (2) are not the subject of pending litigation or a federal government agency consent decree; (3) are not permanently withdrawn from use before the date of the complaint; (4) do not have technical issues that prevent NAD/CARU from conducting a meaningful analysis; or (5) are without sufficient merit to warrant the investigation. If the complaint involves matters other than the truth or accuracy of advertising, it will be forwarded to the NARC president, who considers whether the complaint is appropriate for a consultative panel. NARC states that "complaints regarding specific language in an advertisement, or on product packaging or labels, when that language is mandated or expressly approved by law or regulations; political and issue advertising; and questions of taste and morality are not within NAD/CARU's mandate" (FTC/NARC 1998).

The review process begins when NAD/CARU forwards a complaint to the advertiser. The advertiser may submit a written response within 15 business days after receipt of the complaint. If the advertiser fails to submit a written response, NAD/CARU may make the information available to the public and the press by releasing a "notice" summarizing the complaint and the advertiser's failure to respond. Upon receipt of a written response from the advertiser that provides substantiation for any advertising claims challenged, NAD/CARU forwards the response to the challenger, who must reply within 10 business days. NAD/CARU again forwards the response to the advertiser; within 10 business days, the advertiser must submit a response. Finally, within 15 business days, NAD/CARU formulates its decision. An expedited review can be granted when NAD/CARU determines the matter appropriate for such a review. In the event of an expedited review, the challenger automatically waives the right to reply to the advertiser's substantive written response.

When NAD/CARU finds the advertising claims at issue unsubstantiated, the advertiser shall submit an Advertisers' Statement stating their agreement to modify the advertising, discontinue the advertising, or appeal the decision. Whether the advertiser decides to comply or appeal, the statement should include an explanation of its decision. If the advertiser does not submit an advertiser's statement, NAD/CARU can refer the issue to an appropriate government agency. Upon receipt of the advertiser's statement, NAD/CARU provides copies of the "final case decision" to the parties and the public.

A review of NAD cases from 1973 to 1981 shows that 37 percent of cases were brought by NAD monitoring; 22 percent of cases were filed by consumer and consumer groups; 21 percent of cases were brought by competitors; and 17 percent of cases were made by local Better Business Bureaus. In total, 613 cases were filed from 1971 to 1973; 876 cases were filed from 1974 to 1978; and 420 cases were filed from 1979 to 1981 (Armstrong and Ozanne 1983).

More recently, complaints filed by competitors occupy the majority of those filed. Based on the NAD reports available online, about 66 percent of cases were brought by competitors from 2002 to 2008; 28 percent of cases were made by NAD monitoring; and only 3.4 percent of cases were brought by consumers and consumer groups. Compared to the early years of NAD, a sharp increase in the cases filed by competitors can be seen, as well as a significant drop in filings by consumers and consumer groups. Table 3.1 shows a summary of recent cases from 2007 to 2010. Each year, cases brought by competitors ranged from 56 to 114, while cases by consumers were rare.

Table 3.1

National Advertising Division (NAD) Filings from 2007 to 2010

	2007	2008	2009	2010
Competitor	56	98	114	85
BBB	5	0	0	8
Consumer	1	0	0	0
Monitoring	67	36	24	24
Total	129	134	138	117
	(47 pending)	(45 pending)	(28 pending)	(28 pending)

Source: Advertising Self-Regulatory Council (ASRC) 2012.

Table 3.2

National Advertising Division (NAD) Cases from 2007 to 2010

	2007	2008	2009	2010
Substantiated	14	9	5	8
Modified/discontinued	48	42	42	42
Substantiated/modified/discontinued	25	39	42	42
Administratively closed	19	15	15	6
Compliance	16	24	19	15
Referral to government	7	5	15	4
Pending	47	45	28	28
Total	176	179	166	145

Source: Advertising Self-Regulatory Council (ASRC) 2012.

Compliance from advertisers has been relatively high. From 1973 to 1981, for the ads viewed questionable by NAD, most advertisers (77 percent) substantiated or clarified the ad claims. About 15 percent had already discontinued/modified ads before NAD requested them to, or did so when requested by NAD. When NAD found the ads unacceptable, 68 percent of advertisers discontinued/ modified them (Armstrong and Ozanne 1983). Table 3.2 shows more recent cases according to decisions. Most cases were either modified or substantiated over the years. Very few cases were referred to the government (a low of four cases in 2010 and a high of 15 in 2009).

National Advertising Review Board (NARB)

When an advertiser decides not to comply with the NAD/CARU decision, the advertiser is entitled to appeal to the NARB within 10 business days after receiving NAD/CARU's final case decision.

Table 3.3

National Advertising Review Board (NARB) Cases from 2007 to 2010

	2007	2008	2009	2010
Requested	10	6	12	17
Granted	10	2	12	15
Withdrawn	3	0	0	2
Upheld	5	2	7	8
Overturned	0	6	0	0
Pending	2	3	5	7
Total	10	6	12	15

Source: Advertising Self-Regulatory Council (ASRC) 2012.

The NARB chairperson reviews the appeal and within 10 business days determines whether to proceed to appoint a review panel or not. If a challenger's request to appeal is granted by the NARB chairperson, NAD/CARU forwards the case record to the NARB within five business days. The NARB chairperson appoints a panel of five qualified members, among them advertisers, advertising agency representatives, and public members drawn from a pool of distinguished educators, attorneys, and other public authorities. Each review panel is composed of one "public" member, one "advertising agency" member, and three "advertiser" members. The advertiser and complainant each have the right to object to the inclusion of individual panel members. Such objections are decided by the NARB chairperson. A majority of the panel will constitute a quorum. If any newly discovered evidence that is germane to the issue becomes available, the panel may remand the case back to NAD/CARU for its further consideration.

Within 10 days after receiving the appeal, the panel members confer to resolve the matter. When the panel reaches a decision, it will notify the NARB chairperson, who forwards the decision to NAD/CARU and then to the advertiser. Within five business days, the advertiser has to respond either by accepting or rejecting the decision. In the event that the advertiser fails to comply, the NARB chairperson will issue a Notice of Intent to the advertiser that the full record on the case will be referred to the appropriate government agency. Table 3.3 shows NARB activities from 2007 to 2010. Cases that were overturned were very rare—zero cases in all years except for six cases in 2008.

Electronic Retailing Self-Regulation Program (ERSP)

The Electronic Retailing Self-Regulation Program (ERSP) was formed to provide an expeditious review of matters regarding the electronic retailing industry as a forum of the self-regulation of direct response advertising. Any commercial messages in any electronic medium—i.e., 1–800 numbers, email, or websites—are referred to as "electronic retailing."

Any person or organization can submit an inquiry to the ERSP. Upon receipt of an inquiry, the ERSP forwards the inquiry to the marketer unless it decides to close the case administratively. Within 15 calendar days after receipt of notice of the review, the marketer has to submit a written

Table 3.4

Electronic Retailing Self-Regulation Program (ERSP) Filings from 2007 to 2010

	2007	2008	2009	2010
Competitor	28	3	7	4 (2)
Consumer	6	8 (3)	2	11
Monitoring	26	30(7)	34	24 (7)
Total	60	41	43	39
		(10 pending)		(9 pending)

Source: Advertising Self-Regulatory Council (ASRC) 2012.

Table 3.5

Electronic Retailing Self-Regulation Program (ERSP) Filings from 2007 to 2010

	2007	2008	2009	2010
Substantiated	1	1	0	2
Modified/discontinued	32	19	23	26
Administratively closed	16	15	12	6
Compliance	9	5	5	3
Referral to government	2	1	3	2
Total	60	41	43	39

Source: Advertising Self-Regulatory Council (ASRC) 2012.

response. If a marketer fails to submit a written response, the ERSP will release the information to the press and the public with a "notice" summarizing the advertising claims subject to the complaint. Within 10 calendar days after receipt of the marketer's written response, the challenger should reply. Within 10 calendar days upon receipt of the challenger's reply, the marketer should submit a response. Then, within 15 calendar days, the ERSP will formulate its decision and provide the decision to the marketer, who must write a marketer's statement within five calendar days or face referral to an appropriate government agency for review. Upon receipt of the marketer's statement, the ERSP makes the final case decision.

Table 3.4 shows ERSP filings from 2007 to 2010. Monitoring is the major filing approach, ranging from 34 cases in 2009 to 24 cases in 2010. Except for 2007, ERSP cases filed by competitors were very few. As shown in Table 3.5, the compliance rate is high. Most cases were modified or discontinued across the years. Very few cases were referred to government.

Children's Advertising Review Unit (CARU)

CARU was established to promote responsible advertising directed to children younger than 12 years of age. It assures child-targeted advertising is not deceptive, unfair, or inappropriate. In 1975, CARU formulated its own standards called the Self-Regulatory Program for Children's Advertising. In 1999, CARU adopted guidelines for data collection and privacy on the Internet. Two years later, these guidelines became the first Safe-Harbor program approved by the FTC under the Children's Online Privacy Protection Act of 1998. In 2006, the Children's Food and Beverage Advertising Initiative was developed to address issues involving food advertising.

CARU reviews advertising targeted toward children and receives complaints about advertising practices directed to children. CARU's Academic/Expert Advisory Board consists of experts in education, communication, child development, child mental health, marketing, and nutrition who consult with CARU on individual cases. Nondeceptive children's advertising, according to CARU, meets several basic standards: "The net impression of the entire advertisement, considering, among other things, the express and implied claims, any material omissions, and the overall format, must not be misleading to the children to whom it is directed" (2011, 6). Through the Guidelines for Online Privacy Protection, CARU addresses concerns about the collection of personal data from children. Its provisions are consistent with the Children's Online Privacy Protection Act of 1998 (COPPA) and the FTC's implementing rule.

Specifically, general guidelines address deception; product presentations and claims; material disclosures and disclaimers; endorsements; blurring of advertising and editorial/program content; premiums, sweepstakes, and contests; online sales; sales pressures; and unsafe and inappropriate advertising to children. In addition to the principles of the truth and accuracy of advertising promoted by NAD, CARU assures fairness of advertising given the special vulnerabilities of children. Fairness issues include product presentation, pressure to purchase, endorsements, safety, premiums, and social values.

A review of CARU cases from 1974 to 1982 shows that 80 percent of the 158 CARU cases were made by CARU's monitoring; cases filed by consumers and consumer groups were about 14 percent. Other cases were brought by competitors and local Better Business Bureaus. During this period, about 25 percent were dismissed when advertisers' claims were found acceptable or substantiated. In 37 percent of the cases, ad claims were found unacceptable or unsubstantiated and were discontinued or modified upon CARU request. Thirty-eight percent of the cases were dismissed because the ads in question had been previously discontinued and advertisers assured CARU that they would not be used again. CARU's caseload during the period from 1974 to 1982 varied from year to year: it ranged from a low of five cases in 1974 to a high of 27 cases in 1979 (Armstrong 1984). Table 3.6 summarizes recent cases from 2007 to 2010. Most cases were modified/discontinued across the years.

Table 3.6

Children's Advertising Review Unit (CARU) Filings from 2007 to 2010

	2007	2008	2009	2010
Substantiated	3	1	3	2
Modified/discontinued	38	36	39	29
Administratively closed	4	13	10	8
Compliance	2	0	0	0
Expedited 2.13	3	6	1	0
Noncompliant	1	0	0	0
Referral to government	7	3	10	4
Other referral	11			
Total	58	70	63	43

Source: Advertising Self-Regulatory Council (ASRC) 2012.

Media Industry Clearance

Newspapers and magazines began to review advertisements before publication around 1900, especially after ads on patented medicines prompted many consumer complaints. Publishers developed their own codes as early as 1910, including the "Curtis Advertising Code" by the publisher Cyrus H.K. Curtis in 1910 and "The Printer's Ink Statute" by *Printer's Ink Magazine* in 1911. In 1914, the Standards of Newspaper Practice was developed by the newspaper division of the Associated Advertising Clubs of the World (Rosden and Rosden 1973).

In fact, media organizations in the United States are obligated to review advertising before publication. Based on the First Amendment, the broadcast and print media have a right to decide what advertising they can carry. In *Columbia Broadcasting System Inc. v. Democratic National Committee* (412 U.S. 94, 1973), the U.S. Supreme Court held that the television networks had discretion to accept or reject advertising. For print media, in *Miami Herald Publishing Co. v. Tornillo* (418 U.S. 241, 258, 1974), the U.S. Supreme Court recognized the editorial discretion of a publisher. Accordingly, a medium is subject to liability if it knowingly or recklessly disseminates false advertising.

In 1952, the National Association of Broadcasters (NAB) established the Television Code to regulate the content of television advertising. The Radio Code was also developed, and the Radio Code and Television Code were enforced by the Television and Radio Code Authorities until 1982. They provided the basis for broadcast advertising across the country (Linton 1987; Maddox and Zanot 1984). However, in 1982, the U.S. Justice Department filed an antitrust lawsuit against the NAB. The Multiple Product Announcement Rule of the NAB Code was held to be a violation of the Sherman Act. While an appeal was pending, the NAB decided to suspend enforcement of the NAB Codes in their entirety. Subsequently, each of the major U.S. television networks issued its own set of advertising standards and guidelines and has revised them periodically (Edelstein 2003).

The four major networks review advertising for compliance with the network's advertising guidelines and policies as well as applicable laws and regulations. The networks' guidelines cover their own acceptable and unacceptable advertising practices, including special standards for different product categories. For example, the NBC Guidelines state: "NBC will accept comparative advertising which identifies, directly or by implication, a competing product or service, provided that each substantive claim, direct or implied, is adequately substantiated" (NBC 2011). Fox Guidelines state: "Comparative advertising may not distort or exaggerate differences between competitive products or services or otherwise create a false, deceptive, or misleading impression. False or misleading disparagement of competitive products or services is not acceptable" (Fox Broadcasting Company 2010). Advertising for certain product categories—such as advertising for distilled spirits and firearms, advocacy advertising involving controversial issues, and subliminal advertising—is prohibited by the networks' guidelines. Those advertising guidelines of the networks are generally followed by local affiliates, but not consistently because affiliates have some power to make their own decisions.

Studies show that television stations and cable networks rarely require substantiation of advertising claims (Parsons and Rotfeld 1990; Rotfeld 2001). Radio stations make such requests even less frequently (Rotfeld and Abernethy 1992). A review of clearance policies at 164 magazines showed that the most common interest was a general concern for "good taste," which often equates with degrees of sexual explicitness (Rotfeld and Parsons 1989). Newspapers indicated little interest in consumer protection and were primarily concerned with screening products that consumers find objectionable (Pasternack and Utt 1988). A survey of radio station managers showed that the technical details of the commercial's production quality are the major priority (Rotfeld and Abernethy 1991). Broadcasters' emphasis is FCC regulations, not the consumer protection concerns of the FTC. Although complaints about advertising can be submitted to the FCC to show that a station was failing to serve community interests, the FCC lacks rules or programs to check commercials to make certain their claims are true. Some magazines and newspapers maintain a policy of accepting everything based on a First Amendment rationale (Goldstein 1986; Parsons, Rotfeld, and Gray 1987; Rotfeld and Parsons 1989).

Many trade associations have established advertising codes. For example, the Consumer Healthcare Products Association (CHPA), representing U.S. manufacturers and distributors of nonprescription, over-the-counter drugs and dietary supplements, has a "Code of Advertising Practices for Nonprescription Medicines." Other industry codes include "Codes of Good Practice" of the Distilled Spirits Council of the United States, Inc., and the Direct Marketing Association Guidelines for Ethical Business Practices.

CONCLUSION

Due to the importance of the First Amendment and its application to commercial speech, the regulation of advertising in the United States has focused on truth and accuracy of advertising contents, rather than more subtle taste and decency issues (Boddewyn 1992b; Rotfeld 1992). In addition, due to the strong tradition of antitrust laws, government regulatory bodies are prohibited from entering into industrywide agreements, making any attempts at collaborative and comprehensive advertising regulation unsuccessful.

As mentioned earlier, in the case of tobacco advertising, a comprehensive ban was invalidated by the U.S. Supreme Court. In *Lorillard Tobacco Co. v. Reilly* (2001), the issue was a Massachusetts law banning outdoor ads and point-of-sale ads for tobacco products within 1,000 feet of public playgrounds and schools. The Court agreed that the state had a substantial interest in protecting young children but declared the rule much more extensive than necessary.

The termination of the National Association of Broadcasters (NAB)'s Television and Radio Codes in 1982 left the broadcast industry without an industrywide standard, leading each media outlet to develop its own standards; the development of various codes by trade associations also followed. The fact that each media outlet has editorial discretion over advertising selection also makes them obligated to screen certain advertising. Since a medium is subject to liability if it knowingly or recklessly disseminates false advertising, each medium has its own guidelines as to the types of products and formats it will permit.

The industrywide self-regulatory system has proved to be effective in the United States. Since the advertising industry created the National Advertising Review Council (NARC) in 1971, it has expanded and modified its operating system to meet the changing media environment. The addition of the Electronic Retailing Self-Regulation Program (ERSP) in 2008 is an example of its attempt to tap into new forms of advertising. CARU has revamped its guidelines to protect children from inappropriate online advertising and foods marketing as children's use of the Internet and exposure to food advertising have increased. In the United States, whereas protecting advertising as a type of speech protected by the First Amendment has remained central, a variety of regulatory attempts have been made to protect consumers from inappropriate practices.

BIBLIOGRAPHY

Advertising Self-Regulatory Council (ASRC). 2012. Online Archive. http://www.asrcreviews.org/category/enter-the-asrc-online-archive/.

Armstrong, G.M. 1984. "An Evaluation of the Children's Advertising Review Unit." *Journal of Public Policy & Marketing* 3: 38–55.

Armstrong, G.M., and J.L. Ozanne. 1983. "An Evaluation of NAD/NARB Purpose and Performance." *Journal of Advertising* 12(3): 15–52.

Bachman, K., A. Crupi, M. Shields, L. Moses, and N. O'Leary. 2010. "Forecast 2011." *Media Week* 20(45): 7.

Boddewyn, J.J. 1992a. "Advertising Self-Regulation: True Purpose and Limits." *Journal of Advertising* 18(2): 19–27.

———. 1992b. *Global Perspectives on Advertising Self-Regulation: Principles and Practices in Thirty-Eight Countries.* Westport, CT: Quorum Books.

Central Hudson Gas and Electric Corp. v. Public Service Commission of New York, 1980 447 U.S. 557.

Chemerinsky, E., and C. Fisk. 2004. "What Is Commercial Speech? The Issue Not Decided in *Nike v. Kasky.*" *Case Western Law Review* 54(4): 1143–1160.

Children's Advertising Review Union (CARU). 2011. *Self-Regulatory Program for Children's Advertising.* New York: Council of Better Business Bureaus, Inc. http://www.caru.org/guidelines/guidelines.pdf.

Edelstein, J.S. 2003. "Self-Regulation of Advertising: Alternative to Litigation and Government Action." *IDEA: The Journal of Law and Technology* 43: 509–544.

eMarketer. 2012. "US Online Ad Spend Set to Exceed Print (Update)." http://www.marketingcharts.com/television/us-ad-spend-up-15-year-to-date-20465/emarketer-us-print-v-online-ad-spending-2011–2016-jan12gif/.

Federal Communications Commission (FCC). 2011. http://www.fcc.gov/guides/broadcast-advertising-complaints.

Federal Trade Commission (FTC). 1914/2012. Federal Trade Commission Act. http://www.ftc.gov/ogc/stat1.shtm.

———. 2011. *Fiscal Year 2010 Congressional Budget Justification Summary.* http://www.ftc.gov/ftc/oed/fmo/budgetsummary10.pdf.

———. 2012. "About the Federal Trade Commission." http://www.ftc.gov/ftc/about.shtm.

Federal Trade Commission and National Advertising Review Council (FTC/NARC). 1998. *National Advertising Division, Children's Advertising Review Unit, & National Advertising Review Board Procedures. Voluntary Self-Regulation of National Advertising, Effective November 1, 1998 (as Amended July 30, 1998).* http://www.ftc.gov/bcp/workshops/disclosures/cases/procedur.pdf.

Food and Drug Administration (FDA). 2007. Food and Drug Administration Amendments Act (FDAAA)

of 2007. http://www.fda.gov/RegulatoryInformation/Legislation/federalfooddrugandcosmeticactfdcact/
significantamendmentstothefdcact/foodanddrugadministrationamendmentsactof2007/default.htm.

Fox Broadcasting Company (FBC). 2010. *FBC Advertiser Guidelines.* http://www.fox.com/fbcadvertiser-
guidelines/FBC_Advertiser_Guidelines.pdf.

Goldstein, T. 1986. *A Two-Faced Press.* New York: Priority Press.

Kantar Media. 2011. "Kantar Media Reports U.S. Advertising Expenditures Increased 6.5 Percent in
2010." Press release, March 17. http://kantarmediana.com/intelligence/press/us-advertising-expenditures-
increased-65-percent-2010.

———. 2012. "Kantar Media Reports U.S. Advertising Expenditures Increased 0.8 Percent in 2011."
Press release, March 12. http://kantarmediana.com/intelligence/press/us-advertising-expenditures-
increased-08-percent-2011.

Linton, B.A. 1987. "Self-Regulation in Broadcasting Revisited." *Journalism Quarterly* 64(2–3): 483–490.

Maddox, L.M., and E. Zanot. 1984. "Suspension of the NAB Code and Its Effect on Regulation of Advertising." *Journalism Quarterly* 61(1): 125–156.

Mulligan, Lia. 2011. "You Can't Say That on Television: Constitutional Analysis of a Direct-to-Consumer
Pharmaceutical Advertising Ban." *American Journal of Law and Medicine* 37(2–3): 444–467.

NBC. 2011. *NBC Advertising Guidelines.* http://www.nbcadsales.com/content/programming/pdfs/2011%20
Final%20NBC%20Advertising%20Guidelines.pdf.

Nielsen. 2011. "Global Advertising Rebounded 10.6% in 2010." Press release, April 4. http://www.nielsen.
com/us/en/insights/press-room/2011/global-advertising-rebound-2010.html.

Palumbo, F.B., and C.D. Mullins. 2002. "The Development of Direct-to-Consumer Prescription Drug Advertising Regulation." *Food and Drug Law Journal* 57: 423–444.

Parsons, P.R., and H.J. Rotfeld. 1990. "Infomercials and Television Station Clearance Practices." *Journal of
Public Policy & Marketing* 9: 62–72.

Parsons, P.R., H.J. Rotfeld, and T. Gray. 1987. "Magazine Publisher and Advertising Manager Standards for
Acceptable Advertising." *Current Issues and Research in Advertising* 19: 199–211.

Pasternack, S., and S.H. Utt. 1988. "Newspapers' Policies on Rejection of Ads for Products and Services."
Journalism Quarterly 65(3): 695–701.

Rosden, George Eric, and Peter Eric Rosden. 1973. *The Law of Advertising: A Treatise.* New York: M. Bender.

Rotfeld, H.J. 1992. "Power and Limitation of Media Clearance Practices and Advertising Self-Regulation."
Journal of Public Policy & Marketing 11(1): 87–95.

———. 2001. *Adventures in Misplaced Marketing.* Westport, CT: Quorum Books.

Rotfeld, H.J., and A.M. Abernethy. 1991. "Radio Station Acceptance of AIDS-Related Advertising Messages."
Journal of Health Care Marketing 11(2): 33–40.

———. 1992. "Radio Station Standards for Acceptable Advertising." *Journal of Business Research* 24(4):
361–375.

Rotfeld, H.J., and P.R. Parsons. 1989. "Self-Regulation and Magazine Advertising." *Journal of Advertising*
18(4): 33–40.

Schwartz, V.E., C. Silverman, M.J. Hulka, and C.E. Appel. 2009. "Marketing Pharmaceutical Products in the
Twenty-First Century: An Analysis of the Continued Viability of Traditional Principles of Law in the Age
of Direct-to-Consumer Advertising." *Harvard Journal of Law & Public Policy* 32: 333–388.

Statistica. 2012. "Total Population of the United States, 2003–2013." October. http://www.statista.com/
statistics/19320/total-us-population/.

Valentine v. Chrestensen, 1942 316 U.S. 52.

Virginia State Board of Pharmacy v. Virginia Citizens Consumer Council, 1976 425 U.S. 748.

Warner-Lambert Co. v. FTC, 1977 562 F. 2d 749 (D.C. Cir.).

Zauderer v. Office of Disciplinary Counsel, 1985 471 U.S. 626, 638.

PART II

SOUTH AMERICA

CHAPTER 4

ARGENTINA

MARIA-ELENA GRONEMEYER

Argentina is the second-largest country in South America (after Brazil) with about 40.3 million people. After its military regime from 1976 to 1983, the country returned to a democratic form of government. It is a federal republic, in which voters directly elect their representatives.

The country's economy features export-oriented agricultural activity and a diversified industry. In the 1990s, Argentina adopted a neoliberal model by opening its economy to world trade and international capital. Although one of the world's wealthiest countries just over a hundred years ago, Argentina suffered during most of the twentieth century from recurring economic crises, persistent fiscal and accounting deficits, high inflation, mounting external debt, and capital flight. The Digital Economy Ranking 2010, executed by the Economist Intelligence Unit (EIU) and the Institute for Business Value (IBV), positions the country in fourth place in a ranking of Latin American countries, preceded by Chile, Mexico, and Brazil.

Table 4.1 shows Argentina's evolution in advertising investment during the last decade.

DEVELOPMENT OF LEGAL ADVERTISING REGULATIONS IN ARGENTINA

Following a trend in several South American countries, Argentina is politically and financially open to external world markets and has signed international treaties that encourage the flow of people, goods, and services. In this context, Argentina has sought to be in tune with Western policies concerning legal advertising regulations, supported by an increasing awareness of consumer rights in their relationship with suppliers of goods and services.

The Argentinean Law 26.522 (2009) on Audiovisual Communication Services defines advertising as "any form of announcement broadcast in an audiovisual medium in exchange for a payment or a similar arrangement, or for self-promotion, by a public or private enterprise, or by a person in connection with an industrial, craft or professional business in order to promote, in exchange for a remuneration, the provision of goods or services, including property, rights and obligations."

Argentina has passed recent laws and regulations that define the scope and limits of advertising, and it has adopted new advertising policies related to socially sensitive products, including alcohol, cigarettes and tobacco, and food. The marketing of advertising space in the press began in Argentina in the late nineteenth century, extending gradually throughout the twentieth century as new media outlets appeared. But since the 1980s, more laws and decrees on the regulation of advertising have been approved. For example, Law 22.802, the Argentinean Fair Trading Law, was enacted in 1983 and prohibited any advertising that could lead to consumers' error, deception, or confusion by misleading information or concealment of pertinent data. Decree 1091 of 1988

Table 4.1

Evolution of Advertising Investment in Argentina, 1999–2009 (in US$ million)

Medium	1999	2000	2001	2002	2003	2004	2005	2006	2007	2008	2009
Television	351	309	266	188	262	326	441	565	670	806	956
Print media	425	347	299	213	276	346	407	503	558	694	793
Radio	52	59	57	20	21	24	27	32	39	51	65
Street	52	58	43	29	32	46	59	88	136	166	187
Film	14	14	11	8	9	11	14	17	19	23	25
Online	3	4	6	8	23	33	51	66			
Total	894	787	676	461	604	759	956	1228	1455	1791	2092

Source: AAAP 2010.

demanded the translation of the ads into neutral Spanish (a standard, nonlocalized form of Spanish used in formal communications) as it is commonly spoken in the country.

Argentinean laws on advertising focus especially on matters that might mislead consumers, as well as on the advertising of socially sensitive products and the morality of advertising and messages addressed to vulnerable groups such as minors. In addition to the laws, Argentina has established government agencies to ensure the compliance with the legal norms and to safeguard consumer rights in the face of the excesses of advertising.

In addition, self-regulatory bodies complement this responsibility with a special concern for decency, good taste, and standards of ethical conduct.

CURRENT LEGAL ADVERTISING REGULATION

The foundation for advertising practices in Argentina is laid out in the National Constitution, since misleading or abusive advertising is likely to affect the rights guaranteed therein.

The National Constitution of Argentina (1994) states: "Consumers and users of goods and services are entitled to protection of their health, safety and economic interests, to appropriate and truthful information, to freedom of choice, and to fair and nondiscriminatory conditions during the consumption process." Accordingly, the government is responsible for protecting those rights, for consumer education, for the defense of competition from any form of market distortion, for the control against natural and legal monopolies, for the quality and efficiency of public services, and for the establishment of consumers' and users' associations. The constitution also mandates the establishment of procedures for the prevention and resolution of conflicts and the participation of consumer associations in the monitoring process.

In order to meet these requirements, Argentina passed Consumer Protection Law 24.240 (enacted in 1994 and updated in 2008). It specifies the information that people have a right to obtain, and it commands those who produce, import, distribute, or sell products—as well as suppliers of services—to "provide consumers or users, positively and objectively, truthful, comprehensive, efficient and adequate information on the essential characteristics" of those products or services. This requirement is especially urgent in the case of hazardous goods or services placed on the market. In the case of services, the law says that "those who provide services of any kind are bound to respect the terms, timing, conditions, reservations and other circumstances under which they were offered, advertised or agreed."

Furthermore, Argentina has the Fair Trading Law 25.156 (1999), which regulates the markets and public services and creates the National Court for the Defense of Competition. This court facilitates agreed-upon solutions between the competing parties and signs agreements with associations of users and consumers to promote their participation in the strengthening of competition and market transparency.

Comparative advertising is not explicitly legislated in Argentina and, therefore, not formally forbidden. Jurisprudence supports the fact that advertising may name the competition if it does not lie, does not hurt the consumer, and especially does not confuse consumers' understanding of who owns the brand. Furthermore, there is a bill pending in Argentina's capital to regulate comparative advertising in brochures and public places. This bill defines comparative advertising as all forms of communication about a commercial activity—displayed on the streets by a person or legal entity—that identifies explicitly or by implication a competitor or the goods or services offered by that competitor.

Argentina's Law on Audiovisual Communication Services 26.522 (2009) controls the national and international programs broadcast through radio and television. Regarding advertising, it imposes, among other things, limits on advertising airtime in order to protect the public from excessive commercial breaks. Following parameters of the European Union, Argentina ruled that the radio has a maximum of 14 minutes per hour to broadcast advertising; television, a maximum of 12 minutes; and paid television, a maximum eight minutes per hour.

In addition, the law restricts foreign advertising by dictating that the ads must be locally produced if broadcast on national radio, and limits are considered for paid television channels. Subliminal advertising is prohibited, and the law especially defends minors against ads that play on their inexperience and credulity. Advertisements cannot discriminate on the basis of race, ethnicity, gender, sexual orientation, ideology, socioeconomic status, or nationality, and commercial ads cannot undermine human dignity, offend moral or religious convictions, or induce behaviors harmful to the environment or to the health and morality of children and adolescents.

SPECIAL LEGAL REGULATIONS OF TOBACCO, ALCOHOL, AND FOOD ADVERTISING

Motivated mainly by international health organizations, Argentina has approved and enforced laws specific to the advertising of products such as tobacco, alcohol, and certain foods, all of which can be considered socially sensitive goods.

Argentinean Law 24.344 (1994) establishes limitations on cigarette and tobacco advertising and mandates that a warning be included on each package. The law is concerned primarily with the protection of minors, and it prohibits the advertising of these products from 8:00 A.M. to 10:00 P.M. on radio and television. Furthermore, tobacco and cigarettes ads are prohibited in publications for minors, at theaters or during activities with the presence of children, and in educational establishments. Underage actors cannot be featured in tobacco-related advertising, and ads aimed at minors cannot show people smoking or make claims about the relative safety of low-tar and low-nicotine alternatives to regular tobacco products. Additionally, the law requires the following specific text to appear in the ads: "Smoking is harmful to health; smoking in public places is prohibited."

Furthermore, Argentines have legal provisions that apply to alcohol advertising. The country's fight against alcoholism is supported by Law 24.788 (1997), which establishes requirements for alcohol ads and prohibits advertising that encourages the consumption of alcohol. The law specifies that it is forbidden to show minors drinking alcohol in ads, to address messages specifically to an audience under 18, to suggest that alcohol consumption improves physical or intellectual capacities, or to imply that the use of alcohol enhances one's strength or sexuality. Furthermore, all ads must display the following text in a prominent place: "Drink with moderation," and "Not for sale to persons under 18 years of age."

In 2009, Law 24.788 added restrictions to protect children by banning alcohol advertising on television before 10:00 P.M. The provision extends the ban to films targeting children and minors, as well as to public events (sports, cultural, or artistic) that offer free access to minors and print media aimed specifically at children.

Law 26.396 on Eating Disorders (Obesity Law; 2008) regulates the sale and marketing of food in Argentina as a way to help control the problem of obesity in the country. The law classifies eating disorders such as bulimia, anorexia, and obesity as diseases, meaning their treatment can be covered by health care plans. It also states that "advertising and/or promotion through any media of foods high in calories and low in essential nutrients, must contain the warning: 'The excessive consumption [of this product can] damage your health.'"

GOVERNMENT SUPPORTED BODIES REGULATING ADVERTISING

Argentina has several bodies responsible for ensuring compliance with the provisions of the Consumer Protection Act.

With Law 24.284 (1993), Argentina introduced the National Ombudsman's Office, an independent agency whose mission, among others, is the defense of the rights of consumers. The country also has a Secretariat for Consumer Defense, which is connected with the Ministry of Economy. It deals with receiving and processing consumer complaints, developing mediation opportunities, determining the responsibilities of the providers, and monitoring compliance with Law 24.240 (Consumer Protection) and Law 22.802 (Fair Trading).

The Agencies for the Defense of the Consumers, created by Law 24.240 in 1997, are also familiar with the laws protecting consumers. The National Directorate of Domestic Trade is a registry of associations linked to consumer protection throughout the country. These agencies play an important social function, ensuring the rights of consumers and encouraging their participation in the processes for the exchange of goods and services. The state assigns them the role to defend, inform, and educate consumers. The associations can be contacted both to initiate a joint action or to obtain information and guidance.

In order to implement consumer-oriented policies, in particular to increase transparency and market information, and to balance the relationship between the various participants in the economic process, Argentina established the Consumer Advisory Council in 1998 as a governmental body to advise several ministries. Members of this entity are representatives of the national government and of the consumer protection agencies enrolled in the National Register of Consumers Associations.

The National Institute Against Discrimination, Xenophobia, and Racism, established in Argentina in 2009, helps to control broadcasting content or ads deemed discriminatory. In 2001, during the World Conference Against Discrimination, Xenophobia, and Related Forms of Intolerance in Durban (South Africa), Argentina committed to develop a National Plan Against Discrimination. This plan has the support of an Observatory of Discrimination on Radio and Television, which has issued several reports, including examples of discriminatory advertising, especially against women.

ADVERTISING SELF-REGULATION IN ARGENTINA

As a member of CONARED,[1] the network of advertising self-regulatory bodies in Latin America, advertisers, ad agencies, and the mass media in Argentina agreed on (1) the need to regulate themselves and to have national advertising self-regulatory boards to promote ethical conduct, (2) the importance of public confidence in the advertising business, (3) the value of strengthening corporate loyalty and thereby avoiding a government overregulation of advertising.

In Argentina, the body responsible for self-regulation is the Advertising Self-Regulation Council (Consejo de Autorregulación Publicitaria [CONARP]). It was founded in 2001 by the initiative of its current active members: the Argentinean Association of Advertising Agencies (AAAP) and the Argentinean Chamber of Advertisers (CAA). Predating CONARP in Argentina, the Advertising Self-Regulation Committee operated between 1976 and 1992. The AAAP and the CAA ran their own corresponding ethics committees from 1992 until the formation of CONARP.

THE OBJECTIVES OF THE ADVERTISING SELF-REGULATION COUNCIL

The current council, CONARP, is a civil, legal, and nonprofit association that promotes the practice of advertising self-regulation and the responsible exercise of freedom of commercial expression.

As part of its remedial function, CONARP receives complaints from businesses, agencies, private or state entities, and the general public on advertisements deemed unethical. If the accusations hold up under scrutiny, the council imposes penalties on the advertisers under review.

The specific goals that CONARP aims to achieve are: (1) contributing to the understanding of the role and social responsibility of advertisers and the advertising industry; (2) strengthening the values of advertising as a profession; (3) promoting cooperation between advertisers, advertising agencies, and the media; (4) ensuring compliance with ethical standards; (5) acting as a mediator in industry-related conflicts, using the Code of Ethics as a guide; (6) ensuring cooperation with the authorities in the developments of laws directly or indirectly associated with advertising; and (7) contributing to the training and professional improvement of the advertising industry by collaborating with schools and universities offering these kinds of studies.

THE COUNCIL'S CODE OF ETHICS

The agreed-upon ethical principles and standards that govern commercial speech are defined in the council's Code of Advertising Ethics. To fulfill its mission, the Advertising Self-Regulation Council and its associated entities have a duty to adhere to the code and encourage compliance with it. The mediation task is the responsibility of a special agent within the council, CONARP´s Ethics Committee, whose operating rules are contained in the Code of Ethics. Each reported advertisement is discussed in depth in relation to this code.

The text is based on the International Code of Advertising Practice of the International Chamber of Commerce in Paris. The Argentinean code has incorporated the most relevant aspects of national experience, and the rules and procedures of countries in Europe, North America, and Latin America.

Argentina updated its code in 2001. It emphasizes the concern with respect for freedom and human dignity that should inform all social communications. This stipulation obliges advertisers to become aware of their role in society and to assume the defense of the highest moral and civic values. As underscored in the code, the consideration of human dignity requires advertisers to adhere to the fundamental principles of honesty, fairness, integrity, and good taste in all messages.

CONARP's partners are committed to promoting among their members the responsible exercise of self-regulation and respect for fair competition. None of them can defame or discredit, openly or in veiled ways, any other partner with messages that might cast doubt on their integrity, honesty, ability, or the quality of their products or services. In order to safeguard the prestige of the business and common interests, the members have to compete ethically, basing their actions on professional merit and the exercise of responsibility in advertising.

The Code of Ethics applies to both the content and the display of advertising messages. Specific rules are aimed at safeguarding children and vulnerable groups, including the elderly and the ill who might be especially susceptible to misleading medical advertising. Furthermore, the code handles advertising through new media like the Internet, email, and mobile phone technology.

The norms and principles contained in the Code of Ethics are applicable only to commercial advertising—whatever the medium used to display products or services to a consumer—produced domestically or abroad and issued in the form of traditional or nontraditional advertising.

Advertising business ethics apply to the advertiser and advertising agency that created and placed a given message, the mass medium that disseminates it, and any person who has participated in the planning, creation, or publication of the ad. Given the characteristics of the different forms of media, all versions of an advertisement designed to be published in diverse media must be carefully adapted to the principles and standards set out in the council's code.

THE ADMINISTRATION OF THE COUNCIL AND ITS ETHICS COMMITTEE

The Ethics Committee is alternately chaired by an AAAP or a CAA member for two-year periods. If the content of the advertising under discussion relates directly or indirectly to any member of the Steering Committee of CONARP and/or the Ethics Committee, the person or persons in this situation cannot participate in that particular discussion or meeting.

The agency's intervention in a conflict between private parties requires the parties involved to recognize CONARP's authority on the subject, to adhere to the principles of the Code of Ethics, and to understand its norms and fulfill its resolutions.

PROCEEDINGS OF THE COUNCIL AND ETHICS COMMITTEE

In the case of a complaint, CONARP's Steering Committee decides whether sufficient evidence exists to consider the case a contradiction to the principles of the Code of Ethics. If the minimum requirements for analysis are not met or if the topic is outside the purview of CONARP, the committee informs the applicant and the case ends there.

If instead the committee believes that the message in question is contrary to the principles of the code, the contents of the communication are analyzed by the committee members and they decide by simple majority if the ad is framed according to the principles of the code. The quorum for adopting a valid resolution is five members, with at least two representatives from each entity. The discussion of the committee, be it in person or online (email), is always private and confidential.

If there are grounds for further analysis of the case, CONARP's committee invites the involved parties to submit a written response regarding the content of the advertisement in dispute. The members of the committee to whom this presentation is made should be the same as those who previously analyzed the contents of the communication.

The council may recommend that changes be made to the advertisement, or they may pull the advertisement altogether. The resolutions of the boards and ethics committees can be appealed.

In that case, the interested party must provide new data within fixed time periods to try to reverse the ruling.

COMPLIANCE AND PUBLICATION OF THE RESOLUTIONS

Argentina has agreed on standards to promote compliance with the dictates of its self-regulatory agency and the public dissemination of its resolutions.

In Argentina, if the advertiser and the responsible agency voluntarily accept the committee's request, the investigation ends there. However, in the event that the advertiser or the responsible agency does not respond to or abide by the Ethics Committee's request, the committee reports the fact to the complainant and may proceed to (1) communicate the intervention of CONARP to relevant government agencies and related industry entities, when appropriate; or (2) communicate the intervention through the mass media, publicly stating the decision on the issue and the nonacceptance of the resolution by the advertiser or agency.

STATISTICS FROM CONARP ARGENTINA

On its website, CONARP keeps statistical information on cases handled by the institution. Searches for information can be made using six categories: resolution, observation, claimant, industry, topic, and medium.

According to CONARP, after an upward trend in the number of cases handled by the organization in 2008 (64 cases), complaints fell in 2009, when 46 cases were considered. Statistics for the period January 2001–July 2010 show that CONARP analyzed 295 cases during that time. The complaints were mostly ex officio (30 percent), followed by requests made by individuals (23 percent) and requests made by companies (21 percent).

In that period, CONARP resolved about half of the cases. The majority of the questionable ads were either withdrawn altogether or their content was altered; in the remainder of the cases, either other modifications were called for or the ad could only be broadcast after 10:00 P.M.

In addition, the council reported that 52 percent of the cases of questionable advertisements in the 2001–2010 period dealt with the food and beverage industry. The top three topics that led to the formal treatment of a case by the council were "social sensitivity" (30 percent), "child protection" (14 percent), and "competition" (14 percent). By far the most challenged medium was television (73 percent of the complaints), followed by the press (11 percent).

OTHER INSTANCES OF SELF-REGULATION IN ARGENTINA

Chamber of Liquor Distillers

In Argentina, the Chamber of Liquor Distillers has its own rules of self-regulation on the advertising of alcoholic beverages—rules that are consistent with the self-regulatory organizations and the law. The chamber's rules reinforce the idea that the content of advertisements must be truthful, must not be targeted at children, and must avoid encouraging consumption as a way of achieving health, strength, or longevity or as a means of escaping from anxiety or depression. The Chamber of Liquor Distillers also requires that messages steer clear of any political or religious references and do not offend the standing moral values and institutions in the society. Regarding penalties, the committee may: (1) suspend the representation of the company involved; (2) eliminate from the chamber the company involved; and, in extremely serious cases, (3) document the resolution in the mass media and publicly denounce the sanctioned company.

Chamber of the Tobacco Industry

Argentina's Chamber of the Tobacco Industry is a self-regulating entity that operates according to the Code for Marketing, Sales, and Advertising of Tobacco Products, first published in 1997 and updated in 2001. This document sets out the principles and rules that guide advertising in the tobacco industry—rules that are consistent with and reinforce the norms of the general self-regulatory mechanisms for the field. The code stresses: "Smoking is an adult choice." Consequently, all advertising and promotion has to be developed responsibly and directed exclusively to smokers over 18 years of age. It further states that the purpose of tobacco advertising is to influence brand choice: Audiences change brands, and companies may attempt to improve sales by convincing consumers to switch to their brand; however, promoting the consumption of tobacco among people who have decided not to smoke is strictly prohibited.

In audiovisual media, health warnings must be screened in the final frame of the ad, using a clearly readable font, and be visible for at least three seconds, without background sound, and in a clear and neutral tone of voice. In print media and on street signs, the warning should occupy at least 5 percent of the total area devoted to the ad, in clear and visible letters. On the radio, the warning has to be issued after the ad and should last at least three seconds.

The companies that are members of the Chamber of the Tobacco Industry are responsible for ensuring the reciprocal observance of its rules through a self-regulatory committee composed of representatives of the industry.

Coordinator of the Food Products Industries

The food production industry in Argentina also has a written framework for advertising self-regulation. The project is based on the principles of legality, consumer protection, and fairness. As a general guideline, it establishes and controls the advertising of foods to avoid creating confusion regarding a food's quality, caloric value, flavor characteristics, size, content, and nutritional and health benefits.

Food advertisements to the general consumer should be balanced and accurate, not encouraging the excessive consumption of any food, but promoting instead the importance of eating healthy, varied, and balanced dishes. In addition, ads should not diminish the role of parents and educators as facilitators of healthy eating habits. Food ads should seek to contribute to the positive development of relations between parents and children, students and teachers, and other relationships involving children. Ads from the food industry should also respect children's dignity, naiveté, credulity, lack of experience, and their sense of loyalty, and must pay special attention to the psychological characteristics of children who are less able than adults to discern fact from fiction. Finally, this body stresses that in the advertising of food products for consumption by children, it will adopt the most restrictive interpretation of the industry's self-regulation rules.

CHALLENGES AWAITING REGULATORY MECHANISMS IN ARGENTINA

In Argentina, the government is working to create several additional mechanisms to control the media while maintaining acceptable standards for commercial speech and the industry. During the 2009 CONARED meeting, the delegation of Argentina expressed to their Latin American counterparts their concern about the progress of the Observatory of Discrimination on the Radio and Television (created in 2007), a state agency composed of the Federal Broadcasting Committee (COMFER), the National Institute Against Discrimination, Xenophobia and Racism (INADI) and the National Council of Women (CNM). They noted that COMFER has the power to take out ads and punish those considered responsible for an abuse, but for now the observatory has limited its intervention to calling attention to potential problems and inviting discussion and review.

Representatives of the Argentinean Chamber of Advertisers (CAA) noted in 2009[2] that the country is heading toward greater regulation of advertising with apparently good intentions, but also creating potentially uncertain scenarios for this industry and reflecting a distrust or questioning of self-regulatory mechanisms in that country.

The CAA notes that this situation has begun to affect business ethics and creative advertising, and as a consequence the number of commercial disputes that arise among advertisers in CONARP is rising. In addition, this self-regulatory body has had an increasingly difficult time gaining compliance with its resolutions.

Advertisers in Argentina are pushing for the reconstruction of an environment more favorable to commercial speech, responsible advertising, and advertising self-regulation.

NOTES

1. Once the local councils were founded, Latin American countries proceeded to link these entities in a regional alliance. The first Latin American meeting of national self-regulatory agencies took place in 2008, and from that first meeting, CONARED was created. CONARED is the network of advertising self-regulatory bodies in Latin America. This entity now includes Argentina, Brazil, Colombia, Chile, El Salvador, Guatemala, Mexico, Paraguay, Peru, and Uruguay. Its purpose is to seek the incorporation of a greater number of countries in the network.

The initiative emerged from the interest of the advertising industry in Latin American countries to establish a network of self-regulation. The intent was to unify criteria for the application of the codes of ethics and to foster a regional approach to commercial communication practices for advertisers, advertising agencies, and the media to ensure public safety and trust.

In turn, CONARED is linked to the World Federation of Advertisers (WFA). In its annual meetings in the region, they discuss key global strategic regulatory and media issues and bring together marketers and national advertiser associations from across South America. The WFA has Latin American National Advisers Associations in Argentina, Brazil, Colombia, Chile, Guatemala, Mexico, Paraguay, Peru, Uruguay, and Venezuela.

2. Cámara Argentina de Anunciantes, CAA, "Amenazas a la Actividad Publicitaria." 8ª Reunión Regional Latinoamérica. Encuentro anual de las asociaciones nacionales de anunciantes latinoamericanas [Annual meeting of national associations of Latin American advertisers]. Lima, Peru; 15–17 July 2009. http://info.wfa.be/WFA&ANDAPerú16julio09.ppt.

BIBLIOGRAPHY

Documents

Alcohol Advertising Law 24.788. 1997, last modified in 2009.
Audiovisual Communication Services (Servicios de Comunicación Audiovisual) Law 26.522. 2009.
Cigarette and Tobacco Advertising Law 24.344. 1994.
Code of Advertising Ethics from CONARP. 2001.
Consumer Protection (Protección del Consumidor) Law 24.240. 1994, last modified in 2008.
Fair Trading (Lealtad Comercial) Law 22.802. 1983.
Fair Trading (Lealtad Comercial) Law 25.156. 1999.
National Constitution of Argentina (Constitución Nacional de Argentina). 1994.
Obesity Law 26.396 (Transtornos Alimentarios; Ley de Obesidad). 2008.

Institutions

AAAP. 2010. http://www.webuniversitaria.com/AAAP-Asociacion-Argentina-de-Agencias-de-Publicidad. universidad.987.html#sthash.BWrsiGAK.dpbs.

Advertising Self-Regulation Council/Consejo de Autorregulación Publicitaria (CONARP). http://www. conarp.org.ar.

Agencies for the Defense of the Consumers/Asociaciones de Consumidores. http://www.enargas.gov.ar/ Listados/Detalle.php?Continuar=Listados+de+Entidades.

Argentinean Chamber of Advertisers/Cámara Argentina de Anunciantes (CAA). http://www.anunciantes. org.ar/.

Chamber of Liquor Distillers/Cámara Argentina de Destiladores Licoristas (CADL). http://www.camlic. com.ar.

Chamber of the Tobacco Industry/Cámara de la Industria del Tabaco (CIT). cit@sion.com.

Consumer Advisory Council/Consejo Consultivo de los Consumidores. http://www.consumidor.gov.ar/ consejo-consultivo-de-los-consumidores/.

Consumer Association for the Prevention, Advice, and Defense of the Consumer /Asociación de Consumidores PADEC—Prevención, Asesoramiento y Defensa del Consumidor. http://www.padec.org.ar.

Coordinator of the Food Products Industries/Coordinadora de las Industrias de Productos Alimenticios. www.copal.com.ar.

Economist Intelligence Unit (EIU). http://country.eiu.com/Argentina.

IBM Institute for Business Value (IBV). http://www-05.ibm.com/services/es/bcs/html/ibv/index.html.

National Directorate of Domestic Trade/Dirección Nacional de Comercio Interior. http://www.consumidor. gov.ar.

National Institute Against Discrimination, Xenophobia, and Racism/Instituto Nacional Contra la Discriminación, la Xenofobia y el Racismo (INADI). http://inadi.gob.ar/.

National Ombudsman's Office/Defensoría del Pueblo de la Nación. http://www.dpn.gob.ar/.

Observatory of Discrimination on the Radio and Television/Observatorio de la Discriminación en Radio y Televisión. www.obserdiscriminacion.gov.ar.

Secretariat for Consumer Defense/Subsecretaría de Defensa del Consumidor. http://www.consumidor.gov. ar/la-subsecretaria-de-defensa-del-consumidor/.

CHAPTER 5

BRAZIL

PAULO FAUSTINO

Brazil is the largest country in South America in terms of land mass, economic activity, and population. Unlike most countries in Central and South America, its official language is Portuguese—a holdover from centuries of Portuguese rule. After achieving its independence in 1822, Brazil was led by largely by military regimes. The Constitution of the Federal Republic of Brazil was finally promulgated in 1988 (CIA 2013).

Brazilian industry has several regulatory-type entities. According to Brunetto (2002), the emergence of these bodies occurred at a time when the role of the state was being redefined: The government was no longer directly responsible for developing the means of production of goods and services, and Brazil began adopting a market approach to its economy. Social and political demands followed the dilution of the role of the state as the exclusive supplier of public services. At the same time, a significant attempt was made to regulate productive activities of strategic public interest.

Among the regulatory agencies in Brazil are:

- CADE—Conselho de Administração da Defesa Económica (Brazil's Council for Economic Defense);
- ANATEL—Agência Nacional das Telecomunicações (National Agency for Telecommunications);
- ANVISA—Agência Nacional de Vigilância Sanitária (National Health Surveillance Agency);
- ANEEL—Agência Nacional de Energia Eléctrica (National Agency of Electric Energy);
- ANP—Agência Nacional do Petróleo (National Petroleum Agency); and
- ANCINE—Agência Nacional do Cinema (National Cinema Agency), among others.

However, the only *self-regulatory* entity related to *media and communications* is the National Council for Advertising Self-Regulation (CONAR), which deals with advertising content. Brazil does not have any broad media regulatory agency, although its possible creation is a frequently debated topic. One project concerning media regulation was presented by ex-minister Franklin Martins, but it is not a current priority for the Brazilian government. Their major efforts are related to universalizing broadband access in Brazil.

ANCINE deals with the communications sector. Its purpose is to stimulate the production, distribution, and exhibition of film and videos to several segments of the market and to promote the self-sustainability of the national industry in the various links of the production chain.

From a technical regulation perspective, Brazil's first regulatory agency, ANATEL, was created in 1997 as part of an effort to reformulate the country's telecommunications sector. Administrated independent of the government and financially autonomous, ANATEL plays an important role in the normalization and regulation of pay-television services, promoting the development of the country's infrastructure and encouraging quality services from providers at fair prices. Beyond regulation, ANATEL seeks to universalize access to media services and stimulate industrywide price reductions.

ANATEL was created by the General Communications Law (Law No. 9.472, 1997), and decisions made by the agency can only be contested in court. ANATEL has regulatory, investigatory, and sanctioning powers and acts in the public interest. Its main arm is the Direct Council, which is composed of five counselors nominated by the Senate and confirmed by the president. The 12-member advisory board deals with social participation and is made up of two representatives each from the Senate, the House of Representatives, the Executive Branch, the telecommunications service industry, entities representing users, and entities representing society. Brazilian paid television includes cable television, Mutichannel Multipoint Distribution Service (MMDS) and distributed hash table (DHT). ANATEL also promotes interaction with the administrations of the Common Southern Market (MERCOSUL) to develop common objectives.

In Brazil, legislative concerns about advertising appeared initially in the First Brazilian Congress of Advertising. Held in Rio de Janeiro in 1957, the congress sought to strengthen professional ethics in the advertising business, resulting in the later passage of national legislation—Law No. 4.680 (1965) and Decree No. 57.960 (1966). According to Roberto Correa (2006, p. 229), by that time the increasing presence of advertising and its influence on consumer behavior was readily observable. As Marcus Pereira commented in his column for *O Estado de S. Paulo*: "Advertisement is an unquestionable presence in our life, for readers and nonreaders, listeners and nonlisteners, viewers and nonviewers. Advertisement doesn't spare anyone. Where there is a man, there is an advertisement. And wherever there is an advertisement, we can be sure of the presence of man." (Article: "The Man and the Advertisement"). Still, as Correa (2006) puts it, the consumer of that period had few legal defense instruments beyond those in the Brazilian Civil Code of 1916 (which was replaced by the Civil Code of 2002, presently in use), and some other assorted legal devices concerning specific issues, such as those in the Statute on Children and Adolescents (Law No. 8.069 from July 13, 1990), and in the Medication Law (Law No. 6.360 from September 23, 1976), among others.

The Brazilian Advertising Self-Regulation Code did not appear until 1978—during the Third Brazilian Congress of Advertising—despite the efforts of some pioneers interested in establishing an ethical norm in the country in the 1950s and 1960s. As Correa (2006) suggests, Brazil's Code is wider than the English Code, since it covers all the mass media (including radio and television), not just the press. Mexico, El Salvador, Colombia, and Chile adopted the Brazilian Advertising Self-Regulation Code as a base document and made local adaptations, but the Brazilian system is considered by Interamerican Society for Freedom of Commerical Expression (SILEC) as the continental standard.

INSTITUTIONS AND ADVERTISING REGULATION MODEL IN BRAZIL

The idea of protecting consumers' rights dates back to the Empire of Brazil (1822–1899), but such protections only acquired constitutional status much later, in 1934. The constitutionally mandated Code of Consumer Protection was published on September 11, 1990, and went into effect six months later. Article 37, no. 1 of the code prohibits misleading, offensive, and abusive advertisements. Misleading advertisement may be the result of an omission of facts—when the advertiser fails to include essential information about a product or service. This type of false advertising adversely affects the decision-making abilities of consumers by manipulating them into purchasing the advertised product or service based on erroneous information.

Abusive advertising, defined in Article 37, no. 2 of the Code of Consumer Protection, is offensive to the nation's social values. It concerns the use of discrimination, violence, fear, superstition, disrespect for the environment, exploitation (as in the case of children's lack of judgment and experience), or the encouragement of the consumer to behave in prejudicial, unsafe, or damaging ways.

The Code of Consumer Protection (1990) made the regulation of advertising in Brazil official. Consumers' interests are now protected by a specific legal instrument. Because advertising has a great degree of influence over consumer behavior, advertising messages must comply with the principles laid out in the articles of the code, especially numbers 37 and 63 through 69. Illicit advertising is a crime, according to the code; consumers' rights cannot be violated in the name of easy profit.

National Council for Advertising Self-Regulation (CONAR)

CONAR is a nongovernmental agency that for more than 30 years has defended the freedom of expression and promoted self-regulation of advertising in Brazil. CONAR maintains the balance between the protection of consumer rights, the opportunity for fair competition in the marketplace, and freedom of intellectual creation. Its main objective is the enforcement of the Brazilian Advertising Self-Regulation Code, which came into force in 1978 as a way for the media to avoid previous advertising censorship. The code contains the general rules that govern ethics in advertising (the principles of honesty, fair competition, and social responsibility), as well as specific rules for the regulation of advertising of certain product categories (such as alcoholic beverages, pharmaceutical products, foods, pesticides, and others).

The emergence of CONAR in Brazil followed the adoption of the self-regulation principles in force in other countries, such as England, Portugal, the United States, Canada, and Mexico, and it was largely supported by the major players in Brazilian advertising. The initial agreement between agencies, advertisers, media broadcasters, and members of the public paved the way for the approval of the code, which CONAR has the power to enforce.

CONAR deals with the consumer's complaints by opening up an inquiry into the actions of the advertiser or advertising agency charged with a code violation. Only complaints against already published or aired advertisements are considered.

Aside from handling complaints from consumers, competitors, and public authorities, CONAR can also detect violations through its own monitoring procedures. In these cases, an inquiry is opened and submitted for evaluation by the Ethics Council. Depending on the council's decision, CONAR can suspend the advertisement campaign or impose content changes. According to Article 50, penalties include: (a) a warning, (b) a recommendation to modify or correct the advertisement, (c) a recommendation to the media to suspend the broadcasting of the advertisement, or (d) disclosure to the media of CONAR's position regarding the advertiser, the agency, and the medium for noncompliance with the steps and measures determined by the agency. The agency or the advertiser then has a formal deadline to present a defense. CONAR's decisions are strictly respected by all communication vehicles.[1]

The council does not judge political advertising, which, in Brazil and other countries such as Portugal, is within the jurisdiction of electoral tribunals.

Table 5.1 shows the number of cases evaluated by CONAR in Brazil from 1998 to 2010.

Table 5.1

Cases Evaluated by CONAR in Brazil, 1998–2010

Year	Number of instituted processes	Suspended ads
2010	376	221
2009	343	268
2008	448	180
2007	330	51
2006	303	62
2005	361	77
2004	309	88
2003	368	110
2002	288	59
2001	264	97
2000	229	90
1999	292	124
1998	227	119

Source: Translated from CONAR's website, http://www.conar.org.br/.

Code of Consumer Protection

According to Zulke (1990), consumers' rights in Brazilian society started gaining serious recognition in 1987, with the creation of IDEC (Instituto Brasileiro de Defesa do Consumidor), a civil entity that provides an alternative means of protection for consumers. For example, the payment anticipation of the telephone charges, payment of the stamp-toll, etc. In order to accomplish these activities, other ones, like comparative tests of products and the publication of the obtained results, were also included. The Code of Consumer Protection (Law No. 8.078, 1990), addresses consumer relations in all areas: *civil,* by defining industry responsibilities and the mechanisms for redress; *administrative,* by defining the rights and role of the public in monitoring consumer relations; and *criminal,* by defining specific types of crimes and establishing sanctions for them. The commercial relations between the seller/service provider and the consumer are contained in the Code of Consumer Protection. The government entity known as PROCON (Protection Prosecutor and Consumer Protection) guides consumers through the complaint process, informs them about their rights, and oversees consumer relations.

National Health Surveillance Agency (ANVISA)

ANVISA, created in 1999, is Brazil's National Health Surveillance Agency, charged with protecting the health of the population through production controls and surveillance of processing environments, methods, inputs, and related technologies. Since 2010, ANVISA has also regulated the advertising of foods with low nutritional value and high levels of sugar, saturated fats, and so-dium. According to the agency, the new regulation "forbids advertising that encourages the public, especially children, to consume these foods in amounts . . . incompatible with health standards and . . . adequate nutrition."

The advertisement of beverages with low nutritional content is also regulated. This includes soft drinks, artificially flavored drinks, beverages or concentrates composed of guarana syrup or gooseberry, and ready-to-drink teas. Advertisements for beverages containing caffeine, taurine, glucoronolactone, or any other substance that acts like a stimulant in the central nervous system must carry a warning concerning the health risks posed by their excessive consumption. Advertise-ments should also inform the public, for example, that eating foods high in fat increases the pos-sibility of heart disease and may contribute to the development of diabetes. The consumer should be informed that food with higher quantities of sodium increases the risk of high blood pressure and heart diseases. In the case of food with excess sugar, warnings about the risk of obesity and dental cavities are required.

Federal Constitution

The constitutionally guaranteed right to free speech in Brazil covers all forms of intellectual, artistic, scientific, and social expressions. According to the Brazilian constitution, "The mani-festation of thought, the creation, the expression, and the information—in any form, process, or medium—shall not be subject to any restriction, with due regard to the provisions of this Consti-tution" (Chapter 5, Article 220). The same article characterizes the extent of freedom of speech in the press, prohibiting any kind of political, ideological, or artistic censorship, and provides the constitutional framework for regulation, ownership, and content.

BRAZIL'S HISTORY OF CONTENT REGULATION AND MEDIA BROADCASTS

Media content regulation is often seen as a threat to freedom of expression, especially in a country like Brazil that endured a long period of dictatorship. Media censorship—even though it was never officially acknowledged—was dominant for almost 30 years, and only in the second half of the 1980s was freedom of speech—both political and apolitical—reestablished.

The Federal Constitution of 1988 was pivotal to the process of redemocratization in Brazil. It eliminated some restrictive rules that dominated the years of repression and started a process of political and social liberalization. One example—and maybe the greatest—was the declaration of the Press Law (Law No. 5.250, 1967) as unconstitutional. Approved during the period of dictator-ship in Brazil, the law imposed a series of direct and indirect restrictions on the press.

The Press Law remained in force for more than 20 years after Brazil's constitution was approved in 1988; it was finally declared unconstitutional by the Supreme Federal Court in April 2009. The marks left by the censorship in Brazil are still present, however. Every time the government imposes a new restriction on the media, the reaction is usually defensive and, in a certain way, exaggerated. And when these restrictions focus on the advertising industry, the reaction is even more extreme, due to the pervasive and passionate defense of the freedom of expression in Brazil.

Advertising in Brazil is big business; in fact, Brazil is one of the five biggest advertising markets in the world. To protect their interests, the media, the advertising industry, and in some cases even the public have been very effective in generating lobbies that block attempts to regulate media content. The result is an almost complete absence of regulations for sensitive themes.

Table 5.2

Total of Advertising Investments in Brazil, by Media Type, 2009 and 2010

Medium	January–December 2010		January–December 2009	
	BRL (000)	%	BRL (000)	%
Total	76.256.415	100	64.003.768	100
TV	40.213.791	53	33.524.169	52
Newspapers	16.120.105	21	14.447.244	23
Magazines	6.407.192	8	5.654.658	9
TV subscriptions	6.330.570	8	5.234.276	8
Internet	3.160.863	4	1.815.934	3
Radio	3.056.429	4	2.839.502	4
Cinema	432.677	1	391.221	1
Urban furniture	407.561	1	—	0
Outdoor	127.226	0	96.765	0

Source: IBOPE 2010—Monitor Evolution—37 Markets. Databases: ME10129MEIOS of December 2010 and ME09121T37NET of December 2009. Data for the period January 1–December 31, 2010. Published February 2, 2011.
Note: Data in R§ (000).

EVOLUTION OF ADVERTISING INVESTMENT IN THE BRAZILIAN MEDIA

According to IBOPE (the Brazilian Institute of Public Opinion and Statistics), as shown in Table 5.2, total advertising investments in all types of media in 2010 reached 76.256.415 reais (about 36,082.900 USD), 12.252.647 more reais (about 5,797,680 USD) than the year before. More than half of the investments went to television advertising, but Internet ads saw the biggest year-over-year increase.

Advertising Regulation of Alcoholic Drinks

In Brazil, the advertisement of alcoholic beverages is regulated by the Code of Consumer Protection, specifically by Law No. 9.294 (1996), which established restrictions of the advertisement of tobacco products, alcoholic drinks, drugs and therapies, and agricultural products. Section 3 of the code deals with advertising in general and protection from misleading or abusive advertising, without any reference to alcoholic drinks. Article 4 makes it illegal to advertise alcoholic beverages on radio or television during the period between 9:30 P.M. and 6:00 A.M. Also forbidden is the association of these products with greater success or heightened physical performance and sexual drive. Some leeway is given in cases of sponsorship, however. These products can be mentioned at any time by brand or slogan, without reference to their consumption.

Note that the aforementioned restrictions are not applicable to all alcoholic beverages. Beer, iced drinks, and most wines are too low in alcohol to be considered alcoholic drinks in Brazil. Consequently, their advertisement is not regulated by this law.

No legal mechanism exists to force advertisers to obey the self-regulation code. The state does not have enforcement power over the advertisers, and the observance of these rules is totally voluntary. Complaints are submitted to CONAR, a nongovernmental organization, for arbitration. It is the responsibility of CONAR to determine the appropriateness of commercials throughout Brazil.

The most severe sanction CONAR can impose on a violator of the code is the complete suspension of the advertising campaign. There is no additional sanction for the authors, sponsors, and broadcasters of the ads. Therefore, the advertisers are not afraid to produce bolder and bolder commercials; at the very worst, such commercial spots might be suspended after some weeks, at which point they would have already produced the desired effect in the minds of those who viewed them.

Although Brazil is generally soft on regulating alcohol ads, the use of children or childlike images or sounds in alcohol-related commercials is strictly prohibited in the self-regulation code. Additionally, according to this code, these commercials can be broadcast only between 9:30 P.M. and 6:00 A.M.

Food Advertising Regulation

The National Health Surveillance Agency (ANVISA) Resolution RDC No. 24 (2010) states that warning messages must accompany the advertisement of any kind of food that contains ingredients considered unhealthy by world health standards. ANVISA demanded the inclusion of warnings explaining that such foods can be harmful to health when consumed in excess. According to the agency's text, the rule applies to the distribution and commercial promotion of foods with high levels of sugar, saturated fat, and sodium, along with beverages with low nutritional levels. This broad group includes cookies, chocolates, jellybeans, soft drinks, and other snacks and sweets.

Resolution RDC No. 24, says ANVISA, aims to inform the public about the risks posed by overconsumption of unhealthy foods. The text makes it clear that the measure's main goal is the protection of children's health.

Advertising Regulation Concerning Children

There are few specific advertising regulations concerning the targeting of children by ads on Brazilian television. Restrictions on the audiovisual marketing of products that can damage health—like tobacco, alcoholic beverages, medicine, therapies, and chemical products—appeared only with the Law No. 9.294, which isn't specifically directed at child protection. Beyond that, similar protections can be found in other documents such as the Code of Consumer Protection, the Statute on Children and Adolescents of 1990, or the Brazilian Advertising Self-Regulation Code. Specifically, the Statute on Children and Adolescents states that, depending on the infraction, television broadcasters who violate the statute's terms can be fined and their programs can be suspended.

Article 37 of the Brazilian Advertising Self-Regulation Code explicitly regulates advertisements targeted toward children. Besides a number of prohibitions, it encourages:

- the positive development of relations between children and parents, students and teachers, and other relationships between caregivers and children;
- respect for the ingenuousness, credulity, inexperience, and loyalty so common in children;
- special attention to be paid to the psychological characteristics of the target public, assuming that these individuals have a reduced discerning capacity;

- truth and honesty in advertising over distortions of the facts; and
- upstanding behavior.

Note, however, that this code does not have the force of law. According to André Lacerda, one of the directors of the Association of Advertising Agencies of Minas Gerais (Sinapro), CONAR's recommendations are effective because CONAR has developed a code of rules that, "when not complied with, demands the advertisement to be taken off the air. In a general way, all complaints are answered. But there can be interpretative differences." The Code of Consumer Protection also takes care of this subject and prohibits abusive and misleading advertisement, which includes "taking advantage of children's lack of judgment and experience." In July 2008, the Consumer Defense Commission approved a directive, set forth by Deputy Luis Carlos Hauly (PL-591 [2001]), that mandates the advertising of any product or service must always be targeted to the adult public.

In the approved draft of PL-591, advertising and marketing aimed at children are forbidden. This includes the use of cartoons, children's language, and special effects; children's songs or songs sung by children; the use of people, celebrities, or characters connected with a child audience, including hosts of children's programs; and toys, promotional gifts, or giveaways that would appeal to an audience of children. This draft, still waiting for approval, also sets time constraints on advertising on television, the Internet, or radio (banning them 15 minutes before, 15 minutes after, and during children's programming or programming with predominantly child audiences).

CONCLUSIONS AND CHALLENGES FOR THE REGULATION OF ADVERTISING

All the agents involved in Brazil's advertising (agencies, media, advertisers, creatives, etc.) should identify themselves with the principles of good commercial practices in the communications sector. For their part, the consumers—especially educators and guardians—should be committed to safeguarding the more vulnerable audiences who are most likely to be swayed by the advertising messages.

Since 1937, when the International Chamber of Commerce (ICC) started working to establish a common basis for the development of self-disciplining systems, several countries joined with the intent of instituting advertising regulation entities. Brazil is among the 33 countries with self-regulatory agencies.

Brazil's history of dictatorship has given way to democratic governance, and with it, new economic growth. The purchasing power of the country's middle class has increased; in response, the media has also expanded and joined forces with advertising companies in the broadcasting of ads that stimulate the demand and consumption of products and services.

The importance of ethics in Brazil's advertising industry is paramount because of the tremendous responsibility that advertisers have in shaping the perceptions of their target audiences. Because of its continued growth and tradition of bold advertising campaigns, it is especially important that Brazil maintain an ongoing discussion of ethics and morality in the field. Literacy and education programs are vital for teaching citizens how to decode advertising messages in all media, including online, and how to become savvy consumers.

Looking ahead, the monitoring of electronic advertising will be one of the main drivers to consolidate and extend the role played by advertising's regulatory entities in Brazil.

NOTE

1. For example, two famous court cases involving CONAR were the Zeca Pagodinho case and the Mon Bijoux case. Zeca Pagodinho, a famous Brazilian samba musician, was hired by a beer company, Shincariol, in 2004, to promote a new beer. He broke the terms of his contract with Shincariol by doing an ad for another beer company, Brahma (supposedly his favorite). Brahma's ad clearly mentions and makes fun of Shincariol's ad. The case was brought to CONAR and, in a historical vote (11 to 0), Brahma's ad was pulled and the company was strictly forbidden from mentioning the Shincariol brand. Zeca Pagodinho was forced to honor his original contract or pay a stiff fine.

Another notorious advertising war—this one centering on a laundry detergent—took place in 1988. The advertisement in question compared Mon Bijoux detergent to another brand—Confort—and even featured a bottle of Confort in the ad. When Confort complained to CONAR, Mon Bijoux's parent company remade the ad but maintained the same comparisons (this time, not mentioning the Confort brand by name). The teasing remake featured a bottle of Confort covered by a cap and made fun of the latter's complaint to CONAR. In addition to being legal, the second ad was far more effective. Both ads can be accessed through this URL: http://conectou.blogspot.com/2010/11/guerra-publicitariamon-bijou-x-comfort.html.

BIBLIOGRAPHY

Brunetto, Thiago Cechini. 2002. "Reformas do Estado, Estado regulador," in *Agéncias de regulação do mercado*, Ed. UFRGS Editora.

Central Intelligence Agency. 2013. "Brazil." *The World Factbook Online*. Washington, DC: CIA. https://www.cia.gov/library/publications/the-world-factbook/geos/br.html.

Chaise, Valéria Falcão. 2001. *A Publicidade em face do Código de Defesa do Consumidor*. São Paulo: Saraiva.

Correa, Roberto. 2006. *O Atendimento na Agência de Comunicação*. São Paulo: Global Editora.

Ghiaccheta, André Zonaro, and Larissa Galimberti. 2008. "Novas restrições para a publicidade de bebidas alcoólicas no âmbito do CONAR." May 20. São Paulo: Conselho de Auto-Regulação Publicitária. http://www.migalhas.com.br/dePeso/16,MI60637,101048-Novas+restricoes+para+a+publicidade+de+bebidas+alcoolicas+no+ambito.

Giacomini Filho, Gino. 1991. *Consumidor versus Propaganda*. São Paulo: Summus.

Nunes Júnior, Vidal Serrano. 2001. *Publicidade comercial: Proteção e limites*. São Paulo: Juarez de Oliveira.

Tato Plaza, Anxo. 1993. *Publicidad comercial y libertad de expresión en la jurisprudencia norteamericana*. Actas de Derecho Mercantil. Instituto de Derecho Mercantil de la Universidad de Santiago de Compostela. Tomo XIV, 1991–92. Madrid: Marcial Pons.

———. 1994. *Publicidad comercial y libertad de expresión en la jurisprudencia norteamericana: nuevos desarrollos*. Actas de Derecho Industrial. Instituto de Derecho Industrial de la Universidad de Santiago de Compostela. Tomo XV, 1993. Madrid: Marcial Pons.

Zulke, Maria Lucia. 1990. *Abrindo a empresa para o consumidor*. Ed. Qualitymark, 3, 42–43.

Legal Sources

ANVISA Resolution RDC No. 24 (regarding food labeling). June 15, 2010. http://portal.anvisa.gov.br/wps/wcm/connect/34565380474597549fd4df3fbc4c6735/RDC24_10_Publicidade+de+alimentos.pdf?MOD=AJPERES.

Brazilian Advertising Self-Regulation Code. 1978. http://www.conar.org.br/. Portuguese and English versions available.

Code of Consumer Protection. 1990. http://www.brasil.gov.br/para/invest/brazilian-consumer-rights.

Constitution of the Federal Republic of Brazil. 1988. http://www.wipo.int/wipolex/en/details.jsp?id=8755.

Law No. 9.294 (regarding tobacco control). July 15, 1996. http://www.tobaccocontrollaws.org/files/live/Brazil/Brazil%20-%20Law%20No.%209.294.pdf.

Institutions

Agência Nacional de Telecomunicações (National Agency for Telecommunications) (ANATEL; Brazil). http://www.anatel.gov.br/.

Agência Nacional de Vigilância Sanitária (National Health Surveillance Agency) (ANVISA; Brazil). http://portal.anvisa.gov.br/.

Associação Brasileira das Agências de Publicidade (Brazilian Association of Advertising Agencies) (ABAP; Brazil). http://www.abapnacional.com.br/.

Associação Nacional de Editores de Revistas (National Association of Magazine Publishers) (ANER; Brazil). http://www.aner.org.br/.

Conselho Nacional de Autorregulamentação Publicitária (National Council for Advertising Self-Regulation) (CONAR; Brazil). http://www.conar.org.br/.

Entidade Reguladora Para a Comunicação Social (Regulatory Authority for the Media) (ERC; Portugal). http://www.erc.pt/.

Interactive Advertising Bureau (Brazil). http://iabbrasil.ning.com/.

Intermeios Project (Brazil). http://www.projetointermeios.com.br/.

Sindicato das Agências de Propaganda do Estado de Minas Gerais (Association of Advertising Agencies of the state of Minas Gerais) (SINAPRO-MG; Brazil). http://www.sinapromg.com.br/.

Other Resources

Correio do Brasil (newspaper). http://correiodobrasil.com.br/.

IBOPE (research company). http://www.ibope.com.br/.

Via de Acesso (news website). http://www.viadeacesso.com.br/.

Note: Websites accessed in February 2012.

CHAPTER 6

CHILE

MARIA-ELENA GRONEMEYER

Chile occupies a long, thin band of land in southern South America along the Pacific Ocean. According to 2013 estimates, its population had reached approximately 17 million people (CIA 2013). Chile has a central democratic government that exercises its functions through the three independent state powers: executive, legislative, and judicial. During the military regime in power from 1973 to 1989, the country began to embrace the neoliberal free market economic model that has been maintained since the return to democracy in 1990. This South American nation exhibits a strong cultural, political, and financial openness to other world markets and maintains international treaties with several countries from all continents, encouraging the flow and exchange of people, goods, and services.

Regarding communications, *The World Factbook Online* (CIA 2013) states that Chile has national and local television channels, coupled with extensive cable TV networks; the state-owned Television Nacional de Chile (TVN) network is self-financed through commercial advertising revenues and not under direct government control. The country also has four privately owned TV stations and about 250 radio stations. Furthermore, Chile publishes more than 60 newspapers; the mainstream papers with national reach are *El Mercurio, La Tercera, La Cuarta*, and *Las Últimas Noticias*, all of them published in Santiago (the capital). Additionally, the country has at least two dozen magazines, some of which can only be accessed via the Internet, the main one being *El Mostrador.cl.*

According to data from the Economist Intelligence Unit (EIU), in 2010 Chile was considered the best place in Latin America to do business. Robert Wood, EIU senior analyst for Latin America, was quoted by the Santiago Chamber of Commerce as saying that Chile is a pioneer in consolidating macroeconomic stability and promoting the kind of structural reforms that made the current business climate possible.[1] Wood argues that Chile's ranking is based on its longstanding commitment to economic liberalization; although its economy is small, this is partly mitigated by its position on free trade agreements and exports. In 2012, Chile's GDP was US$319.4 billion and achieved a real growth rate of 5 percent (CIA 2013).

Table 6.1 shows Chile's evolution in advertising investment during the last decade.

DEVELOPMENT OF LEGAL ADVERTISING REGULATIONS IN CHILE

Chile has developed its legal advertising regulations in concert with the trends of the West, which have contributed to an increased awareness of consumer rights when dealing with providers of goods and services. The Consumer Protection Law in Chile defines advertising as "the communication that the provider addresses to the public in any suitable medium for that purpose, to inform and motivate to buy goods or services."

Table 6.1

Evolution of Advertising Investment in Chile, 2000–2009 (in US$ million)

Medium	2000	2001	2002	2003	2004	2005	2006	2007	2008	2009
Television	324	341	371	389	408	430	454	488	458	464
Print media	299	251	256	245	264	285	294	310	289	245
Radio	80	73	71	70	66	72	68	68	66	65
Street	51	48	48	50	61	74	81	93	79	66
Film	3	3	3	3	3	3	3	3	2	3
Online	7	7	10	12	16	21	24			
Total	757	716	749	764	809	874	912	978	915	867

Source: ACHAP 2010.

The scope and limits of advertising are enforced in Chile by specific laws and regulations, including recent supplements related to advertisements for products perceived as especially sensitive, among them alcohol, cigarettes and tobacco, and food. These new regulations also respond to the demands placed upon the country by international treaties that Chile has signed, for example, with the World Health Organization (WHO).

Although today's advertising business is subject to several rules and norms, the legal regulation is a rather recent phenomenon in Chile, as in many South American countries. During colonial rule in Chile in the sixteenth century, some protective measures existed, but only in the early to mid-twentieth century were new rules established for the Chilean market. Consumer protection laws came even later: The first such law (Law 18.223) was enacted in 1983 and later revised. Law 19.496 on consumer rights and advertising was passed in 1998.

Although still in force, Law 18.223 has been supplemented with provisions regulating newer and more specific types of advertising such as spam or unwanted advertising emails, and logo and trademark infringements that might create confusion for consumers.

Following the model of other Western countries, laws on advertising in Chile regulate misleading advertising, the treatment of socially sensitive products, and the morality of advertising and messages addressed to vulnerable groups such as minors. In addition to laws and regulations, Chile has government agencies to ensure compliance with legal norms and to protect consumers against the excesses of advertising.

The self-regulatory bodies add to these issues a further concern for decency, good taste, and standards of ethical conduct.

CURRENT LEGAL ADVERTISING REGULATION

In Chile, as in some other countries in Latin America, consumer protection still has no constitutional status. In 2002, legislators proposed a law to incorporate consumers' rights as a constitutional guarantee. The proposal stated that Chileans had the right to high "quality . . . goods and services . . . ; the protection of their health, safety and economic interests; the repair of [any] damage caused to them [by substandard goods]; and the right to information, education, and organizations to defend their interests." However, this law has not yet been added to the nation's constitution.

Chile's Consumer Protection Law 19.496 was last supplemented in 2004 with Law 19.955, which makes it easier for victims of misleading advertising to seek justice and gives more power to the National Consumer Service (SERNAC) to act as a mediator. In addition, the rule expressly recognizes the application of the Consumer Protection Law to health care, education, and housing sales.

As a general rule, Chilean Law 19.496 establishes as basic and inalienable rights of consumers the free choice to purchase a good or service; the right to accurate and timely information about goods and services offered; freedom from arbitrary discrimination by providers of goods and services; safety in the consumption of goods or services; protection of health and the environment; and the repair of or compensation for damages caused by a good or service. In Chile, the local police courts are the pertinent authorities to deal with all actions emanating from the Consumer Protection Act.

The law on consumer protection establishes financial penalties for the dissemination through the media of false or misleading advertising. The amount of those sanctions increases in cases of recidivism and in cases involving products or services that affect the health or safety of the public or the environment. In the case of false advertising, the court may order the suspension of the ads or require the advertiser to place corrective advertising appropriate to amend errors or falsehoods. In Chile, only financial penalties have been enforced under this law.

Regarding newer advertising methods such as email, the law specifies that the word *advertising* must be included in the subject line of the message, the identity of the sender must be clear, and the message must contain a valid address to which the recipient may request suspension of the emails, which from then on will be banned.

Comparative advertising is allowed in Chile, but with certain restrictions. The ads must not be misleading, very high standards of proof must be supplied by those who make the advertisements, and self-regulatory bodies must have a role in controlling this kind of advertising. The Unfair Competition Law 20.169 (2007) in Chile defines unfair competition as "any comparison of goods, services, activities, or businesses . . . based on facts that are not true and provable."

GOVERNMENT SUPPORTED BODIES REGULATING ADVERTISING

Several different types of organizations exist in Chile for the defense of consumers' rights. The official body is the National Consumer Service (SERNAC), created in 1990 to educate, inform, and protect consumers in Chile. Formed under the terms of Law 19.496, SERNAC is a government agency that mediates consumer disputes with suppliers. According to data from this agency, in 2009 it received 170,000 complaints from consumers. Most of the cases were related to the telecommunications industry, banks, retailers, and insurance agencies.

SERNAC follows three guiding principles linked to advertising: loyalty, accuracy, and testability. The organization has no oversight powers. The identification of misleading advertising by SERNAC has to be reported by the regulator to the courts. A complaint in court can take between four and six months to resolve, and an additional year if the first decision is appealed.

SERNAC can ask the court for the following actions and sanctions against advertisers: suspension of the advertisement, publication of a corrective advertising, and the imposition of fines. Of the three sanctions, the court in Chile has applied only the third. However, the fines have apparently been too low to discourage advertisers from breaking the law. Therefore, it is estimated that the actual penalty imposed in these cases is public exposure of the complaint made by SERNAC through the media, thereby affecting the public image of the denounced companies.

There are also consumer associations in Chile that are nonprofits, with no commercial or political ends. Their aim is to protect, inform, and educate consumers, and to represent and advocate for their members and for consumers who request their help. These associations cannot receive aid or subsidies from companies or groups of companies who provide goods or services to consumers, or do advertising or disseminate communications about goods or services unless those communications are merely informational. To finance themselves, these consumer associations apply for a grant administered by SERNAC.

A governmental National Television Council (Consejo Nacional de Televisión [CNTV]) operates in Chile as a regulator of the content released by broadcast television and cable television; this includes the contents of ads. Its Special Rules on the Content of Television Broadcasts were agreed upon by the council in 1993 and updated in 2009.

Founded in 1989 by Law 18.838, the National Television Council has among its many functions the control of the content of foreign and national advertising. Its powers include preventing the spread of advertising that threatens morals, good customs, or public policy, and applying the provisions on advertising abuses to television broadcasts. It also has powers to punish transgressions of special laws such as those regulating the advertising of tobacco and alcohol.

Regarding advertising, the CNTV safeguards Chile's moral and cultural values—the dignity of individuals, families, pluralism, democracy, peace, protection of the environment, and the spiritual and intellectual formation of children and youth. To that end, the council prohibits advertising containing excessive violence, barbarism, or pornography, the participation of children or adolescents in messages at odds with good values, and all forms of advertising related to drug use or consumption.

ADVERTISING SELF-REGULATION IN CHILE

The international experience, Western trends, and Chile's status as a member of the network of advertising self-regulatory bodies in Latin America, CONARED,[2] pushed Chilean advertisers, ad agencies, and the mass media to agree on the need to regulate themselves. National advertising self-regulatory boards promote ethical conduct and public confidence in the advertising business, consolidate corporate loyalty, and thereby decrease the likelihood of government over-regulation of advertising.

In 1986, the Chilean Association of Advertising Agencies (Asociación Chilena de Agencias de Publicidad [ACHAP]) and the National Advertisers Association (Asociación Nacional de Avisadores [ANDA]) merged their conduct codes. Together, they created and approved the new original text of the Chilean Code of Advertising Ethics, a regulatory policy that endures through today with minor modifications and contains the principles and ethical standards that should prevail in advertising practice. In 1987 in Chile, ACHAP and ANDA founded the National Council for Advertising Self-Regulation (Consejo Nacional de Autorregulación Publicitaria [CONAR]) with the participation of the mass media represented by the National Press Association (Asociación Nacional de la Prensa [ANP]), the Association of Chilean Radio Broadcasters (Asociación de Radiodifusores de Chile [ARCHI]), and the National Television Association (Asociación Nacional de Televisión [Anatel]).

Considering the development of digital media and their new place in advertising, in early 2010 the CONAR incorporated a new foreign institution, the Interactive Advertising Bureau (IAB), as a member for online advertising. It was considered an important step that will help online marketing meet the established parameters of legality, honesty, decency, truthfulness, and the rules of the Chilean Code of Advertising Ethics.

CONAR's mediation task is the delegated responsibility of a special agent within it. Additionally, CONAR established the Advertising Standards Court (Tribunal de Ética Publicitaria) in 1994 for backup on mediation.

The council rules on traditional and nontraditional commercial advertising for products and services produced domestically or abroad, regardless of the medium used for its display to a consumer. The responsibility for abuses in advertising sanctioned by CONAR may lie with the advertiser and advertising agency that created and placed the message, the mass medium that disseminated it, or any person who participated in its planning, creation, or publication.

According to CONAR, there are several advantages to having advertising self-regulatory boards. The first is that the advertising industry itself knows its own weaknesses and is best suited to devising its own solutions to its problems; regulation by specialists in the field is more expeditious and less expensive than it is through the ordinary courts. Second, self-regulation allows for continuous updating of standards and evaluation criteria, and it does not require actual prejudice against consumers or competitors be proved to make self-regulatory mechanisms operate. The interest of the industry is that advertising takes place within an ethical framework freely agreed upon. CONAR considers compliance with its standards to be in the best interest of advertisers because such standards establish a framework of trust and good relations between stakeholders in advertising. Furthermore, self-regulation allows for specialized treatment of topics that, in the legal domain, would be difficult to regulate (taste and sensuality, among others). Finally, as mentioned earlier, an efficient and socially validated mechanism of self-regulation prevents overregulation by the state.

THE OBJECTIVES OF THE COUNCILS OF SELF-REGULATION

The main purpose of CONAR in Chile is to defend the freedom of commercial expression through self-regulation. CONAR seeks to make advertising a reliable and credible tool that helps consumers make informed decisions and facilitates fair competition among advertisers. The council's members are united in their belief that companies have the right to advertise their products and services freely, and that consumers have the right to make well-informed purchasing decisions.

In order to achieve these goals, the advertising self-regulatory board assumes three roles: a guiding and preventive role, a corrective role (by resolving complaints), and a cautionary role that serves as a precedent for future publications. The main ethical principles and standards that govern commercial speech are defined in the Code of Advertising Ethics.

The main topics discussed and reviewed by CONAR are misleading advertising, the consumer's ability to discern truth from fiction, accepted levels of exaggeration, verification of promises made through advertising, the particular sensitivities of certain individuals and groups, unfair competition, appropriation of others' ideas, and the use and possible manipulation of children in advertising.

THE COUNCIL'S CODE OF ETHICS

In order to fulfill its mission, the board of advertising self-regulation and its associated entities have a duty to adhere to its Code of Ethics. This code, like many other such international documents, is based on the International Code of Advertising Practice of the International Chamber of Commerce (ICC) in Paris (1937). Necessary supplements and adaptations relevant to the Chilean experience were blended with the rules and procedures of other countries in Europe, North America, and Latin America. It is always being reviewed and updated to accommodate new methods of communication and sociocultural changes.

The Ethics Code of Chile, in its most recent version from 2007 (it is the fourth updated version), declares that advertising should be framed within the law; it should be decent, honest, and truthful; and it should respect the family as the fundamental unit of society. Additionally, it establishes that "no advertisement or commercial statement should be presented in ways that could undermine public confidence in advertising."

The Administration and Proceedings of the Council and Its Ethics Committee

CONAR is headed by a board of nine members and nine alternates elected by the institutions associated with the council—all the major entities and private companies in the country related to advertising and communications: ANDA, ACHAP, ANP, ARCHI, and ANATEL. In addition, CONAR has an executive secretary and assistant general. This board meets weekly or as requested.

In accordance with the procedures of CONAR in Chile, a complaint can be filed by any person, company or entity—public or private—who considers a given advertisement ethically questionable. The breaches of the Ethics Code can also be reported ex officio by CONAR's own initiative when requested by at least two of the council's members. CONAR also performs arbitrations and conciliatory procedures, and the organization can disseminate doctrinal pronouncements.

Complaints activate a process that includes an initial review of the advertising by the board of CONAR, who accepts or rejects the claim. When CONAR decides to handle a complaint, the advertiser or the agency has a formal deadline of three working days for defense and clarifications. If an ad is considered unethical, the council may recommend that the advertisement be changed or pulled from distribution altogether.

Generally, in the Chilean procedure, the final decision does not take more than two weeks. If the case warrants it, the advertisement under discussion may be suspended before the final decision is reached. The resolutions of the board and the ethics committee may be appealed to CONAR's Court of Advertising Ethics. In that case, the advertiser must provide new data within three working days to try to reverse the ruling.

COMPLIANCE AND PUBLICATION OF THE RESOLUTIONS

Chile has agreed on standards to promote compliance with the rules of its self-regulatory agency and the public dissemination of its resolutions. While claims are being processed, the record is kept in reserve, but once the resolution has been handed down, it can be made public. CONAR issues a newsletter of its decisions on a quarterly basis. In addition, the files are available online through a subscription service.

Since 1987 in Chile, CONAR has handled more than 700 complaints for violations of advertising ethics. Its decisions are useful to the academic community, to government, to businesses, and to the general public. Though they do not have the force of law, CONAR's decisions are almost always respected. In the few cases when they are ignored, CONAR may publicly disclose information on the offender's noncompliance.

STATISTICS FROM CONAR CHILE

According to CONAR data, Chile runs 60,000 ads each year. The nation's advertising investment in 2009 was US$869 million (0.53 percent of GDP) and consisted of ads on television (broadcast and cable), radio, in the press (newspapers and magazines), on the streets, in film, and in online media. Only a few dozen of the 60,000 ended in formal complaints and were presented to the self-regulatory body.

Public information is available regarding 765 cases submitted to CONAR between 1987 and 2009. In Chile, the years with the most cases were 1998 (85) and 1999 (70). The average load during most years in the period 1987–2009 was 29 cases.

CONAR reports that most of the complaints originated with companies or advertising agencies (nearly 70 percent), followed by claims made by individuals (another 20 percent). The remainder is split between allegations originated ex officio, from government organizations, from trade associations, and from nonprofit organizations.

Institutional claimants in Chile include the Senate, political parties, the Chilean Book Chamber, the National Television Council, ARCHI (Association of Chilean Radio Broadcasters), Citizen Action (NPO), the police, the Plastic Surgery Society, the Association of Private Health Insurance, the National Traffic Safety Commission, the Superintendency of Electricity and Fuels, and SERNAC.

CONAR has ruled on cases that involve the defense of threatened patriotic values, aggression against the competition (by denigrating the image and the campaign of a competitor), harm to a profession (to dentists in the Chilean case), discrimination against a minority (in this case, the Rastafarian community), misuse of a personality (making use of an individual's image and/or voice without consent), and the use of gratuitous violence.

The Most Frequent Complaints

Within the period 1995–1999 (no data is available from previous years), CONAR cases have focused primarily on three areas: (1) plagiarism or imitation, (2) unproven advertising claims designed to deceive the consumer, and (3) disparagement or denigration of products or people. Since 1999, more cases have centered on the issue of accuracy, presentation, and possible misinterpretations of advertising. In more recent years, 2007 and 2008, new topics have become matters for self-regulation: comparative advertising, previously forbidden in Chile, and fair competition. The advertising of foods and beverages, recently covered by more specific and stringent regulations, also saw an increase in complaints in 2007–2008.

The Most Frequently Violated Articles of the Code of Advertising Ethics

The article of the Code of Ethics that appears to be violated most frequently is Article 4, related to Accuracy, Presentation and Interpretation, with a total of 141 cases. It is followed by the articles relating to Comparative Advertising, the Subject of Law, Morality and Respect for People, and Imitation or Plagiarism.

Certain articles have been violated very sporadically throughout the period observed, reaching a maximum of only three cases. They are:

- Article 3—Violence;
- Article 15—Identification of the ad as such;
- Article 20—Responsibilities;
- Article 22—Promotional advertising;
- Article 24—Standards for planning and preparing advertising targeting children; and
- Article 25—Advertising of medicines.

There are articles that do not appear to have been violated at all throughout the period 1996–2008. They are:

- Article 2—Public trust and exploitation of fear;
- Article 18—Advertising of alcohol and tobacco;
- Article 19—Education and training;
- Article 21—Advertisement of offers;
- Article 23—Guarantee and certification; and
- Article 26—General statements on drug advertising.

OTHER INSTANCES OF SELF-REGULATION IN CHILE

Editorial Principles of the Media

In Chile, the media generally have embraced as their own standards and principles those contained in CONAR's Code of Ethics, an entity associated with almost all the media in the country.

However, television channels that have been defined as public or university media, as opposed to commercial channels, have in some cases provided additional standards according to their editorial policy and program guidelines. Thus, Televisión Nacional de Chile (TVN), the public channel in Chile, places special emphasis on safeguarding pluralism, tolerance, and respect for minorities in all television content, including advertising.

Channel 13, which until mid-2010 belonged to the Catholic University in Chile, also had special provisions for advertising and programs under its editorial policy.

Special Legal Regulations of Tobacco, Alcohol, and Food Advertising

Following in the footsteps of other countries in the region, Chile has taken steps to adopt the proposals of international health organizations (WHO, for example) in approving and enforcing laws specific to the advertising of tobacco, alcohol, and food.

The Chilean Tobacco Law 20.105 (2006) states that tobacco and cigarette advertisements can be displayed only within the stores in which the product is sold and broadcast on television in timeslots for adults (from age 18 on), between 10:00 P.M. and 6:00 A.M. As a way of protecting minors from consuming tobacco, the law prohibits any form of advertising of tobacco products in places that are within 300 meters of a school.

In any advertising message for a tobacco-containing product, the use of words like "soft," "light," "low tar," "low nicotine," "low carbon monoxide," or similar terms is prohibited. Instead, the advertising of all kinds of tobacco and cigarettes disseminated through any medium must carry a visible, clearly worded warning of injury, disease, and other damaging effects to health from cigarette smoking.

The Alcohol Law 19.925 (2004) on Expense and Consumption of Alcoholic Beverages concerns legal provisions applying to alcohol advertising. It penalizes advertisers for encouraging underage alcohol consumption. Following the Western trend of tightening regulatory standards relating to advertising and alcohol consumption, the Chilean Congress passed a bill in September 2012 that introduced changes to Law 19.925 by setting more specific standards regarding the dispensing and labeling of alcoholic beverages.

Warnings against excessive consumption must be in every graphical advertising (newspapers, magazines, or other print media) in a block of at least 15 percent of the total area of the ad. Certain specifications also apply for audiovisual or radio advertising formats.

Since 2007, the Chilean Ministry of Health has been advocating for stricter regulations of food advertising aimed at children. A bill on the nutritional composition of food and its advertising was approved by the Health Commission of the Chamber of Deputies in 2010. The bill prohibits the advertisement of certain items to an audience of children under 12 years of age. These include ads for foods high in calories, fat, or salt broadcast on television, radio, and other mass media, as well as promotions and information advancing the consumption of such a product. These foods cannot be promoted or advertised in any school or kindergarten, and the use of toys or other accessories as commercial hooks is absolutely forbidden. Law 20606 on Nutritional Composition of Food and its Advertising was passed in July 2012. It allows advertising to target adults and adolescents, but the ads must be accompanied by a message that promotes healthy lifestyles and encourages the consumption of healthy food, along with engagement in sports or other physical activity.

CHALLENGES FACING REGULATORY MECHANISMS IN CHILE

In a conversation about advertising regulation with the author of this chapter, Chilean lawyer Jaime Lorenzini, a consumer law specialist with 14 years' experience in consumer protection regulatory matters and former chief of staff of the National Consumer Service, highlights the main achievements and tasks that still need to be accomplished.

According to Lorenzini, advertising self-regulation in Chile has allowed companies to find the most suitable ways to solve the problems that affect them. Self-regulation has given companies an opportunity to manage and share the costs involved in building a reputation in the market, and may be viewed as a tool to enhance the prestige of an entire industry or sector. Under certain circumstances, it has helped the industry avoid regulatory overload and obviate the need for strong formal controls. In the case of nutritional labeling and advertising of foods, advertising self-regulation drew on the contents of formal regulation.

There is a high degree of compliance with CONAR's verdicts. However, this does not necessarily mean that unethical behaviors will not be repeated later. Lorenzini suggests that the self-regulatory mechanisms be complemented by positive incentives from regulators.

In many cases, allegations from SERNAC related to misleading advertising (or breach of duties of information on promotions and offers) may also have been reviewed by CONAR. Although the Chilean Code of Advertising Ethics could have been applied in certain cases, the application of self-regulation has not always worked; consequently, the state body is forced to intervene in these cases and exercise the formal mechanisms of regulation and punishment in advertising. More and better coordinated work by SERNAC and CONAR must be done in the future.

NOTES

1. Robert Wood in "Chile tiene mejor ambiente de negocios de la región y se ubica en el 17 del mundo," http://www.chilexportaservicios.cl/ces/default.aspx?tabid=404 (accessed December 10, 2010).

2. Once the local councils were founded, Latin American countries proceeded to link these entities in a regional alliance. The first Latin American meeting of national self-regulatory agencies took place in 2008, and from that first meeting, CONARED was created. CONARED is the network of advertising self-regulatory bodies in Latin America. This entity is now integrated by Argentina, Brazil, Colombia, Chile, El Salvador, Guatemala, Mexico, Paraguay, Peru, and Uruguay. Its purpose is to seek the incorporation of a greater number of countries in the network.

The initiative emerged from the interest of the advertising industry in Latin American countries to establish a network of self-regulation. The intent was to unify criteria for the application of the codes of ethics and to foster a regional approach to commercial communication practices for advertisers, advertising agencies, and the media to ensure public safety and trust.

In turn, CONARED is linked to the World Federation of Advertisers (WFA). In its annual meetings in the region, they discuss key global strategic regulatory and media issues and bring together marketers and national advertiser associations from across South America. The WFA has Latin American National Advisers Associations in Argentina, Brazil, Colombia, Chile, Guatemala, Mexico, Paraguay, Peru, Uruguay, and Venezuela.

BIBLIOGRAPHY

Documents

Alcohol Law 19.925 (Ley de Alcoholes). 2004.
Central Intelligence Agency. 2013. "Chile." *The World Factbook Online*. Washington, DC: CIA. https://www.cia.gov/library/publications/the-world-factbook/geos/ci.html.
Code of Advertising Ethics from CONAR. http://www.conar.cl/.
Consumer Protection Law 18.223 (Ley de Protección del Consumidor). 1983.
Consumer Protection Law 19.496 (Ley del Consumidor). 1998.
Consumers' Rights Protection Law 19.955 (Ley de Protección de los Derechos de los Consumidores). 2004.
Draft Law on Protection of Consumer Rights (to give constitutional protection to consumers); Chamber of Deputies. June 2009. http://www.camaradediputados.cl/pley/pley_detalle.aspx?prmID=6936&prmBL=6543–03.
Tobacco Law 20.105 (Ley del Tabaco). 2006.
Unfair Competition Law 20.169 (Ley de Competencia Desleal). 2007.

Institutions

Association of Chilean Radio Broadcasters/Asociación de Radiodifusores de Chile (ARCHI). www.archi.cl.
Chilean Association of Advertising Agencies/Asociación Chilena de Agencias de Publicidad (ACHAP). www.achap.cl.
Chilean National Television/Televisión Nacional de Chile (TVN). www.tvn.cl.
Consumer Associations/Asociaciones de Consumidores. http://www.sernac.cl/vinculos/chile_organizaciones_Metropolitana.php.
Economist Intelligence Unit (EIU). http://country.eiu.com/Chile.
Interactive Advertising Bureau (IAB). www.iab.cl.
National Advertisers Association/Asociación Nacional de Avisadores (ANDA). www.anda.cl.
National Consumer Service/Servicio Nacional del Consumidor (SERNAC). http://www.sernac.cl.
National Council for Advertising Self-Regulation/Consejo Nacional de Autorregulación Publicitaria (CONAR). www.conar.cl.
National Press Association/Asociación Nacional de la Prensa (ANP). www.anp.cl.
National Television Association/Asociación Nacional de Televisión (ANATEL). www.anatel.cl.
National Television Council/Consejo Nacional de Televisión (CNTV). www.cntv.cl.
Santiago Chamber of Commerce/Cámara de Comercio de Santiago. www.ccs.cl.
Television Channel 13 (Canal 13). www.canal13.cl.

CHAPTER 7

COLOMBIA

MERCEDES MEDINA

Colombia is a democratic republic located in northern South America with a population of about 45 million as of 2012. The country has endured decades of conflict and guerilla influence that threatened civil liberties. Since 1991, however, it has had a written constitution, where the people's fundamental human rights are recognized.

The economic recession affected advertising investment in Colombia in 2009 (see Table 7.1), but the impact was not as great as in Europe or the United States. The growth in 2010 was 12 percent, which is rather good taking into account a 2 percent inflation rate and economic growth of around 4.5 percent. Radio and television experienced the highest growth, while investment in magazines decreased by 16.1 percent since 2007.

GOVERNMENT REGULATION

Colombia followed in the footsteps of the democratic transition in Spain. Advertising regulation in Colombia reflects the constitutionally guaranteed right to freedom of expression.

The following rights are recognized and protected in Colombia: the freedom to express and disseminate thoughts, ideas, and opinions through words, writing, or any other means of distribution; the production of literary, artistic, scientific, and technical works; academic freedom; and the right to freely communicate or receive truthful information via any media (Article 20). Regarding freedom of information, there are two other fundamental principles to consider: advertising, which is considered a type of speech protected under freedom of expression (Article 78), and the copyright of works (Article 61). Both are recognized and protected under Law 182 (1995). The law recognizes both the clause of conscience and professional secrecy in the exercise of these freedoms, which cannot be restricted by any form of censorship. It regulates the organization and parliamentary control of the state-dependent media or any other public body and grants access to such media by significant social and political groups, respecting the pluralism of the society and the diversity of languages. These freedoms may be limited by the requirement to recognize other rights, such as privacy, personal reputation, and the protection of youth and children.

HISTORY OF ADVERTISING REGULATION

There is no specific advertising law in Colombia. Instead, there are different agreements that define some principles of behavior in the field. Moreover, there are a great number of public bodies that regulate advertising. Rules cover issues such as unfair competition, consumer protection, copyright restrictions, self-regulation, television advertising, health, and bank and finance information.

Table 7.1

Advertising Gross Investment, 2005–2010 (in millions of current Colombian pesos and millions of US$)

	2005	2006	2007	2008	2009	2010
Magazines	83,439	105,912	118,890	108,196	93,488	99,876
Radio	257,507	294,505	345,592	352,518	365,762	419,008
TV, local and regional	36,741	47,228	59,306	58,633	58,794	65,275
TV NAC	673,409	763,408	863,885	858,225	823,611	919,366
Total TV	710,151	810,636	923,191	916,857	882,404	984,640
Total	1,051,098	1,211,052	1,387,673	1,377,571	1,341,654	1,503,525
In millions of USD	575.8	663.5	760.2	754.7	735.0	823.7

Source: ASOMEDIOS 2010.
Note: 1.00 USD (U.S. dollars) = 1,825.20 COP (Colombian pesos)
1.00 COP = 0.000547885 USD

In the absence of a specific advertising laws, it is necessary to turn to laws that deal with unfair competition (Law 256 [1996]), consumer protection (Decree 3466 [1982]), intellectual property (Law 565 [2000]), and of course media-specific regulations. (The difference between a *law* and a *decree* as used in this article is the procedure for their authorization: Decrees are written and approved more quickly than laws.) Examples of laws related to advertising but not specific to the industry are Law 140 (1994) on outdoor advertising (known as "independent advertising" to distinguish it from "dependent media" such as radio, television, and print media); Law 29 (1944) on political propaganda and the press; Law 74 (1966) on time restrictions for radio broadcasting; Law 182 (1995) on television, later reformed by Law 335 (1996); and finally, Laws 527 (1999) and 545 (1999), which regulate the Internet, electronic commerce, and intellectual property, based on the World Intellectual Property Organization (WIPO).

In Colombia, outdoor advertising has special regulations related to environmental protection. It is regulated at a local rather than a national level. The main aspects of the rules deal with the duration and size of the ads, with an eye toward protecting the trees, landscape, and airspace. Some of the cities in Colombia have a high level of outdoor advertising, but changing business conditions will likely result in a decrease in its use.

According to the Press Statute (29 [1994]), the advertiser bears responsibility for the advertising, but the medium should reject ads that violate basic rules of truthfulness, honor, morality, and decency. Under the guidelines on ethical behavior and professional practice, ads in Colombian newspapers should be located at the bottom of the printed page and cannot take up more than 20 percent of the space. Informative content is always given priority over ads.

In Colombia, there are three models of radio stations: community radio stations that can broadcast ads every 75 minutes; commercial stations without advertising restrictions; and public radio stations that may not broadcast ads. Community radio that is financed through public funding has an educational mission and, usually, a geographic- or interest-based niche based on shared experience; commercial radio is entertainment oriented and financed by advertising; public radio focuses on issues of public service and political interest.

GOVERNMENT REGULATION

Monitoring of advertisements is carried out by the Ministry of Information and Communication Technologies, which has legal authority to impose fines on those radio stations that break the law. The National Spectrum Agency, created in 2010, controls and allocates the nation's telecommunications licenses. The ministry develops the telecommunication policies and the agency ensures their implementation.

The creation of private television channels was allowed by Law 182 (1995), which underwent a reform a year later (Law 335 [1996]) and was finally launched in 1999. The Comisión Nacional de Television (National Television Commission [CNTV]) was formed to oversee advertisers' compliance with copyright rules. It also held the power to withdraw those ads found to violate the rules for television and to apply appropriate sanctions. However, in 2011 the mission of CNTV was revised, and by 2012 the commission disappeared completely.*

The Colombian national government viewed CNTV as being inefficient and overly politicized. The creation of a new regulatory body for the telecommunications market has been in the works for some time.

Prior to its liquidation, the National Television Commission (CNTV) signed a series of agreements to regulate advertising activity, including Commission Agreement 010 (1997) on commercial television; Commission Agreement 017 (1997), which regulates sex and violence on television; and Commission Agreement 042 (2005), which regulates tobacco and alcohol advertising on television. The aforementioned Law 140 (1994) on outdoor advertising and Decree 3466 (1982), establishing the quality, prices, guarantees, and proper labeling of goods and the responsibilities of producers and providers of any good or service, also originated with CNTV. The general principle that frames the content of television advertising states that the message must be truthful and provable, must respect the rules of fair competition and fair trade, and must obey the principles governing public service television.

Responsibility and Penalties

In 1994 it was established that media are obliged to review the content they disseminate—including paid advertising—and that they should reject any ads that violate fundamental rights or existing regulations. Broadcasting operators are responsible for every transmitted commercial. The control is exercised by the Ministry of Communication, but a debate exists about the efficiency and enforceability of these agreements. A debate was launched in 2009, triggered by a television spot that included explicit sex, incited voyeurism, and damaged the reputation and image of educators. CNTV maintained that advertising content is part of television content. The commission encouraged a self-regulation agreement in which all industry agents would be involved. Questions were raised regarding the relative weight of freedom of speech versus claims of censorship, and further issues arose concerning the restrictions necessary on the advertisement of particular goods such as alcohol and tobacco. According to Ricardo Galán (2009), then commissioner of CNTV, there were too many rules and controls imposed on the advertising industry.

---

*The Comisión Nacional de Television (CNTV) was dissolved on April 10, 2012. It no longer regulates Colombian television. Oversight of broadcasting and advertising rules is now carried out by the National Television Authority (www.antv.gov.co), the Communications Regulation Commission (www.crcom.gov.co), the Superintendency of Industry and Trade (www.sic.gov.co), and the National Spectrum Agency (www.ane.gov.co).

SELF-REGULATION

The Advertising Self-Regulation Code was enacted in Colombia on October 24, 1980. The Code was signed by ASOMEDIOS (National Media Association), ANDA (National Association of Advertisers), DIRIVENTAS, UCEP (Colombian Union of Advertising Agencies), and IAA (International Association of Advertising) and updated in 1987. It covers topics such as comparative advertising, references, and the reproduction and use of images of living people in ads.

Article 4 of the code explains the ethical responsibilities of advertisers. The most important of these principles concern decency, honesty, and truthfulness; protection of private life, intellectual property, and environment; and concern for health, safety, and the protection of children. The principle of truthfulness in this context prohibits advertisers from making false claims about a product, service, or activity's benefits or guarantees. Furthermore, verifiable references must be included when citing research or statistics in an advertisement. According to Agreement 010 (1997), advertising messages cannot be used to injure the reputation of persons, institutions, or national symbols.

The National Council of Self-Regulation and Advertising Ethics (CONARP) was established in 1994. It is part of the CONARED, which includes nine other countries, among them México, Brazil, Argentina, Peru, and Chile. The actions that the council can take are: suggesting the modification or withdrawal of an ad; admonishing a violator; and informing the media about the unacceptable behavior.

CONARP receives between 10 and 12 complaints each year. The complaints come from advertisers, advertising agencies, media, the government, and consumers. According to J.E. Andrade, the General Secretary of UCEP (Advertising Agencies Association 2011), most of the complaints come from consumers and competitors. If CONARP pursues the complaint, the advertisers have a period of five days to justify their ad. If the advertisers refuse to review the ad, they have to present a review claim in the next three days. Regarding the issuing of complaints, sanctions include (1) an order to withdraw the ad or to compensate for damage caused by violations of the law against unfair competition, as issued by the Courts of Justice of the Republic of Colombia; (2) fines against the advertiser for violation of consumer protection rules (Decree 3466 [1982]), according to Colombia's Consumer Protection Commission (SIC); or (3) the aforementioned censures by CONARP, which include the modification or withdrawal of the ad, or reprimands for the advertiser, the agency, and the media, who are to assume their responsibility jointly.

SIC is the organization that imposes most of the sanctions, typically in response to cases of misleading advertising or unfair comparative advertising. The majority of past sanctions have been for telecommunications companies.

According to Carlos Delgado Pereira, the president of ANDA (National Association of Advertisers), one of the factors that have contributed to the durability and authority of CONARP has been its task as mediator—saving the involved parties from long and tortuous legal proceedings. The president of the advertising agency Publicis CB noted that although CONARP is a laudable initiative, issues like "the time taken for processes in which the media do not adhere to the judgments and the fact that these judgments will not be made public, are factors against its effectiveness." Other agency managers also look upon CONARP's lack of legal power as a stumbling block.

There is a current desire among advertising industry members to create a self-regulatory body similar to Spain's.

PARTICULAR TYPES OF ADVERTISING

Children

Child protection is one of the most sensitive issues in this country, because Colombia is characterized by a certain level of social, economic, and political insecurity (Chiswell 2010; "Colombia's Victims Law" 2011). In fact, the Colombian Constitution (1991) gives children a superior status over others in terms of rights. The fundamental rights of children are life, physical integrity, health, social security, a balanced diet, their name and nationality, having a family and not being separated from it, care and love, education and culture, recreation, and free expression of opinion. They shall be protected against all forms of neglect, physical or moral violence, kidnapping, sale, abuse, labor exploitation, and hazardous work (Article 44). The law defines children as those individuals who have not yet reached the age of 12. The Children's Code Decree 2737 (1989) encourages advertisers to show the role of the family in children's education through ads.

In 2008, ANDA—formed by advertisers, ad agencies, the CNTV, UNICEF, and other foundations and institutions—signed a commitment to ensuring quality television for the children of Colombia. The agreement is concerned with (1) promoting the production of children's programs on both public and private TV channels; (2) encouraging the process of citizen participation in children's TV programs; (3) extending the public debate on television (questioning the role of TV and their educative mission), childhood, and teenagers in Colombia; (4) fostering alliances with international organizations to exchange information and research methodologies; and (5) cofinancing joint projects. However, the problem is that this kind of agreement is not enforceable; it is only a goodwill agreement.

Tobacco and Alcohol

The advertising of tobacco, cigarettes, alcohol, sex, violence, pornography, arms, and war tools was banned from television during family and children time slots by the CNTV; sports sponsorship is allowed (Agreement 04 [2005]), yet only from 9:30 P.M. to 6:59 A.M. For television stations, the advertising income derived from alcohol, beer, and tobacco ads accounted for almost 3 percent of their overall budget; that is why media managers do not agree with the prohibition of these ads during the time established by the law.

In addition to this restriction, warnings of the harmful effects of these products must be issued along with the advertisement. Examples of such messages include: "Too much alcohol is harmful to health," and "Sales to minors are prohibited." Commercials showing consumption of these products must not be associated with success or achievement of personal, sexual, professional, economic, or social goals, nor may they state or imply that consumption is a desirable or viable option for solving problems, or that abstinence or moderation are to be rejected. Furthermore, television broadcasters are encouraged to air information on preventive campaigns—ones that highlight the risks and negative effects of alcohol consumption—in time slots considered suitable for all audiences.

Scenes of violence should be excluded not only from the children's time slot, but also from the time considered suitable for all audiences (from 7:00 A.M. to 9:30 P.M.). Commercials for condoms have some special restrictions: They must not encourage promiscuity in condom users or suggest that the use of condoms is the only way to avoid sexually transmitted diseases. In addition, these commercials should be broadcast when the children's time slot is over.

CONCLUSION

One of the most important aspects of the Colombian constitution is its recognition of freedom of ideas and information. The fear of censorship by the national government remains very real in Colombia because of its history. Perhaps this is the reason for the nation's lack of specific regulation for advertising; for years before its dissolution, Colombia relied instead on CNTV—the independent National Television Commission—to control the advertising standards on television. CNTV played an important role in promoting quality television content and advertising and in advancing the social function of television.

Self-regulation through the National Commission of Advertising Self-Regulation (CONARP) is generally thought to be inefficient. Although the advertising regulations in Colombia include a clear reference to constitutional principles of public service and child protection, there is no specific advertising law.

The biggest governmental worry is child protection. Because Colombia is a country where civil society is very active, there is hope that the industry will take the initiative in improving advertising practices.

BIBLIOGRAPHY

Andrade, J.E. 2011. General Secretary UCEP (Advertising Agencies Association). Email correspondence with the author, June 9.

Arauz, Adriana. 2009. Director of ANALPEX (National Association of Outdoor Advertising). "Queremos reglas claras para la publicidad exterior visual." *Revista ANDA* 39 (September 25): 58–59. http://www. andacol.com/php/index.php?searchword=sanciones&ordering=newest&searchphrase=all&limit=20&ar eas[0]=content&option=com_search#content (accessed May 29, 2011).

Asociacion Nacional de Medios de Comunicación (ASOMEDIOS). 2010. Estudio Inversión Publicitaria Neta 2010, Bogotá. February.

Buitrago López, E. 2008. *Derecho de la Publicidad, Librería ediciones el profesional.* Bogotá.

Chiswell, John. 2010. "Violencia en TV ante los ojos de los menores." *Revista ANDA* 16, no. 42: 40–43.

"Colombia's Victims Law: Feeling Their Pain." 2010. *The Economist.* June 2. http://www.economist.com/ node/18775093?zid=305&ah=417bd5664dc76da5d98af4f7a640fd8a.

Communications Regulation Commission (CRC). 2011. http://www.crcom.gov.co/ (accessed November 14, 2011).

Compromiso Nacional por una Televisión de Calidad para la Infancia en Colombia. n.d. http://www.com-minit.com/es/node/270004 (accessed August 8, 2011).

Galán, Ricardo. 2009. "¿Quién responde por los contenidos de la publicidad en TV? [Who is responsible for the content of advertising?]" July 9. http://www.cntv.org.co/cntv_bop/noticias/2009/julio/22_07_09. html (accessed May 27, 2011).

Gómez, Leonardo. 2008. "Todo el que venda pauta en TV tendrá que pagar a la CNTV." Conexionista blog, July 10. http://www.conexionista.com/2008/07/todo-el-que-venda-pauta-en-tv-tendr-que.html (accessed October 17, 2011).

———. 2009. "SIC sanciona a Movistar por publicidad engañosa." Conexionista blog, January 20. http:// www.conexionista.com/2009/01/sic-sanciona-movistar-por-publicidad.html (accessed October 17, 2011).

———. 2011a. "Cultura de autorregulación." *Conexionista TV Journal* 1, no. 1 (April-May): 41.

———. 2011b. Professor of Media Convergence at School of Communication, University of La Sabana (Colombia). Email correspondence with the author, November 14.

Jaeckel, Jorge. "Publicidad en los canales de televisión: De cubrimiento nacional." [Advertising television channels: national coverage."] http://www.teleley.com/articulos/PUBLICI1.html (accessed February 22, 2013).

National Television Commission (CNTV). 2004. "Inversion publicitaria de cerveza, bebidas alcohólicas y tabaco en la TV colombiana." http://www.cntv.org.co/cntv_bop/estudios/cerveza.pdf (accessed June 24, 2011).

————. 2009. "¿Quién responde por los contenidos de la publicidad en TV?" http://www.cntv.org.co/cntv_bop/noticias/2009/julio/22_07_09.html (accessed May 27, 2011).

————. 2011a. http://www.cntv.org.co/cntv_bop/basedoc/arbol/1000.html (accessed May 25, 2011).

————. 2011b. "Project of law to regulate the DTT services." http://www.cntv.org.co/cntv_bop/tdt/documentos/22082011_proyecto_acuerdo_tdt.pdf (accessed November 14, 2011).

Osorio, Eduardo. 2011. "Balances y retos para el desarrollo de los servicios audiovisuales en la era digital." *Conexionista TV Journal* 2 (July-August): 6–8.

Publicidad, mercadeo y medios. 2005. "La CONARP: hay que dotarla de colmillos." August 2. http://www.artedinamico.com/portal/sitio/tips_mo_comentarios.php?it=2101&categoria=1 (accessed June 2, 2011).

Ramírez, Augusto. 2011. "A Colombia le va bien este año." *Revista ANDA* 16, no. 43 (January 13): 6–13.

Superintendencia de Industria y Comercio (SIC). 2012. http://www.sic.gov.co/en/.

Tapias, Ximena. 2009. "III Reunión de Organismos de Autorregulación Publicitaria de América Latina 'CONARED.'" *Revista ANDA* 15, no. 40 (January 18): 32–33.

CHAPTER 8

PERU

MARIA-ELENA GRONEMEYER

Peru is located in western South America and borders the southern Pacific Ocean. Today it has a democratic government, with independent state powers: executive, legislative, and judicial. However, the country had fairly recent experiences with dictatorships. Between 1968 and 1975, Peruvians lived under the Revolutionary Government of the Armed Forces, commanded by Juan Velasco, and another dictatorship under Alberto Fujimori between 1992 and 2000. According to 2013 estimates, Peru has about 29.5 million inhabitants, 45 percent of whom are indigenous (CIA 2013). Clearly, this country is a multicultural and multiethnic nation.

Regarding communications, *The World Factbook Online* (CIA 2013) states that in 2010, Peru had 10 major television networks, one of which was state owned (Televisión Nacional de Perú); multichannel cable TV services; and as many as 2,000 radio stations, including a substantial number of indigenous language stations. Additionally, 22 newspapers are published in Lima (the capital), and 60 other papers are published in regions throughout the country. Peruvian mainstream newspapers are *El Comercio, Perú 21*, and *La República*.

The country's economy began adopting the neoliberal free market model during the Fujimori regime, maintaining it to the present. Therefore, Peru emerges today as politically and financially open to world markets. It maintains international treaties with several countries that encourage the flow of people, goods, and services between them. According to records from the National Institute of Statistics and Informatics of Peru (Instituto Nacional de Estadística e Informática [INEI]), in 2010 the country's economy showed high productive capacity; in fact, the Peruvian economy is largely perceived as among the fastest growing in the world. Peru is ranked 47 in the world ranking of countries considered attractive to business, according to a report by the Economist Intelligence Unit (EIU). In 2012, Peru's GDP was US$325 billion and achieved a real growth rate of 6 percent (CIA 2013).

Figure 8.1 shows the percentage of ad investments by medium in Peru during 2009; the total amount spent was US$527 million.

DEVELOPMENT OF LEGAL ADVERTISING REGULATIONS IN PERU

In this political and economic context, Peru, along with other countries in South America, has sought to adapt its legal advertising regulations to the standards and the trends of the West, with an increasing awareness of consumer rights when dealing with providers of goods and services. Law 1.044 on the Repression of Unfair Competition (2008) defines advertising as "any form of communication disseminated through any media, and . . . aimed at promoting—directly or indirectly—images, brands, products, or services of a person, company, or entity in the exercise of their trade, business, or profession, within the framework of a concurrent activity, promoting

Figure 8.1

Percentage of Advertising Investment by Medium in Peru, 2009

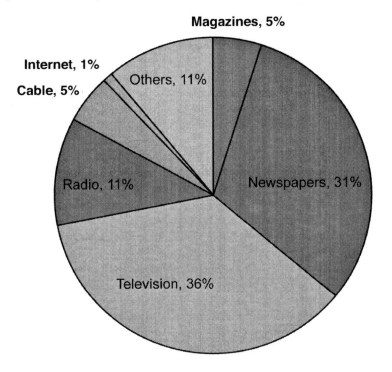

Source: "Inversión publicitaria en Perú fue US$527 millones el 2009, informa AAM." Peru.com, June 4, 2010. http://www.peru.com/economiayfinanzas/portada20100604/100433/Inversion-publicitaria-en-Peru-fue-US527-millones-el-2009-informa-AAM (accessed December 10, 2012).

the procurement or conducting transactions to meet their business interests." To be considered as such, commercial advertising must be directed to an audience of potential consumers, and must have the purpose or effect of encouraging the recipient of the message to consume the goods or contract the advertised services.

Peru has passed very recent laws and regulations that define the scope and limits of advertising. Furthermore, following worldwide trends and as required by international treaties, it has established additional policies related to products perceived as especially sensitive, such as advertising of alcohol, cigarettes, and other forms of tobacco. Although the first advertising agencies were set up in Peru during the 1940s and the Peruvian Association of Advertising Agencies was founded in 1954 as a self-regulatory entity, before the 1990s there were no specific laws for consumer protection. The basic principles for the advertising of goods and services were first made explicit in Peru with the Consumer Protection Law (DL 716) of 1991, followed by the Law of Advertising Standards for Consumer Protection (691), enacted in 2000. These laws were followed by a new regulation in 2010, which is discussed next. As in other countries of the region, the legal rules of

Peru have stressed the need for advertising to deliver accurate information to prevent consumer deception or confusion.

Today, Peru has laws and government regulations on advertising that focus especially on misleading advertising, socially sensitive products, the morality of advertising, and messages addressed to vulnerable groups such as minors. Additionally, Peru has government agencies to ensure compliance with the legal norms and to protect consumer rights from the excesses of advertising.

Self-regulatory bodies in the advertising field in Peru have been strengthened since the country returned to democracy and as a consequence of the growing importance of consumer rights. These bodies are also concerned with decency, good taste, and standards of ethical conduct.

CURRENT LEGAL ADVERTISING REGULATION

Peru's constitution (1993) lays out the fundamental bases of advertising in the country and gives institutional status to consumer rights. "The State defends the interests of consumers and users," according to Article 65 (1993). "Therefore, it guarantees the right to information about goods and services that are available on the market. It also ensures, in particular, health and safety of the population."

In addition, Article 61 protects free enterprise and trade, and safeguards Peruvian citizens and businesses from monopolistic actions. The constitution notes: "The State facilitates and oversees free competition. It opposes any practice that limits it and the abuse of dominant or monopolistic positions. . . . The press, radio, television and other means of expression and social communication—and, in general, enterprises, goods and services related to freedom of expression and communication—cannot be subject to exclusivity, monopoly or hoarding, directly or indirectly" (1993).

The constitutional rights of consumers are fortified by Law 29.571, enacted in September 2010 to counteract deception and abuse. This Code of Consumer Protection and Defense is the most recent and comprehensive regulation and the only rule in this matter, previous laws having been repealed.

Law 29.571 recognizes the vulnerability of Peruvian consumers in their relationship with suppliers of goods and services. Therefore, this law works to correct the imbalance of information between consumers and providers, and it devotes an entire subchapter to the protection of consumers against advertising abuses.

Specific goals of the law are to prevent abuses in the provision of services and goods, and to create mechanisms for consumer protection as a means of preserving the constitutional mandate set forth above. The law explicitly says that "protection is interpreted in the sense most favorable to the consumer" (2010). The Code of Consumer Protection and Defense also serves as a way of bolstering the quality of products and services offered in the Peruvian market.

Article 13 of the law makes it clear that advertisements in Peru must be truthful, accurate, and free from "any misleading or false advertising, including the presentation or the omission of relevant information, that can induce or mislead [consumers] about the origin, nature, mode of manufacture or distribution, features, usability, quality, quantity, price, terms of sale or purchase and, in general, [the] attributes, benefits, limitations or conditions that apply to products, services, institutions or transactions."

Regarding the possible impact of advertising on behavior, Peruvian law states that no advertisement may encourage or promote any kind of racial, sexual, social, political, or religious discrimination. Furthermore, it is prohibited for advertising to encourage antisocial, criminal, or illegal activities, or to appear to support, enhance, or encourage such activities.

With regard to the quality and conditions of business information contained in advertising, this new code states that it must be truthful, fair, easily understood, appropriate, timely, and easily accessible, in addition to the requirement that it has to be in Spanish. Even in the case of foreign manufactured products, all information has to be delivered in Spanish when dealing with ingredients, components, conditions of warranties, manuals, warnings and the foreseeable risks, and care to follow in case damage occurs.

Peruvians advocate strongly for informed consumers by establishing that ads should not contain information or images that directly or indirectly—or by omission, ambiguity, or exaggeration—could mislead consumers, especially concerning the characteristics of the product, the price, or the sales conditions. Moreover, advertising of dangerous goods must warn consumers against the risks involved.

Peruvian law defines *relevant information* as any data necessary for the consumer to make an informed decision, or omitted information that might have changed a consumer's mind about making a purchase or contracting for a service. In addition to the need for all required information to be available to the consumer, that information must be written in clear, easily understandable language.

Concerning the control of advertising, the same law discloses the mechanisms that the state guarantees for the solution of conflicts. The rule promotes direct and rapid resolutions of the disputes with the use of alternative mechanisms such as mediation, conciliation and voluntary arbitration, and self-regulatory systems. It also ensures access to quick administrative and judicial procedures, and it facilitates access to collective actions. Finally, the state promotes citizen participation and organization of consumers to protect and defend their rights.

Another new rule that affects Peruvian commercial activity, including advertising, is the Law for the Repression of Unfair Competition (DL 1.044, 2008), which unifies previous regulations. The law seeks to prohibit and punish acts of unfair competition, as well as specific violations of commercial advertising, and strengthens the regulatory framework for the defense of fair competition, which, according to the preamble of the rule, will "encourage economic efficiency in the national market, promote economic competitiveness, and improve consumer welfare by establishing an appropriate environment for investment."

DL 1.044 considers advertising at odds with this standard if it employs deceptive testimonial advertising or any other unsupported or false claims. The law says that it "constitutes a breach of this principle to broadcast advertising disguised as news or opinion journalism . . . without explicitly and remarkably expressing that this is an infomercial or contracted advertisement."

Regarding the attribution of responsibility for acts of unfair competition through advertising, Law 1.044 holds liable the advertiser, the mass media, and the advertising agency.

Furthermore, Peruvian Law 28.293 (2005) regulates the use of unsolicited commercial emails (SPAM). It provides that all unsolicited commercial, promotional, or advertising email that originates in the country must contain the word "advertising" in the subject field of the message; the sender of the message must be fully identified; and the email should indicate a valid and activated email address for the recipient to notify his or her desire to be removed from the solicitor's list. Failure to comply with these requirements makes it an illegal advertisement, and the responsibility lies, according to the law, with anyone who sends unsolicited emails containing commercial advertising, companies or individuals directly benefiting from the widespread publicity, and intermediaries of unsolicited emails (such as providers of email services).

GOVERNMENT SUPPORTED BODIES REGULATING ADVERTISING

Peru has created a consumer protection agency that also relates to advertising, the National Institute for the Defense of Competition and Protection of Intellectual Property (Instituto Nacional de Defensa de la Competencia y de la Protección de la Propiedad Intelectual [INDECOPI]). Established in 1992 through Law 25.868, it promotes within the Peruvian economy a culture of fair and honest competition and protects all forms of intellectual property. Its role is to oversee the competition and ensure the development of a free market policy. INDECOPI is the body that monitors the fulfillment of the provisions of the Consumer Protection Act. It also has a Consumer Protection Commission whose function is to guide and protect the interests of consumers if they believe their rights have been violated.

INDECOPI's Oversight of Unfair Competition Commission prohibits and sanctions instances of unfair competition in Peru's advertising industry. It has the power to evaluate the legality of commercial ads and impose sanctions when appropriate. INDECOPI's Consumer Protection Commission is charged with protecting consumers from unsuitable goods and services. Law 29.571 recognizes INDECOPI as the nation's consumer authority and the governing body of the Integrated National Consumer Protection System (Sistema Nacional Integrado de Protección al Consumidor). In order to improve the organizational structure of INDECOPI to execute the actions required to strengthen consumer protection at a national level according to the Code of 2010, the institute is expressly empowered to make investments in people, goods, and services required to meet all the tasks under the new law. According to INDECOPI's statistical records from 2010, the Oversight of Unfair Competition Commission investigated 1,444 cases between 2000 and mid-2009.

The Code of Consumer Protection and Defense recognizes and supports consumer associations in Peru. In early 2010, INDECOPI had registered 11 consumer associations, five of them in Lima, the capital, and the other six throughout Peru. The law defines them as nongovernmental organizations (NGOs), established to protect, defend, inform, and represent consumers and users. They may introduce complaints to authorities on behalf of their members and individuals who have given them the power of representation, and in defense of collective interests of consumers in accordance with the code's provisions.

ADVERTISING SELF-REGULATION IN PERU

The international experience, Western trends, and Peru's status as a member of the network of advertising self-regulatory bodies in Latin America, CONARED,[1] pushed Peruvian advertisers, ad agencies, and the mass media to agree on the need to regulate themselves. National advertising self-regulatory boards promote ethical conduct and public confidence in the advertising business, consolidate corporate loyalty, and thereby decrease the likelihood of government over-regulation of advertising.

In Peru, the Advertising Self-Regulation Council (Consejo de Autorregulación Publicitaria [CONAR]) was founded in 1998 in a ceremony attended by the then first vice president of the country and the nation's ombudsman. CONAR consists of three closely related associations: the National Association of Advertisers (Asociación Nacional de Anunciantes [ANDA]), the Peruvian Association of Advertising Agencies (Asociación Peruana de Agencias de Publicidad [APAP]), and the National Society of Radio and Television (Sociedad Nacional de Radio y Televisión [SNRTV]). They are united by the desire to promote fairness between competitors and to protect consumers.

The mediation task is a delegated responsibility of a special agent within the council, the Ethics Standing Committee, which operates according to the Code of Ethics of the organization. The establishment of implementation standards and the creation of the Permanent Ethics Committee with functions and powers to constantly monitor the proper implementation of the code are included within the code structure.

The council rules on commercial advertising displayed in any medium aimed at reaching consumers of products or services, produced domestically or abroad, and issued in the form of traditional or nontraditional advertising, be it from affiliated member agencies or from outside the CONAR.

Individuals and entities that can be held responsible for an abuse or violation of the code are the advertiser and the advertising agency that created and placed the message; the mass medium that disseminates it; and any person who has participated in the planning, creation, or publication of the ad.

THE OBJECTIVES OF THE SELF-REGULATION COUNCIL

The main goal of CONAR in Peru is to promote the development of the advertising industry, ensuring that its use and practice conforms to a set of basic principles, including lawfulness, decency, truthfulness, and loyalty.

As part of its corrective function, the council receives complaints from businesses, agencies, and private or state entities, and from the general public on advertisements that allegedly may be unethical. The main ethical principles and standards that govern commercial speech are defined in the Code of Advertising Ethics. Each reported advertisement is discussed in depth in relation to this code.

The Council's Code of Ethics

To fulfill its mission, the board of advertising self-regulation and its associated entities have a duty to adhere to its Code of Ethics, pledging to honor and encourage compliance with its tenets. This code, like many other international texts, is based on the International Code of Advertising Practice of the International Chamber of Commerce (ICC) in Paris, with the necessary adaptations for use in Peru.

Given the need for legislation in Peru that standardizes the ethical guiding principles of advertising, advertisers, agencies, and mass media grouped in their respective guilds—ANDA, APAP, and SNRTV—the industry decided to publish its own Code of Advertising Ethics. In 2007, after 19 years, CONAR updated its Peruvian ethics code. The council worked under the assumption that consumers are increasingly concerned about the ethical behavior of the company that sells a product, requiring consumer associations and the media to be more alert and proactive in identifying and disseminating ethical aspects of advertising. In addition, industry and civil society are rewarding and recognizing advertising that promotes good values. The Peruvian approach is said to be oriented toward the development of advertising to benefit the consumer, without whom it would be pointless to advertise in the first place. Furthermore, they promote fair competition in the market, without which advertisers would compete in a jungle without rules. The code includes specific rules for advertising of cigarettes, tobacco, and alcohol.

The general principles underlying this code are the recognition that (1) the Peruvian freedom of industry and trade operates in the context of a social market economy, and (2) information promotes transparency in the market and empowers consumers by allowing them to make informed and rational purchasing decisions. Again, considering the welfare of the audience, the Code of Ethics stresses that in advertising the duties and obligations to the community are translated into rules of behavior that must be accepted voluntarily for the common good. It also acknowledges that advertising is both informative and persuasive.

The code specifies that self-regulation works effectively when all those involved in the advertising business actively comply with the principles and rules of advertising, and when this observance takes place at all stages of the advertising process, including planning, design, production, implementation, and dissemination. It also stresses that the primary objective of self-regulation is to monitor the quality of information provided through ads, in addition to preserving and enhancing the credibility of advertising. Furthermore, the code places responsibility for updating and observing the existing advertising principles and rules of legality, decency, truthfulness, and loyalty squarely on the industry itself. This responsibility has to be assumed with consideration of the Peruvian society and in response to particular economic, cultural, and educational circumstances.

The Administration of the Council and Its Ethics Committee

In Peru, the CONAR board consists of nine persons, three representatives appointed by each guild: ANDA, APAP, and SNRTV. Chosen from these nine is a president (rotated between representatives of the guilds), a vice president, a secretary, a treasurer, and two members at large.

The Standing Committee on Ethics of the Peruvian CONAR also consists of nine members, all outstanding professionals from various sectors of the industry; they are appointed by the board. Any member who knows about a case from its inception is obliged to participate in its deliberations until a conclusion is reached. Conflicts of interest are avoided by excluding from deliberations any member of the Committee on Ethics who is involved in the conflict.

Proceedings of the Council and Ethics Committee

The CONAR proceedings can be initiated by request from a party or ex officio. But unlike other countries, the Peruvian Council stipulates that if the claim is made by a legal expert, a payment to CONAR of about US$200 must be made to file it. In the case of complaints filed by individuals, the procedure is free.

The complainant can give up his or her claim at any stage of the proceedings. However, if the Standing Committee on Ethics finds that the issue affects consumer rights, it may continue the proceeding on its own.

Complaints originating with INDECOPI can be processed simultaneously with complaints by CONAR against the same ad and for the same offense. But if the Ethics Committee of the National Association of Advertisers (ANDA) in Peru is conducting an investigation on an advertisement that is the subject of a complaint to the CONAR, ANDA must refer the proceedings to CONAR.

CONAR in Peru has a technical secretariat in charge of classifying a complaint as *admissible* or *inadmissible* within one working day after its receipt. If acceptable, the case goes to the Standing Committee on Ethics, and the accused has three business days after the notification of the complaint to answer it. Once answered, a decision is rendered within seven working days. Failure on the part of the defendant to answer the complaint does not prevent the Standing Committee on Ethics from deciding the case.

In Peru, CONAR attempts to achieve amicable resolutions to advertising complaints. Additionally, CONAR tries to convince the advertiser to amend a message under dispute or to willingly withdraw it from circulation. The sanctions imposed by the Standing Committee on Ethics consist of either a written reprimand to the advertiser, the medium, or the advertising agency or a public admonition of the complainant or medium or advertising agency in the Peruvian press.

Additionally, the commission may order the following measures, by account, cost, and risk of the denounced:

1. Modify the advertising to eliminate the infringement. The amendment must be submitted for approval prior to its dissemination.
2. Remove or cease the dissemination of the ad containing infringement.
3. Remove or cease the dissemination of all advertising.
4. Place ads rectifying the matter of infringement.

All mass media in Peru must ensure the strict enforcement of the commission's judgments. The resolutions of the boards and ethics committees can be appealed. In such cases, the interested party must provide new data within fixed time periods to try to reverse the ruling.

COMPLIANCE AND PUBLICATION OF THE RESOLUTIONS

Peru has agreed on standards to promote compliance with the dictates of its self-regulatory agency and the public dissemination of its resolutions. All resolutions and even the pending cases are available to the public in the CONAR offices. Anyone may request copies of these documents, with the sole obligation of paying the shipping or mailing costs. CONAR may also publish the decisions in the media and on its website.

OTHER EXAMPLES OF SELF-REGULATION IN PERU

In addition to the existing self-regulatory mechanisms from CONAR, the National Association of Advertisers (ANDA) in Peru promotes best practices in advertising through "Ethics Stoplight." Its main promoter is ANDA's Committee of Ethics in Programming, whose objective is the promotion of ethical investment options for advertisers, thereby strengthening the growth of different brands and products.

SPECIAL LEGAL REGULATIONS FOR TOBACCO, ALCOHOL, AND FOOD ADVERTISING

In line with the views of international organizations like the World Health Organization (WHO), Peru has very recently approved and enforced laws specific to the advertising of products such as tobacco and alcohol.

Law 29.517 (Law Against Tobacco Consumption) was approved in early 2010. It regulates cigarette and tobacco sales and advertising, using a previous law—28.705 (2006) on the Prevention and Control of Risks from Tobacco Consumption—as its basis. The new law makes explicit Peru's compliance with requirements set forth in international agreements. A Framework Agreement for the Control of Tobacco from the World Health Organization (WHO) was signed by Peru in 2004 and enacted in 2006.

The Law Against Tobacco Consumption stipulates that the advertising, promotion, and marketing of tobacco and cigarettes be directed only to adults and must adhere to the principle that all adult users know the risks of its consumption.

Article 6 mandates that advertisements for tobacco products cannot contain messages or images that are targeted to minors, nor can they suggest that one's success and popularity increases because of smoking. In addition, cigarette packets and the packaging of other tobacco products should carry printed phrases and images warning about the damaging effects of the product on consumers' health. These warnings must occupy a predetermined amount of space on each package and be accompanied by the phrase "Not for sale to persons under 18 years." Article 8 prohibits the use of certain terms in tobacco advertising, among them "light," "ultra light," "mild," "super," "light" written in English, "ultra light" written in English, as well as synonyms or other similar words.

In relation to the spaces where this kind of advertising is allowed, the law states that tobacco may be advertised inside print media—newspapers, magazines or the like—only if the target audience is over 18 years of age. Tobacco ads can never be placed on the front or back cover of print media, nor can any event or activity aimed at minors be sponsored by any brand of tobacco product.

Ads for tobacco products cannot show a minor using the product or suggest that most people in the ad are smokers. Finally, in Article 17, the Law Against Tobacco Consumption prohibits direct or indirect advertising of tobacco products on broadcast television, radio, or similar media; in buildings dedicated to health or education (public or private); or in public buildings. Furthermore, tobacco ads cannot be placed in a radius of 500 meters around schools of any kind, or appear in venues during any sports activities, or in exhibitions, shows, and the like that cater to people younger than 18. Finally, no tobacco ads can be exhibited on apparel.

The year 2006 saw the enactment of Law 28.681, which regulates the marketing, consumption, and advertising of alcoholic beverages in Peru. Its goal is to protect minors and minimize damage to citizens' health due to alcohol abuse, family disintegration, and threats to others caused by drinking. This law complements a 2009 regulation that also deals with the advertisement of alcoholic beverages of all alcohol levels, making it a very serious offense to use in advertising elements that lead minors to the consumption of alcoholic beverages.

The law states that at least 10 percent of the total area of the packaging and/or labels of alcoholic beverages must contain the phrase "Drinking to excess is harmful." The same phrase must also occupy at least 10 percent of the total area of print ads, and the audiovisual media should legibly display the warning for at least 3 seconds. On radio ads, the same sentence has to be spoken clearly and slowly at the end of the spot.

Also as a way to protect minors, the promotion and free distribution of alcoholic beverages at activities aimed at them is forbidden, as is the promotion and distribution of toys that are shaped like or refer to alcoholic beverage products.

The Peruvian Association of Consumers and Users (ASPEC) is urging the country's authorities to review the draft law regulating food advertising aimed at children. Advocates claim that food-related ads should reflect the requirements and limits imposed by WHO concerning advertising of foods high in calories, fat, and salt aimed at children—requirements that have already been approved in several countries in the region. The Supreme Decree 009 (2006) regulates the advertising of infant formulas. The text prohibits, for example, any advertising to the general public and to mothers in particular of products identified as breast milk substitutes.

CHALLENGES FACING REGULATORY MECHANISMS IN PERU

Critical voices have been raised in Peru regarding advertising. Some observers believe that standards are being set by the biggest companies and that advertising, rather than serving the consumer, is solely a mechanism to promote competition. However, it has also been said that citizen responsibility is essential in the free market and that civic action—still very underdeveloped in Peru—should be promoted.[2] This would also discourage advertising behaviors that are harmful to society.

In cases where civil actions or the actions of self-regulatory organizations do not control advertising abuses, INDECOPI is considered an alternative, but it still lacks a high level of efficiency.

NOTES

1. Once the local councils were founded, Latin American countries proceeded to link these entities in a regional alliance. The first Latin American meeting of national self-regulatory agencies took place in 2008, and from that first meeting, CONARED was created. CONARED is the network of advertising self-regulatory bodies in Latin America. This entity is now integrated by Argentina, Brazil, Colombia, Chile, El Salvador, Guatemala, Mexico, Paraguay, Peru, and Uruguay. Its purpose is to seek the incorporation of a greater number of countries in the network.

The initiative emerged from the interest of the advertising industry in Latin American countries to establish a network of self-regulation. The intent was to unify criteria for the application of the codes of ethics and to foster a regional approach to commercial communication practices for advertisers, advertising agencies, and the media to ensure public safety and trust.

In turn, CONARED is linked to the World Federation of Advertisers (WFA). In its annual meetings in the region, they discuss key global strategic regulatory and media issues and bring together marketers and national advertiser associations from across South America. The WFA has Latin American National Advisers Associations in Argentina, Brazil, Colombia, Chile, Guatemala, Mexico, Paraguay, Peru, Uruguay, and Venezuela.

2. Óscar Súmar Albújar, "El sinsentido trascendental de la protección al consumidor 'pro-empresa' y alternativas." *Enfoque Derecho*, July 20, 2010. http://www.enfoquederecho.com/?q=node/407 (accessed December 10, 2010).

BIBLIOGRAPHY

Documents

Advertising of Infant Feeding Supreme Decree 009 (Reglamento de Alimentacion Infantil). 2006.
Advertising Standards for Consumer Protection Legislative Decree 691 (Decreto Legislativo Normas de la Publicidad en Defensa del Consumidor). 2000.
Central Intelligence Agency. 2013. "Peru." *The World Factbook Online*. Washington, DC: CIA. https://www.cia.gov/library/publications/the-world-factbook/geos/pe.html.
Code of Consumer Protection and Defense Law 29.571 (Código de Protección y Defensa del Consumidor). 2010.
Constitution of Peru. 1993. http://www.congreso.gob.pe/_ingles/CONSTITUTION_29_08_08.pdf.
Consumer Protection Law (DL 716) (Ley del Protección del Consumidor). 1991.
Regulations on the Marketing, Consumption and Advertising of Alcoholic Beverages Law 28.681 (Comercializacion, Consumo y Publicidad de Bebidas Alcohólicas). 2006.
Regulations on the Use of Nonrequested Commercial Emails Law 28.293 (Uso del Correo Electrónico Comercial No Solicitado, SPAM). 2005.
Repression of Unfair Competition Legislative Decree 1.044 (Decreto Legislativo 1044 Ley de Represión de la Competencia Desleal). 2008.
Tobacco Law 28.705 on the Prevention and Control of Risks from Tobacco Consumption (Prevención y Control de los Riesgos del Consumo del Tabaco). 2006.
Tobacco Law 29.517 Against Tobacco Consumption (Ley Contra el Consumo del Tabaco). 2010.

Institutions

Advertising Self-Regulation Council/Consejo de Autorregulación Publicitaria (CONAR). www.andaperu.org/conar.
Economist Intelligence Unit (EIU). http://www.eiu.com/PublicDefault.aspx.
National Association of Advertisers/Asociación Nacional de Anunciantes (ANDA). www.andaperu.org.
National Institute of Statistics and Informatics of Peru/Instituto Nacional de Estadística e Informática (INEI). www.inei.gob.pe.
National Institute for the Defense of Competition and Protection of Intellectual Property/Instituto Nacional de Defensa de la Competencia y de la Protección de la Propiedad Intelectual (INDECOPI). www.indecopi.gob.pe.

National Society of Radio and Television/Sociedad Nacional de Radio y Televisión (SNRTV). www.snrtv. org.pe.

Peruvian Association of Advertising Agencies/Asociación Peruana de Agencias de Publicidad (APAP). www.apap.org.pe.

Peruvian Association of Consumers and Users/Asociación Peruana de Consumidores y Usuarios (ASPEC). www.aspec.org.pe.

PART III

THE NORDIC COUNTRIES

CHAPTER 9

DENMARK

MARY ALICE SHAVER

Advertising regulation in Denmark is covered by both legal and self-regulatory bodies. In the latter, the advertising industry itself provides guidelines as well. There is a Consumer Ombudsman (*Forbrugerombudsmanden*) and a Marketing Practices Act, both of which fall under the legal regulation framework. The Danish system follows the Codes of the International Chamber of Commerce (ICC).

The Danish Marketing Practices Act (consolidated in July 2000) contains the essential rules of Danish advertising. Its primary purpose is to protect consumers and to regulate competition. It states that all business must be conducted according to the standards of good marketing practice. The act is central to the business of advertising and must be followed regardless of the way in which the advertising is promulgated.

The Marketing Practices Act covers marketing as well as all advertising. Some specific provisions deal with false or misleading advertising and comparative advertising (which cannot discredit a competitor or be misleading). Competitive advertising must be objective and truthful. The Marketing Act's focus is on private business and public responsibility.

There is a separate rule for ad displays and prices, requiring tags to reflect the price and the value-added tax (VAT), along with any other fees. Other legislation includes the Danish Radio and Television Broadcasting Act (2002) and the Executive Order Concerning Radio and Television Advertising and Programme Sponsorship (2003).

There is a particular section of the Danish Marketing Practices Act that covers covert advertising. Covert advertising (defined as not specifically distinguishable as advertising) is not allowed. All advertising—regardless of the source of transmission—must be clearly identified as such. The provision also states that the target audience for the advertising must be appropriate. Violations of this section are punishable by a fine; other rules or laws may impose a more severe punishment.

Similarly, product placement generally is not allowed in programming, and sponsorship notice is only allowed at the beginning and end of any broadcast program. Such credit may not appear within the program. Furthermore, the sponsor's name or logo may not be accompanied by any soundtrack or music that could be related to the sponsor.

The Consumer Ombudsman (established in 1974) is charged with making certain that advertising is compliant with the provisions of the Marketing Practices Act. It is a governmental agency and not a self-regulatory body. The role of the Consumer Ombudsman is to protect consumers; it can institute legal proceedings in the Danish Commercial Court. The Consumer Ombudsman issues specific guidelines to ensure the protection of society and the consumers.

The Consumer Ombudsman can issue orders to advertisers if they do not follow the provisions of the Marketing Practices Act. It can institute legal proceedings for noncompliance. Although it can pursue legal action, the final decision or confirmation must come through the Danish courts.

The Danish government does not keep track of the cases brought to court by each of the governmental bodies; however, the Consumer Ombudsman has been charged with bringing cases forward since 2004. The number of cases brought forward between 2004 and 2011 is in excess of 200; 37 of these have resulted in fines.

The cases are separated into different areas; some are reviewed according to the stipulations of the Marketing Act, others under an Act for Payment, and still others under the Tobacco Advertising Law and other branches not related to advertising. Most of the cases are related to a real or potential misinterpretation of information in the advertising, price comparisons that proved to be untrue, or specific pricing that was advertised in one media but was different in other media applications.

The Radio and Television Board is an independent authority in a range of media matters. The board's seven members must have expertise in legal, media, business, and cultural fields. Board members are appointed by the Minister of Culture for a four-year term. However, the decisions of the board cannot be appealed to the ministry.

INDUSTRY-BASED SELF-REGULATION

An Advertising Forum was established by members of the Danish advertising industry, which also funds it. Its role is to apply codes and rules regarding advertising content. This self-regulatory body receives complaints about advertising. Should the complaint be found to be accurate, the advertiser in question is asked to withdraw or amend the advertising to meet the norms of the Advertising Forum. The Danish Advertising Forum is a member of the European Advertising Standards Alliance.

A number of Danish associations collaborate to form the Forum of Responsible Food Marketing Communication. This forum includes the Danish Food and Drink Federation, the Federation of Retail Grocers, TV2/DENMARK, Danish Brewers' Association, Danish Newspaper Publishers' Association, Association of Danish Advertisers, Association of Danish Internet Media, Danish Association of Advertising and Relationship Agencies, and the Danish Magazine Publishers' Association.

This forum has put together the Code of Responsible Food Marketing to Children (2008). Its purpose is to reduce the number of child-directed advertisements for food and drinks that contain high amounts of sugar, fat, or salt. Within a year of the code's establishment, this type of advertising largely disappeared in Denmark. There has been a reduction in Internet advertising of this nature, as well.

ADVERTISING TO CHILDREN

The Consumer Ombudsman states that businesses must take into account the lack of experience and critical sense of children and young people when targeting advertising to this group. Laws exist concerning product placement in films and television shows directed at a young audience. Online games featuring brands and products used by the games' characters must adhere to sound and responsible marketing practices.

According to the Marketing Practices Act, advertisers and marketers must not take advantage of the credulity or lack of experience of children, must not include in their advertisements any information detrimental to children, and must encourage parents to supervise children's online activities. Information should be provided to show parents ways to protect their children's privacy online.

Advertising must not promote excessive use of consumable products. Soft drinks may not be marketed in schools or in after-school associations. Marketers may not target small children or preteens.

Advertising to children must not undermine social values. For example, no advertisement should imply that the use of the product may give the user power over others. Nor may advertisers imply that *not* owning or using a given product will put the consumer at a disadvantage. Beyond this, no advertising should enjoin children to attempt to persuade anyone to purchase the advertised goods.

In addition, advertising may not be misleading as to size, performance, or durability of products. The advertisements must make it very clear as to what is included in the purchase. For example, no picture on the box or in the ad may suggest that little people are included with a train or auto set.

The advertising must not state or imply that the product is affordable to all families. Phrases that encourage children to ask their parents to buy an advertised good are forbidden. No advertisement for sweets such as candy or cookies may state or imply that the product is a replacement for regular meals.

Special rules for the protection of children and those under 18 are covered in the Executive Order concerning the protection of children. Advertisements must not undermine social values or suggest that a purchase will increase popularity or success. They must not be misleading. Advertisements must indicate the size of toys and be explicit in stating if anything else is required to make the toy perform as shown in the ad (such as batteries). Packaging must be truthful; for example, figurines shown on the package must either come with the toy, or it must be clearly stated that they are only available as a separate purchase.

ADVERTISEMENTS FOR ALCOHOL

Three regulations mandate alcohol advertising in Denmark. They are the Executive Order Concerning Radio and Television Advertising and Programme Sponsorship, the Marketing Practices Act, and the Regulation for Marketing Alcoholic Beverages. The last is a self-regulation, and it is the most stringent of the three. The final (self-) regulation pertains to beverages containing 2.8 percent or more of alcohol. (Beverages of 2.0 percent or less are sold in grocery and similar stores.) The Regulation for Marketing Alcoholic Beverages contains the following stipulations: Advertisements and sponsorships may not target children; advertising may not claim or imply that the product is good for one's health; and advertisements and sponsorships may not appear in conjunction with sports or any medium targeted to young people. Advertising is banned from the areas around schools, playgrounds, or youth clubs.

TOBACCO

As of January 2002, all tobacco advertising in Denmark was prohibited in any form. This includes all print media, broadcast media, social media, and direct mail.

AUTOMOBILES

While there are no specific regulations prohibiting automobile advertisements in Denmark, the Executive Order Concerning Radio and Television Advertising and Programme Sponsorship mandates that no television advertisement may show behavior that would be in violation of traffic safety or might be harmful to the environment. Furthermore, there are detailed rules that state that all pricing must appear in auto advertising and that the pricing must show the VAT and other taxes. The pricing rules for a car bought with payments must show all interest, the amount of the down payment, and the price and number of installments. The pricing rules apply to both new and used vehicles as well as any parts bought separately. The intent of the order is to ensure that all costs associated with buying and paying for a car are clearly revealed before the point of sale.

OTHER ISSUES AND GROUPS

The Executive Order Concerning Radio and Television Advertising and Programme Sponsorship also states that television advertising may not discriminate on grounds of gender, race, religion, or political beliefs. Groups such as trade unions are prohibited from advertising, as are those that express political or religious opinions.

Medical Advertising

Advertisements for drugs and other health products may not be misleading or deceitful. Denmark specifically bans drug or health advertising to children. There is a general ban of this kind of advertising on television as well as some restrictions on radio advertising.

Teleshopping

An amendment to the Danish Consolidated Act on Consumer Contracts provides guidelines for teleshopping, whether by telephone or other means. Two main stipulations are that adequate information must be provided to the consumer before any contracts are made; if such information is not provided, the contract is void and consumers may withdraw from the contract without penalty.

In the case of withdrawal, the consumer must return the product in its original condition. The decision and notice that the consumer wishes to withdraw from the contract must be made within two weeks of delivery. However, it is the duty of the supplier to tell the consumer of the right to withdraw. If the company fails to inform the consumer of his rights, the time for withdrawal may be extended.

The full name and contact information must be given to the prospective customer. The main characteristics and attributes of the product must be fully explained. All pricing must be disclosed, including all taxes, terms of payment, and delivery costs. The consumer must also be provided with all information concerning complaints, and all guarantees, warrantees, and rules regarding repairs must be specified.

CULTURAL ISSUES

Denmark requires that the advertising industry and advertisements themselves be attentive to the country's cultural norms. This drives the issue of ethics in advertising to children and the requirement that the consumer be given all possible information about a product prior to purchase. While the advertising industry accepts the regulations, it is felt that the growth or profit of the advertiser may be limited by such strict rules. Denmark, as a society, places value on family—especially children—and is not consumption minded. The right of children to be protected from many types of advertising and the right of the consumers to know all the factors involved in a product, including all price information, mirrors Danish values. Another illustration of this mindset is the prohibition of both religious and political advertising.

Advertising cannot encourage audiences to compromise on safety. For instance, promoting illegal behavior, irresponsible actions, actions that may be detrimental to the environment, or recklessness of any kind goes against Danish law.

The tenets of the Marketing Practices Act clearly state the guidelines in advertising related to alcohol, issues of discrimination in marketing, retailers awards and promotion, credit purchases, loyalty programs, and the avoidance of violence and misleading content. Advertising must be in good taste and respect human dignity. It may not be disparaging to any nationality, race, or religion or be offensive to any religious or political convictions.

AGENCIES/ACTS

Danish Consumer Ombudsman (*Forbrugerombudsmanden*). Danish: http://www.forbrugerombudsmanden. dk/; English: http://www.consumerombudsman.dk/.

Danish Marketing Practices Act. http://www.consumerombudsman.dk/Regulatory-framework/ Danish-Marketing-Practices-Act.

Danish Ministry of Culture. 2010. The Radio and Television Broadcasting Act. Act no. 477, June 4 (as amended). http://kum.dk/Documents/English%20website/Media/Promulgation%20of%20the%20 Radio%20and%20Television%20Broadcasting%20Act%202010.pdf.

Forum of Responsible Food Marketing Communication. 2008. *Guide: Code of Responsible Food Marketing Communication to Children.* January. http://kodeksforfoedevarereklamer.di.dk/SiteCollectionDocuments/ Foreningssites/kodeksforfoedevarereklamer.di.dk/Downloadboks/Kodeks%20eng%20sep%202008%20 samlet.pdf.

BIBLIOGRAPHY

Campaign. 2006. "Scandinavia: The Rules of Nordic Exposure." August 4. http://www.campaignlive.co.uk/ news/575994/.

Danish Consumer Ombudsman. 2012. "About the Consumer Ombudsman." http://www.consumerombuds-man.dk/About-us.

———. 2012. "Danish Marketing Practices Act." http://www.consumerombudsman.dk/Regulatory-framework/ Danish-Marketing-Practices-Act.

EuroCare—European Alcohol Policy Alliance. 2012. "County Profiles: Denmark." http://www.eurocare.org/ resources/country-profiles/denmark.

European Advertising Standards Alliance. 2012. "What Is a Self-Regulatory Organisation?" http://www. easa-alliance.org/Issues/page.aspx/323.

European Centre for Monitoring Alcohol Marketing. 2012. "Regulations: Denmark." http://www.eucam. info/eucam/denmark/.

European Consumer Centre Denmark. 2004. "Act on Certain Consumer Contracts." June 9. http://www. consumereurope.dk/Menu/Consumer-laws/Danish-laws/Act-on-Certain-Consumer-Contracts.

Food Drink Europe. 2010. "Marketing Communications: Self-Regulatory Codes (industrywide self-regulatory measures)." http://www.active-lifestyle.eu/php/today/marketing/index.php?doc_id=425.

Foreningen af Danske Interaktive Medier (FDIM) [Danish Interactive Media Association]. 2011. "Vedtægter [Statutes]." June 1. http://www.fdim.dk/om-fdim/vedtaegter.

International Federation of Pharmaceutical Manufacturers & Associations (IFPMA). 2007. Guidance on Advertising, etc., for Medicinal Products, Guidance No. 29 of 24/05/2007 (in force). May 24. http:// www.ifpma.org/fileadmin/content/About%20us/2%20Members/Associations/Code-Denmark/1_DK_ EN_Code1%5B1%5D.pdf.

Statens Netbibliotek. 1997. "The Ministry of Culture's Executive Order No. 489 of June 11, 1997: Executive Order Concerning Radio and Television Advertising and Programme Sponsorship." http://www.aeforum. org/gallery/9256481.pdf.

CHAPTER 10

SWEDEN

MARY ALICE SHAVER

The primary role of oversight of advertising and consumer rights in Sweden relies on an ombudsman system along with a Market Council, rather than with the more usual formal or self-regulatory bodies—although the system has some aspects of each. While Sweden had quite workable regulations at the time of the initiation of the ombudsman role (1970), these were replaced by the newly introduced ombudsman position, complemented by a Market Court that includes representatives from business. There are separate ombudsmen for specific advertising such as alcohol and children's products. There is a Council for Market Ethics and a consumer ombudsman, among others.

The Market Court (Marknadsdomstolen) handles cases that have not been resolved at a lower level. Cases brought to the Market Council may be related to the Competition Act or may arise in violation of the Marketing Act. The Association of Swedish Advertisers is the only formal industry organization in Sweden, and it (1) protects the interests of the advertising community, (2) interprets the laws and regulations in the field, and (3) provides information and education for members. The advertising rules and practices are always open to change, and business is well involved in the system.

How all of this comes together as a workable plan to serve both business and the consumers is detailed below.

Sweden is a constitutional monarchy with the power invested in the Riksdag or legislature. Although the country has accommodated over a million refugees from other areas of the world (primarily the Balkans and the Middle East), Sweden remains a relatively homogeneous country of 9 million. The Swedish behavioral mode of making decisions is generally a group effort, using consensus rather than conflict to solve problems in business and other areas of life.

The Swedish culture is defined by process, compromise, and lack of argument or public confrontations. The Swedish word *lagom* describes the philosophy: "It is better for us to have too little rather than some have too much. Beyond legislation, the social mores or rules define behavior and society at large."

Although Sweden has existed as a country for centuries, many actions and governmental functions are empowered at the local or *kummon* area. *Kummon* may be explained as a county area, with specific powers and decisions which may vary by location. In other words, the Swedish system supports nationwide regulations but gives local *kummons* the empowerment to make their own decisions in many areas. So even though many decisions and some rulings come from Stockholm, the capital of Sweden, it is the empowering duty of the *kommunfull* in each area to develop and enforce local rules.

HISTORY OF ADVERTISING REGULATION IN SWEDEN

Sweden had a workable plan of advertising self-regulation and consumer guides starting in the 1930s with a perceived need to make consumer issues a part of the self-regulatory task. Funke (2009) states that the process began as a need to check plagiarism in advertising. A review of the process in the 1950s and 1960s led to some self-regulatory bodies merging and some new ones being created.

At the start of the 1970s, there were radical changes. The newly elected Social Democratic government mandated "an extensive consumer legislation, also regulating advertising and marketing, and in the process largely replacing the self-regulation system" (Funke 2009). The current ombudsman and Market Council system was introduced, and the previous plan was set aside (Boddewyn 1985). Boddewyn offers a colorful explanation, stating that the Social Democrat program saw in consumerism "a new vehicle to revive good old-fashioned anti-business agitation, which ultimately culminated in the creation of the Consumer Ombudsman as St. George fighting the dragon advertisers" (1985, 150).

Before the implementation of the current system in Sweden, there were four associations. Funke argues that conflicts developed among the four, leading to an inefficient system that needed to be replaced. The self-regulatory model was exchanged for what is now one association working within an ombudsman role, with a council functioning as the last resort if allegations cannot be resolved at a lower level.

CURRENT SYSTEMS

An updated Marketing Act was initiated in June 2008 in accord with a "decision by the Riksdag" (the *Riksdag* is the legislative body in Sweden) (Parliament of Sweden 2008). This very comprehensive Code of Statutes is meant to protect and promote the interests of consumers and to prevent or censure unfair or deceptive marketing at all levels.

The Marketing Act applies to any Swedish market transaction as a business, to television broadcasts by satellite regulated by the Radio and Television Act, and to actions of the Consumer Ombudsman in the work for consumer protection.

All advertising practice is covered by the updated 2008 act, which includes guidelines for marketing practice. Violations include aggressive or unfair portrayals of competitors, misleading advertising, coercion in advertising or marketing practices, unfair representation of goods and services, and contact with the target market by electronic (email) means (unless there is previous consent). The penalties for violating any of the act's provisions are also clearly stated.

The purpose of the Marketing Act is "to promote the interests of consumers and business in connection with the marketing of products and to prevent marketing that is unfair to consumers and traders" (Barnombudsmannen 2010).

One provision of the act is to define unfair practice and also good marketing practice. Unfair marketing occurs when goods or services are sold in such a manner that the consumer cannot make a valid judgment before deciding on a purchase. The fact that the selling points are a matter of marketing the product or service must be clear. The provisions against aggressive marketing and misleading marketing are encompassed in the definition of the term *unfair*. No incorrect statements or claims may be made about a product. In addition, the consumer must be able to tell if a sale or promotional offer is a marketing tactic, and there can be no bolstering in the marketer's claims. Goods and services must be offered for a specific product with a stated price, and the goods must be from regular stock, be offered during a specific time, and clearly be priced lower than is usual for the piece and type it is.

Comparative advertising is allowed, but only with the following provisions: (1) Advertisements are not misleading and truly represent comparative goods or services; (2) ads refer to actual and verifiable characteristics of the product; and (3) they do not discredit the other vendor or take advantage of the other company's reputation. Nothing may be marketed that is an imitation of the other product if it has its own trademark or logo.

Several of the provisions cover warranties and the ways in which unfair marketing may be penalized. In the case of the warranty, it must be provided to the buyer and must state clearly under what circumstances the buyer may appeal for some redress for a nonperforming function of the product. The warranty information must be available to the consumer, and the seller must make clear the circumstances for claiming a refund or replacement. Sanctions against traders may take the form of a fine, an order to provide more and better information to the public or new packaging that shows the product more fully, or a fine along with an injunction to cease the unfair marketing.

There is also a separate clause called a Market Disruption Charge, which applies in cases where an advertiser uses aggressive means of comparing products, uses an ad that would be misleading or could affect the ability of the consumer to make an informed choice, or purposely discredits a competitor and his product. The seriousness and duration of the illegal practice determines the severity of the charge. The amount shall be between 5,000 and 50 million Swedish Kronor and may not be more than 10 times the company turnover for a year.

The Swedish ombudsman and Market Court systems, along with the specific regulation targeted to advertising to children and alcohol advertising, work to assure that the consumer is protected and informed and that members of business and the public are involved in the systems and its consideration of advertising in the market.

The Association of Swedish Advertisers has close to 500 members, representing a full array of Swedish companies of all sizes (Sveriges Annonsörer 2012). The association monitors and is present during all negotiations, market legislation, media development and dissemination of related information. It works for the good of the advertising community.

Should an advertiser be judged as guilty of violating a regulation, he or she will be asked to either withdraw or amend the advertisement in question. The advertiser may be fined for noncompliance. The advertising industry expects the Market Council to apply codes and rules about the copy and illustrations for an advertisement in question. (Note that the Council is a member of the European Advertising Standards Alliance [EASA]). Other ombudsman positions are quite specific. Examples of ombudsmen are a Discrimination Ombudsman (Diskrimineringsombudsmannen, or DO), a Consumer Ombudsman (Konsumentombudsmannen, or KO), and a Press Ombudsman (Pressombudsmannen, or PO). The job of Parliamentary Ombudsman dates from the early nineteenth century. Each position has its particular role. The Discrimination Ombudsman, for instance, promotes equality and the enforcement of the antidiscrimination law, and the Consumer Ombudsman oversees advertisements and can intervene if a faulty or dangerous product is advertised to the public. The Press Ombudsman oversees press ethics, and the Parliamentary Ombudsman handles complaints from anyone who feels that they were wronged or that they have been abused by a public servant. When considering these various roles, one must remember that anyone, including children, may bring a complaint to any ombudsman. Every citizen is equal according to Swedish law and practice. Sweden recognized press freedom as early as the late eighteenth century and has worked hard to promote both the free press and the responsibility that it entails. Sweden also permits everyone—Swedish citizens and Swedish press—full access to official records. An exception would be if official documents were protecting citizens and the law or if revealing information might put the state at risk.

Beyond the cases brought to the attention of the National Board of Consumer Policies, there is national monitoring of advertising. If an advertiser is found to be in violation of a policy, the board first talks to the advertiser. In the vast majority of cases, that is all it takes for the advertiser to make the required change. If the advertiser does not comply, the case will move to the appropriate ombudsman. If the problem cannot be settled at that level, the ombudsman will take the case to the Market Court, where the advertisements or practice will be studied further and where a recommendation to resolve the problem will be made.

In all cases, much effort is made to resolve the difficulty at the lowest possible level. There are cases that may be taken to a local consumer board and resolved there, so they do not appear on the national level at all. It is most important that the complaints or problems be solved as quickly as possible with fairness to all parties, including, perhaps most of all, the consuming public.

Both the relevant ombudsman and the Market Court follow the Marketing Act created in 1970, most recently updated and revised in 2008, as discussed further on in this chapter. Very few advertisements overall get as far as the Market Court for a ruling.

For example, the Advertising Ombudsman (Reklamombudsmannen, or RO) received 400 complaints in 2009, which resulted in 298 cases. All but 14 were resolved at this level, either by changing or withdrawing advertising. The majority of the unresolved cases (nine) were sent to the Consumer Agency. The RO also rejects cases that are judged to be noncommercial instances. No political, moral, or religious cases are reviewed. The Advertising Ombudsman is the industry representative, working for ethical and good (nonviolent) advertising that serves an informative marketing role. One example that was removed was a commercial where a fireworks rocket was placed in the mouth of someone portrayed in the ad and the fuse was lit: It was deemed that the advertising was unsuitable because a viewer could imitate the advertising situation. In no case may violence be permitted in Swedish advertisements.

PUBLIC COMMITTEES AND COUNCILS IN SWEDEN

Three bodies are considered as public.

1. The Market Court

The Market Court is the highest court of appeal for cases that involve competition. Areas covered involve competition and cases under the Marketing Act. The Market Court has the greatest power; cases that the ombudsmen cannot solve are taken to the Market Court, which can apply injunctions and level fines. The Market Court includes nine members—three representatives from business, three from consumer and labor organizations, and three independent members—along with a consumer affairs representative, a vice-chairperson, and a chairperson. The findings of the Market Court may not be appealed. Any unresolved breach of the Marketing Practices Act may result in fines and, in the case of egregious behavior against the public or a refusal to pay the levied fined, jail terms. Because the Market Court acts to protect consumers, it also rules on labeling and information supplied by the advertiser to the buyer of the company's products. The defendant may be asked to add wording about the use of a product so that a consumer will be fully informed.

2. The Ombudsman/Consumer Agency (Konsumentverket/ Konsumenttombudsmannen)

This is a state agency that deals with consumer complaints against a business. It may pursue legal action in consumer interest areas. The agency is headed by a director who serves as the Consumer Ombudsman as well. This is a particularly important agency in Sweden, where a great deal of emphasis is placed on fairness to consumers.

3. Children's Ombudsman (Barnombudsmannen)

Protection of children is a valued and important function in the Swedish system. The role of the Children's Ombudsman is to "promote the rights and interests of children and young people as set forth in the United Nations Convention on the Rights of the Child." The Barnombudsmannen is appointed for a term of six years by the Swedish government (2010).

Aside from representing children and young people in Sweden, the main duty of the Children's Ombudsman is to interact with other nations through international activities.

SELF-REGULATION COMMITTEES AND COUNCILS

The following agencies and committees could be considered as self-regulatory, although they have no real power to prosecute.

Council on Market Ethics (Marknadsetiska Rådet)

The Council on Market Ethics is funded by the advertising industry. Its primary function is to apply rules on advertising content. The council provides information on complaints to both industry and the media. If a complaint is upheld, the offending advertiser is asked to either withdraw or modify the advertisement. There is no appeals process.

This council is a member of the EASA.

Marketing Act

This provides guidance on marketing practice. It does not provide rules for advertising to children, although other Market Court decisions prohibit direct mail advertising to anyone under the age of 16.

The Marketing Act's purpose is to protect the interests of consumers and to "counteract marketing which is unfair" to the public in general, to business, or to both. It stresses good marketing practices, which "should be stated fairly and should give useful and viable information to both consumers and businesses" (Barnombudsmannen 2010). It addresses the need for clear identification of the advertiser and prohibits misleading advertising.

The International Chamber of Commerce (ICC) marketing rules are used as a measure of advertising in many areas, including advertising to children. ICC rules are also followed in rulings on the advertising of food and drink. Likewise, the Swedish Marketing Act is in compliance with the EASA (European Union) guidelines.

The number of cases brought to the Market Court in the past 10 years have been fairly consistent (see Table 10.1).

Table 10.1

Cases Adjudicated by the Swedish Market Court from 2001 through 2010

Year	Number of Cases
2001	97
2002	99
2003	94
2004	94
2005	92
2006	86
2007	98
2008	82
2009	83

ADVERTISING TO CHILDREN

Advertising either targeting children directly or considered to be appealing to child viewers is very carefully monitored in Sweden. As previously noted, there is a special ombudsman appointed to supervise issues relating to children and to young people.

The ombudsman may submit bills to the legislature and may seek changes for the greater good for the nation's children. Public relations is a key role, and participating in public meetings and debate is important in this position. The office of the Barnombudsmannen tries to "promote public interest . . . regarding key issues" (EASA 2010). However, by law, the ombudsman may not consider individual cases. The ombudsman or delegates visit schools and social clubs to gather firsthand reports on the views of young people; in addition, a yearly questionnaire is sent out. Each year, a report is made to the government outlining the concerns—and also the opportunities—for children in Sweden. It should be noted that the Barnombudsmannen's role is to consider children and youths up to age 18. There is a website where young people can contact the office of the Barnombudsmannen.

A 2009 report on the United Nations Committee on the Rights of the Child stated that Sweden had a national strategy for implementing the suggestions that came from the convention. A recommendation to protect children who use media—broadcast, the Internet, and games—resulted in an initiative shared by the private sector, national authorities, and NGOs. The initiative would establish an Internet portal to provide access to all to learn how Sweden protects the rights of children when using any form of media (Office of the United Nations High Commissioner for Human Rights [OHCHR] 2009). On July 1 of that same year, Sweden assumed the presidency of the European Union. A high priority was to bring the rights of children prominently forward and to write a resolution for the European Union on this subject. The Children's Ombudsman played a key role in these tasks.

As can be seen, the role of the Children's Ombudsman extends further than Sweden itself. International cooperation and membership in the European Network of Ombudspersons for Children

(ENOC) connects Sweden to the other EU countries. The functions of this network are supported administratively by UNICEF. The group works to establish more ombudsmen within the European countries. At present, there are 23 members (ENOC 2012). The Right to Be Heard Project and an International Training Program were held in several countries (ENOC 2011, 2–3). The Swedish ombudsman for children has organized the training program since its founding in 1998.

Consumer Ombudsman

The Consumer Ombudsman also plays a role in the practices of advertising to children. Section 4 of the Swedish Marketing Act forbids advertising to children under the age of 12. Violating this prohibition can lead to a fine and, in some cases, to a market disruption penalty as well. The penalties may be levied against the advertiser, the agency, and film or broadcast producers.

What follows are the interpretive guidelines from the Consumer Ombudsman. By statutory law, no commercials targeted to children may be shown during or after any program that is deemed to be for children under the age of 12. Personalities on children's programming may not appear in any advertising in that program role. Actors appearing in children's programs may appear in other commercials in another role; it is the possible confusion with children recognizing them and the enhanced element of persuasion that is forbidden. The statute assumes that children under the age of 12 may not be able to distinguish the characters in their commercial role apart from the program. This prohibition stands regardless of the type of product being advertised.

The introduction of a commercial is relevant to its judging. If it contains children's music, children's voices, or anything that would be aimed at drawing children into the advertisement, it is forbidden under law. A similar ruling would apply if the advertisement shows children's games or toys.

If the voice in the advertisement appears to be directed at a child audience, it is forbidden. This applies to any childlike voice, especially if the voice is recognizable to children from another context. Cartoon characters are considered to attract young audiences and must not be used to encourage children to purchase any goods. Similarly, a recognizable cartoon character may not be used in any company logo or trademark.

Context and time are important considerations. The time that the program is aired is crucial in deciding its appeal to those under 12 years of age. The commonly accepted time for children to watch is until 9:00 P.M. However, if the program is of a nature that would be especially interesting for children (sports, for example), the time may logically be later than usual. The ombudsman also views the peak time as being later on weekends, when children are not going to school in the next morning.

The ombudsman provides examples to illustrate the interpretations of the statute. One example is for a chocolate bar with packaging that features popular children's characters. No cartoon characters may be shown as promoting the product, and children's music is not allowed to accompany the ad. A second example is a breakfast cereal preferred by children. Again, the context is important. If there are cartoon characters in the ad, it should not be scheduled to air during programs directed toward children. To be acceptable for other advertising, the commercial must have a neutral voice-over or speaker and be informational rather than persuasive. Yet another example is an advertisement for a zoo. Recognized as a form of entertainment for the whole family, zoos and other attractions must not be advertised during a sports or family program. The commercial must address parents, not children. In all cases, persuasion must not be a part of any commercials that show goods or services for children. Information is the desired effect.

Other Swedish Consumer Organizations

While there is no official definition of consumer institutions at a national level, two organizations are devoted to this cause: the Swedish Consumers' Association and the Swedish Consumer Agency.

The Swedish Consumers' Association (Sveriges Konsumenter 2009) has member organizations and is also open to individual membership. Its main goals are to strengthen consumers' power, to bring consumer matters into the open, and to effect changes that will benefit the consumer. The Swedish Consumers' Association is an independent and nonpartisan organization and consists of a number of other, smaller organizations, whose mission is to inform and assist consumers in making their needs known and in giving them market power. The association works on both national and international consumer issues.

A white paper written by the association addressed the subject of children and marketing (von Haartman 2009). Noting the need for children to be protected from assertive advertising and marketing messages and techniques, the paper advocates a total ban on advertising to children under the age of 16. Modern technology makes the messages in advertisements more difficult to separate and also more manipulative. The organization states that democracy in Sweden involves both local and regional input and decisions, and it calls for the EU to mandate a similar program in member states so that all are involved, informed, and invited to consider and contribute ideas for action to the national commissions. The paper states that the EU consumer mandates must always include consumer input. It calls for more coordination among the involved constituents and a strategy for including other directorships and organizations. The power and decisions must be transparent and incorporate the voice of the consumer (von Haartman 2009).

A 2009 survey by the Swedish Consumers' Association found that young people notice only 10 percent of all Internet advertisements during their time online. However, studies indicate that "it only takes a few milliseconds for a viewer to perceive and process information. Young people spend increasingly more time in front of the computer than watching TV," and companies have responded by investing "enormous amounts into commercials on the Internet" (Sveriges Konsumenter 2009). The Swedish Consumers' Association recommends close scrutiny of the "hidden influence" of Internet ads aimed at young people (2009).

Another important Swedish consumer organization is the Swedish Consumer Agency (Konsumentverket). Founded in 1994, it is nonprofit and nongovernmental in membership. Its members work for the common interest by monitoring consumer issues and bringing them to public notice. Their statement of policy states that they aim:

- to strengthen the position and influence of consumers in the market.
- to help households make the best possible use of their money and other resources.
- to strengthen the protection of consumer health and safety.
- to promote patterns of production and consumption that contribute to long-term sustainable development.
- to increase consumer access to good advice and assistance, information, and education (Konsumentverket 2009).

Consumer issues or problems about food are of particular importance to the Swedish Consumer Agency. Quality of all goods versus quantity is stressed. The organization states that consumers have the right to "a wholesome environment and a fundamental quality of life" (Konsumentverket 2009). As with other organizations, it is agreed that consumers need access to honest and complete information to make good decisions about goods and services in the marketplace. In Sweden, consumers are included in policy matters.

While the Swedish Consumer Agency works to develop relationships on the national and local level, the primary focus is on the local level.

A key belief in Sweden—one that distinguishes it from many other countries—is that consumers are far less powerful than the manufacturer or business owner and that governmental and other advocates are needed to level the playing field.

PUBLIC FUNDING FOR CONSUMER ORGANIZATIONS

In 2009, Sweden developed a system that allows public interest organizations to apply for public funding and project support. The criteria are quite detailed, but the organization must be democratic, independent of politics, and have the goal of safeguarding Swedish consumers and of representing them on the national market or the EU or some other international forum. Project support is given to finance projects that have a major goal of initiating or supporting consumer interest or understanding of rights.

The Consumer Omsbudsman is the head of this agency, which identifies "misleading advertising and marketing, unfair contracts, incorrect price information and dangerous products and services" (Thorelli and Thorelli 1997, chap. 7).

The Consumer Ombudsman may represent a consumer in court seeking redress for a business's unlawful practice. The National Board for Consumer Complaints investigates conflicts, supports mediation, and serves in an advisory capacity in a legal case.

The board may suggest how a dispute should be resolved, but it has no power of law. Most businesses do respect the board's decision. Unresolved cases may be brought in an open court.

FREEDOM OF THE PRESS

In considering the rights of the public to be informed about all the issues of the advertising industry and the rights of consumers, one must look to the state of freedom of the press in Sweden. The first article on the freedom of the press in Sweden spells out the right of the citizen to publish written material without hindrance or prosecution afterward. The goal is to exchange true and comprehensive information and to encourage a sharing of opinions and facts. The act applies to all written material, regardless of where published.

However, there are several bans on commercial advertising. First, it is forbidden in the marketing of alcohol or tobacco products. This includes products that may have some relationship to alcohol and tobacco. There is a ban on advertising for the protection of health and the environment in accordance with the EU regulations. Also prohibited are publications dealing with credit information, and untrue or misleading advertisements.

Documents published must be readily accessible to every Swedish citizen. This applies to documents or information about governmental business, as well as more private communication.

Of course, there are provisions against material that may be construed as treasonous, or the unauthorized trafficking of secret information, or material that goes against civil liberty. Liability in these cases lies with the person identified as the editor of the publication.

EVOLVING SWEDISH ADVERTISING REGULATION

Sweden has a long history of consensus building. A key right is that every party in every discussion or committee is allowed (and encouraged) to express its own view.

As noted earlier, Sweden's advertising regulations are embedded in a number of ombudsman positions, which attempt to resolve difficulties with solutions that all parties can agree upon. In line with Swedish custom, there is a great emphasis on consensus. Everyone is allowed to express an opinion, and the resolution process generally takes all ideas into consideration.

Still, there may be areas of total disagreement (examples could be apparent trademark violations, alleged competitive violations, and such). It is at that point that the case may be moved into the Market Court.

SWEDISH AGENCIES AND ASSOCIATIONS

Advertising Ombudsman (Reklamombudsmannen, or RO)
Association of Swedish Advertisers (Sveriges Annonsörer)
Children's Ombudsman (Barnombudsmannen)
Consumer Ombudsman (Konsumentombudsmannen, or KO)
Council on Market Ethics (Marknadsetiska Rådet)
Discrimination Ombudsman (Diskrimineringsombudsmannen, or DO)
The Market Court (Marknadsdomstolen)
The Ombudsman/Consumer Agency (Konsumentverket/Konsumenttombudsmannen)
Parliament of Sweden (Riksdag)
Press Ombudsman (Pressombudsmannen, or PO)
The Swedish Consumers' Association (Sveriges Konsumenter)

BIBLIOGRAPHY

Barnombudsmannen [Children's Ombudsman]. 2010. Interview with the author, December.
Boddewyn, Jean J. 1985. "The Swedish Consumer-Ombudsman System and Advertising Self-Regulation." *Journal of Consumer Affairs* 19(1): 140–162.
European Advertising Standards Alliance (EASA). 2010. "Sweden." In *Blue Book*, 6th ed., 152–161. Brussels, Belgium: EASA.
European Network of Ombudspersons for Children (ENOC). 2011. *Consultation Document: European Commission's Communication on the Rights of the Child (2011–2014).* http://ec.europa.eu/justice/news/consulting_public/0009/contributions/public_authorities/026_enoc_part7.pdf.
———. 2012. "What We Do." http://crin.org/enoc/whatwedo/index.asp.
Funke, Michael. 2009. "Swedish Business Associations and Self-Regulations of Advertising 1950–1971." In *Marketing History: Strengthening, Straightening, and Extending. Proceedings of the 14th Biennial Conference of Historical Analysis and Research in Marketing.* University of Leicester, May 28–31.
Konsumentverket. 2009. "Swedish Consumer Policy: Consumer Agency." December 4. http://www.konsumentverket.se/otherlanguages/English/.
Marknadsdomstolen [The Market Court]. 2012. "The Swedish Market Court." http://www.marknadsdomstolen.se/default.aspx?id=1225.
Office of the United Nations High Commissioner for Human Rights (OHCHR). 2009. "Committee on the Rights of the Child: Monitoring Children's Rights." http://www2.ohchr.org/english/bodies/crc/.
Parliament of Sweden [Riksdag]. 2008. The Marketing Act. Swedish Code of Statutes, SFS 2008:486, June 16. http://www.government.se/content/1/c6/05/03/14/6c7aa374.pdf.
Reklamombudsmannen (RO) [Advertising Ombudsman]. 2012. "The Swedish Advertising Ombudsman." http://www.reklamombudsmannen.org/eng.
Sveriges Annonsörer [Association of Swedish Advertisers]. 2012. "In English: Welcome to the Association of Swedish Advertisers." http://www.annons.se.
Sveriges Konsumenter [The Swedish Consumers' Association]. 2009. "Young people notice 10 percent of all

Internet advertisements." Press release, October. http://www.sverigeskonsumenter.se/Documents/Projekt/
Engelska/091016.MarketingProject.PressRelease.pdf.

Thorelli, E.B., and S.V. Thorelli. 1977. *Consumer Information Systems and Consumer Policy.* Cambridge,
MA: Ballinger.

von Haartman, Filippa. 2009. *Stakeholder Views on Policy Options for Marketing Food and Beverages
to Children: Findings from the PolMark Project in Sweden.* Report, September. Karolinska Institutets
folkhälsoakademi [Karolinska Institute School of Public Health]. http://ki.se/content/1/c6/08/19/17/
KFA_2009_9.pdf.

PART IV

OTHER EUROPEAN COUNTRIES

CHAPTER 11

FRANCE

JEAN-PIERRE TEYSSIER

Advertising in France operates amid a comprehensive and complex set of public laws and professional regulations. In this way, the country's advertising industry can be distinguished from that of most other democracies in the world; it has developed into a unique system of *coregulation*. Public regulation in France, as elsewhere, consists of laws enacted by the legislature, decrees and orders of the executive branch, or rules made by independent administrative authorities. The courts adjudicate disputes involving these entities. Private regulation refers to a body of professional rules (standards of practice and ethics) developed by the three branches of the advertising industry—advertisers, advertising agencies, and the media. Since 2008, the Professional Advertising Regulation Authority (Autorité de Régulation Professionnelle de la Publicité, or ARPP)—the successor to the Advertising Verification Bureau (Bureau de Vérification de la Publicité, or BVP)—issues and implements these professional standards and rules.

There is no uniform definition of advertising in France. European Union directives refer to advertising as "commercial communication." In Directive 2007/65/EC, commercial communication refers to "images with or without sound which are designed to promote, directly or indirectly, the goods, services or images of a natural or legal entity pursuing an economic activity. Such images accompany or are included in a program in return for payment or for similar consideration or for self-promotional purposes. Forms of audiovisual commercial communication include . . . television advertising, sponsorship, teleshopping and product placement" (European Union 2007).

In French legislation, the definition of advertising depends on the type of medium used to disseminate information or the type of product being sold. For example, the legislation on misleading ads includes advertising in "commercial practices." The law governing the advertising of alcohol equates advertising with "propaganda." We will settle for the definition used by the International Chamber of Commerce (ICC) in its code: "Any form of marketing communication carried by the media," which is also the one used by the advertising industry in France (ICC 2012).

In France, legislation regulating advertising is abundant, perhaps more so than in any other European country. Increased concern about public health and the environment continue to generate even more rules and regulations. Nevertheless, this large body of public regulation did not hinder the development of advertising self-regulation, or "professional regulation" as it is termed today. French advertisers began regulating themselves in 1935, with the founding of the Office for the Control of Advertisements (Office de Contrôle des Annonces, or OCA). Now operating as the Professional Advertising Regulation Authority, it administers about 40 different recommendations that address standards and practices. Its organizational structure was recently broadened with the integration of consumer associations.

The French model refutes the common perception that self-regulation can thrive only when the volume of legislation in a country is small. In France, where official rules applying to advertising are numerous, one would expect limited self-regulation. However, the French advertising industry has embraced self-regulation and established strong professional ethics codes precisely because public authorities and civil society have been highly critical of advertising. Indeed, in France, "culture" has traditionally opposed "commerce," resulting in a deep-seated suspicion of advertising. A substantial number of French consumers dislike and distrust advertising. Their disaffection, in turn, spurs public authorities to regulate advertising even more. Meanwhile, the industry strives to demonstrate its own sense of social responsibility through new initiatives in self-discipline. As a result, the advertising profession is highly controlled by more and more rules imposed from several directions.

PUBLIC REGULATION OF ADVERTISING IN FRANCE

French law acknowledges freedom of expression. However, the first article of the Freedom of Communication Law (No. 86–107, 1986) grants great discretionary power to the French government: "Audio-visual communication is free. The exercise of this freedom may be limited, only to the extent required, to maintain respect for human dignity, the freedom and property of other people, [and] the pluralistic nature of the expression of ideas and opinions. Regulation can also be imposed for protection of law and order, for national defense and public-service reasons, for technical reasons inherent in the means of communications, as well as for the need to develop a national audio-visual production industry" (Boddewyn and Loubradou 2011).

The government has not shied away from using its authority to impose stringent regulations on advertising, and it has done so for several reasons. Advertising is viewed with suspicion because of perceptions that it "pollutes" the airwaves—hence, the banning of advertising on public radio stations and after 8:00 P.M. on public television. Many fear that advertising can manipulate vulnerable segments of the audience, such as children. Regulations prohibit advertisements for certain products on channels or in publications aimed at children. Online money games (gambling) were banned on such channels and publications in 2010.

Until the 1980s, television channels were entirely owned by the French government. Commercials were not allowed until 1968, and then only for certain sectors. The printed press—worried about competition—did its best to prevent advertising on television. Moreover, the budgets for certain campaigns were thought to be excessive and seen as a source of corruption, leading to major inequity among competing advertisers. This explains strict limitations on political advertising in France during the months preceding an election.

Consumers themselves have organized to monitor and criticize advertising in France. Since the 1970s, labor unions, family associations, and consumer groups have created watchdog organizations. Nowadays, 18 of these associations are recognized and subsidized by the Consumer Affairs Ministry. Together with environmental nongovernmental organizations (NGOs), they challenge the advertising industry on many issues, such as *greenwashing* (the deceptive use of PR or advertising to suggest that a company's practices and products are environmentally friendly); food and beverage marketing; and the portrayal of women. Pressure groups are active in other fields, including women's rights (Les Chiennes de garde) or the portrayal of obese persons (Allegro Fortissimo). Finally, public health concerns efficiently relayed by associations, NGOs, and public officials have resulted in limiting or prohibiting the advertising of certain products, such as alcohol (Evin Law of 1991), something of an irony given that French wines and brandies are the envy of much of the world.

Altogether, French laws pertaining to advertising are numerous and strict. While they also cover the intellectual property aspects of advertising (copyright, unfair competition, etc.), this analysis will focus on advertising content in terms of such issues as misleading advertising and the promotion of certain products (e.g., alcohol).

Sources of Regulation

European Union (EU) directives must be reflected in French laws, which apply to all ads issued in France, although the French legislature can reinforce EU regulations in specific cases. Under European Union rules, advertising is considered to be a service that benefits from the "free movement" principle, according to Articles 30 and 59 of the Rome Treaty of 1957. Commercial communications, which include advertising, also benefit from the freedom of speech guaranteed by Article 10 of the European Convention on Human Rights. This freedom can be abridged only in the cases explicitly specified under the law. In general, concerns regarding consumer protection and fair competition in the context of a free market have inspired the EU advertising legislation. For example, the Directive on Misleading Advertising (1984) closely resembles the French law of 1973, particularly in defining the concept as "any advertising which in any way, including its presentation, deceives or is likely to deceive the persons to whom it is addressed or whom it reaches and which, by reason of its deceptive nature, is likely to affect their economic behavior or which, for those reasons, injures or is likely to injure a competitor" (Directive 8450, 1984). It is worth noting that—even before the passage of the EU directive—in France and most other European countries, individual self-regulatory codes had required accuracy and honesty in consumer advertising.

The Directive on Comparative Advertising (1997) authorizes, under certain conditions, ads that "explicitly or implicitly identify a competitor or the products or services offered by a competitor."

The Directive on Unfair Business-to-Consumer Commercial Practices (2005) adds to the list of unfair commercial practices those considered "aggressive" and "contrary to professional diligence." For example, this directive forbids a professional from claiming that he is signatory to a good-conduct code when he is not. This prohibition thereby recognizes the existence and validity of professional self-regulatory rules. The directive was incorporated into French law in 2008.

Other European directives regulate specific fields such as television advertising. The 2007 directive concerning television broadcasting replaced the 1989 Television Without Borders directive and was incorporated into French law in March 2009. Direct marketing is regulated through a 1995 directive that protects personal data and electronic commerce (2000). EU directives also limit advertising for certain products such as pharmaceuticals. A 1992 directive prohibits the advertising of prescription drugs, and a 2003 directive ended advertising and sponsorship for tobacco products after 2005 in all European countries. However, alcohol advertising is not yet regulated by a harmonized EU rule.

French Public Rules on Advertising

In many fields, French legislators have been more restrictive than the EU and other countries regarding advertising and its practitioners.

France Regulates Relations Between Advertisers and Their Advertising Agencies

The January 1993 Sapin Law (named after Michel Sapin, the Secretary of the Treasury who drafted it) aimed at establishing transparency in the relations among advertisers, advertising agencies, and media companies, including media buyers. This law obliges agencies and media buyers to act as intermediaries commissioned by the advertiser, and it prohibits any compensation other than the amount specified in the written contract, thereby eliminating the former practice of using discounts or other perks to compensate intermediaries. Nevertheless, the law has created some problems because it does not apply to nonmedia advertising such as direct marketing or flyers; therefore, it complicates the legal status of advertising agencies, which varies depending on the type of media used for an advertising campaign.

France Prohibits Some Industries from Advertising on Television

Bowing to pressure from print media's concerns about competition, the French legislature has only slowly widened access to television. TV advertising was authorized in 1969, but it took until 2003 for the French to allow large retailers to run commercials for supermarkets on television (Decree of October 2003). The cinema sector still cannot advertise, except on channels dedicated to movies, and publishing firms cannot advertise on privately owned TV channels.

France strictly controls the advertising of alcohol. The 1991 Evin Law (named after Health Minister Health Claude Evin, who authored the law) severely limited advertising for beverages containing more than 1.2 percent alcohol by volume. Banned from television advertising since 1987, alcohol advertising is now forbidden in all media except print and then not in publications aimed at children, on radio at certain hours, on the Internet, and in postings at points of sale. Even when advertising for alcohol is allowed, the law authorizes mention of only a few specific qualities, such as the amount of alcohol by volume, its origin, its composition, and the name of the product. Alcohol ads must not encourage the "dangerous consumption" of alcohol and must carry the warning that alcohol abuse is dangerous to health.

This law has become one of the most difficult to enforce and has triggered confusion and perplexity. For example: How can one entice people to buy a product without also encouraging its consumption? Because advertising goes beyond simply informing consumers, it is easy to break the law, making ad creation for alcoholic beverages risky and difficult.

Alcohol ads, and even news content about alcohol, are frequent targets of anti-alcohol associations, which often lodge complaints or file suits under the Evin Law. Judges who must apply and strictly interpret the law have been very severe—and often contradictory—in their interpretations. One of the more bizarre examples involved a feature story in the daily newspaper *Le Parisien* titled "The Triumph of Champagne." A state-sponsored association, the National Association for the Prevention of Alcoholism and Addiction (NAPAA), sued the paper under the Evin Law, complaining that the 2005 article encouraged drinking and failed to carry the warning—mandatory for ads—that alcohol abuse can be hazardous to health. The newspaper argued that the article was strictly its own editorial content and not an advertisement. Nevertheless, the judge ruled that the article should have carried the mandatory warning and fined the paper 5,000 euros (BBC 2008).

The same group also prevailed in a suit against the Dutch brewer Heineken over the promotional material on its French website. The NAPAA argued that Heineken's beer promotions were illegal because the 1991 Evin regulation did not include the Internet among the media allowed to carry alcohol ads. A French appeals court agreed and ordered Heineken to remove all promotion of its products on the site or face a fine of 3,000 euros a day (AFP 2008). Finally, in July 2009 a law was passed specifying that the Internet is a legal medium for alcohol advertising, except on websites aimed at persons under the age of 18. However, the only types of information authorized are those listed in the Evin Law.

France Mandates Many Other Legal Warnings in Advertisements

The French legislature is very fond of warnings to alert consumers or protect them against the risks of excessive consumption and the uncontrolled purchase of particular products and services. These warnings, which accompany the principal message of the advertiser, risk confusing or befuddling consumers, but they have multiplied in recent years in many sectors. There are two types of compulsory legal warnings: banners and legal notices. Banners—the size of which is often specified in the law—warn, promote, or admonish: "The abuse of alcohol is dangerous for your health"; "Energy is our future, let's save it!"; "For your health, avoid eating too much fat, too much sugar, too much salt." Since 2010, advertising for gambling or games of chance have also come under the law, which mandates several notices including: "Playing involves some risks: debt, dependence . . . Call this number if you need help"; "You are committed by a credit transaction, and it must be repaid. Check your ability to pay your debt before committing yourself."

Legal notices must be included in an ad as a reference or a footnote; for example, automobiles ads must include information about gas consumption, performance, and CO_2 emissions. Consumer credit ads have to include notices of the rate of interest offered and whether that rate is promotional or permanent. Telecommunication service ads must include rate information. The expansion of legal notices in recent years has led to concerns about their unproven effectiveness, while the cost of their production and publication is significant for the industries concerned.

France Insists That Advertisers Respect the French Language in Advertisements

The 1994 Toubon Law (named after the Minister of Culture at the time, Jacques Toubon) requires that all non-French expressions be translated into French, although this obligation does not apply to trademarks and slogans when they are part of the advertiser's identity. Such translation aims to provide correct information to consumers and to prevent the Anglicization of advertising. It applies to all media, including television, but its "soft" implementation is entrusted to professional regulation and to the self-regulatory body ARPP in order to ensure the understandability and correct translation of advertising texts.

France Strictly Limits Political Advertising During an Election Campaign

Since 1990, French law has prohibited all political advertising for a candidate or a party during an election campaign in all media except radio and television. Previously, candidates could advertise on billboards and in the printed press, but now political ads are allowed only on radio and television and on posters in front of polling stations. Only during the periods between elections can the public officials and political groups advertise in other media, which, of course, is of no interest to them. This French peculiarity can be explained by the fear that excessive spending during election campaigns will lead to inequity and undue influence—especially in presidential elections. However, restrictions on campaign spending imposed by the legislature in 1990 seem to have limited this risk, even without prohibitions on nonbroadcast media advertising.

Court Decisions

Although there have been many court cases in other areas of advertising and marketing—including many cases bearing on brands, agency property, copyrights, privacy and image rights, lotteries, and sales promotions from 2008 through 2010—court cases addressing advertising content have been relatively infrequent. The Heineken case in 2008 raised the novel legal issue of the legality of alcohol ads on the Internet, but the few other content cases of the period have focused on familiar legal issues.

Alcohol and Tobacco Advertising

Most content cases deal with alcohol and tobacco products. For instance, a recent decision prohibited the reference in an advertisement to the taste or color of an alcoholic product, concluding that such descriptions could be interpreted as an improper inducement to drinking (Cour de cassation 2010).

Comparative Advertising

A recent decision validated websites that compare prices because these ads respected the EU law on comparative advertising (*JDN: Journal du Net* 2008).

Misleading Advertising

There have been decisions against breaches of French and EU laws applying to marketing and commercial practices. The Tribunal de Grande Instance de Paris (2009) ordered Google to pay 200,000 euros to Voyageurs du Monde (Travelers of the World) and 150,000 euros to Terres d'Aventure (Lands of Adventure), even though the judge acknowledged that the commercial harm to the companies was marginal. When Web users typed the trademarked terms "voyageur du monde" and "terres aventure" into Google, the search results were accompanied by ads for the companies' competitors. The court said that, although the commercial harm was marginal, it had denied the companies some customers by directing them to other sites.

Google appealed the case to the Paris Court of Appeals (Out-law.com 2009).

Unfair or Insensitive Advertising

Cases have dealt with brand or company names being used or denigrated through advertising campaigns.

Despite the numerous and strict government advertising rules mandating respect for human dignity and beliefs, it is difficult for the French judiciary to use criminal laws against free speech. Nevertheless, it is worth mentioning the 1996 case involving a graphic international advertising campaign mounted by the Benetton apparel company. A billboard campaign by Benetton about AIDS was condemned on the basis of the Civil Code's Article 1382, which obliges whoever injured someone else to pay damages to the victim. In 1991, Benetton displayed three huge posters showing an elbow, a pubic area and a pair of buttocks stamped "HIV positive." A French governmental AIDS-awareness agency (AFLS) sued Benetton and won damages. The court held that Benetton undermined the human dignity of those affected by HIV by using images that evoked the way meat is stamped and the tattooing of concentration camp inmates during World War II, while marginalizing a group of people by representing them as a marked population (Cour d'Appel de Paris 1996).

A 2005 case raised the issue of illegally insulting religious beliefs. The fashion house Marithe and Francois Girbaud erected giant billboards in Paris, Milan, and New York that parodied Leonardo da Vinci's *The Last Supper* to advertise blue jeans. The billboard portrayed Christ and all of the disciples but one as women. The Catholic Church, outraged by the ad, successfully won a ban on the ad first in Milan and then in France. A judge in Paris ruled that the ad was offensive to Catholics, calling the parody "a gratuitous and aggressive act of intrusion on people's innermost beliefs." Judge Jean-Claude Magendie ruled, "The offence done to Catholics far outweighs the desired commercial goal." He ordered that all ads on display be taken down within three days (Cour d'Appel de Paris 2005). However, the Higher Appeals Court struck down Magendie's ruling, finding that that the advertiser had not intended any harm (Cour de cassation 2006).

Still other recent court decisions took note of professional or deontological rules in several advertising cases, adding legal credibility to France's professional regulations devised by the advertising industry itself. For example, the Paris Appeals Court ruling in a case involving alcohol advertising stated, "Recommendations from the ARPP, even though they have no legal character, are professional practices that the judge must take into account if they do not contradict a legal or statutory measure" (Cour d'Appel de Paris 2010). A court in Versailles confirmed a decision of the Tribunal de Commerce de Nanterre, stating that an ad was not unfair according to a provision of the International Chamber of Commerce's Advertising Code (Article 16 on Imitation) (Cour d'Appel de Versailles 2010).

French Professional Regulation of Advertising

The ethics rules set by the advertising industry's professionals are very old in France, where the same association has led self-regulation for 75 years, first, under the name of Office for the Control of Advertisements (Office de Contrôle des Annonces, or OCA, 1935) at the initiative of the press, then as the Advertising Verification Bureau (Bureau de Vérification de la Publicité, or BVP, 1953) when advertisers joined agencies and the media in this tripartite association, and finally as the Professional Advertising Regulation Authority (ARPP) after an extensive revision of the association's statutes in June 2008.

The ARPP is a nonprofit professional association with about 1,000 members—mostly from advertising's three branches: advertisers, agencies, and media. All television commercials must be precleared by the ARPP, and, because this preclearance is less costly for ARPP members than for nonmembers, all major advertisers and agencies plus all the media are members, whether individually or through their own organizations (ARPP 2012).

ARPP is managed by a 30-member board of directors representing equally the professional organizations of the three advertising branches. The board elects a president or chair who is always someone from outside the advertising industry. Since 2008, a nine-member independent Advertising Deontology Jury (Jury de Déontologie Publicitaire, or JDP), chaired by a member of a high court, adjudicates all complaints. Its members have no links with industry or consumer associations. In addition, another group, the Joint Advertising Council (Conseil Paritaire de la Publicité, or CPP) has brought together various stakeholders, including consumer and environmental associations as well as industry associations, to consider the need for new recommendations (JDP 2012). The Advertising Ethics Council (Conseil de l'Ethique Publicitaire, or CEP) operates within the ARPP. An independent academic chairs the ethics council, which is charged with advising the ARPP board of directors about the evolution of societal issues concerning advertising. The ARPP has both legislative and enforcement authority.

The ARPP's bylaws impose strict procedures for the drafting of new ethics rules. The process must include stakeholders from industry and from society, even though professionals themselves ultimately write and adopt their own rules of ethics. Nevertheless, democracy demands that professionals consult with representatives of French civil society. This is why, since 2008, the Joint Advertising Council (CPP) has brought together the representatives of advertisers, agencies, and media and of consumer and environmental associations when changing an ethical rule or drafting a new one. The CPP chair offers advice and counsel, but it is the ARPP board of directors, which is made up strictly of advertising professionals, that determines whether any changes are appropriate and signs off on the final language of rule changes or new rules.

Establishing and Promulgating Rules of Good Practice

The ARPP's rules, together with the Code of the International Chamber of Commerce (ICC)*, are the only ones recognized in France governing the content of advertisements. They consist of about 40 best practice guidelines called *recommendations* that aim to ensure responsible commercial communications and to guarantee to the public that ads are truthful, culturally sensitive, and protective of society's most vulnerable groups.

Truthfulness in Advertising

Ensuring honest and accurate marketing communication is a principle set in the law, but the practical details are spelled out in professional rules. For example, *Développement Durable* (the Sustainable Development Recommendation) governs ads that make environmental claims. The recommendation was developed to quell *greenwashing,* which environmental groups and the government consider abusive and misleading. The recommendation was recently strengthened after consultation between the ARPP and environmental NGOs. In order to guarantee implementation of the recommendation, advertising professionals and the government agreed in writing in 2009 to submit to the ARPP, before publication, all of their advertising projects involving environmental claims, whatever the media used.

Cultural and Religious Sensitivity in Advertising

In the area of cultural and religious sensitivity, where public values can change quickly, self-regulation has proved to be more nimble and adaptable than legislation. For example, *Image de la Personne Humaine* (the "Images of Human Beings" Recommendation) sets professional rules for maintaining the dignity of individuals. For example, an ad cannot show a model in scanty attire unless the nature of the product—lingerie or a bathing suit, for example—justifies the portrayal and only if the ad does not feature any scene of violence, humiliation, or subordination.

Sensitivity to Potential Risks to Society

Several ARPP recommendations set rules to protect the public, especially its most vulnerable groups, from manipulation or risk. For example, the Automobile Recommendation bans references to speed or power in car ads. The Health Allegations Recommendation bans any presentation or assertion that a food is medicinal or can cure disease. In January 2010, a new Eating Habits Recommendation set strict rules for food ads, which, for example, cannot show unbalanced diets or people snacking between meals.

---

*The ICC codes for a long time were the only rules applying to the French advertising industry. Then, in the 1970s, the BVP and later the ARPP promulgated specific rules. The latest ICC Code of Advertising and Marketing Communication Practice, published in 2006, still inspires the ARPP recommendations, and it figures among the rules recognized in France—notably by the Advertising Deontology Jury (JDP).

Implementing and Enforcing the Rules

To ensure that advertisers and agencies comply with its rules, the APRR reviews all advertising campaigns and creative material before distribution and adjudicates complaints afterward.

Before distribution, two different types of consultation are possible. During the creative phase, all ARPP members can freely ask for copy advice. In less than 48 hours, the ARPP will let them to know whether a television spot, radio message, or an image for press ads complies with the law and professional rules. In 2009, more than 15,000 requests for copy advice were received and answered within the allotted time.

All television commercials must be submitted to the ARPP for prebroadcast review before acceptance by television channels. This obligation, also imposed on non-ARPP members, resulted from a request by the French public authority for audiovisual regulation, the Conseil Supérieur de l'Audiovisuel (CSA), and French television channels. In 1991, ARPP began its preclearance process. In 2009, it delivered more than 20,000 television preclearances. Altogether, about 150 advertising projects are submitted each day to the ARPP. About one-third require modification. In most cases, the requested modifications are made.

After an ad is broadcast, any consumer can file a complaint with the Advertising Deontology Jury (JDP), which will determine whether the ad in question complies with the ARPP professional recommendations. Created in 2008 and chaired by a member of the top French legal body, the Conseil d'Etat, the JDP is totally independent of the advertising industry. Even though the ARPP houses and funds the JDP, the jury must rule with impartiality. In 2009, it received 502 complaints and discussed 36 of them in plenary session, finding 25 ads to be in violation of ARPP recommendations. In such cases, two penalties are imposed: withdrawal of the ad and publication of the decision. The jury publishes its decisions on its own website and issues a news release in serious cases. The jury's decisions are generally quoted in the press, thereby causing embarrassment and at least some damage to the advertiser's reputation, illustrating that the "name and shame" approach is a very effective sanction.

The ARPP can decide on its own to intervene if a campaign is obviously breaching a professional rule. Such actions take place only about three or four times a year, often when an ad triggers controversy that generates considerable press coverage. The JDP can intervene only if it receives a complaint, but the ARPP can prevail on its professional members to stop the condemned ad's distribution. Most of the media, including French Internet companies, are members of the ARPP and are committed to withdrawing ads that contravene professional rules. In March 2010, for example, three flyers issued by an antitobacco association were taken out of circulation within three days of their distribution. The flyers showed an adult touching an adolescent boy and an adolescent girl, which the ADPP believed implied sexual abuse.

Advertisers generally comply with withdrawal requests from the ARPP because brands and companies do not want to be damaged by controversy or threatened with a lawsuit. The significant impact of web buzz and pressure groups encourages advertisers to comply, lest their brand images and their firms' reputations get hurt by public controversy.

The ARPP also monitors advertising by periodically conducting studies to check compliance with its professional rules. All ads distributed by a specific medium during a given period (for example, three or six months) are analyzed in order to detect violations of ARPP recommendations. This monitoring is done to prove to the government, stakeholder associations, and the media that ARPP rules are effective. Such assessments, which are sometimes required by various Commitment Charters between government ministries and ARPP, are mainly conducted in three sensitive fields: (1) the portrayal of human beings; (2) environmental claims, and (3) food advertising. Through these monitoring studies, thousands of ads are analyzed to detect possible rule violations and to assess their importance. If a violation is found, the advertiser is warned and asked to stop using the ad. These studies, which are checked by independent organizations, such as the Public Agency for the Environment, are published and presented to the appropriate government ministry and they are widely distributed. Annual surveys prove the efficiency of the self-regulatory system and serve as a barometer of industry compliance with ARPP recommendations.

CONCLUSIONS

The French self-regulatory system has gone through significant changes in recent years. In 2008, it moved from self-regulation—considered by nonprofessionals, stakeholder associations, and the government as a closed and opaque system without credible controls and sanctions—to professional regulation with a transparent and disinterested system. The old Bureau de Vérification de la Publicité (BVP) became the ARPP, the first private regulatory authority in France. The reinvention of the ARPP, along with the creation of its ancillary Advertising Deontology Jury (JDP) to handle external complaints; its Advertising Ethics Council (CEP), which monitors social developments affecting advertising; and its Joint Advertising Council (CPP), which is involved in the drafting of new recommendations, added weight and strength to the self-regulation concept .

Outside participation in the ARPP helps to strengthen its credibility and acceptability among NGOs and the public officials. The French system has been opened to: (1) stakeholders (consumer and environmental associations) who are consulted before any writing or rewriting of the ARPP recommendations through the CPP, and (2) nonindustry and independent personalities from the courts or universities through the JDP.

In recent years, agreements called Commitment Charters (Chartes d'Engagement) have been signed with relevant French ministries. These charters acknowledge the existence and use of professional advertising regulation in the sensitive area of the portrayal of women (2003), environmental claims (2008), and food and beverage advertising (2009). Under such charters, the government agrees to not regulate or ban certain practices but, in exchange, requires effective professional regulation with adequate standards and accountability evidenced by periodic and transparent monitoring. These agreements have led to a form of coregulation between public and private sectors working together in the public interest.

The French legislature has recognized ARPP's system of private regulation through specific legislation. For example, a March 2009 law, which imported into French law the EU directive on audiovisual services, authorized the Superior Audiovisual Council (CSA) to use the ARPP for the preclearance of television commercials. In August of 2009, a law titled *Grenelle I* (enacted after the television-related Grenelle of the Environnement of 2007–2008—National Environmental Forum), recognized the improved French self-regulatory system as the best way to control ads that made environmental claims.

The now officially recognized private regulation of advertising can more easily complement, codify, or even replace public regulation in a field where the freedom of the media and of the advertising industry must be defended and promoted. It gives a sense of responsibility to advertising professionals, who are now convinced that their industry cannot claim its freedom unless it can demonstrate responsibility.

AGENCIES

Advertising Deontology Jury (Jury de Déontologie Publicitaire, or JDP).
Advertising Ethics Council (Conseil de l'Ethique Publicitaire, or CEP).
Advertising Verification Bureau (Bureau de Vérification de la Publicité, or BVP).
Joint Advertising Council (Conseil Paritaire de la Publicité, or CPP).
Office for the Control of Advertisements (Office de Contrôle des Annonces, or OCA).
Professional Advertising Regulation Authority (Autorité de Régulation Professionnelle de la Publicité, or
    ARPP).

BIBLIOGRAPHY

Listed below are a few English-language publications analyzing the French advertising control system:

Autorité de Régulation Professionnelle de la Publicité [Professional Advertising Regulation Authority]
    (ARPP). Website (www.arpp.org) with summaries in English.
Boddewyn, J.J. 1992. *Global Perspectives on Advertising Self-Regulation: Principles and Practices in Thirty-
    Eight Countries.* Westport, CT: Quorum Books.
———. 1998. *Advertising Self-Regulation and Outside Participation: A Multinational Comparison.* West-
    port, CT: Quorum Books.
Caffagi, F. 2006. *Rethinking Private Regulation in the European Regulatory Space.* Florence: European
    University Institute.
European Advertising Standards Alliance (EASA). 2010. *Blue Book*, 6th ed. Brussels, Belgium: EASA.
———. *EASA Focus.* Newsletter. http://www.easa-alliance.org/page.aspx/269.
European Union Commission, Director General for Health and Consumer Affairs (DG SANCO). "Self-
    Regulation in the Advertising Sector." http:/eur-lex.europa.eu/LexUriServ.
International Chamber of Commerce (ICC). 2006. *Advertising and Marketing Communication Practice:
    Consolidated ICC Code.* Paris. August. www.iccbo.org.
Neeklankavil, J.P., and A.B. Stridsberg. 1980. *Advertising Self-Regulation: A Global Perspective.* New York:
    Communication Arts Books.

SOURCES

Agence France-Presse (AFP). 2008. "French court rules online alcohol ads illegal." February 14. http://afp.
    google.com/article/ALeqM5jcR9gUWQNh_PLQCqjWlyhtZplWmw.
Autorité de Régulation Professionnelle de la Publicité [Professional Advertising Regulation Authority]
    (ARPP). 2012. http://www.arpp-pub.org/.
BBC. 2008. "Paper fined over champagne 'ad.'" January 9. http://news.bbc.co.uk/2/hi/europe/7179562.stm.
Boddewyn, J.J., and E. Loubradou. 2011. "The Control of 'Sex in Advertising' in France." *Journal of Pub-
    lic Policy & Marketing* 30, no. 2: 220–225. http://www.journals.marketingpower.com/doi/abs/10.1509/
    jppm.30.2.220?journalCode=jppm.
Cour d'Appel de Paris. 1996. *Agence Française de Lutte contre le SIDA v Benetton.* May 28.
———. 2005. The *Girbaud* case. April 8. *Recueil Dalloz,* no. 20 (2005): 1327–1328.
———. 2010. *Association Nationale de Prévention en Alcoologie et Addictologie (ANPAA) v Conseil Inter-
    professionnel des Vins de Bordeaux* [National Association for the Prevention of Alcoholism and Addiction
    v. Interprofessional Counsel of Bordeaux Wines]. February 26.
Cour d'Appel de Versailles. 2010. The *Rogé Cavaillès* case. June 17.
Cour de cassation. 2006. The *Girbaud* case. November 14. *Légipresse,* no. 238 (January/February 2007): 11.
———. 2010. *L'association Nationale de Prévention en Alcoologie et Addictologie v Gérard Z. . . . and
    Alain Y. . . . .* No. 08–88134, January 26.
European Union. 1980. "Summary." *Procureur du Roi v Marc J.V.C. Debauve and others.* March 18. http://
    eur-lex.europa.eu/LexUriServ/LexUriServ.do?uri=CELEX:61979J0052:EN:NOT.
———. 2007. Directive 2007/65/EC of the European Parliament and of the Council of 11 December 2007
    amending Council Directive 89/552/EC on the coordination of certain provisions laid down by law,

regulation or administrative action in Member States concerning the pursuit of television broadcasting activities. December 11. http://www.wipo.int/wipolex/en/details.jsp?id=7881.

International Chamber of Commerce (ICC). 2012. "ICC Commission on Marketing and Advertising." http://www.iccwbo.org/advocacy-codes-and-rules/areas-of-work/marketing-and-advertising/.

JDN: Journal du Net. 2008. "Leclerc remporte son bras de fer 'comparatif' contre Carrefour" [Leclerc wins his 'comparative' standoff against Carrefour]. June 19. http://www.journaldunet.com/ebusiness/commerce/actualite/leclerc-remporte-son-bras-de-fer-comparatif-contre-carrefour.shtml.

Jury de Déontologie Publicitaire [Jury of Advertising Ethics] (JDP). 2012. http://www.jdp-pub.org/.

Out-law.com. 2009. "French court fines Google over trademarked keywords." *The Register,* February 3. http://www.theregister.co.uk/2009/02/03/google_france/.

Tribunal de Grande Instance de Paris. 2009. *Voyageurs du Monde et Terres d'Aventure v. Google.* January 7.

CHAPTER 12

PORTUGAL

Luísa Ribeiro

Portugal, a member of the European Union, is a small country located in southwestern Europe. A colonial empire for centuries (its largest and most notable holding was Brazil, which achieved independence in 1822), Portugal had given up most of its overseas territories by the mid-1970s. Sovereignty over the last of its colonies, Macau, ended in 1999 (CIA 2013).

Only within the past several decades have regulatory agencies for the advertising industry emerged in Portugal. The country's first advertising law (Law 421) dates back to September 1980. Although the first advertising agency, Hora, was established in 1927, television broadcasting was not available on a regular basis until 1957 (20 years after the dawn of the BBC). Almost immediately, TV became the prevailing media in Portugal. Until that time, advertising was based on printed press, outdoor ads, and cinema.

After the 1950s, multinational brands such as Lever, Nestlé, and Procter & Gamble had substantially increased their investment in advertising, with a new focus on providing information to increase consumption. The following decade saw the growth of radio advertising, supported by live shows. International advertising agencies started operating in Portugal around this time, thereby professionalizing the industry.

In April 1974, following a military coup that put an end to a 48-year-long dictatorship in Portugal, an important part of the economy was nationalized. Advertising activities, largely equated with liberal economies, had a bad reputation in the ensuing years. Additionally, advertising budget cuts and the end of local adaptations for international campaigns led to the closure of most international advertising agency branches in Portugal such as Thompson and Leo Burnett.

After the mid-1980s and in the early 1990s, social appeasement and a rising economy supported by the European Union market allowed domestic consumption to increase. By that time, multinational companies had returned to the country and advertising activity was growing. Along with the proliferation of radio frequencies and the emergence of specialized press came the influence of new technologies, mainly in the production and publishing areas. Also, advertising activities became more professional and popular with the appearance of undergraduate courses in marketing, advertising, and public relations.

The end of the 1980s was also marked by consolidation in the advertising industry, with the acquisition of national agencies by international groups. The expansion of businesses into new markets led to the international alignment of advertisers' accounts. The characteristics of advertising agencies also changed with the advent of creative and media planning. In the 1990s, two privately held television networks began to broadcast, and satellite and cable operators emerged, taking the advertising scene even further.

According to figures from Marktest (2009), advertising investment reached around 4.8 billion euros in Portugal. Using prices before commercial discounts, a positive trend for investment can be drawn from 2005 to 2009 (except for newspapers), as seen in Table 12.1.

Table 12.1

Advertising Revenues by Media Type, 2005–2009

							(in thousand euros)			
	2005	%	2006	%	2007	%	2008	%	2009	%
Television	2,483,635	68.3%	2,840,206	70.1%	3,085,780	70.3%	3,330,911	71.3%	3,517,230	73.4%
Press	700,606	19.3%	733,912	18.1%	816,546	18.6%	835,223	17.9%	741,717	15.5%
Outdoor	250,590	6.9%	276,730	6.8%	283,984	6.5%	303,504	6.5%	311,407	6.5%
Radio	187,322	5.2%	184,883	4.6%	183,458	4.2%	178,760	3.8%	196,229	4.1%
Cinema	13,596	0.4%	14,491	0.4%	21,976	0.5%	23,427	0.5%	22,864	0.5%
Total	3,635,749	100.0%	4,050,222	100.0%	4,391,744	100.0%	4,671,825	100.0%	4,789,447	100.0%

Source: Based on data from Marktest.

Another clear conclusion is the consistent and increasing domination of television over the total advertising market, capturing 73.4 percent of overall revenues in 2009.

BASIC PRINCIPLES AND REGULATIONS CONCERNING ADVERTISING IN PORTUGAL

Advertising regulation in Portugal has three branches: national, international, and industry self-regulation.

Besides having to comply with the rules of commercial and civil law, advertising is controlled on a national basis in Portugal by the Advertising Code (Law 330). This code underwent considerable reform in 1995 (Law 6) and 1998 (Law 275); since then, it has been modified by eight pieces of legislation in order to harmonize national rules with the European Community directives (namely the directives 84/450/CEE and 89/552/CEE and with the Television Without Borders Directive).

International legislation (namely, European Community directives) has also influenced important subjects such as misleading and comparative advertising, television broadcasting rules, the advertising of medicinal products for human use, and advertising and sponsorship of tobacco products.

The legislative definition of *advertising activities* is wide, including "any communication form by individuals or institutions (including state owned) that occurs in the scope of a commercial or industrial activity or service, with the purpose of commercializing any goods or services or to promote ideas, principles, initiatives or institutions [except political propaganda]. " The Advertising Code highlights two main principles with which advertisers must comply:

1. Truthfulness—advertising cannot, directly or indirectly, by omissions, ambiguities, or means of exaggeration, falsify the claims of a good or service, and
2. Legality—advertising has to respect values, rights, and principles recognized in Portugal's constitution and any applicable legislation.

Notwithstanding the possible intervention of courts and administrative authorities, it is the public body known as the Directorate General of Consumer Affairs (DGC) that supervises Advertising

Law compliance (reporting directly to the Portuguese Government). DGC can instigate legal proceedings, which are then referred to the Advertising Regulatory Commission (CACMEP), chaired by a judge, whose decisions are subject to judicial review.

Sanctions for violating the Advertising Law can be applied not only to the advertising agency and its client but also to other parties working on the release of the advertising message—from the media owner to every member of the creative team. (Portuguese law, notes Chaves [2005], includes the following among advertising media: television, the press, digital, mobile, air-supported devices [airplanes, zeppelins, and balloons], radio, outdoor media, direct marketing, cinema, product packaging and labels, and catalogs and brochures.) According to Pereira (2009, 87) the reason for such wide coverage in terms of responsibilities is that "advertising agencies in their creative function . . . involve team work where individual contribution is sometimes difficult to determine."

Failure to comply with the law can result in sanctions such as fines; the suspension, cessation, or prohibition of a campaign; or, in the case of a more serious violation, accessory sanctions. Accessory sanctions can include the seizure of equipment, a ban on advertising activities for a period of up to two years, exclusion from consideration of public subsidies or other benefits for up to two years, closure of premises where the advertising activity took place, and the cancellation of licenses for up to two years. Also, depending on the severity of the violation, the sanction itself can be broadcast at the guilty party's expense.

Misleading Advertising

Misleading or deceptive advertising is strictly forbidden in Portugal. Advertising is considered misleading if it misrepresents goods' or services' characteristics or prices, or attempts in any way to trick consumers into making a purchase.

When an instance of misleading advertising practices is identified, protective and suspension measures can be taken by DGC, which can demand evidence to support the claims made in a given message. In such a case, the burden of proof always falls on the advertiser.

Other Cases of Prohibited Advertising

There are six types of products or services that cannot be advertised in Portugal: religion, politics (at least, not in radio or television), gambling and games of chance, tobacco, miraculous goods or services, and medical treatments and prescription drugs.

Contrary to the common practices in other countries, Portugal does not allow advertisements of a religious or political nature, with the exception of specific programming during certain times (e.g., before elections) under the law.

Gambling and games of chance cannot be the focus of an advertising message, with the exception of those promoted by the state-run lottery Santa Casa da Misericórdia, a nonprofit institution that has the gambling monopoly outside casinos.

All forms of tobacco advertising are forbidden in Portugal. To avoid indirect advertising, tobacco manufacturers and distributors and their derivatives cannot sponsor events or programs.

It is also illegal to advertise miraculous goods or services (1) that take advantage of ignorance, fear, beliefs, or superstitions held by the target audience; (2) that present goods or services as having curative effects on health; or (3) that attribute well-being, luck, or happiness to the purchase of a given product. The burden of proof regarding a product's scientific effects and benefits is on the advertiser.

Also, due to their complex characteristics, and to prevent a general audience from reaching erroneous conclusions, medical treatments and prescription drugs can only be advertised in specialized magazines addressed to health care–sector professionals.

Also, as a general principle, Portuguese advertising laws forbid ads that encourage or glorify violence or any illegal or criminal activity or that encourage consumers to engage in behaviors that might damage their health or compromise their security. Also prohibited is any advertising that compromises human dignity, uses obscene language, or discriminates against race, religion, or gender. Additionally, national or religious symbols or historical characters cannot be used in a denigrating way.

RESTRICTED ADVERTISING

Comparative Advertising

In Portugal, comparative advertising (implicit or explicit) was forbidden until 1990. Nowadays, following the harmonization with European directives, comparative advertising is allowed only if some very restrictive principles are obeyed, namely:

1. the comparison has to involve goods and services answering the same needs or with the same purposes;
2. it has to make objective comparisons of the main, pertinent, demonstrable,* and representative characteristics of such goods and services (including price);
3. it cannot discredit a competitor's brand; and
4. it cannot present a good or service as being an imitation or reproduction of another one with a protected brand or commercial designation.

Advertising Targeting Minors

Advertising targeting individuals less than 18 years of age cannot exploit minors' inexperience and credulity, or include elements that might jeopardize their physical or moral integrity, health, or security (namely in the form of pornography or violence). Advertising cannot directly induce young people to persuade their parents or others to buy goods or services, or exploit the special trust that minors have in parents, mentors, or teachers.

Other specific limitations regarding advertising for children are set in the Advertising Code for Children: Food and Beverage, adopted by the advertising self-regulation authority.

Other Restricted Advertising: Language and Alcohol

As a general rule, advertising in Portugal must use the Portuguese language. Foreign words can be applied exceptionally, but only if they are considered necessary to attain the effect intended by the advertiser.

Advertising testimonials should be based on genuine and provable statements in connection with the personal experience of the individual making the claim.

---

*The burden of proof regarding truthfulness of comparative advertising also lies with the advertiser.

In Portugal, alcoholic beverages can be advertised only if the ad includes the warning: "Be responsible. Drink in moderation." All the same, the content of such advertisements cannot encourage excessive consumption or suggest any relationship between alcohol consumption, success, or the consumer's possession of special skills. It is never acceptable to advertise alcohol when minors are the specific targets of the ad, or to mention any (implicit or explicit) brand of alcoholic beverage at events in which minors participate, such as sports or cultural events. It is forbidden in primetime radio or television to advertise alcoholic drinks (between 7:00 P.M. and 10:30 P.M.), although sometimes manufacturers use nonalcoholic products to promote the brand associated with alcoholic drinks during that period.

Advertising Specifications for Television

The powerful influence television exercises over society led to the creation of Television Law 13, where advertising rules are specified.

Basically, all television advertising must be preceded and followed by visual or acoustic separators that let the viewer know where the content of each message begins and ends. Regarding the maximum advertising time allowed, the law distinguishes between pay-TV and free television: For pay-TV channels, advertising time cannot exceed 10 percent of the daily transmission time; free TV channels have a limit of 15 percent (rising up to 20 percent when teleshopping is included). Also, the maximum advertising time between two-hour units is 10 minutes in the case of subscription television and 20 minutes in the case of free-to-air channels.

Another way to advertise on television—sponsoring—must be well identified by the name or logo of the sponsor at the beginning or the end of programs. News and information television programs cannot be sponsored.

SELF-REGULATION IN THE ADVERTISING INDUSTRY

In Portugal, advertising is one of the few economic activities where the most visible conflicts and claims are decided by a self-regulatory entity: the Civil Institute of Commercial Communication Self-Regulation (ICAP). Although it is possible to carry on a civil lawsuit regarding advertising matters (and, in fact, there is some jurisprudence in this area), the growing use of ICAP stems from its easy access, low costs, and quick decisions.

Established in 1991 by the most important players in the industry, ICAP has 78 members, whose contributions finance 80 percent of the institute's needs (the remaining 20 percent of the budget comes from copy advice and competitor complaints handling services).

ICAP's members are advertisers (and advertising associations), agencies, and media (television, press, radio, outdoor, digital, mobile, direct marketing, and cinema) representing most of the Portuguese advertising industry. According to its bylaws, the institute's main purpose is "to defend ethical and deontological principles of commercial communication"; furthermore, its members are committed to "promote lawfulness and transparency in advertising communication, benefiting from honest competition and thus preserving consumers' rights."

In practice, ICAP's members follow an Advertising Code of Conduct (advertising has to be legal, decent, and truthful) and agree to respect the ruling of the decision committees associated with ICAP (the Ethical Jury, Technical Legal Cabinet, and Mediation procedures). When advertisers have doubts regarding the legality or appropriateness of content they want to transmit, ICAP can also provide copy-advice services.

Table 12.2

Total Number of Complaints Analyzed Yearly by ICAP

Year	# Complaints
2009	31
2008	22
2007	49
2006	43
2005	38

Source: Based on data from ICAP.

ICAP allows individuals, corporations, and consumer associations to file a complaint when they believe advertising does not follow national ethical and legal norms. If the Ethical Jury, composed by independent experts, concludes that ICAP's Code of Conduct or current legislation was violated, it can order the modification or termination of the advertising campaign. It should be noted that ICAP's decisions are generally respected even when they mean the end of a campaign.

CIVIL INSTITUTE OF COMMERCIAL COMMUNICATION SELF-REGULATION (ICAP) COMPLAINTS-HANDLING PROCESS

When ICAP's decisions are not obeyed, sanctions (other than suspending, modifying, or terminating a campaign) can be established, according to the gravity of the case. These can include (a) warnings, (b) censures, or (c) suspension or expulsion from the institute's membership.

Every year, ICAP analyzes and decides dozens of complaints; the period covering 2005 through 2009 is summarized in Table 12.2.

A review and classification of the decisions made by ICAP during 2009 is shown in Figure 12.1. Twenty-nine of the total 31 claims made that year were available to the public, representing a coverage of 93.5 percent. The main reasons for filing complaints were accusations of misleading advertising (17 claims) and lack of truthfulness (12 claims).

In terms of complaints by type of industry, telecommunications takes the lead, representing more than 52 percent of the total complaints. The other three relevant industries were: food and beverage (21 percent of total), retail (10 percent), and hygiene and health care (7 percent). It is curious to observe that the number of generated complaints is not directly correlated to each industry's investment in advertising (see Figures 12.2 and 12.3). According to Marktest, in 2009, the telecommunications industry accounted for just 8.2 percent of total advertising revenues, food and beverage represented 10.7 percent, and retail accounted for 10.3 percent of advertising revenues (2010).

The majority of complaints to ICAP (59 percent) were driven by individuals, while 31 percent of files were originated by institutional industry players, and the remaining 10 percent by associations.

Figure 12.1

Main Types of Complaints Analyzed by ICAP, 2009

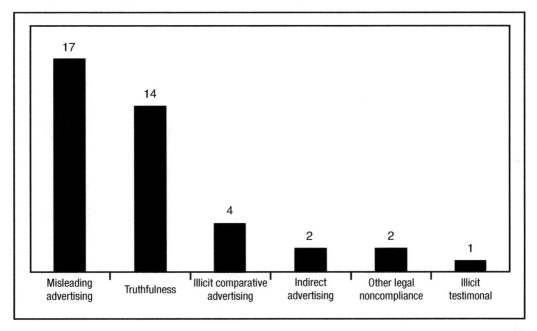

Reflecting the growth of advertising on the Internet, electronic media generated 16 complaints, while advertisements on television prompted eight, ads in catalogs and pamphlets sparked six, and text on packaging and labels led to another five.

Just over three-quarters of ICAP's decisions in 2009 required termination of the campaign in question (see Figure 12.4). Apparently, decisions were generally considered fair, as only 28 percent of the cases pursued the appeals mechanism (and only one in four appeals was successful).

SPECIAL REGULATIONS: ADVERTISING OF FOOD AND BEVERAGES AIMED AT CHILDREN

The dangers of childhood obesity were acknowledged when, in 2006, the World Health Organization (WHO) adopted the European Charter on Counteracting Obesity. Similarly, in Portugal, the Directorate-General for Health has established the Platform Against Obesity. Realizing the importance of the food and beverage industry in total advertising revenues (more than 512 million euros in 2009, making it the second-biggest spender), on May 2010, advertising professionals and industry players approved a self-regulatory code on commercial communication (including advertising) of food and beverage targeting children. The text recommends a set of general and specific rules as it recognizes that communications—including advertising, promotions, sponsorships, and direct marketing—targeting an audience of children under 12 years old require clear and simple language due to the vulnerability of audience.

Portugal's code for advertising to children is probably best explained by what the ads cannot do; for instance, ads cannot condone or encourage a sedentary lifestyle, nor can they use testimonials

Figure 12.2

Complaints' Source

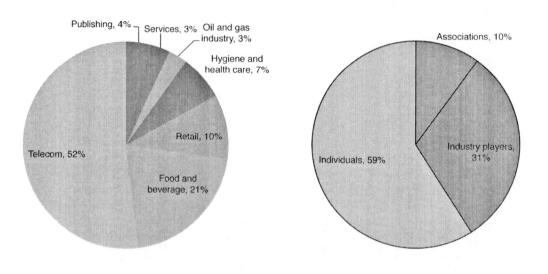

Figure 12.3

Distirbution of Complaints by Type of Advertisment

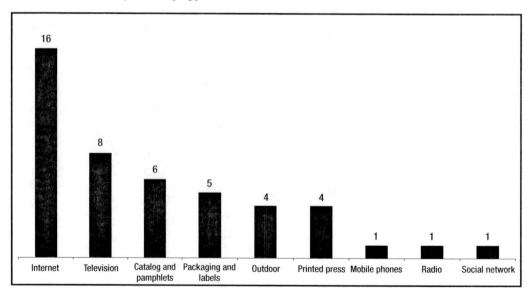

Figure 12.4

ICAP Decisions and Appeals

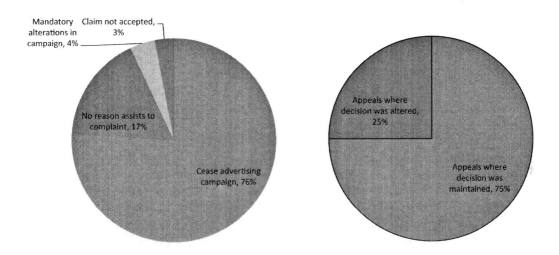

that might exploit children's trust or use deceptive claims about potential benefits of such products. Advertisers must always have available scientific proof to back up data in product descriptions, statements, and illustrations.

Furthermore, advertisers are not allowed to manipulate children through advertising, or have them appeal to the adults in their life to purchase advertised goods, or to suggest that the acquisition of a good or service will provide users with special advantages. Several recommendations are also included concerning the use of story characters popular among children.

CONCLUSIONS

Although advertising law still exerts considerable control over ad content and form in Portugal, self-regulation is strongly endorsed by the advertising industry, with a respectful history of extrajudicial decisions. Notwithstanding the acceptance of self-regulation, there is some industry skepticism regarding the timing of ICAP decisions and thus its ultimate effect. Often an advertising campaign is already completed by the time ICAP issues a decision. Thus, an advertiser can put a campaign in the market even knowing that it probably will be withdrawn after some time.

The purpose of this chapter is to give readers a sense of Portugal's advertising regulations in the twenty-first century. However, more fragmented advertising (such as Internet ads) presents challenges to regulators. The search for a balance between efficiency and innovation will probably lead to a more cohesive approach from regulating entities in the future.

BIBLIOGRAPHY

Central Intelligence Agency. 2013. "Portugal." *The World Factbook Online*. Washington, DC: CIA. https:// www.cia.gov/library/publications/the-world-factbook/geos/po.html.

Chaves, R.M. 2005. *Código da Publicidade Anotado*. Coimbra, Portugal: Edições Almedina.

Diário da República. 2011. "Lei da Televisão no. 8/2011." April 11, 2139–2175.

European Advertising Standards Alliance (EASA). 2010. "Section 3—Self-Regulation in Europe: Portugal." In *Blue Book*, 6th ed., 133–138. Brussels, Belgium: EASA.

Instituto Civil da Autodisciplina da Comunicação Social [Civil Institute of Commercial Communication Self-Regulation] (ICAP). 2010. *Código de Conduta do ICAP em Matéria de publicidade e outras formas de Comunicação Comercial*. http://www.icap.pt/images/memos/Novo_CodConduta_ICAP_Pub_Com-Comercial.pdf.

———. 2011. ICAP (website). www.icap.pt (accessed September 2012).

Leitão, A.M. 2000. *Estudo de Direito Privado Sobre a Cláusula Geral de Concorrência Desleal*. Coimbra, Portugal: Edições Almedina.

Marktest. 2009. *Anuário de Media & Publicidade, 2009*. Lisbon, Portugal.

Official Journal of the European Communities. 1992. "Council Directive 92/28/EC." OJ L 113, April 30, 13–18.

———. 1997a. "Council Directive 84/450/EC." Altered by Directive 97/55/EC, OJ L 290, 18–22.

———. 1997b. "Council Directive 89/552/EC." Altered by Directive 97/36/EC, OJ L 202, July 30, 60–70.

———. 1998. "Directive 98/43/EC of the European Parliament and of the Council." OJ L 217, August 5, 18–24.

———. 2010. "Directive 2010/13/UE of the European Parliament and of the Council." OJL 95, April 15.

Pereira, S. (coord.). 2009. *A televisão e as crianças—Um ano de programação na RTP1, RTP2, SIC e TVI*. [Television and children—A year of programming in RTP 1, RTP 2, SIC and TVI.] Lisbon, Portugal: Entidade Reguladora da Comunicação Social (ERC).

Ribeiro, L.C. 2007. *A Televisão Paga*. Lisbon, Portugal: Media XXI.

World Health Organization (WHO). 2006. "European Charter on Counteracting Obesity." EUR/06/5062700/8, November 16. http://www.euro.who.int/__data/assets/pdf_file/0009/87462/E89567.pdf.

CHAPTER 13

SPAIN

MERCEDES MEDINA

Spain is a democratic country, organized as a parliamentary government under a constitutional monarchy. In 1978, at the end of the dictatorship, a written constitution was adopted. Since then, Spain has been divided into 17 autonomous communities, each one having its own regional government. In 2010, the Spanish population was 47 million. Spain has been a member state of the European Union since 1986.

ADVERTISING EXPENDITURES

Most media depend greatly on advertising; that is why the global economic recession of 2008–2009 has negatively affected many of them. In 2008, the rate of ad spending fell by 7.5 percent (total ad spending was €16,108 million in 2007 and €14,915.3 million in 2008). In 2009, revenues decreased another 14.9 percent, and the spending amounted to €12,699.4 million. This was mainly due to lower investment in strategic sectors such as housing and automotive, which represent a significant part of the global investment in the advertising industry.

The top ten advertisers in Spain in 2010 were Procter & Gamble (€676.62 million), Danone (€350 million), L'Oreal (€269.60 million), Reckitt Benckiser (€266.45 million), Telefónica (€199.25 million), Nestlé (€144.07 million), Vodafone (€126.27 million), Unilever (€123.03 million), Henkel Ibérica (€118.61 million), and Orange (€114.19 million).

During the worst years of the recession—2008 through 2009—media ad spending decreased by 27 percent. Media expenditures in 2009 were more than €2,300 million less than in 2007, as shown in Table 13.1. Although television remains one of the most attractive media for advertisers, its loss of advertising investment has also been the largest. In recent years, television channels have earned 33 percent less in advertising than they did in prerecession years. Although in 2010 a slight recovery was seen, investment was still less than in 2005, despite the fact that the number of television channels increased in 2010 due to the digital switchover. In 2012, the television market continued to decline, dropping 19 percent from 2011. Meanwhile, the decrease of advertising in cinema was significant—with the medium losing 79 percent of advertising income from 2005 to 2009. Only Internet advertising expenditures increased, from €162 million in 2005 to €748 million in 2010. Online advertising was 2.4 percent of the advertising pie in 2005, but rose to 12 percent in 2010.

One of the big changes in the market has been the growth of investment in nonconventional media (below the line), which more than doubled from 1997, when it accounted for only 25 percent of ad spending, to 2009, when it reached 55.7 percent. In this year, investment in conventional media was €5,621 million and in nonconventional media €7,078 million.

Table 13.1

Media Advertising Expenditure in Spain, 2005–2010 (€ million)

Media	2005	2006	2007	2008	2009	2010
Television	2,951	3,188	3,468	3,082	2,368	2,516
Newspapers	1,666	1,791	1,894	1,507	1,174	1,141
Magazines	674	688	721	617	401	175
Radio	610	636	678	641	537	538
Outdoor	493	529	568	518	401	415
Dominicals	119	123	133	103	68	293
Internet[a]	162	310	482	610	654	748
Cinema	43	40	38	21	15	24
Total	6,721	7,309	7,985	7,102	5,621	5,851

Source: Infoadex 2010.
[a]Desktop and mobile devices.

HISTORY OF ADVERTISING REGULATION

In 1964, the Advertising Statute went into force through Law 61/1964, regulating the overall aspects of advertising in various media.* The statute created the Advertising Central Board and the Advertising Jury to oversee the interests of all the different players in the industry: advertisers, agencies, media, and consumers. In 1988, the General Law of Advertising 34/1988 was published, and shortly thereafter the first private television channels were launched. The 1988 law stated that the conflicts of interest were to be solved through a judicial rather than an administrative process (as the law from 1964 stated). Article 25 rules that any natural or legal citizen who is affected and, in general, anyone who has a subjective right or legitimate interest may request from the advertiser the cessation of a campaign or, where appropriate, the correction of illegal advertising.

According to the General Law of Advertising (Law 34/1988, art. 2), advertising is any form of communication carried out by a natural or legal citizen, public or private, in the exercise of a trade, business, craft, or profession, in order to promote directly or indirectly the hiring of goods, services, rights, and obligations. Under this definition, then, direct marketing is also considered advertising.

Advertising is considered illegal if it violates fundamental rights. Hence, misleading advertising, surreptitious advertising, and subliminal advertising are prohibited. Subliminal advertising is defined in the new audiovisual law (7/2010) as that advertising that uses persuasive techniques to produce stimuli that are not consciously perceived by the audience.

The General Law allows comparative advertising, provided certain requirements are met, the most important being:

---

*Laws in Spain are named with the correlative number of the laws published in a year and the year of publication.

1. The goods or services compared must have the same purpose or meet the same needs.
2. The comparison must be made in an objective way between one or more essential, relevant, verifiable, and representative feature of the goods or services, among which price may be included.

The prohibitory aspects of the law apply to both direct and indirect advertising. Indirect advertising does not specifically mention competitors by name, but it makes use of the trademarks, emblems, or other distinctive features of such products.

The General Law of Advertising also aims at protecting the rights and images of women. Advertisers who use of the image of a woman in a discriminatory or disparaging way may be told to cease or amend their campaign. The complainant in such cases may be the Government Delegation on Violence Against Women, the Women's Institute (or the equivalent in the autonomous communities), any legally established associations dedicated to defending the interests of women, and any holder of a right or legitimate interest.

For other general topics, the agents that may act as a complainant are the National Institute of Consumer Affairs, the relevant bodies or entities under the autonomous communities, and local corporations responsible for consumer protection. The consumer and user associations that meet the requirements of Law 26/1984, Defense of Consumers and Users (or, where appropriate, regional legislation on the defense of consumers), can also ask for the modification or cancellation of an ad. The request shall be in writing, in a manner that allows reliable recording of the date of its receipt and its contents.

The General Law of Advertising 34/1988 was modified by the Law 39/2002, which brought the Spanish ordinance in line with various EU directives on the subject of protection of consumers' and users' interests, and by Law 29/2009, which modifies the regulation of unfair competition and advertising. In order to protect consumers, the law distinguishes the relationship between consumers and competitors and explains in detail the meaning of fraud and aggressive practices—those that coerce, harass, or unduly influence a consumer's buying patterns.

Television is the most regulated media in Spain. As in other European countries, the first television channels were public—that is, managed by the public administration. However, contrary to practices in other European countries, most of their income derived from advertising rather than from public subsidies. According to the RTVE (the Spanish public television) Statute from 1980, advertising was looked upon as a limited source of funding. But this rule was largely ignored until 2010, when a new General Law on Audiovisual Communication was published, changing the funding system of RTVE: Advertising was completely banned from national public channels.

In 1994, the European Directive 89/552 Television Without Borders was incorporated into the Spanish regulation system through the publication of Law 25/1994. The new General Law on Audiovisual Communication 7/2010 regulated the commercial time slots and banned ads for products such as tobacco, alcohol, and medicines.

In summary, Spain's legal framework on advertising is quite profuse. The following are the most important ad laws in force:

- General Law of Advertising (LGP 34/1988, November 11)
- Laws Regulating Electoral Advertising (2/1988) and Terrestrial Broadcasting of Electoral Propaganda by Local Television Stations (14/1995)
- Unfair Competition Law (1991; amended in 2009)
- Legal Protection of Minors Act (Law 1/1996)
- Retail Trade Act (Law 7/1996)
- Law on Universal Postal Service (Law 24/1998)

- Law on Protection of Personal Data (Law 15/1999)
- Law on Information Society Services and Electronic Commerce (Law 34/2002).
- General Telecommunications Law (Law 32/2003)
- Spanish Law of E-Commerce (Law 292/2004)
- Law on Guarantees and the Rational Use of Medicines and Health Products (Law 29/2006)
- Amendments to the Unfair Competition Act, modifying the Spanish legal system of unfair competition and advertising to enhance consumer and user protection (Law 29/2009)
- European Directive 89/552 Television Without Borders, incorporated to the Spanish Law (Law 25/1994) and modified by the General Law on Audiovisual Communication (Law 7/2010)

An advertising self-regulation body was formed in Spain in 1977, but it had a small impact on the industry. Its role increased since 1994, and it was given the name Autocontrol (AC). In 2000, the body was again renamed—becoming the Asociación de Autocontrol de la Comunicación Comercial or AACC (the Spanish Self-Regulatory Association for Commercial Communications)—and assumed a broader commercial scope, including fields such as e-commerce, Internet domains, promotional material, labeling, and packaging.

SELF-REGULATION

Beyond the legal framework, the Spanish advertising system is bound by ethical principles laid out in professional codes. The most important one, the Code of Advertising Practice from 2002, is based on the Code of the International Chamber of Commerce (ICC). Its basic ethical principles apply to all advertising communication activities which, directly or indirectly, encourage the trading of goods or services or promote trademarks or trade names, whichever medium is used. The first of these principles is the principle of legality, which means that advertising must respect current legislation and especially all values, rights, and principles recognized under the Spanish constitution. In addition, advertising shall not incite violence or promote illegal behavior. Advertisements must never undermine a consumer's good faith and must not include content that offend prevailing standards of good taste, social decorum, and accepted customs. Another important principle is that of truthfulness, which means that advertising will not be misleading. Misleading advertising manipulates consumers with inaccuracies, ambiguities, omissions, or erroneous conclusions regarding the characteristics of goods, services, and prices. Other principles relate to respect for others and human dignity; for instance, denigration of competitors will not be tolerated, nor will discriminatory advertising that offends on the basis of race, nationality, religion, gender, or sexual orientation. Furthermore, comparisons between one's own activity, services, or establishment and those of others must be based on essential, similar, analogous, and objectively demonstrable characteristics that are truthful.

The aforementioned self-regulatory body AACC is dedicated to the promotion of truth and accuracy in advertising. Its activities and procedures are reflected in the Code of Advertising Practice, signed in 1996 and updated in 2002. According to this code, advertising must serve as a particularly useful instrument in the economic process, ensure respect for ethics, and protect consumer rights.

The AACC is one of the youngest member bodies in the European Advertising Standards Alliance (EASA). The EASA system, which handles cross-border complaints, allows any European Union consumer to submit a complaint to the relevant foreign advertising self-regulation body through the equivalent body in his or her own country.

Currently, the AACC has more than 300 members, which represent more than 70 percent of the Spanish advertising investment; these members include all the television broadcasters and other media, more than 100 advertisers, 30 advertising agencies, and the most important advertising associations. The AACC also has ties to other public and administrative divisions, such as SETSI (State Secretary of Telecommunications and Information Society) and many other consumer and producer associations.

The AACC has an Advertising Jury, which consists of 21 members. This specialized body is composed of independent experts in consumer affairs; academics in the fields of law, economics, sociology, and commercial communications; retired advertising practitioners; ex-civil servants; and the like. Twenty-five percent of its members are nominated by the Spanish National Institute of Consumer Affairs (Instituto Nacional de Consumo).

By applying the Code of Conduct and the procedural rules governing the jury's adjudication activity, the AACC Advertising Jury resolves all the complaints and controversies submitted against specific ads. The complaints can be submitted by anyone with a legitimate interest and need not be a member of the association. Complaints may originate from consumer associations, competitors, the general public, or AACC monitoring. The system is free of charge for consumers, consumer associations, and public authorities. After reviewing the questionable advertisements, the AACC may request advertisers to withdraw or modify the advertisement at issue. However, the council's decisions are not legally binding, and affect only AACC members. The only penalty for noncompliance is losing the privilege of being an AACC member.

In spite of the voluntary nature of the system, the moral strength that accompanies the jury's pronouncements is undeniable. The technical knowledge and impartiality demonstrated by the jury's decisions have generated a high level of credibility and confidence from the advertising industry, the government, and society in general. A good example is that, to date, less than 5 percent of the companies who have come under scrutiny have refused to comply with the jury's decisions. When those parties started new proceedings in the Courts of Justice after the AACC's Jury made a decision, the judicial pronouncements have substantially agreed with the content of the pronouncements previously passed out by the jury.

Once a complaint is filed, the AACC Advertising Jury notifies the advertiser; most cases are resolved within 15 days. A monthly newsletter publishes the full case transcripts, and decisions are posted online. The latest amendments to the jury's actions were approved in May 2006. According to the General Manager of Autocontrol, J. Domingo Gómez, the Spanish Self-Regulatory Association for Commercial Communications is the only Spanish private body recognized by the European Commission for fulfilling the requirements and principles of transparency, independence, efficiency, legality, freedom of election, and representative rights for consumers. This evaluation is based on the European recommendation 98/257/EC on principles applicable to the bodies responsible for out-of-court settlement of consumer disputes.

In 1996, the AACC's copy advice service started operations. It offers a technical opinion and/or advice on the legal and ethical correctness of a specific advertisement before it is launched. The service reduces the likelihood that an ad will fail to comply with advertising regulations. It is voluntary, confidential, nonbinding, and free for AACC members. Nonmembers may partake in the copy advice service for a fee.

Figure 13.1 tracks the evolution of copy advice consultations since 1996. In 2001, the AACC received 390 requests for consultation, whereas in 2010 the number had risen to 8,162. On the other hand, the number of possible violations cases decreased from 247 in 2001 to 143 in 2010. Thirty percent of the claims were resolved through mediation, and their resolution was accepted by the complainant; therefore, no jury decision was necessary.

Figure 13.1

Number of Cases and Requests for Copy Advice Made to the AACC, 1996–2009

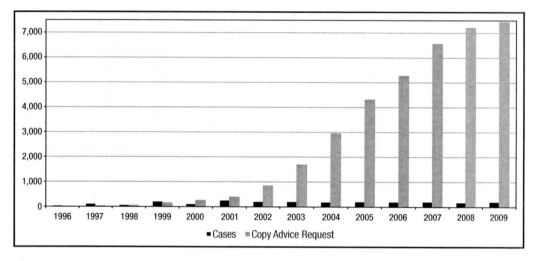

Source: AACC (2011) Annual Report.

In 2010, the copy advice team revised, before their broadcast, 5,220 television advertisements. The most common reasons for AACC advice typically relate to advertising aimed at children, especially the presentation of children in hazardous situations; violations of the principle of legality; rules regarding specific sectors, such as alcohol, financial deals, drugs, unauthorized health claims, road safety, games and betting, food, and promotions; misleading advertising; ads that might incite violence and antisocial behavior; discriminatory advertising or advertising prejudicial to people's dignity; abuse of consumers' good faith; unlawful comparative advertising; and surreptitious advertising.

In 2009, claims stemmed mainly from consumer associations or individual consumers (78.6 percent), other companies (16.1 percent), public authorities (4.6 percent), and cross-border complaints from EASA (0.5 percent). The following year, 54 percent of the claims directed to Autocontrol came from consumers and other citizen organizations, 40 percent came from companies or company associations, and 4 percent from different public authorities. The distribution of ads at issue in these years was as follows: 40 percent appeared on television, 29 percent in newspapers and magazines, 11 percent on Internet and new media, 9 percent through direct marketing and promotional material, 3 percent on labeling and packaging, 2 percent on the radio, and 1 percent outdoors (Medina and An 2012). This distribution is directly proportional to the advertising investment in media, as can be seen in Figure 13.2.

The AACC has signed more than 14 codes with different professional associations. These include the Code for Children's Advertising, signed with the Spanish Association of Toy Manufacturers; the Code of Advertising Deontology, with the National Association of Advertising Pharmaceutical Specialties; the Code of Television Advertising, with the State Department for Telecommunica-

Figure 13.2

Percentage of Advertising Investment in 2009

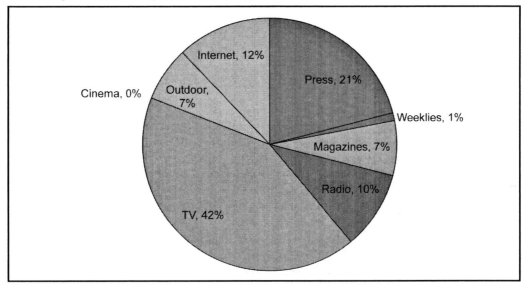

Source: Infoadex (2010).

tions and the Information Society; the Code of Online Confidence, with the Spanish Association of E-Commerce and Relationship Management; and the Self-Regulatory Code of Practice for the use of environmental arguments in commercial communications, signed with the Ministry of Environment, and Rural and Marine Affairs, as well as with companies within the energy and automobile sectors. (Note that the Spanish Association of E-Commerce joined Ecommerce Europe, Europe's leading online retailer organization, in 2013.) In 2009, an agreement was signed in the presence of the Ministry of Health, Social Policy, and Equality between Spanish television channels, the Spanish Agency of Food Security and Nutrition, and Autocontrol (Medina and An 2012). The agreement forced television broadcasting companies to collaborate in the application of the Code of Self-Regulation on food advertising aimed at children under 12 for the prevention of obesity and other health issues (PAOS Code).

According to the industry, advertising is an activity that should be practiced in compliance with basic ethical and legal principles. The difference between laws and codes is that laws are approved by the government and can be legally enforced, whereas codes are agreements among professional parties about professional behavior and ethics (Fernando 2008).

The advent of new media and its commercial use led authorities to create a seal of quality and a regulating scheme in order to protect consumers against potential abuse. Confianza Online's blue and green trustmark was thus launched in 2002, through an agreement between Autocontrol and the Spanish Association of E-Commerce and Relationship Management. Its main goal was to increase the confidence of consumers in relatively new interactive media and to promote and reinforce the confidence of web page users through a joint self-regulatory system. This agreement was made with openness toward different institutions, both public and private, seeking to join the initiative.

Confianza Online was awarded the "Trustworthy Public Emblem" prize in 2005 by the Spanish Government because it meets the requirements established by the Spanish Law of e-commerce (Law 292/2004). Currently, more than 500 corporate websites adhere to the agreement and thus display the Confianza Online seal as a sign of the company's adherence to the agreement and its commitment to responsibility.

PARTICULAR TYPES OF REGULATION

Children

In the Spanish context, and from the point of view of a special legal protection, children are individuals who have not yet reached the age of 18 (Law 1/1996, Legal Protection of Minors Act, art. 1). Some specific rules on children and advertisements include the avoidance of images of violence and exploitation in personal relationships, or images reflecting degrading or sexist treatment.

The Television Law 25/1994 (art. 17.2) states that programs (and advertising) that might affect the physical, mental, or moral development of minors can be broadcast only between 10:00 P.M. and 6:00 A.M., and they must include warnings about their content through audible and visual means. The time slot spanning from 5:00 to 8:00 P.M. has special treatment regarding children's protection: if broadcasters show content deemed inappropriate for children during this time slot, they must pay a fee to the Ministry of Industry.

An interesting example of this took place in November 2001. The company Nintendo Spain broadcast a TV spot launching a new game. The TV ad showed four adults standing on the deck of a boat playing with the game. When one of the players realized that a female competitor was about to win, he tied a rope around her leg and dragged her across the deck until she fell into the water. Then the following message appeared on the screen, "Mario Kart Super Circuit for Game Boy Advance. Four players. No rules." The jury agreed with the claim against this television ad and with the argument that it violated rights and values recognized in the constitution regarding respect for children and young people. According to the jury, children and adolescents might interpret this advertising message in a literal way. Moreover, the use of violent scenes could instigate violence in them by diminishing their social disapproval of violent acts (Volz et al. 2005, 71).

The regulation of advertising for children on television is also stricter. Ads directed to children must always avoid the exploitation of their naivety, immaturity, or natural gullibility; they must not take advantage of children's sense of loyalty; and they must not contain statements or visual representations that might result in mental, moral, or physical harm among young viewers. Commercials must not instigate the purchase of a service or product, or exploit the special confidence of children in their parents, guardians, or other persons; they cannot show children in dangerous situations, and children's programs cannot be interrupted by commercials unless the program is longer than 30 minutes (Television Law 25/1994).

There are also very specific norms regarding the making of ads featuring children: (1) Small children must not be shown with toys that are not suitable for their age and are only safe for older children; (2) when products or activities can be dangerous to their safety, children must not be shown using them or engaging in those activities without adult supervision; (3) advertisements must not portray children in unsafe situations or in activities that are harmful to them or others; (4) advertisements must avoid messages or representations that encourage the dangerous or inappropriate use of a product; and (5) children must not be used to give testimony about a product or service.

Additionally, advertisements for toys cannot contain inaccurate information regarding the characteristics or safety of the product, nor may they contain any misleading information regarding its safe use by children. When advertising games for children, advertisers must not give unrealistic expectations of the possibilities of winning a prize. Prizes and possibilities of winning must be clearly indicated and all prizes must be appropriate for children.

According to the report on the Christmas Toy Advertising Campaign 2003/2004, 16 specific cases of violation of the self-regulation codes and the applicable legislation were detected. Compared with previous years, there was an increase in violence in advertising spots (Volz et al. 2005, 76).

The sanction provided by the General Law on Audiovisual Communication for these violations is a fine ranging from €100,001 to €500,000, which represents a considerable increase from the provisions in the previous legislation (Law 7/2010, art. 57 and 60). The sanction provided does not include the revocation of the license conferred to the audiovisual media service, as it was before.

TELEVISION ADVERTISING REGULATION

Product Placement

As opposed to other European countries such as the United Kingdom or France (Fine 2007), product placement on television is allowed in Spain, except in children's programs. The new General Law on Audiovisual Communication 7/2010 defines the term *product placement* as: "any form of audiovisual commercial communication consisting of the inclusion, display, or reference to a product, service, or trademark so that it is shown on a program" (art. 2), and distinguishes it from *surreptitious commercial communication,* which is prohibited. The latter is defined as the "verbal or visual presentation . . . of goods, services, names, [and] trademarks [for a] misleading [purpose]" (Law 7/2010, art. 2).

However, it is important that the audience is clearly informed of the product placement at the beginning and the end of the program, and when it resumes after a commercial break (Corredoira 2010). The sign to indicate a product placement is shown in Figure 13.3. The producer should include "Emplazamiento publicitario" or "EP" on the show when a product appears for promotion.

Commercial Slot Limits

According to the General Law on Audiovisual Communication (Law 7/2010), for a broadcasting company the overall time devoted to advertising its own programs shall not exceed five minutes per hour; commercial slots and teleshopping shall not exceed 12 minutes per hour. Sponsorship and product placement are excluded, and this limitation does not apply to radio or Internet ads.

The Ministry of Industry, Tourism, and Commerce imposed sanctions worth €2.48 million to television companies for committing a total of 98 violations of advertising rules and protection of minors in 2010. In terms of excessive advertising time (the offense for which the greatest sanctions are traditionally imposed, with over €15 million collected since 2005), six operators were fined €1.5 million that year. However, these sanctions are far from significant for television companies whose earnings are above €200–500 million. The Audiovisual Law (7/2010) establishes sanctions between 500,000 and 1 million euros for violating women's dignity on television, and 100,001 and 200,000 euros for the same offense on radio. Hence, the system is not as efficient as needed.

Figure 13.3

Sign of Product Placement (Law 7/2010)

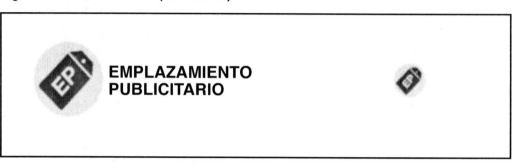

TOBACCO, ALCOHOL, AND MEDICINES

Any television advertising of tobacco and spirits containing over 20 percent of alcohol is prohibited (Law 25/1994), and the use of minors in ads for alcoholic drinks is also prohibited. Consequently, any advertising campaign addressed to minors that directly or indirectly encourages the consumption of alcohol and tobacco is prohibited. Such advertising cannot be associated with education, health, or sporting events. There is an interesting case dealing with the illegal advertising of the renowned whisky brand *Ballantines* promoting sports played mainly by minors. The Madrid Court of First Instance decided that their advertising postings at bus stops violated the law in two ways—first, because they were featured at public transport checkpoints, and second, because they were featured at places where the delivery, sale, and consumption of alcohol were prohibited (Volz et al. 2005, 72).

The advertisement of prescription medicines, medical treatments, and prescription medical devices is also prohibited on television (Law 25/1994). Ads for over-the-counter medicines cannot be directed exclusively or mainly to children. Products relating to personal hygiene cannot be advertised in such way that children would use them without parental supervision.

CONCLUSION

The restrictions and limitations on advertising in Spain are more stringent than those applied to other forms of expression. The main reasons for this include the need to protect consumers' rights and the realization that advertising makes use of direct and persuasive techniques, and therefore has great power to exert influence.

The first Advertising Statute in Spain dates from 1964. The General Law of Advertising was published in 1988 and later reformed in 2002, in order to adapt the Spanish system to the European Union's system of regulation. The main change introduced by the 1988 law was to replace the administrative proceedings with judicial proceedings in the process of settling conflicts.

Other regulated aspects aim at the protection of consumers, children, the image of women, e-commerce and so on.

Advertising directed toward children is bound by specific requirements, in addition to the more general principles of looking after the children's physical, moral, and psychological welfare. For instance, advertising may not directly incite children to purchase a good or service or ask their parents or guardians to make such a purchase; nor can children be portrayed in hazardous situations. Furthermore, advertisements for medicines must include a sign stating that the advertised product is a "medicine," and that "it must be kept out of the reach of children."

Regarding media, regulation deals chiefly with television advertising through the General Law on Audiovisual Communication 7/2010. There is no specific regulation for the rest of the media. The current government in Spain wants to eliminate personal contact ads in newspapers in order to put into force the prohibition of prostitution, and it filed a proposal in Parliament in July 2010. This proposal has not yet reached bill status.

Television advertising of tobacco, alcoholic beverages, and prescription medicines is prohibited. Some companies, such as Marlboro (cigarettes) or Larios (gin), reacted to this prohibition by launching various lines of business or sponsoring events in order to increase the visibility of their trademarks.

Although the Ministry of Industry sanctions those companies that break the law, these fines seem quite insufficient to prevent further breaches of the advertising regulation by the companies responsible for the infringements. Another problem with the advertising activity is the lack of transparency regarding fees and negotiations between advertising agencies, media, and advertisers. The Spanish regulatory system has not yet solved this problem. According to Sánchez-Tabernero and Corredoira (1994) there should be a rule to guarantee the transparency of rates, eliminating discounts and double bills.

The Spanish Self-Regulatory Association for Commercial Communications covers marketing and online activities. Its Code of Advertising Practice is a good example of how legality has to be based upon ethics, since the first ethical principle is to respect the laws already in place.

As one of the most efficient systems of self-regulation, AACC has become an example for other industrial sectors and countries because it has proved able to involve advertisers, consumers, and competitors in forming a truthful and respectful advertising industry. One of the successful goals of AACC has been the increasing involvement of advertisers and agencies in self-regulation activities.

However, the work of the association still needs to improve. Advertisers criticize Autocontrol's efficiency in resolving cases—some cases take more than 30 days to work out.

Finally, advertising regulation opens the debate about the limits between freedom of expression and consumer rights. The Spanish system has tried to solve this dilemma through ethical standards and self-regulation in advertising.

BIBLIOGRAPHY

Autocontrol [Spanish Self-Regulatory Association for Commercial Communications]. 2010. "Trabajamos por una publicidad responsable." Annual Report, March 17. http://www.autocontrol.es/pdfs/balance%2009 %20AUTOCONTROL.pdf.

———. Autocontrol [Spanish Self-Regulatory Association for Commercial Communications, or AACC]. 2012. Rules of the Jury. http://www.autocontrol.es/pdfs/regl_ingles.pdf (accessed March 14, 2013).

———. 2012. "We work for responsible advertising." http://www.autocontrol.es/pdfs/folleto_ingles.pdf.

Corredoira, Loreto. 2010. "Apuntes para un nuevo Derecho de la Televisión en España: La ley 17/2010." *Comunicación y Pluralismo*, no. 9, 104–133.

Cunningham, A. 2000. "Advertising Self-Regulation in a Broader Context: An Examination of the European Union's Regulatory Context: An Examination of the European Union's Regulatory Environment." *Journal of Promotion Management*, 5(2), 61–83.

Europa Press. 2011. "Industria impuso 2,48 millones de euros en multas por infracciones en publicidad." *El Mundo*, April 14. http://www.elmundo.es/elmundo/2011/04/14/comunicacion/1302792230.html (accessed July 27, 2011).

Fernando Magarzo, R. 2008. "La consolidación de la autorregulación publicitaria en España: Fomento normativo y reconocimiento jurisprudencial." *Estudios sobre consumo*, 84, 71–83.

Fine, J. 2007. "Product Placement in Europe: Changes Coming?" *Business Week*, April 16. http://www.businessweek.com/innovate/FineOnMedia/archives/2007/04/product_placement_in_europe_changes_coming.html (accessed July 27, 2011).

Gómez, J.D. 2010. "Autocontrol. Herramienta que hace más rentable la publicidad." *Anda Revista*, no. 43, 22–23.

Infoadex. 2010. Estudio Infoadex de la inversión publicitaria en España 2010. http://www.infoadex.es/Resumen_Estudio_Inversiones_InfoAdex_2010.pdf.

Medina, Mercedes, and Soontae An. 2012. "Advertising Self-Regulation Activity: A Comparison Between Spain and US." *Zer*, 17(33), 13–29.

Medina, Mercedes, and Teresa Ojer. 2010. "The New Spanish Public Service Broadcasting Model." *Comunicación y Sociedad*, XXIII(2), 329–359.

Muñoz, Mercedes. 2011. "Algunas reflexiones sobre las novedades en materia de regulación publicitaria en España en 2010." *Sphera Publica*, 11, 41–55.

Palomera, E. 2010. "El Gobierno eliminará los anuncios de sexo en prensa." *El Mundo*, July 15. http://www.larazon.es/noticia/5327-zapatero-afirma-que-los-anuncios-de-contactos-en-la-prensa-deben-eliminarse (accessed March 14, 2013).

PAOS Code [Self-Regulatory Code for Advertising Directed at Minors]. 2005. Código de autorregulación de la publicidad de alimentos dirigida a menores, prevención de la obesidad y salud, FIAB (Spanish Food and Drink Industry Federation).

Patiño, B. 2007. *La autorregulación publicitaria: Especial referencia al sistema español.* Barcelona, Spain: Bosch.

Sánchez-Tabernero, A., and L. Corredoira y Alfonso. 1994. *Transparencia y control de los medios informativos: Informe sobre la situación española y perspectiva europea.* Madrid, Spain: Fundación de la Comunicación Social.

Semova, Dimitrina Jivkova. 2010. "Financing Public Media in Spain: New Strategies." *International Journal on Media Management,* 12(3–4), 141–157.

Taylor, R.E. 2002. "Inside the Asociación de Autocontrol de la Publicidad: A Qualitative Study of Advertising Self-Regulation in Spain." *Journal of Intercultural Communication Research*, 31(3), 181–190.

Villanueva, Ernesto. 1997. *Régimen constitucional de las libertades de expresión e información en los países del mundo.* Madrid, Spain: Fragua.

Volz, Gerhard W., Felipe B. Handschuh, and Dora Poshtakova. 2005. "Advertising to Children in Spain." *Young Consumers: Insights and Ideas for Responsible Marketers*, 6(2), 71–76.

CHAPTER 14

THE UNITED KINGDOM

MARY ALICE SHAVER

HISTORY OF REGULATION

The United Kingdom has a long history of advertising regulation. Although the industry evolved with the development of the mass audience, it was not until the beginning of the nineteenth century that advertising first became widely available to the general public through newspapers, posters, and other printed forms. Between 1800 and midcentury, the volume of newspaper advertising insertions increased threefold. Newspapers were taxed through the Stamp Act of 1797; however, some illegal publications operated below the authorities' radar, carrying some volume of advertisement that we cannot fully measure. Perhaps the most popular advertising used at this time was billposting (Nevett 1982, 20). Whatever the medium, there was a dearth of what we would term consumer goods advertising.

Posters were not subject to taxation, which—along with the ease of distributing them—made them a popular venue. The elimination of the tax stamp requirement in 1855 led to a sizeable increase in advertisement volume and expenditure. Household goods and food were advertised in the UK, as were many branded items. The advertising audience spread to the working classes. From around 1880, advertisements increased, not only for foods but also for housing products, many of which could be purchased on credit terms.

Regulation of advertising, though not formalized, was accomplished by the newspapers themselves in refusing advertising that seem untruthful or obscene and through other laws that had the effect of limiting some of the advertising placement. Of course, there were some newspapers—notably *The Times* (London)—that had higher standards than others.

RELEVANT LAWS

In 1909, a contributor to the London *Times* wrote: "A variety of staple products are now chiefly or largely sold through advertising of specific brands" (Nevett 1982, 70). Aside from copy in newspapers and magazines, advertising took a number of forms, including posters, ads projected against buildings, sampling, and even telegrams sent to residences.

With the growth of advertising and some questionable products being promoted to the public, the media became concerned.

Self-regulation began in the UK in the 1880s—in the poster industry. The first codes of advertising were developed in 1925 by the Association of Publicity Clubs. The very next year saw a more stringent monitoring introduced by the Advertising Association, which delegated its newly formed Investigation Department to monitor advertising and to respond to claims brought by the industry, competitors, and the public. The International Chamber of Commerce (ICC; see chapter 21) introduced an international code of practice in 1937.

The Committee of Advertising Practice (CAP) was formed in 1961. It covered all nonbroadcast advertising. The Advertising Standards Committee (ASC) formed to enforce the codes.

For nearly 50 years, advertising regulation for print advertising in the UK has been handled by the Advertising Standards Authority (ASA). From 2004 on, the ASA has handled regulation for all media, including Internet ads, which are subject to the same regulation standards as all other media.

The ASA adjudicates complaints to ascertain if the advertising in question is breaking any of the international industry codes. All complaints—whether by a consumer, a competitor, a member of the general public, an industry representative, or an advertising agency—are reviewed to determine compliance or a breach of compliance. Each complaint is considered and reviewed. The length of time required to settle a claim depends upon the nature of the complaint and the behavior of the accused when notified (typically within 10 days). In a minor complaint, the case may be closed quite quickly. If the advertiser charged with the breach challenges the complaint, the case goes to the ASA Council for judgment. The council, two-thirds of which consists of lay people and the remainder of industry representatives, decides whether the advertising has broken the code. If the judgment is that it did, the council may recommend withdrawal or amendment of the advertisement. As always, it is the responsibility of the advertiser and the agency to prove the veracity of statements and graphics in their advertising. This evidence is considered in the inquiry by the ASA.

Council judgments may be appealed within 21 days, but any appeal must be in writing and must bring forward new evidence. An independent reviewer decides if the appeal is justified. If so, the council is asked to review the appeal and new evidence. The council's decision in each case is final.

A number of sanctions can be invoked for advertisers who breach the codes. The advertiser may be asked to modify the ad itself, the media may be asked not to run an ad, and advertisers may be required to obtain preclearance for a period of up to two years. The ASA will publish all decisions, and the negative publicity may also affect an advertiser. Industry and professional organizations have the right to cancel support for an advertiser, particularly if the record of offenses is high or the advertiser simply refuses to comply with sanctions. For outdoor advertising, a recommended two years of copy advice may be required. For broadcast advertising, the matter may be referred to the Office of Fair Trading (OFT). In extreme or repeated advertising breaches, the most severe penalty involves revoking the advertiser's license.

For the majority of cases, the lower sanctions are agreed upon: The advertiser modifies the offending copy or visual and the matter is resolved.

Any advertisements brought into the UK by an international firm must conform to ASA standards, even if the material is allowed in another country. The agency or advertiser that wants to use an ad from a foreign venue may apply for preclearance, which is given a fast turnaround.

As recently as 2009, 10 percent of total ad cases brought to the ASA were changed or withdrawn as a result of unfavorable ASA reviews. However, millions of advertisements, promotions, and other publicity are produced every year, so of the actual amount of complaints (28,929 in 2009) (Hobson, 2010), only 2,397 were acted upon. Only 1 percent of all ads produced throughout the UK are ever brought to the ASA. Ninety-seven percent of ads are found to be within the codes.

Beyond public or industry complaint reviews, the ASA conducts its own mentoring for compliance with the various codes as developed and enforced. The UK advertising codes are comprehensive and strict.

DEVELOPMENT OF CODES

The Committee of Advertising Practice (CAP) was founded in1961. Its purpose was to investigate complaints against all nonbroadcast advertisements. A year later, the Advertising Standards Authority (ASA) was founded as an independent agency to enforce all codes of practice for nonbroadcast advertisements. Its role is to protect the customer in purchasing behavior. In 1988, ASA remained the principal self-regulatory body in the UK, but it gained statutory strength through the Office of Fair Trading.

The CAP Code of Nonbroadcast Advertising states that "it makes due allowance for the public sensitivities, but will not be used by the ASA to diminish freedom of speech unjustifiably" (CAP 2010, 9).

In 2003, the Communication Act gave a new body, the Office of Communications (Ofcom), statutory power for broadcast regulations. Ofcom then gave the responsibility for meeting advertising standards for broadcasting to a related body, ASA (broadcast). Another related but separate body—the Broadcast Committee of Advertising Practice (BCAP)—has responsibility for the existing radio and television codes. Sanctions for failure to comply with the codes include removing the offending advertisements from the air, amending the advertisements, and requiring pre-vetting for all advertisements before they are run. The ASA may refer broadcasts that fail to meet the standards to Ofcom.

The primary goal of the ASA in overseeing both the CAP and BCAP codes is that all advertisements and marketing communication conform to the codes. The driving force is that the public and consumers receive information that is "legal, decent, honest, and truthful" (CAP 2010, 3). When advertisers conform to the high standards of the CAP and BCAP codes, the public receives marketing data that informs them and ensures that they can make reasonable marketing decisions. The codes also ensure that advertisers, agencies, and the media are all playing by the same rules. The Compliance Team has the role of making sure that advertisers work within the parameters of the codes. "It enforces ASA adjudications, disseminates any ramifications of them for an industry sector and acts against marketers that persistently break the Code" (CAP 2010, 84).

Both the CAP and BCAP codes are exhaustive, listing areas they do cover and also ones that they do not. The codes cover nonbroadcast media such as newspaper, billboards, posters, email, and others. The TV advertising codes cover content and scheduling of television ads and also interactive television. The radio codes cover radio advertisement. The advertising codes are supported by consumer legislation.

Since the ASA does not have legal authority, some complaints may be turned over to the Office of Fair Trading (OFT) for nonbroadcast ads or Ofcom (ASA's partner) for broadcast ads. These committees can apply sanctions such as fines, mandatory termination of ads, or—in the case of broadcast—withdrawing the license of the offending medium. Because most advertisers comply with ASA recommendations, referral to the OFT or Ofcom is relatively rare.

The ASA Council adjudicates complaints brought about advertising. Their decisions are final with the exception of the appeals process. The council consists of 15 appointed members, 10 of whom are not in the advertising industry. Members may serve for two three-year terms. ASA findings and adjudications are published in the media. This action informs the public while serving as a sanction for the offending advertisers.

There is a Compliance Committee that ensures that the CAP sanctions are enforced. In cases where an advertisement contains a claim that is misleading or could do harm to the public or to a competitor, the committee acts quickly so that the offending advertisement is stopped. The committee also issues Ad Alerts both to CAP members and to the media, apprising them of the sanctions and, in the case of the media, asking them to deny advertising space to the company that is out of compliance.

Since the 2010 BCAP-CAP change, ASA and Ofcom have become partners in coregulation.

The Advertising Standards Authority (ASA) is funded by a tax on advertising buys. It is collected by two bodies independent of ASA. Membership in the ASA consists of industry organizations that represent advertisers, agencies, media, and others. Membership is by industry professionals; no lay people are involved with this function.

An important service offered by the ASA is detailed guidance for both the broadcast and nonbroadcast advertisements. A separate service—copy advice—checks copy for nonbroadcast advertisements and marketing communications to ensure compliance with the codes. Two other associations, Clearcast (for television ads) and the Radio Advertising Clearance Centre (for radio spots) also check for compliance with the codes. Both Clearcast and the Radio Advertising Clearance Centre provide prepublication surveillance. They publish newsletters with the latest information on advertising regulations and practices.

The ASA mission now includes marketing communication, website audits, and evaluations. In addition, as a part of its educational mission, the ASA holds seminars and other events for members.

The ASA sanctions are not enforceable by law. A very effective sanction by the ASA is the printing of weekly adjudications, which are widely read. It should be stressed that the majority of advertisers respond to this first level of sanctions and comply with them.

Although the ASA sanctions do not carry the weight of law, they apparently carry enough weight to deter advertisers from noncompliance with the codes. Specific sanctions are recapped here:

- *Ad Alerts*—CAP can issue alerts to its members, including the media, advising them to withhold services such as access to advertising space.
- *Withdrawal of trading privileges*—CAP members can revoke, withdraw, or temporarily withhold recognition and trading privileges. For example, the Royal Mail can withdraw its bulk mail discount, which can make running direct marketing campaigns prohibitively expensive.
- *Pre-vetting*—Persistent or serious offenders can be required to have their marketing material vetted before publication. For example, CAP's poster industry members can invoke mandatory pre-vetting for advertisers who have broken the CAP Code on grounds of taste and decency or social responsibility. The pre-vetting can last for two years.
- *Sanctions in the online space*—CAP has further sanctions that can be invoked to help ensure marketers' claims comply with the codes both on their own websites and in other non-paid-for space under their control. (ASA 2012a)

Media owners can refuse to run ads that do not comply with the CAP Codes. In persistent cases, the ASA can refer the advertising to the Office of Fair Trading (OFT) or, in the case of broadcasters, to Ofcom. However, these measures are rare because the offending advertisers tend to comply with the standards. For those who refuse to comply, the matter may be referred to the OFT for legal proceedings. For broadcast offenses that cannot be resolved at the lower level, the matter may be transferred to Ofcom, which has the ability to impose fines and, in extreme cases, to take away licenses.

It must be noted that the ASA is independent and not a part of any UK governmental unit. It exists to make certain that advertisements are in line with both consumer and legal codes. Its work upholds the law by resolving cases brought by either the consuming public entity, an individual, or a competitor. By reviewing the advertisement in advance or by seeing it as part of ongoing monitoring, the ASA can stop an actual, more formal, complaint from arising. The code and all

self-regulatory provisions complement the legal aspects of British law. While companies are required to have the backup tests and other verification of claims made within the advertising itself,
if there are actual legal problems, the case is referred to the proper legal authorities.

It should be noted that the ASA may investigate a claim of code violation if there is but a single
complaint. Anyone may make a complaint to ASA concerning advertising. The identity of individuals is maintained with the privacy rules of the ASA. Anyone should be able to bring forward
a complaint to be investigated.

The BCAP Code

BCAP is the equivalent of CAP in the broadcast sphere. In 2010, it merged with the CAP code
for many functions. BCAP was separate for many years, but as the two areas' communication
delivery grew closer, CAP and BCAP became more similar and merged what had previously been
four separate codes.

Compliance Team

Depending on the initial ruling, the case proceeds by notifying the advertiser of what must be done
to become compliant. On many occasions, it goes no further as the advertiser complies with the
ruling. For some cases, the committee finds that the complaint has no merit.

SPECIFIC CATEGORIES

Weight Loss and Slimming Products

Particularly important in the marketing and advertising of products promoting loss of weight
is solid documentation of all claims. There should be no suggestion that the product will work
without an accompanying decrease in caloric intake. Marketing for any weight loss product shall
not make claims that the program is safe absent a nutritious diet. At no time should an advertisement claim that being underweight is desirable or promise that a specific number of pounds can
be lost using the product. Marketers must have the results of actual trials of the product conducted
in an acceptable scientific manner. (Testimonials that cannot be backed up by trial results are not
considered acceptable.) Advertisements must not target those under 18 years of age. Suggested
diet plans to follow while taking the weight loss product must be nutritious.

Financial Advertising

Advertisers of financial products must provide advertising that is understandable to the common
reader both in words and concepts. The copy must provide current interest rates and state that
investments may increase or decrease (be variable) and that past performance is not a guarantee
since the marketplace is dynamic.

Food and Nutrition

Marketing communication (all print publications) must be very clear on claims regarding nutrition and benefits of supplements as well as advertising for food products. Documentary material
supporting claims in these areas must meet the conditions as specified by the EU for this type of

product. Any benefits claimed must be supported. Any claims that imply a lowering of the risk of disease must be in line with the EU guidelines.

Banned as well are any claims that would feature a recommendation for a specific practitioner or a specific firm. The only permissible references to groups are to charities or national, appointed groups.

There must be no mention or inference that would disparage a competing product or company. Put simply, any advertiser must put forward its own work factually and without referring to any advantage over any kind of category competition.

Tobacco

No tobacco products are allowed to appear in any advertisement to the public in the UK.

Alcohol

Any advertising or communication regarding alcoholic products must be clearly aimed at consumers over 18 years of age. Advertising for alcoholic products must not imply that it would be safe to drink while driving, using machinery, or indulging in any behavior where the use of alcohol could be construed to enhance any risky behavior (examples include swimming, boating, and the like). Ads may show flirtatious behavior, but not sexual activity. Alcohol must not be advertised as a mood-enhancing substance, nor as a product to overcome loneliness. It must never be portrayed as any kind of a nutritional aid.

While factual claims may be presented (such as how the alcoholic beverage is made or the number of years it has been produced), such claims may not use comparative statements concerning competing brands.

The marketing of low alcohol products is somewhat more lenient. Drinks containing 1.2 percent alcohol or less by volume may state their strength in the advertisements. However, the low alcohol content cannot be used as a sales tactic to appeal to younger drinkers or to encourage more than moderate consumption.

At no time may the consumption of alcohol be linked to social success, to increased confidence on the part of the user, or to increased ability in sports or other activities. Children may appear in advertisements for low-level alcoholic beverages, but only if the scene is portraying a family getting together. However, anyone who is or appears to be under 18 years of age may not be depicted as a drinker of alcohol, and that must be clear in the advertising.

Gambling

The code for gambling advertisements is similar to that for drinking, with some specific prohibitions. For example, gambling may never be depicted as a solution to financial or personal difficulties. And, of course, such advertisements must not appeal to children or imply that gambling is a necessary rite of passage to move into adulthood. Any messages concerning gambling must be socially responsible.

Working from Home

Any business advertising work-from-home positions must include the name and address of the employment business as well as a realistic portrayal of the work itself. Any limitations to the work must be included, as must any financial outlay by the clients. Statements about average income from the work cannot be given unless the company is able to use actual figures that have been earned by those already employed. All of these matters must be spelled out in the initial contact between likely buyers and the company itself.

Advertising Directed Toward or for Children

Codes and rules concerning advertising to children are strict. Age and possible impressions of the advertising are taken into account for this more vulnerable segment of the public. The code concerning children notes that what may be acceptable and understood by older children may not be suitable when younger children are involved.

Specific sections of the code address the issue of safety. Children must not be shown alone in environments where they would not be safe—on a busy street, talking to strangers, or attempting to use products that normally would not be used by small children. Children must not be encouraged, through ad copy or pictures, to attempt to use products unsuitable for them.

Children must not be made to feel that they will be unpopular if they do not own something shown in an advertisement. This sort of ad is seen as exploiting a child's lack of experience and judgment (Hilton 2003, 66).

Ads must not encourage—or even suggest—that children should pester their parents for a product. In addition, children must see the product as it really is and not with any enhancements.

LEGAL REGULATION

Relationship Between ASA and Laws with Legal Force

There are many laws concerning specific types of goods and services. ASA provides a link to them for the members on their website.

At the initial evaluation of questionable advertising (ads that allegedly are deceptive, contain an untrue comparison or other contents that are misleading, or are not in compliance with the ASA Council), the case may be forwarded to the Office of Fair Trading for further adjudication under the 2008 Consumer Protection from Unfair Trading Regulations and the 2008 Business Protection from Misleading Marketing Regulations (ASA 2012b). If discontinuation of the advertisement is recommended but not honored, a court order may be obtained to stop the advertising. Noncompliance at this stage will be taken to court. It should be noted that a guilty verdict would affect the developer of the questionable advertising, including the agency, and also the media responsible for carrying the advertisements—all of which could receive sanctions under the OFT regulations. Before the sanction takes place, the offenders are encouraged to once again work with the ASA to make the advertising acceptable under all existing consumer laws. The ASA is the primary regulation body and, through its process, succeeds in resolving most complaints.

CONSUMERISM

The first organized consumer movements in the UK occurred in the years following World War I, when food was in short supply. In 1918, a short-lived Consumer's Council was created as a means of understanding and addressing the public's concerns. Formed by the government and not citizens, the council was seen as a means of understanding and addressing the public's concerns. Although the council was primarily an advisory body, some of its opinions and debates made their way into policies. Founded during a period of rationing and scarcity following the war, it was viewed as a political body—one that was closer to the interests of business than the people. The council was dissolved in 1921.

In the period following World War II, modern-day consumer movements began to emerge. These councils were tied to various segments of industry and were not perceived as effective by the consuming public. The forerunner to the UK Consumers' Association (1956) was an advisory committee of consumer goods (1946), established by the National Council of Women to oversee food standards.

From all of these various efforts and organizations, it is the Consumers' Association (CA), started in 1956, that is looked to today as the industry's standard bearer. It performs testing of products and recommendations for the best value. CA serves as an adviser to governmental agencies and, from its very beginnings, has stressed its independence from business interests. Its monthly magazine, *Which?* publishes ratings and comparisons among products. CA saw its role as empowering the consumer. Education is an important aspect of the Consumers' Association.

FREEDOM OF SPEECH

Britain includes the Freedom of Expression in Article 10 of its Human Rights Act. However, there is no mention or inclusion of commercial speech in this article. What is mentioned is that this freedom of expression is not meant to deny the right to requirement of licensing of "broadcasting, television or cinema enterprises."

It is up to the advertiser and the agency (if there is one) to ensure that any advertising created and put before the public is lawful. There are governmental agencies that ensure that communication delivered to the public follows the law.

THE ADVERTISING REVIEW PROCESSES

Advertising reviewing started early in the UK. Today's regulations, including the ASA functions, are a result of many years of monitoring. Advertising is encouraged to operate within the legal framework. The development of the codes and the subsequent CAP and BCAP merger appear to be the logical results of more and more technology and more advertisers entering the market. It should be noted that the CAP Codes do not operate across borders: The new EU directives perform that function.

AGENCIES AND CODES

Advertising Standards Authority Ltd. (ASA). http://www.asa.org.uk/.
Committee of Advertising Practice (CAP). http://www.cap.org.uk/.
Committee of Advertising Practice (CAP). UK Code of Broadcast Advertising (BCAP Code). http://www.cap.org.uk/Advertising-Codes/Broadcast-HTML.aspx.
Committee of Advertising Practice (CAP). UK Code of Non-Broadcast Advertising, Sales Promotion and Direct Marketing (CAP Code). http://www.cap.org.uk/Advertising-Codes/Non-broadcast-HTML.aspx.
Office of Communications (Ofcom). Independent regulator and competition authority for the UK communications industries. http://www.ofcom.org.uk/.
Office of Fair Trading (OFT). Business Protection from Misleading Marketing Regulations, 2008. http://www.oft.gov.uk/business-advice/treating-customers-fairly/advertising/business-protection.
United Kingdom. The Consumer Protection from Unfair Trading Regulations, 2008, No. 1277. http://www.legislation.gov.uk/uksi/2008/1277/contents/made.

BIBLIOGRAPHY

Advertising Standards Authority Ltd (ASA). 2012a. "Non-broadcast sanctions." http://www.asa.org.uk/Industry-advertisers/Sanctions/Non-broadcast.aspx.
———. 2012b. "Our history." http://www.asa.org.uk/About-ASA/Our-history.aspx.
Committee of Advertising Practice (CAP). 2010. *The CAP Code: The UK Code of Nonbroadcast Advertising, Sales Promotion and Direct Marketing*, Edition 12. London, UK: The Committee of Advertising Practice. http://www.cap.org.uk/Advertising-Codes/~/media/Files/CAP/Codes%20CAP%20pdf/CAP%20Code%209%20oct%2012%281%29.ashx (accessed June 2011).
Hilton, M. 2003. *Consumerism in 20th Century Britain: The Search for a Historical Movement.* Cambridge, UK: Cambridge University Press.
Hobson, W. 2010. "ASA sees record numbers of complaints in 2009." *UK Marketing News,* June 2. http://www.ukmarketingnews.com/asa-sees-record-number-of-complaints-in-2009/ (accessed June 17, 2011).
Nevett, T.R. 1982. *Advertising in Britain.* Norwich, UK: William Heinemann.

CHAPTER 15

GERMANY

DAN SHAVER

Germany is a federal, parliamentary republic of 16 states where the primary role of advertising and consumer rights relies on a combination of legal and voluntary self-regulation. Because of the federate structure, some regulatory powers derive from the German constitution, and others are specified in treaties agreed upon between the states.

Reacting to the negative influences of advertising and media control experienced in the first half of the twentieth century during two world wars, the German approach to media content regulation is characterized by the desire (1) to maintain independent voices, (2) to clearly identify the distinction between advertising and editorial content, and (3) to prevent misleading or harmful content.

HISTORY OF ADVERTISING REGULATION IN GERMANY

German advertising regulation traces its roots to a 1909 Law Against Unfair Competition (hereafter known as the UWG), which established legal standards for business communication. The essence of the law was contained in two all-purpose prohibitions—the banning of advertising that was misleading or that violated accepted moral standards. The courts generally interpreted misleading advertising to exist if 10 to 15 percent of consumers questioned misunderstood the advertiser's claim based on public surveys. The Federal Supreme Court used the "morals" clause to ban unsolicited telephone sales calls, since it violated people's privacy without their consent. In 1932, two additional regulations were added to the UWG—both designed to prevent consumers from being enticed into buying something through free gifts or high discounts. The Ordinance Regulating Free Gifts restricted giveaways to a value of two German marks. The Rebate Law restricted discounts to 3 percent of the price of the article. In 1938, a ruling by Germany's highest civil court effectively banned comparative advertising (Dr. Schotthöfer & Steiner 2012).

The framework for court decisions about advertising began to shift after Germany joined the European Union. Decisions by the European Court of Justice forced abandonment of the assumption that consumers should be considered "superficial, uninformed and uninterested" when considering issues of misleading advertising; rather, it fostered the notion of consumers as "reasonably well informed, reasonably observant and circumspect." Other court rulings and EU regulations regarding competition forced further adaptations, and in 2004 a new version of the UWG went into effect.

CURRENT REGULATORY SYSTEMS

Enforcement power is concentrated at the state level through 14 state media authorities that cover the 16 German federated states. State-level initiatives and policies are coordinated through the

Association of State Media Authorities for Broadcasting (ALM). Its primary role is to harmonize the interests of state media authorities in broadcasting regarding programming, legal matters, technology, research, media competence, and financial support. It is also assigned social responsibilities in areas such as agreements over the regulatory framework affecting advertising and sponsorship in broadcasting (ALM 2012c). The ALM works through four commissions and in additional collaboration with the national Commission for the Protection of Minors in the Media (KJM) and the Commission on Concentration in the Media (KEK, dedicated to diversity of opinion in media) (ALM 2012b).

The Kommission für Jugendmedienschutz der Landesmedienanstalen (Commission for the Protection of Minors in the Media, or KJM) consists of at 24-person board of directors. Twelve of the directors are appointed by state media authorities, eight are appointed by the supreme state authorities responsible for the protection of minors, and four are appointed by the supreme federal authorities responsible for minors (KJM 2012). The mandate for this group is founded in Germany's constitutional provision that identifies the protection of children, adolescents, and human dignity as fundamental rights and obligations under the Interstate Treaty on the Protection of Minors in Broadcasting and in Telemedia (JMStV), which was signed by all 16 German federated states in 2002 and has been in force since 2010 (Mann 1999). A second major influence on commission activities comes from the need to harmonize German regulation with EU treaties and directives. In general, this has resulted in a slow liberalization of Germany's restrictive approach to advertising regulation.

The primary responsibilities of the KJM are the structural protection of minors (risk avoidance), educational protection (informing minors about risks and providing guidance on dealing with them), and providing legal protection to regulate exposure to dangers. To achieve these goals, they (1) review media content to determine whether it might impair minors in their development, (2) formulate guidelines to ensure that appropriate content is accessible to minors in specified age groups within specific time frames, and (3) approve encryption and blocking systems. The commission determines whether content providers have breached the laws and regulations regarding content and decides measures to be recommended to state authorities. State media authorities have a range of sanctions available, including fines of up to 500,000 euros for a breach of sponsorship or advertising rules but generally prefer more informal solutions (Hitchens 2009). The KJM files applications for Internet content to be listed on an index of problematic media and responds to applications from the Federal Department for Media Harmful to Young Persons (Bundesprüfstelle für jugendgefährdende Medien, or BPjM). It is also charged with stimulating public discourse regarding protection of minors and must certify organizations dealing with self-regulation.

The BPjM is a federal agency charged under the Youth Protection Law with monitoring videos, DVDs, computer games, audio recordings, CDs, print media, and Internet sites for content harmful to children and adolescents. The BPjM only acts at the request of other administrative institutions such as the KJM or state youth welfare departments. It consists of 12 representatives from eight different social organizations such as the artistic community, the educational arena, religious groups, and the entertainment industry, as well as three representatives from federal states and the BPjM chairperson (Hitchens 2009).

If the content in question is deemed harmful, it is placed on an index and subject to a range of distribution restrictions. These include not being sold or otherwise made accessible to minors, not being displayed where it can be seen by minors, not being sold by mail order, not being rented in a store accessible to minors, banned for import, and not being advertised in a place where minors may see the advertisement.

THE REGULATORY ENVIRONMENT AND FINANCIAL MODELS

Print and broadcast media are the primary sources of advertising in Germany. Many specific advertising regulations are targeted at broadcast media but general standards and rules apply across the board, even to in-store retail advertising in some categories.

German regulators distinguish between three forms of advertising based on the Interstate Treaty on the Protection of Minors in Broadcasting and in Telemedia. These are:

- Advertising—Any self-promotional content delivered in connection with a trade, business, craft or profession intended to promote the sale of goods or services.
- Sponsorship—Any contribution from an entity not engaged in broadcasting or audio-visual production which directly or indirectly supports program financing with the intent to promote the contributor's brand, product, or service.
- Surreptitious Advertising—Any allusion or reference to brands, goods, or services within program content intended to promote the brand, goods, or services in a way that may mislead the public. In the United States, this is called *product placement* or *embedded advertising.*
- In addition, the Interstate Treaty defined a new broadcast activity called *teleshopping.* This is defined as "direct offers broadcast to the public with a view to selling goods or services, including immovable property, rights, and obligations, in return for payment." (ALM 2010, Section I, Article 2[2])

Fundamental to the German approach to advertising regulation is the *distinction rule,* which requires that advertising should be clearly separated from other content in a way that consumers can easily distinguish. There is also a prohibition on advertisers influencing programming. Infomercials are permitted as long as they are clearly recognizable and must be identified as such when they are broadcast. Sponsorship rules require disclosure so the audience recognizes that a commercial relationship exists and that there is no editorial influence (Petrenko 2000).

The German television system is often called *dual* because public and private broadcasting coexist—but with marked differences, including some in regulation. The Association of Public Broadcasting (ARD) network of regional public stations, also called Channel I, was founded in 1954 and began transmitting both local and national programming. In 1967, a second public network Zweites, Deutsches Fernsehen (ZDF) or Channel II, began transmission in collaboration with the federal states. Finally, Channel III was established in 2000 (Herold 2012).

Commercial competition began after the Federal Constitutional Court granted states the right to issue broadcast licenses to privately owned companies in 1981. The first commercial television networks—Radio Television Luxemburg (RTL plus) and SAT 1—began programming in West Germany in 1984 and, just over a decade later, there were 28 private broadcasters. While the public broadcast channels are available across Germany, the commercial channels tend to concentrate on metropolitan markets. By 2008, Germany had 365 combined public and commercial licensed channels, though the public channels remained dominant. In 2011, eight top channels claimed 68.2 percent of German viewership, with the two leading public channels, ARD and ZDF, having a combined reach of 24.5 percent of total viewing (The Library of Congress, 1995). Although commercial cable channels have proliferated, there is currently a single pay-TV satellite operator in Germany, Sky Deutschland.

Funding models for the two types of broadcasters differ significantly, and this was codified in the Interstate Treaty. Commercial broadcasters finance their operations almost exclusively through advertising (FRG 1991, Section II). Public service broadcasters are funded primarily through license fees from the owners of broadcast receivers with advertising revenue as a supplement. With guaranteed funding through licensing, there came restrictions on advertising activities. Key provisions included:

- Broadcasts of religious services or children's programs cannot be interrupted by advertising.
- While advertising may be inserted in blocks between programs, they can only be inserted during programs of more than 45 minutes in duration or during intervals in sporting events.
- The annual average for the entire duration of advertising on public service channels cannot exceed 20 minutes on working days and advertisements cannot be broadcast on Sundays, national holidays, or after 8:00 P.M.
- The amount of television spot advertising during any one-hour period cannot exceed 20 percent.
- Teleshopping advertising is banned on public channels. (FRG 1991, Section III, Subs. 5, Art. 44)

The treaty specifies that commercial broadcasters shall be financed through advertising and consumer fees such as subscriptions (FRG 1991, Section III, Subs. 5, Art. 43). Key provisions include:

- Somewhat more flexible advertising insertion rules, though similar to those for public broadcasters.
- Total advertising time should not exceed 20 percent of transmission time and spot advertising is limited to 15 percent of transmission time and 20 percent of any given hour.
- Direct offers to the public for the sale, purchase, or rental of products or for services should not exceed one hour per day. (FRG 1991, Section III, Subs. 5, Art. 45)

SELF-REGULATION IN GERMANY

Self-regulation of advertising has a long history in Germany, and the Interstate Treaty introduced the concept of "regulated self-regulation," requiring industry-based regulatory organizations to be certified by KJM. However, the operations of German self-regulatory organizations are not always as transparent as in other countries. Because published self-regulatory principles for an industry have often been interpreted as working legal obligations, some industry organizations prefer to deal with disputes and penalties through confidential arbitration (Deutscher Werberat 1979, 2).

Although there are a number of industry-related self-regulatory bodies, two deserve special attention because of their prominence: Deutscher Werberat (The German Advertising Standards Council, or DW) and Zentrale zur Bekämpfung unlauteren Wettbewerbs e. V. (Centre for Protection Against Unfair Competition, or WBZ).

The German Advertising Standards Council is primarily concerned with issues of taste and decency. Founded in 1972, its goal is to reconcile complaints between the German public and the advertising industry (Loitz 2012). It acts in two ways—providing a mechanism for conflict resolution and the development of voluntary codes of conduct for commercial advertisers in sensitive areas. It consists of, and is funded by, 40 organizations representing advertisers, media, advertising agencies, advertising professionals, and researchers represented by the German Advertising Federation (ZAW). Its 10-member panel includes four members representing commercial advertisers, three representing media, two from advertising agencies, and one representing advertising professionals. Complaints can be submitted by anyone. Although anonymous complaints are not processed, complainants' names are treated confidentially. Advertisers who are the subject of the complaint are notified and offered an opportunity to respond. If the complaint is upheld, the advertiser is notified and asked to change or discontinue the ad. If the violation is suspected of violating legal guidelines, referrals are made to the appropriate German authority with enforcement powers. If no legal violation is suspected and the advertiser fails to respond, Deutscher Werberat (DW) issues a public reprimand and a request to the media to reject the advertising until the ad is modified. The organization reports a high level of compliance from advertisers before the public reprimand step is reached (DW 2012). In 2000, the Council received 1,139 complaints (Loitz 2012, 31).

The DW has established broad guidelines for commercial communication that are based on prevailing social values and notions of decency and morals, fair competition, and responsibility to society. Specific requirements include:

- Consumers must not be exploited.
- Children and juveniles must not be subjected to physical or psychological harm.
- Discrimination in any form must not be fostered or tolerated.
- Violent, aggressive, or antisocial behavior must not be fostered or tolerated.
- Fear, unhappiness, and suffering should not be instilled.
- Behavior that threatens consumers' safety should not be tolerated. (DW 2007)

Additionally, the DW has developed specific guidelines dealing with the advertising of alcohol, children's products, and food and beverages, along with issues of personal denigration and discrimination and the use of traffic noises in radio advertising, among others. Although these rules were developed primarily for broadcast media, they have frequently been applied to other media.

Unlike the Advertising Council, the Centre for Combating Unfair Competition (WBZ) does possess legal, though civil, authority based on the Act Against Unfair Competition (UWG). The law assumes that companies, rather than the government, are best prepared to identify and intervene in instances of anticompetitive behavior and authorizes competitors, certain trade associations, consumer associations, and chambers of commerce to enforce statutory law through the Centre for Protection Against Unfair Competition (WBZ 2012). Founded in 1912, WBZ is an association of chambers of commerce, most trade associations, around 750 industrial and commercial associations, and approximately 1,200 companies. It handles more than 15,000 complaints a year. Its objectives are to maintain and support competition through legal research and public education, pursue violations of competition law, and develop competition law through test cases and expert consultation with governmental bodies regarding proposed legislation at both the national and European level.

WBZ accepts complaints from the consumers, competitors, and public authorities such as the police, trade, and health authorities. If the complaint is considered valid, the agency asks the advertiser to sign an agreement to amend or discontinue the practice. If the advertiser rejects the agreement, WBZ's executive directors decide whether to pursue legal recourse or seek to resolve the issue before the Board of Conciliation of the regional Chamber of Commerce. On average, the complaint is resolved within one to two weeks. If the complaint cannot be settled out of court, WBZ is authorized to seek a preliminary court injunction or main court proceedings. In 2011, court proceedings were initiated in more than 600 cases out of 14,000 complaints filed. In cases involving complaints by German companies regarding foreign competitors, the complaint is referred to the Federal Office for Consumer Protection and Food Safety (Bundesamt für Verbraucherschutz und Lebensmittelsicherheit, or BVL).

SPECIAL REGULATORY CASES

Minors

Under German law, children under the age of seven are considered to be in the preoperational stage of development, meaning they are not yet able to understand the consequences of their actions. Individuals over the age of 7 but under the age of 18 are considered to be of limited legal capability (EC 2012). This leads to age-based gradations in regulation. The following restrictions apply to advertising directed at children. The key restrictions are:

- The advertisement cannot directly or indirectly suggest that the child should ask parents or others to purchase the product.
- The advertising cannot exploit the trust minors place in persons of confidence such as parents or teachers.
- Unless there is valid justification, the advertising cannot show minors in dangerous situations.
- The advertising cannot depict criminal or other wrong acts which may injure or harm people in a way that may be considered imitable or acceptable.
- The advertising cannot use techniques such as free lotteries or quizzes to mislead the consumer and attract them to activities that might harm them.
- The advertising cannot represent minors as sexual objects.
- The advertisement must be free from terminology that does not correspond to the natural expression of children.
- The advertisement cannot appear immediately before or after a children's program.
- Commercial communications targeted to children should not suggest that a particular product is irreplaceable in a balanced diet or deter children from pursuing a healthy and balanced diet.
- Advertisements for food and beverages should not discourage children from pursuing a healthy and active lifestyle. (DW 1998)

Alcohol

There are a number of restrictions on the advertising of products containing alcohol, with some especially aimed at protecting minors. Key issues include:

- Commercials may not encourage, promote, or trivialize excessive alcohol consumption through such means as "all you can drink" offers or display a person who is obviously intoxicated in a way that gives the impression that such behavior is acceptable.
- Alcoholic drink advertising should not create any association between consumption and dangerous, violent, or aggressive behavior.
- Alcoholic beverage advertising should not disparage abstinence and should promote responsible consumption.
- Alcoholic beverage advertising should not show minors in the act of drinking or promote drinking by minors or appear in media whose audience consists primarily of minors.
- Alcohol-related ads should make no claims or representations to encourage drinking by minors or show persons claiming to have consumed alcoholic beverages as minors. Nor should they show figures wearing sports gear associated with teams comprised of minors.
- Athletes should not be shown drinking or promoting drinking.

- No advertising should show or in any way encourage consumers to drink alcohol and operate a vehicle or engage in any other unsafe activity.
- No alcohol advertisement should imply or claim any positive health effects or feature individuals who appear to be in health-care professions.
- Advertisements must neither boast of high alcohol content as a reason to purchase or low alcohol content as a factor that prevents alcohol abuse.
- No claims related to the relief of anxiety, the relaxation of inhibitions, improved physical performance or psycho-social conflicts, or improved social or sexual success are allowed.
- Any individual appearing in an alcohol-related commercial must clearly appear to be an adult. (DW 2009)

Originally intended primarily for media outlets, the provisions were extended in 2009 to include producers of alcoholic beverages and retailers.

Social Considerations

Advertising images and texts that violate human dignity or common decency are forbidden. This is the modern incarnation of the "morals" standard in early German advertising regulation, modified by the need to harmonize with EU regulations and directives.

Specifically forbidden are representations or claims that:

- it is appropriate to discriminate on the basis of gender, descent, race, language, place of origin, creed, political opinions, age, or appearance.
- include or condone violence. This prohibition includes the use of Nazi symbols in advertising content.
- any person or classes of people are "available for sale."
- conflict with prevailing basic standards, that reduce any person to a purely sexual function, or are pornographic in nature (e.g., excessive nudity). (DW 2004)

OVERVIEW AND LOOKING AHEAD

The German regulatory environment is extremely complex and in a state of flux. The issue of complexity stems from the governmental system, which allows each of the 14 media governance bodies representing the 16 federated states to make their own decisions about media and advertising policy. Although the ALM's primary goal is to harmonize policies across Germany, it has no power to enforce a consensus.

The second issue is related to the role of the European Union and its directives, either directly or through decisions of the EU courts. Germany has had, from the beginning of the twentieth century, an orientation toward tight regulation of advertising and media. That tendency was reinforced by the country's experiences with media control and propaganda, particularly during the Nazi era. The institutions that emerged since then have focused on maintaining editorial independence—both from a central government and from private influences, including advertisers. Harmonizing those tendencies and rules with EU directives based largely on the experiences of countries with different experiences has resulted in a significant reorientation of legal issues without resolving the core concerns of the German political and public constituencies about the need to ensure that social values are protected. How that will play out in the future is a matter of conjecture.

An example of this can be seen in the Germany versus EU conflict over tobacco advertising.

Although tobacco product advertising had been banned on broadcast media in Germany since 1975, Germany resisted a 2003 ruling that barred tobacco advertising in other venues because of concerns about the impact on kiosks, gas stations, and tobacco stores. Their concern was heightened by the fact that print media and the advertising industry were expected to lose up to 118 million euros if the ban was implemented. Ultimately, they accepted the ruling, but many more issues of a similar nature are likely to develop in the future.

A third issue involves the complexity and interdependence of the advertising regulatory structure. Key decisions about enforcement and some regulatory issues remain in the hands of the federated states. Although the Association of State Media Authorities for Broadcasting (ALM) is charged with harmonizing these policies, it is a difficult task, particularly when there are political shifts within the individual states that can lead to significant changes in interpretation and application of rules and penalties. Self-regulatory agencies, representing major segments of the advertising constituency, are in turn regulated by the Kommission für Jugendmedienschutz der Landesmedienanstalen (KJM), which has no other sanctioning power than public opinion. The Zentrale zur Bekämpfung unlauteren Wettbewerbs e. V. (WBZ) does have the authority to pursue violations of advertising standards in civil court but it cannot act unless a complaint has been filed.

It seems likely that significant differences in social experience and regulatory attitudes toward media and advertising issues between Germany and the EU representatives in Brussels are likely to produce turbulence and change in the future.

BIBLIOGRAPHY

Arbeitsgemeinschaft der Landesmedienanstalten [Association of State Media Authorities for Broadcasting] (ALM). 2010. Interstate Treaty on Broadcasting and Telemedia (Interstate Broadcasting Treaty) in the version of the 13th Amendment to the Interstate Broadcasting Treaties. April 1. http://www.kjm-online.de/files/pdf1/RStV_13_english.pdf (accessed June 7, 2010).
———. 2012a. "Commission for the Protection of Minors in the Media (KJM)." Die medienanstalten. http://www.die-medienanstalten.de/profile/organisation/commission-for-the-protection-of-minors-in-the-media-kjm.html (accessed June 7, 2010).
———. 2012b. "Organisation." Die medienanstalten. http://www.die-medienanstalten.de/profile/organisation.html (accessed June 7, 2010).
———. 2012c. "Tasks." Die medienanstalten. http://www.die-medienanstalten.de/profile/tasks.html (accessed June 7, 2010).
Bundesprüfstelle für jugendgefährdende Medien [Federal Department for Media Harmful to Young Persons] (BPjM). 2012. "General Information." http://www.bundespruefstelle.de/bpjm/information-in-english.html (accessed June 8, 2012).
Deutscher Werberat [German Advertising Standards Council] (DW). 1979. "Deutscher Werberat Rules of Procedure." September 24. http://www.werberat.de/sites/default/files/uploads/media/rules_of_procedure.pdf (accessed June 8, 2012).
———. 1998. "German Standards Advertising Council Rules of Conduct on Advertising with and for Children on Radio and Television." http://www.werberat.de/sites/default/files/uploads/media/dw_adv_with_and_for_children_en.pdf (accessed June 8, 2012).
———. 2004. "German Standards Advertising Council Code of Conduct on Personal Denigration and Discrimination." http://www.werberat.de/sites/default/files/uploads/media/dw_personal_denigration_en.pdf (accessed June 8, 2012).
———. 2007. "German Standards Advertising Council Rules on Advertising and Its Appraisal." October. http://www.werberat.de/sites/default/files/uploads/media/dw_general_principles_en.pdf (accessed June 8, 2012).
———. 2009. "German Standards Advertising Council Code of Conduct on Commercial Communication for Alcoholic Beverages." April. http://www.werberat.de/sites/default/files/uploads/media/dw_code_of_conduct_alcoholic_beverages_2009_en.pdf (accessed June 8, 2012).

———. 2012. "English Key Facts: German Advertising Standards Council." http://www.werberat.de/keyfacts (accessed June 8, 2012).

Dr. Schotthöfer & Steiner. 2012. *A "revolution" in German advertising laws?* http://www.schotthoefer.de/downloads/Revolution_in_german_advertising_law.pdf (accessed June 8, 2012).

European Commission (EC). 2012. "Regulation and Self-Regulation of Advertising Directed at Minors—Germany." http://ec.europa.eu/avpolicy/docs/library/studies/finalised/studpdf/tab_de.pdf (accessed June 8, 2012).

Federal Republic of Germany (FRG). 1991. Rundfunkstaatsvertrag [Interstate Broadcasting Agreement]. August 31 (incorporating the third amendment adopted between 26 August and 11 September 1996). http://www.iuscomp.org/gla/statutes/RuStaV.htm (accessed June 8, 2012).

Herold, Frank. 2012. "TV-Sender: Marktanteile in Deutschland 2011" [TV Stations: Market Share in Germany 2011]. Reichweite, January 3. http://archive.is/jKkw (accessed March 12, 2013).

Hitchens, Lesley. 2009. *International Regulation of Advertising, Sponsorship and Commercial Disclosure for Commercial Radio Broadcasting*. Research Report Prepared for the Australian Communications and Media Authority, June 15. University of Technology, Sydney.

Kommission für Jugendmedienschutz der Landesmedienanstalen [Commission for the Protection of Minors in the Media] (KJM). 2012. "Organisation." http://www.kjm-online.de/en/pub/the_kjm/organisation.cfm (accessed June 7, 2010).

The Library of Congress. 1995. *Germany: A Country Study*. Report, August. Washington, DC: The Library of Congress. http://lcweb2.loc.gov/frd/cs/detoc.html (accessed June 8, 2012).

Loitz, Kurt-Michael. 2012. "Evolution of New Advertising Techniques: Germany." Summary, June. http://ec.europa.eu/avpolicy/docs/library/studies/finalised/bird_bird/pub_de.pdf (accessed June 8, 2012).

Mann, Roger. 1999. "German Advertising Standards Under Pressure from Europe." *European Intellectual Property Review* 21, no. 10 (October): 519–521.

Petrenko, Maria A. 2000. "Alcohol Advertising in Germany: What Do You Need to Know Before Going Internationally." MA thesis, Michigan State University, East Lansing, MI, 2000.

Zentrale zur Bekämpfung unlauteren Wettbewerbs e. V. [Centre for Protection against Unfair Competition] (WBZ). 2012. "The Role of the Wettbewerbszentrale in the Enforcement System Against Unfair Commercial Practices in Germany." May. http://www.wettbewerbszentrale.de/de/englishinfo/ (accessed June 8, 2012).

PART V

THE PACIFIC RIM

CHAPTER 16

AUSTRALIA

GAYLE KERR

Australians are a little bit different, from the language they use to the way they live to the advertising they create. The "She'll be right" attitude, which optimistically implies that all will work out well, has seen Australia evolve from a penal settlement in the late 1700s to a modern free-thinking nation, which embodies values such as "mateship" and egalitarianism. These values are inherent in the way Australians govern their society and in the way they do business.

Australia is the sixth largest country in the world. It is about the same size as the 48 mainland United States. Despite this, it has a comparatively small population of about 23 million and one of the lowest population densities on the planet at 2.9 people per square kilometer (Australian Bureau of Statistics 2012a, 2012b; Australian Government 2012a, 2012b). Australia is part of the Asia Pacific region, but it has strong historical, legal, and cultural connections to the United Kingdom and the United States.

Rich in resources and a magnet for tourism, Australia earns a modest GNP and has fostered a vital and well-organized advertising industry. Although hit by the global financial crisis in 2009, which saw advertising expenditure contract by 8 percent to A$12.6 billion, the industry recovered well in 2010 with a predicted 5.3 percent growth in main media expenditure (Sinclair 2010). While most of this expenditure is still devoted to traditional media such as television and newspaper, the real growth is in the online sector. Growing by around 23 percent, it is expected to exceed A$2.2 billion in 2010, giving it an almost 20 percent share of total advertising revenue (Canning 2010). Most of this growth online is coming from search, video content creation, social networking, and IPTV. Nielsen's *2010 Social Media Report* (Nielsen 2010) suggests there were 9 million Australians (41 percent of the total population) on social networking sites in 2009. Most of these (78 percent) were sharing content or visiting profiles (73 percent). Activity on Twitter increased by 400 percent in 2009, and 92 percent of Australians over the age of 12 owned a mobile phone.

More than 6,000 people work in jobs in the top 150 advertising agencies (The Communications Council 2012). The infrastructure of the advertising industry is similar to that of many developed nations, with advertising agencies, advertisers, media, digital marketers, consultants, production houses, and government and self-regulatory bodies. The Australian advertising industry has produced the world's most highly awarded campaign in "The Best Job in the World," sponsored by Tourism Australia, as well as more controversial and more conventional iterations. In all of these cases, the advertising is regulated both by government and the advertising industry—and leveraged by empowered consumers.

THE REGULATORY FRAMEWORK IN AUSTRALIA

Successive federal governments in Australia have supported minimal government intervention in the market and the mechanism of self-regulation through codification of best practice. Henderson,

Coveney, Ward, and Taylor (2009) describe this as neoliberalism, "evident in the decentralization of responsibility for regulation, the codification of practice standards and individualization of responsibility" (p. 1408).

Self-regulation is also the advertising industry's system of choice. It is often seen as a preemptive strategy to avoid harsher government regulation in response to community pressure, and it is frequently defended using the ideals of "free enterprise" (Henderson et al. 2009).

To facilitate this structure of minimal government intervention supporting an active self-regulatory system, there are two independent statutory authorities responsible for regulation of media and compliance with laws of competition, fair trade, and consumer protection.

The first of these is the Australian Communications and Media Authority (ACMA), a statutory authority within the federal government portfolio of Broadband, Communications and the Digital Economy. Its mandate, as set out in the Australian Communications and Media Authority Act of 2005, includes the regulation of broadcasting, the Internet, radio communications, and telecommunications. It achieves this through broadcast license conditions set out in the Broadcasting Services Act of 1992 and industry codes of practice. In the area of television, the Commercial Television Industry Code of Practice covers issues such as the placement of advertisements, the amount of nonprogram material allowed per hour, the loudness of the advertisements, and the disclosure of any commercial agreements such as the endorsement of products in programs. Special provisions for the amount and content of advertisements directed toward children are outlined in the Children's Television Standards, while the amount of foreign-produced advertising is covered by the Television Program Standard for Australian Content in Advertising (TPS 23). Similarly, the Commercial Radio Australia Code of Practice covers provisions such as the content of advertisement and also addresses issues similar to the Australian Association of National Advertisers Code of Ethics such as violence, racial vilification, decency, and language.

A second independent statutory authority is the Australian Competition and Consumer Commission (ACCC). It was formed in 1995 to administer the Trade Practices Act of 1974 (renamed the Competition and Consumer Act of 2010 on January 1, 2011) and other acts and to promote competition and fair trade. A strong advocate for consumer rights, the ACCC is primarily concerned with ensuring that individuals and businesses comply with the commonwealth's competition, fair trading, and consumer protection laws.

In addition to these legal requirements, specialist industries have their own codes of ethics, which are managed by individual industry groups, including the Therapeutic Goods Code (TGC), the Alcoholic Beverages Advertising Code, and the Weight Management Industry Code. All other advertising is self-regulated by the advertising industry through the Advertiser Code of Ethics and the Advertising Standards Bureau (ASB 2010a). This system of self-regulation has changed from a tripartite system involving media, agencies, and advertisers to the current advertiser-driven model.

1974–1996: A TRIPARTITE SYSTEM OF SELF-REGULATION

When the Media Council of Australia (MCA) was formed as an incorporated voluntary association of mainstream media in 1967, its agenda was twofold: First, it sought to establish a media accreditation system for advertising agencies. Second, the MCA developed a system of advertising self-regulation (Harker 2004, p. 70). For 22 years, from 1974 to 1996, the MCA Advertising Code set the guidelines for self-regulation in Australia. This code was monitored, evaluated, and enforced by the Advertising Standards Council (ASC 1996). This "strictly independent and autonomous" complaint-handling system had the tripartite support of the media (Media Council of Australia), the agencies (Advertising Federation of Australia), and the advertisers (Australian Association of National Advertisers) (ASC 1993).

Self-regulation, under this system, was a simple and effective process. Those offended by advertising complained in writing to the Advertising Standards Council. If the board upheld the complaint, the MCA directed its member agency to remove the offending advertisement from the media and the public domain. The ASC handled between 1,000 and 1,300 individual complaints per year, with an average turnaround time of 20.9 days. In doing so, its rulings were rarely controversial. The executive director of the ASC, Colin Harcourt (quoted in Kerr and Moran 2002, p. 191) said: "The system, including the ASC, whilst not without its critics, was regarded as a world model of self-regulation. In fact, the systems in place in New Zealand, Singapore, India, South Africa and even the UK and Canada, include many components adapted from Australia."

By the mid-1990s, the Australian Association of National Advertisers (AANA) had shifted its position from supporter of the self-regulation system to its fiercest critic. It opposed the system of media accreditation and the payment by the media of commissions to advertising agencies—considering the practice anticompetitive. (The AANA contended that the cost of the commissions was borne by advertisers in the inflated price of the media.) The AANA sought to weaken the codes by challenging the charter of the board and consistently opposing its funding.

The AANA found support in its quest for control of the self-regulation process from the government body responsible for competition matters and Trade Practices Act compliance. The Trade Practices Tribunal (TPT), which became the Australian Competition and Consumer Commission (ACCC) in 1995, joined the AANA in its criticism of the self-regulatory system. The ACCC chair, Professor Allan Fels, suggested that the self-regulatory system had outlived its mandate, charging it with a lack of compliance, inadequate administrative control, and dwindling confidence and commitment. He branded the codes as outdated and unresponsive to changes in community needs; on August 19, 1996, the ACCC served notice of a review of authorization of advertising codes (ACCC 1996a).

This review led to the decision to revoke the authorization of the agency accreditation system, one of the initial drivers for establishing the MCA. Despite the argument of the Media Council and the advertising agencies led by the AFA that the loss of accreditation would substantially weaken the codes and their enforcement, the ACCC considered the benefit to the public was insufficient to outweigh the anticompetitive process (ACCC 1996b). As a result, the MCA announced it would disband the Advertising Standards Council and the self-regulatory process by the end of 1996. In his final report, ASC chair Paul Toose (ASC 1996, 8) responded: "To this day, no real evidence has ever been provided by anybody including the TPT (now ACCC) to show that the accreditation system and the Advertising Codes were truly anticompetitive in their effect, in alone causing or likely to cause a substantial lessening of competition as contemplated by Section 45 of the Trade Practices Act."

1998–PRESENT: THE ADVERTISER-DRIVEN SYSTEM

The Australian Association of National Advertisers (AANA), the most vocal critic of the old system, became the architect of the new system. AANA's Robert Koltai stated, "I think it's time advertisers stepped up to the plate and managed this part of their affairs. After all, it's their advertisements" (Burrett 1998). While the AANA saw the control of the self-regulatory process as its mandate, others construed this as evidence of their vested interest in the control and regulation of the advertising process (Kerr and Moran 2002).

The Self-Regulatory Process

The current system of self-regulation in Australia became operational in 1998. Responding to research conducted in consultation with industry, government, and consumers, and filling the remit of the Australian Parliament, the AANA introduced an independent complaint resolution process (ASB 1999).

As shown in Figure 16.1, complaints about offensive advertising can be made to the Advertising Standards Bureau by members of the general public or competitors. These are measured against the AANA-authored Advertiser Code of Ethics and a deliberation made by the Advertising Standards Board (ASB) to uphold or dismiss the complaint.

If the complaint is upheld, the advertiser is asked to modify or withdraw the offending advertisement. It is here that the current system differs from its predecessor. While the Media Council of Australia, authorized by the Trade Practices Tribunal and subsequently the ACCC, could ask its members (the media) to remove the offending advertisement, the current system has no enforcement mechanism. Upon finding an unfavorable determination, the ASB prepares a case report to the advertiser, who has five business days to respond. The advertiser must advise the board of its intention to modify or discontinue the advertising. If the advertiser decides to disregard the ASB recommendations, the board has no other recourse. To date, most advertisers have complied with the ruling of the ASB, although some have taken as long as 11 days to withdraw their advertising.

> Only one advertiser, Windsor Smith Shoes, has refused to comply and remove a sexist billboard advertisement. The offending advertisement is perhaps best described by one of the complainants, "The woman is barely clothed, dressed provocatively with legs apart and her face in line with the man's genitals. In contrast, the man is fully clothed, holding her face. It suggests the woman is "servicing" the man in a sexually exploitative way." (ASB 2000) Despite the soft-pornographic nature of the advertisement, the advertiser responded: "Windsor Smith have decided to stand by their belief that the billboard campaign that started from March 1 is not inappropriate and to leave the billboards up. Although we hold a high respect for the Board, we feel that in this case that the Board has made a bad judgement and used Windsor Smith as an example as a result of complaints we feel is from a minority." (ASB 2000)

The ASB could do nothing further within its prescribed powers and process. However, the media decided to enforce the ruling of the ASB and removed the offending billboards. It is important to note that when the new system failed, the enforcement mechanism of the previous system was enacted. Dann and Dann (2001, p. 3) argue that the media's "actions reestablished the balance of self-regulation without resorting to heavy-handed prosecutions, new legislation or any other form of government intervention," and therefore the integrity of the Australian self-regulation system was restored. This is perhaps an optimistic assessment, as others had described the current system as a "toothless tiger" (*AdNews* 2008, p. 6) because it lacks an enforcement mechanism. It has also been suggested that this incidence demonstrates the need for the tripartite support of the media, agencies, and advertisers in the self-regulation process.

However, it is equally possible that the strong compliance with the system by advertisers is an artifact of their control of the code. Members of the Australian Association of National Advertisers, which includes all major advertisers in Australia, may feel obligated to support a system developed and administered by advertisers. Noncompliance is more likely to come from smaller advertisers who are not AANA members, such as Windsor Smith.

Figure 16.1

Australian System of Self-Regulation

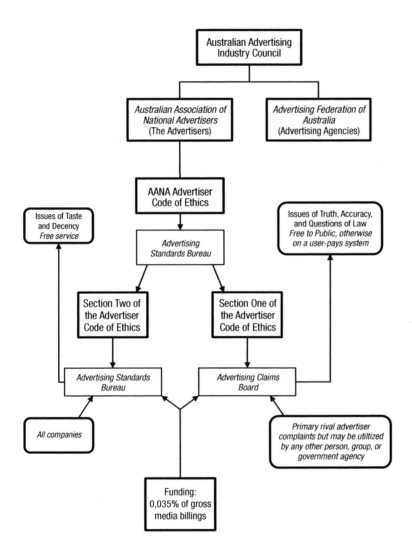

Source: Volkov, Harker, and Harker 2005, 300.

At the end of 2010, the Advertising Standards Bureau Chief Executive Officer, Ms. Fiona Jolly, reported, "This year, as in previous years, all advertisers have complied with Advertising Standards Board decisions. I applaud advertisers for [their] consistent support of the system" (ASB 2010c).

Structure of the Boards

The duality of complaints (from consumers and from competitors) created the need for a structure with two boards—the Advertising Claims Board and the Advertising Standards Board. The Advertising Claims Board (ACB) adjudicates on complaints between competitors on a user-pays basis. It deliberates on matters of truth, accuracy, and questions of law as contained in Section 1 of the Advertiser Code of Ethics (ASB 2010a).

The second section of the Advertiser Code of Ethics deals with the larger number of complaints, which come from the general public. This is handled by the Advertising Standards Board (ASB), which deliberates—on a cost-free basis—on issues of health and safety, the use of language, the discriminatory portrayal of people, the protection of children, and portrayals of violence, sex, sexuality, and nudity (ASB 2010a).

The initial aim of the current system of self-regulation was to make the ASB completely independent from the advertising industry and more representative of the general public to address the criticisms of the previous system (Kerr and Moran 2002). However, many board members rely upon the media for their living (ASB 2010a). They are journalists, actors, filmmakers or reviewers, marketing communication consultants, and former politicians. In addition, there are many advocates for the rights of children and women and antidiscrimination campaigners. While they represent a diversity of opinions and ideals, there is still a substantial social and economic divide between the board and the general public, who are the primary complainants of advertising. This is a common criticism of many self-regulation systems and an issue discussed at length by Boddewyn (1988).

Harker (2003) makes the point that board members may need two types of expertise: "First, communication expertise to understand the message received by consumers and, second, product specific expertise to determine if the message is accurate or not. Whilst ASR complaint determination committees have traditionally comprised the 'great and the good' (Boddewyn 1983, p. 83), it might be more useful to select members with this dual expertise instead" (p. 71).

Others propose an equal number of board members drawn from industry and the public or representatives from government and consumer organizations (Moyer and Banks 1977; La Barbera 1980). Current board members include representatives from all of these groups. However it is unclear as to whether this makes their views more representative of the general public, or better equipped to understand the effects of advertising.

The ASB meets twice a month, and the position of chairperson is rotated on a meeting-to-meeting basis to guarantee greater flexibility and equality among members (ASB 2010a). The operations of the board are monitored by a board of directors, which is made up of between three and six members and currently includes advertisers, market researchers, and agency and media representatives.

All ASB decisions are publicly available as case reports within 10 business days of deliberation, via the website. The boards are industry funded and administered by the AANA. The boards make deliberations on the Code of Ethics, which is detailed in the next section.

Advertiser Code of Ethics

The AANA Advertiser Code of Ethics is shown in Figure 16.2. The AANA states: "The object of this Code is to ensure that advertisements are legal, decent, honest, and truthful and that they have been prepared with a sense of obligation to the consumer and society and fair sense of responsibility to competitors" (AANA 2010).

Figure 16.2

AANA Advertiser Code of Ethics

1.   Section 1: Competitor Complaints
1.1   Advertising or Marketing Communications shall comply with Commonwealth law and the law of the relevant State or Territory.
1.2   Advertising or Marketing Communications shall not be misleading or deceptive or be likely to mislead or deceive.
1.3   Advertising or Marketing Communications shall not contain a misrepresentation, which is likely to cause damage to the business or goodwill of a competitor.
1.4   Advertising or Marketing Communications shall not exploit community concerns in relation to protecting the environment by presenting or portraying distinctions in products or services advertised in a misleading way or in a way which implies a benefit to the environment which the product or services do not have.
1.5   Advertising or Marketing Communications shall not make claims about the Australian origin or content of products advertised in a manner which is misleading.

2.   Section 2: Consumer Complaints
2.1   Advertising or Marketing Communications shall not portray people or depict material in a way which discriminates against or vilifies a person or section of the community on account of race, ethnicity, nationality, gender, age, sexual preference, religion, disability, mental illness or political belief.
2.2   Advertising or Marketing communications should not employ sexual appeal in a manner which is exploitative and degrading of any individual or group of people.
2.3   Advertising or Marketing Communications shall not present or portray violence unless it is justifiable in the context of the product or service advertised.
2.4   Advertising or Marketing Communications shall treat sex, sexuality and nudity with sensitivity to the relevant audience.
2.5   Advertising or Marketing Communications shall only use language which is appropriate in the circumstances (including appropriate for the relevant audience and medium). Strong or obscene language shall be avoided.
2.6   Advertising or Marketing Communications shall not depict material contrary to Prevailing Community Standards on health and safety.

3.   Section 3: Other Codes
3.1   Advertising or Marketing Communications to Children shall comply with the AANA's Code of Advertising & Marketing Communications to Children and section 2.6 of this Code shall not apply to advertisements to which AANA's Code of Advertising & Marketing Communications to Children applies.
3.2   Advertising or Marketing Communications for motor vehicles shall comply with the Federal Chamber of Automotive Industries Code of Practice relating to Advertising for Motor Vehicles.
3.3   Advertising or Marketing Communications for food or beverage products shall comply with the AANA Food & Beverages Advertising & Marketing Communications Code as well as to the provisions of this Code.

Source: AANA 2012.

As mentioned earlier, there are two sections to this code. The first one relates to competitive communications and the second to issues such as discrimination and vilification; sex, sexuality, and nudity; the portrayal of violence; the protection of children; the use of language; and health and safety. While this appears to be a long list, perhaps the best way to evaluate the scope and content of the code is to compare it with an international benchmark.

The International Chamber of Commerce (ICC 2011), the world business organization, provides a comprehensive international benchmark as a code of self-regulation. The Advertising and

Table 16.1

Outcome of Complaints by Number of Complaint, 1998–2009

	1998	1999	2000	2001	2002	2003	2004	2005	2006	2007	2008	2009
Dismissed	927	1553	1971	1291	1191	1770	1349	1753	2648	1730	2263	2278
Upheld	73	111	162	47	11	23	55	94	164	280	477	521
Withdrawn	0	0	0	0	16	113	236	139	20	15	57	56
Outside charter	382	401	425	367	354	714	656	970	1212	577	799	941
Total	1382	2065	2558	1705	1572	2620	2296	2956	4044	2602	3596	3796

Source: ASB 2010b.

Marketing Communication Consolidated ICC Code (2011) contains 26 articles that cover basic principles such as legality, truthfulness, taste, and decency. It encompasses the spirit of fair competition and the mandate of social and professional responsibility. The ICC code is broader and deeper than its Australian counterpart and covers many new issues such as environmental claims and data protection and privacy issues. There is also evidence that the current Australian code is less comprehensive than its predecessor (Kerr and Moran 2002).

In its favor, the AANA Advertiser Code of Ethics has evolved with the dynamic marketing communication industry, addressing the growing concerns of the community and the threat of government advertising bans. This has been reflected in a number of investigations and the formulation of special codes of practice. For example, the original self-regulatory code, the Advertiser Code of Ethics, has been supplemented by the AANA Code of Advertising and Marketing Communications to Children (2008) and AANA Food and Beverages Advertising and Marketing Communications Code (2008). Both new codes represent a major initiative by the Australian advertisers. Australia was the first country in the world to respond to the challenges of obesity through the implementation of the Food and Beverages Code in 2008 (Stuart and Kerr 2009). It appears that, although the current Advertiser Code of Ethics is not as comprehensive as either its predecessor or the international benchmark, it has been strengthened in areas of community concern—such as advertising to children and the advertisement of junk foods—through community consultation with lobby groups and other organizations.

Nature of Complaints

As well as adjudicating on complaints, the Advertising Standards Board (ASB) tracks the number and nature of advertising complaints and publishes annual reports. Table 16.1 shows the outcome of these complaints since the inception of the ASB in 1998. It is important to note that the number of complaints has increased more than 2.5 times since then. In 1998, 67 percent of complaints were dismissed and 5.3 percent upheld. This compares with the most recent 2009 figures, which show a similar dismissal rate (60 percent), but the upheld rate has more than doubled (13.7 percent). This is comparable to the data from the last year of the previous system (1997), where 12 percent of complaints were upheld and 84 percent dismissed. In 2010, more than 520 advertisements attracted complaint, and over 40 of these were determined by the board to have breached the AANA Code of Ethics or other codes administered by the ASB (ASB 2010c).

Table 16.2

Percentage of Complaints by Issue, 2005–2009

Section		2005	2006	2007	2008	2009
2.3	Sex, sexuality, nudity	26.49	22.23	37.91	25.61	40.54
2.1	Discrimination or vilification	27.13	23.25	28.05	22.76	16.31
2.2	Violence	17.38	18.01	8.42	17.67	7.93
Other		14.59	14.69	4.86	15.84	17.04
2.5	Language	4.36	7.55	1.68	7.24	5.35
2.6	Health and safety	6.46	9.70	10.85	6.04	8.38
2.7	FCAI code	3.38	1.84	4.91	3.09	1.19
2.4	Advertising to children code	0.20	2.73	2.95	0.49	0.63

Source: ASB 2010b.

Table 16.3

Media Attracting Complaint, 1998–2009

	1998	1999	2000	2001	2002	2003	2004	2005	2006	2007	2008	2009
TV	84.10	71.7	71.9	66.4	58.2	80.6	85.3	84.8	85.8	75.1	68.6	59.8
Outdoor	1.90	11.7	18.7	14.0	29.8	9.2	6.3	6.7	3.7	12.8	16.5	23.9
Radio	2.00	3.6	1.2	1.4	2.1	1.7	1.7	2.1	4.1	2.4	2.8	3.1
Print	10.70	11.8	7.4	13.6	8.8	4.5	5.5	4.8	3.9	4.1	4.7	1.9
Pay TV	0.0	0.0	0.1	0.0	0.2	0.0	0.0	0.3	0.2	0.4	1.5	5.6
Internet	0.0	0.0	0.0	0.0	0.0	0.0	0.0	0.0	0.3	1.1	1.1	2.6
Transit	0.0	0.0	0.0	0.1	0.4	0.6	0.6	0.5	1.7	1.6	3.6	2.5
Cinema	0.6	1.20	0.3	0.4	0.2	0.4	0.5	0.6	0.4	2.5	0.8	0.1
Mail	0.0	0.0	0.0	0.0	0.0	0.0	0.0	0.0	0.0	0.0	0.0	0.3
Other	0.7	0.0	0.0	0.0	0.0	0.0	0.0	0.0	0.0	0.0	0.4	0.2
Multiple	0.0	0.0	0.5	4.2	0.4	3.0	0.1	0.4	0.0	0.0	0.0	0.0

Source: ASB 2010b.

ASB CEO Jolly commented: "Through its complaints, the community has again shown its concerns about sex, sexuality, and nudity content of advertising. The Ad Standards Board found that three of the 10 most complained about ads breached the AANA Code of Ethics, and advertisers have now withdrawn those ads from use. Seven of the ads in this year's list relate to concerns about section 2.3 of the AANA Code of Ethics (sex, sexuality, and nudity) and include the three ads which the Board determined breached the Code" (ASB 2010c).

Table 16.4

Percentage of Complaints by Product Category, 2005–2009

	2005	2006	2007	2008	2009
Food and beverage	20.9	28.1	33.3	14.4	24.1
Clothing	6.2	4.3	2.2	5.8	7.7
Household goods/services	11.2	2.2	6.0	7.6	6.7
Community awareness	8.0	12.3	3.4	9.3	6.0
Vehicles	15.2	8.4	9.9	5.3	5.2
Professional services	2.6	5.6	10.8	5.1	4.9
Entertainment	0.0	2.9	3.1	3.3	4.4
Sex industry	0.0	0.0	0.0	0.4	4.4
Health products	3.5	8.0	1.4	1.5	4.0
Alcohol	7.1	3.1	2.4	6.4	3.5

Source: ASB 2010b.

Table 16.2 shows the most complained about issues across time. As in 2010, sex, sexuality, and nudity topped the list, followed closely by complaints of discrimination or vilification.

Television is the medium most likely to be the magnet for complaint (see Table 16.3). This is largely because of its pervasiveness in terms of its universal appeal and its accessibility by people of all ages. Outdoor likewise attracts complaints for its huge, colorful, and sometimes unavoidable canvas on public display. In 2010, for example, half of the top ten most complained about advertisements were television advertisements, four were on billboards, and one was an Internet advertisement (ASB 2010c). Surprisingly, the Internet has attracted few complaints, despite its lack of regulation globally.

Food and beverages (excluding alcohol) have been the most consistently complained about products over the last five years. In Table 16.4, we see that that category has attracted twice and sometimes three times as many complaints as any other. Yet what we might consider to be more controversial product categories, such as alcohol or the sex industry or health products, attract relatively few complaints.

Nature of the Complainant

The records of the ASB from 1998 to 2009 describe the typical complainant as female (60 percent), most likely 30 to 54 years of age (52 percent) and living in New South Wales or Victoria. Email is the favorite medium of complaint, growing from 10 percent in 2001 to 85 percent in 2009.

A more extensive study of complaint behavior was conducted by Volkov, Harker, and Harker (2005), who profiled 1,210 ASB complainants using the MOSAIC software program. They concluded that those who complain to the self-regulatory board are much more likely to be highly educated, earn a higher income, and work in a professional occupation. Typical complainants are older and female, while noncomplainants are younger, lower-income, or possibly unemployed.

According to the researchers, "The implication is that those more disadvantaged consumers may lack a voice in this complaint process" (Volkov, Harker, and Harker 2005, p. 308).

INTO THE FUTURE: A SELF-REGULATION SYSTEM BUFFETED BY OTHER FORCES

The current system of self-regulation, like many of its international counterparts, was designed as a closed system. That is, the self-regulation board enforces a code of ethics and holds the power to uphold or dismiss complaints, removing the offending advertisement from the public domain and protecting society from misleading and deceptive advertising.

New Media Changes the Balance of Power

The power to remove offensive advertising no longer rests with regulators alone. The online environment provides a platform to share links and opinions and even offensive advertising. Video-sharing sites such as YouTube allow consumers to post and share advertising material. Some of this material may have been deemed offensive by self-regulation boards, or may be so culturally different as to be unpalatable, or may contain adult themes inappropriate for an underage audience. Yet in this new media environment, consumers have become the de facto regulators, with the power to make judgments about advertising to a global audience or to make offensive advertising universally available.

Advertisers can also share in this power and regulate the distribution of advertising. Many create purpose-built websites with the intention of promoting their goods or services as widely and indiscriminately as possible. A recent example of this is Tourism Australia's "Where the Bloody Hell Are You?" campaign (Tourism Australia 2006). This 30-second television commercial contained offensive language, a religious reference, a half-full glass of beer, and a girl in a bikini. Complaints were received by self-regulatory bodies in five countries, and the television commercial was banned in the UK (for 10 days) and modified in Canada, and the offensive language was removed in four Asian countries (Japan, Korea, Thailand, and Singapore). Over 70,000 hits were recorded on the memorable, purpose-built wherethebloodyhellareyou.com website on the day the television advertisement was banned. Kerr, Mortimer, Dickinson, and Waller (2012), who researched the case, concluded that the traditional process of self-regulation was being circumvented, as bloggers discussed and distributed banned advertising online. This suggests that bloggers may be an alternative and exponentially powerful group of complainants in the self-regulation process. It also highlights the fact that the good work of self-regulation boards in protecting the public interest may be undone with a single upload.

Well-Funded and Organized Lobby Groups

Community concern for advertising regulation is often voiced through lobby groups. While one might think a lobby group such as the Parents' Jury is made up of parents, this international network is funded by VicHealth, Diabetes Australia, the Cancer Council, and the Australian Society for Study of Obesity. In fact, most of the groups lobbying for restrictions on advertising are government funded, and many have an anti-advertising agenda, tracing their lineage to the fight against all forms of tobacco marketing in Australia (*AdNews* 2008). For example, Cancer Council Australia and Cancer Council of NSW are the most active fund-raisers and campaigners against food advertising, defending their involvement on the premise that obesity can contribute to cancer.

The Cancer Council provides funding to the Coalition on Food Advertising to Children, Young Media Australia, and the Parents' Jury, with all lobby groups joining in the Cancer Council NSW marketing campaign to "Pull the Plug" on children's television advertising.

Former Executive Director of AANA, Collin Segelov, observed: "Australia is also being seen as something of a test case for other places in the world, where similar accusations are being leveled and a change in government might initiate a similar reexamination around the regulation of the industry. While we have to recognise that community standards are never static, and as an industry we have to respond, government regulation doesn't work for us, the economy, or, ultimately, the changes some of the activist groups seek" (*AdNews* 2008, p. 6).

The AANA has formed a coalition of marketing, advertising, and media groups called Marketing and Media Industry Forum to engage and debate lobby groups. This has led to an inclusive review of the codes on children's advertising and advertisements for food and beverages. However, following the release of the Advertising to Children Code, Elizabeth Handsley of Young Media Australia described the code as a "toothless tiger" (*AdNews* 2008, p. 6). This was despite consultation with this lobby group during the process, including the introduction of specific standards at its request. "It is greatly frustrating that some of the lobby groups do not display the same ethical standards that they demand of us," stated Segelov. "In some cases, we are dealing with people who simply don't like advertising of any sort and there is little room for compromise" (*AdNews* 2008, p. 6).

Globalization

Another issue for advertising self-regulation is the impact of globalization. This concern was raised at the American Academy of Advertising Conference in Milan in 2010. In a special session entitled "Sleeping Beauty: Global Advertising Self-Regulation Awakens," Kerr, Avery, and Zabkar (2010) posed the following questions, "Is it still possible to target advertising for a local context? How do we manage the risk when advertising is seen by audiences for which it was never intended? What responsibility do consumers have as distributors of advertising? Who is the guardian of this process?"

These are important and urgent questions. Advertising campaigns have in many cases become global, and the appropriateness of the creative idea to transcend cultures and geographic boundaries must be considered. However, of perhaps more concern is the fact that advertising is reaching audiences for which it was never intended via video-sharing sites. An example of this was the KFC cricket campaign for the West Indies tour of Australia in 2010 (Kerr 2010). KFC, a sponsor of Australian cricket, developed a television advertisement called "Cricket Survival Guide," in which a fan named Mick is the only Australian supporter in a sea of cheering West Indies fans. He says, "Need a tip when you're stuck in an awkward situation?" His answer is to share a bucket of KFC with those around him.

The ad was not perceived as racist in Australia and received no complaints to the Advertising Standards Board, until a user called Thundercurls posted "Racist KFC Ad" on a video-sharing website. Drawing on U.S. stereotypes and seeing the crowd as "black" rather than West Indian, he lamented, "How do you survive a crowd of 'awkward' black people? According to KFC's latest advertisement, a bucket of fried chicken will do the trick." The post attracted 200,000 views, 2,900 comments, and international media attention (Kerr 2010).

KFC released a statement in response stating that the ad had been "misinterpreted by a segment of people in the U.S. It is a light-hearted reference to the West Indian cricket team. The ad was reproduced online without KFC's permission, where we are told a culturally-based stereotype exists, leading to the incorrect assertion of racism. We unequivocally condemn discrimination of any type and have a proud history as one of the world's leading employers for diversity" (Anonymous 2010).

There are many challenges for advertising self-regulation within Australia and into the future. Kerr, Mortimer, Dickinson, and Waller (2012) provide an excellent summation: "There is no doubt that the advertising environment has changed, and with it, the process of self-regulation has been irrevocably altered. New media has increased the power of the general public by providing them with a worldwide unregulated form of communication and information transfer. In such an environment, one could argue that the impact of any traditional self-regulatory controls have the opposite effect, that is, the banning of an advertisement leads to an expansion in exposure and distribution. As long as these advertisements are being consumed by people who chose to consume them, and removed from the view of people who do not, then perhaps the self-regulatory system is still operating effectively and fulfilling its remit. However, if the advertisement is creating offense, such as degrading women or depicting racist images, then its distribution is of concern from a societal viewpoint."

Just as the advertising codes must evolve in accordance with community standards, we must also continually redefine the scope and the responsibilities of the self-regulation system in Australia. The process up until now has almost exclusively focused on the content and the execution of the message, and its impact within a defined geographical location. A more enlightened system must also look at the new channels, the new power of consumers as media distributors and regulators, and the global nature of the communication.

CONCLUSIONS

In conclusion, many underlying factors have shaped Australia's advertising self-regulation system. These include a robust legal system from our British heritage; an understanding and easy adoption of many aspects of U.S. business and culture; and even our geography as a large, under-populated island in the Asia-Pacific region. These factors have defined a sense of national identity and business practice that believes in egalitarianism, opportunity, and a fair go for all. As such, Australians demand a system of advertising self-regulation that protects every stakeholder's basic rights, encourages best practice and continual reinvention by advertisers and their agencies, and requires minimal government intervention. Our trust in business, government, and the rights and voice of consumers assures us that when it comes to advertising self-regulation, "She'll be right."

BIBLIOGRAPHY

Advertising Standards Board (ASB). 1999. Annual Report. Sydney, Australia.
———. 2000. Case Reports of the Advertising Standards Board. Sydney, Australia.
Advertising Standards Bureau (ASB). 2010a. "Ad Standards." Retrieved from www.adstandards.com.au.
———. 2010b. "Complaint Statistics 2009." Table. http://www.adstandards.com.au/storage/55eb81b8b615 d57e0ab73ce5b2f33ed8.Stats2009Graphs%20-%20finalx.pdf.
———. 2010c. "Most complained about ads for 2010." Media release, December 14. http://post.cre8ive. com.au/t/ViewEmail/r/CCB9053E36AFD998/C67FD2F38AC4859C/.
Advertising Standards Council (ASC). 1993. "About the ASC." July. Sydney, Australia: ASC.
———. 1996. "Twentieth Report." Sydney, Australia: ASC.
AdNews. 2008. "Advertising under siege." AdNews, May 16, 6.
Anonymous. 2010. January 8. http://adland.tv/content/kfc-australia-pulls-cricket-survival-guide-ad-after-us-viewers-finds-it-racist.
Australian Association of National Advertisers (AANA). 2010. "Regulatory Review." http://www.aana.com. au/pages/regulatory-overview.html.

———. 2012. "AANA Code of Ethics." January 1. http://www.aana.com.au/data/Documents/Codes/AANACodeofEthics_1Jan2012.pdf.

Australian Bureau of Statistics. 2012a. "Geographic Distribution of the Population." In *1301.0 Year Book Australia, 2012*. May 24. http://www.abs.gov.au/ausstats/abs@.nsf/Lookup/by%20Subject/1301.0~2012~Main%20Features~Geographic%20distribution%20of%20the%20population~49.

———. 2012b. "Population Size and Growth." In *1301.0 Year Book Australia, 2012*. May 24. http://www.abs.gov.au/ausstats/abs@.nsf/Lookup/by%20Subject/1301.0~2012~Main%20Features~Population%20size%20and%20growth~47.

Australian Competition and Consumer Commission (ACCC). 1996a. "ACCC announces review of advertising standards." Media Release (MR) 116/96, August 19. http://www.accc.gov.au/content/index.phtml/itemId/86835/fromItemId/378002.

———. 1996b. "ACCC welcomes tribunal upholding media council decision." Media Release (MR) 102/96, July 26. http://www.accc.gov.au/content/index.phtml/itemId/86848/fromItemId/378002.

Australian Government. 2012a. "About Australia." http://australia.gov.au/about-australia/our-country.

———. 2012b. "Australia's Size Compared." http://www.ga.gov.au/education/geoscience-basics/dimensions/australias-size-compared.html.

Boddewyn, Jean. 1983. "Outside Participation in Advertising Self-regulation: The Case of the Advertising Standards Authority (UK)." *Journal of Consumer Policy*, 6(1), 77–93.

———. 1988. *Advertising Self-Regulation and Outside Participation: A Multinational Comparison*. Westport, CT: Quorum Books.

Burrett, Tony. 1998. "AANA enters new era." *B&T Weekly*, June 5, 17.

Canning, Simon. 2010. "Online advertising spending stagnant." *The Australian*, May 10.

The Communications Council. 2012. "Information on an Advertising Career." Careers in Advertising. http://www.communicationscouncil.org.au/public/content/ViewCategory.aspx?id=525.

The Daily Telegraph. 2010. "KFC Australia's West Indies cricket advertisement called racist in the US." *The Daily Telegraph*, January 7. http://www.dailytelegraph.com.au/news/kfc-australias-west-indies-cricket-advertisement-called-racist-in-the-us/story-e6freuy9-1225816779180.

Dann, Susan, and Stephen Dann. 2001. *ANZ Supplement to Accompany Advertising and Promotion: An Integrated Marketing Communications Perspective*. Sydney: McGraw-Hill.

Harker, D. 2003. "The importance of industry compliance in improving advertising self-regulatory processes." *Journal of Public Affairs*, 3(1), 63–75.

———. 2004. "Educating to improve the effectiveness of advertising self-regulatory schemes: The case of Australia." *Journal of Current Issues and Research in Advertising*, 26(1), 69–84.

Henderson, J., J. Coveney, P. Ward, and A. Taylor. 2009. "Governing childhood obesity: Framing regulation of fast food advertising in the Australian print media." *Social Science and Medicine*, 69(9), 1402–1408.

International Chamber of Commerce (ICC). 2011. *Advertising and Marketing Communication Practice Consolidated ICC Code*. http://www.icc.se/reklam/english/consolidated_icc_code_2011.pdf.

Kelly, Tony. 1998. "11 days to pull ad." *B&T Weekly*, June 19, 1 & 4.

Kerr, G. 2010. "Controversial advertising: Is it ever black or white?" Case Material AMN421. Brisbane, Australia: Queensland University of Technology.

Kerr, G., and C. Moran. 2002. "Any Complaints? A Review of the Framework of Self-Regulation in the Australian Advertising Industry." *Journal of Marketing Communications*, 8(3), 189–202.

Kerr, G., J. Avery, and V. Zabkar. 2010. "Sleeping Beauty: Global Advertising Self-Regulation Awakens." Special Session, Proceedings of American Academy of Advertising European Conference. Milan, Italy.

Kerr, Gayle, Kathleen Mortimer, Sonia Dickinson, and David S. Waller. 2012. "Buy, Boycott or Blog: Exploring online consumer power to share, discuss, and distribute controversial advertising messages." *European Journal of Marketing*, 46(3/4), 387–405.

La Barbera, P. 1980. "Analyzing and advancing the state of the art of advertising self-regulation." *Journal of Advertising*, 9(4), 27–38.

Moyer, M., and J. Banks. 1977. "Industry self-regulation: Some lessons from the Canadian advertising industry." In *Problems in Canadian Marketing*, ed. D. Thompson, 185–202. Chicago, IL: American Marketing Association.

Nielsen. 2010. *Nielsen 2010 Social Media Report*. http://www.nielsen-online.com (accessed April 14, 2010).

Sinclair, L. 2010. "Advertisers turn on to television again." *The Australian*, March 29. http://www.theaustralian.com.au/media/advertisers-turn-on-to-television-again/story-e6frg996-1225846632701.

Stuart, H., and G. Kerr. 2009. "Marketing to Children: The Premium Effect." Proceedings of the Australia and New Zealand Marketing Academy Conference. Sydney, Australia.

Tourism Australia. 2006. *Annual Report 2005/2006*. Report, September 29. http://www.tourism.australia.com/en-au/downloads/TA_AnnualReport_2005.pdf.

Volkov, M., D. Harker, and M. Harker. 2005. "Who's complaining? Using MOSAIC to identify the profile of complainants." *Marketing Intelligence and Planning,* 23(3), 296–312.

CHAPTER 17

THE PEOPLE'S REPUBLIC OF CHINA

LIU JING

HISTORY OF CHINA'S ADVERTISING REGULATIONS

Prior to 1949, China's advertising regulation system was mainly the self-restraint of the newspaper advertising industry. The emergence of advertising regulation was closely related to modern commercial newspaper ads and the arrival of somewhat deceptive, immoral advertisements. Thus, many newspapers began to formulate self-regulatory provisions. In May 1920, the National Federation of the Press adopted a regulation to ban all kinds of unacceptable ads. In 1927, six advertising agencies in Shanghai set up the China Advertising Association, the first advertising industry guild organization: It aimed to protect common interests, to resolve disputes between agencies, and to facilitate contact with newspapers. During the 1930s, some media simply enacted self-regulatory provisions, banning ads that were thought to damage the reputation of others, or were deceptive, immoral, or absurd. Harmful drugs ads, offensive book ads, fortune-telling ads and superstition ads were also banned.

Before joint state-private ownership, major cities in China retained the association of private businesses, including the advertising industry guild. In the socialist transformation of capitalist industry and commerce, national advertising has all been managed as a joint public-private venture.

In general, the earlier advertising regulation system was very basic. No national legal system had been established for the industry, and there were only a few industrial rules and self-regulation provisions, scattered in civil law, criminal law, traffic law, and publishing law. Advertising regulation was mainly used to protect social morality, ethics, and customs. The advertising legal system during this period was arbitrary and without any real standards.

The Early Days of New China: 1949–1965

The period between 1949 and 1965 was the initial stage of development for China's advertising legal system. There were neither uniform national advertising regulation laws nor a regulatory body; there were no significant differences between the management of commercial advertising and noncommercial advertising. In 1949, Tianjin and Shanghai published "Advertising Management Codes." Later, Guangzhou, Chongqing, Xi'an, Wuhan, and other cities issued advertising administrative codes. These advertising codes established the scope of advertising specifications, content, and restrictions.

Cultural Revolution Period: 1966–1976

From 1966 to 1976 in China, almost all of the advertising industry was dismissed as a "propaganda tool for the service of capitalism" or "performance of capitalist management and waste" (Chen 2009) and advertising was strictly prohibited. Radio stations and newspapers were ordered to stop publishing ads. Only the theaters' opera ads, a few book ads, and ads published by the *People's Daily* were permitted. Window ads, neon signs, and other outdoor advertising were replaced by political slogans and posters. A large number of advertising management and historical data files were destroyed or lost, rendering the nation's advertising industry nonexistent.

Since the Reform and Opening Up: 1976 to the Present

With the Third Plenary Session of 1978, which opened up and invigorated the domestic economic policy, China's advertising business developed rapidly. In 1980, the State Council identified an advertising management authority, the State Administration for Industry and Commerce (SAIC), to implement overall management of the advertising industry. The SAIC is made up of the Advertising Secretary and the formally established advertising management body: the Advertising Management Divisions. The advertising industry began to form a management system from central to local authority, with the integration of various departments and regions. In 1982, the SAIC in Beijing held the first national advertising conference and started a national survey of advertising agencies.

At the same time, advertising regulations were being enacted into law. As early as 1979, China promulgated the first foreign investment law, the Sino-Foreign Joint Venture Law. This law has some provisions relating to the protection of the joint venture product sales and product information dissemination processes.

On February 6, 1982, the State Council passed the Interim Regulations on Control of Advertisement—the first national integrated advertising legal regulation. In 1987, the State Council approved Regulations on the Administration of Advertising, which set down the conduct code of advertising management in the form of legal regulations. It also proposed a "business agent fee" concept, laying the foundation for management and practice policies that would inform future ad agency systems.

During the 1990s, deceptive ads and misleading ads became a serious problem in China's advertising market. On October 27, 1994, the National People's Congress adopted the Advertisements Law of the People's Republic of China (People's Republic of China 1995). More commonly known simply as the Advertisements Law, it regulates advertising activities "to promote the sound development of the advertising sector, to protect the lawful rights and interests of consumers, to maintain the social and economic order, and to let advertisements play an active role in socialist market economy" (1995). According to this law, an *advertisement* is defined as any commercial announcement for which a supplier of goods or services pays to introduce their goods or services, whether directly or indirectly, through the media to the public at large. The Advertisements Law is an administrative law in China's legal system; its passage marked a milestone in the development of China's advertising industry. In addition, SAIC both singularly and/or jointly, with the relevant bureaus, drew up special provisions on the advertisement of tobacco, alcohol, drugs, medical products and services, cosmetics, and food to further enrich and improve the legal system of advertising regulations. In 1994, the China Advertising Association passed China's first advertising industry self-regulations.

At present, China has formed a multilevel advertising legal system with the Advertisements Law at its core. It is the basic law regulating commercial advertising. Regulations on the Administration of Advertising (1987) complements this law; these are administrative rules and regulations formulated by SAIC and relevant departments, covering specific areas such as Methods on the Administration of Advertising for Alcohol (People's Republic of China 1995).

Advertising as an element of economic activity and business communication behavior is also regulated by China's "Criminal Law," "Civil Law," "Law Against Unfair Competition," "Consumer Protection Law," "Intellectual Property Protection Act," "Product Quality Law," "Drug Administration Law" and "Environmental Protection Law." These laws regulate advertising activities in a direct or indirect way and play a supporting role in the vast and complex advertising legal system.

CHINA'S CURRENT ADVERTISING REGULATIONS

China's current advertising management system is government oriented; industry self-regulations are supplemental. The government supervises and manages advertising activities through the formulation and promulgation of advertising management policies, regulations, and laws by relevant state departments. The overall management lies with government administration, which is mainly implemented by SAIC's advertising management divisions working with other government departments' assistance.

Together, the China Advertising Association and China Advertising Association of Commerce guide their members to follow advertising laws and rules and, at the same time, try to set industry standards and establish national self-regulatory rules. Advertising industry self-regulation includes the China Advertising Industry Self-regulation Rules, the Milk Powder Advertising Industry Self-Regulation Rules, as well as regional industry rules and conventions such as the Shanghai Advertising Association of Self-Regulation and the Zhejiang Newspaper Advertising Industry Self-Regulation Conventions.

The China Advertising Association (CAA) and the China Foreign Economic and Trade Advertising Association (later called the China Advertising Association of Commerce, or CAAC) are the two most important self-regulatory organizations in the industry. CAA is currently the only national self-regulatory organization for advertising. Established in December of 1983, CAA is directly under SAIC and led by local trade and commerce administrations and advertising associations. CAA publishes *Modern Advertisement* magazine. Its members include the professional advertising industry and close to 700 members from other industries.

CAAC, which was established in 1981, is the oldest national advertising industry organization. *International Advertisement* is the main periodical published by CAAC.

The public plays a role in monitoring China's advertising industry through criticism, suggestions, complaints, and reports that may lead to prosecution. The media, competitors, consumers harmed by illegal advertising, and consumer organizations all contribute to this task. Finally, the judiciary deals with false and misleading advertisement in accordance with the law.

China has regulations that apply to ads before, during, and after their creation. These will now be discussed.

Prior Control

Prior controls, which come into play before an ad is even created, include the following:

Administrative Permission

Among the administrative requirements are obtaining an Advertising Business License, an Administrative Investigation on Special Advertisements, and Routine Approval and Registration. In China, advertisements requiring Routine Approval and Registration are cigarette and tobacco products, fixed form printed advertisements, and outdoor advertisements.

(Technical) Issuance of Certification

Prior to placing certain types of advertisements, including Western medical ads and advertisements related to qualification standards, the advertiser must secure a certification from the proper authorities.

Recording

Recording is a weaker method of prior control. The SAIC promulgated the Outdoor Advertising Registration Administrative Regulations on December 8, 1995 (first amendment). Article 14 stipulates that "outdoor advertisements must be reported to local government."

Information Regulations

For most advertisements, there is a mandatory restriction on information disclosure. Article 9 of the Advertisements Law stipulates that "the functions, place of production, application, quality, price, producer, and expiration date . . . should be clearly stated in [all] advertisements. If gifts are promised in the promotion, the goods and number should be clearly stated." Article 10 stipulates, "Data, statistical information, . . . and quotes used in an advertisement shall be factually true and accurate, and their sources mentioned." The effectiveness of such measures is only as strong as the method used to enforce them; therefore, the Advertisements Law includes rules regarding liability if the system is violated (Article 40).

Midway Control

Midway controls apply to advertising as it is being formulated. These controls help detect questionable issues and practices in advertisements before they reach the public, curbing and modifying potentially illegal ads at an early stage.

Post Control

Post control of advertising remedies problematic ads once they've reached their target audience. Typical controls of this type include annulling or retracting Advertisement Business Licenses or issuing some sort of administrative penalty.

THE ORIGIN OF CHINA'S CONSUMERISM AND THE INTERACTION BETWEEN CONSUMERISM AND ADVERTISEMENT

Twenty years after China began its period of reformation, the country began witnessing some social similarities with the Western world of the 1960s—the abundance of commodities brought by rapid economic development, a dynamic market economy, and a thriving world trade. Although overall wealth is increasing, there is great inequality among China's people—and especially between those in rural and urban areas. The social divergence caused by a shift in systems and benefits has created many social strata in the country, and so the issue of consumption has become the most important topic in twenty-first-century China. Compared to the Western world, Chinese consumerism has a different origin, expression, and nature. It is the product of both globalization and a not-yet fully developed market economy expanding in the shadow of the West.

First, China is undergoing an all-around transformation from a traditional society to a modern society, from a social planning economy to a social market economy, from an agricultural society to an industrial society. Social transformation has changed the concept of consumption and behavior in China. The notion of a "foundation based on people" has changed to one of a "foundation based on materialism."

Second, globalization is displaying a consumption-based ideology to developing countries like China, sending the message that the meaning of life is in the things we own. Driven by multinational cooperation and organizations, through mass media like newspapers, television, and the Internet, the Chinese people have gotten a taste of the luxury of developed countries. China's consumer psychology is not based on rational judgment; eager for an increase in their standard of living, the Chinese have taken on a new economic life. This willingness to follow the Western trend has allowed consumerism to enter China and develop into an influential cultural ideology.

Survey data has shown that 60 percent of families in their mid-30s, living in the cities of Shanghai, Guangzhou, and Beijing, with a household income of 3000 Yuan, believe well-known brands can promote users' social status. Similarly, 50 percent of this same cohort believe money is the best way to measure success (Kantar Media, 2012; KPMG, 2006). These data reveal the perspective of high-end customers: They are the group most willing to spend, and they are the target of the largest segment of advertising.

MAIN TYPES OF ILLEGAL ADVERTISEMENTS IN CHINA

In recent years, the rampage of false and misleading advertisement has become a serious social problem. As the State Administration of Industry and Commerce (SAIC) statement (2009) shows, in 2004 alone, more than 60,000 illegal advertisements were inspected with a fine of 107 million Yuan. Nearly 35,000 advertisements were deemed inaccurate and ordered to make a public correction; 16,628 advertisements were pulled altogether; 149 agents were suspended; 97 business licenses were revoked; and 34,869 advertisers, 7,968 advertisement operators, and 10,893 advertisement publishers were punished. In 2004, half of the 113,508 advertising agents in China had violated the law.

At present in China, drugs, medical care, health food, cosmetics, and beauty services are the hardest hit by false and misleading advertisements. Why? There is an overabundance of drugs and medical equipment advertisements in TV, newspapers, and periodicals, most of which deceive consumers by exaggerating their effects or minimizing possible side effects. Because these ads generate the main income of the news media, violations are often overlooked. Furthermore, while the mass media are forbidden from promoting products in the form of news reports, drug and medical equipment promotions are often highlighted in special news reports and interviews.

In addition to the aforementioned penalties against illegal advertisement (mandating modifications; ceasing publication; confiscating advertisement income; paying fines; and closing the specific business), the government can also circulate a notice of criticism. There are two types of notices: The first one is governed by advertising supervision organizations that report on typical violation cases in order to remind advertisers to follow the rules and to inform consumers about how to identify illegal ads. The second one, governed by the Food and Drug Administration, is called the Provisional Regulation on Health Food Advertising.

REGULATION FOR SPECIAL COMMODITY AND SERVICE ADVERTISEMENTS

Special commodity and service advertisements include advertisements for various items including drugs, medical apparatus and instruments, pesticides, food, tobacco, cosmetics, medical treatment, veterinary drugs, wine, real estate, forest tree seed, gene-transfer plant seeds, crop seeds, investment, overseas study, overseas service, enrollment, and art exhibitions.

The regulation of drug advertisements in China is found in the Advertisements Law, in the Pharmaceutical Administration Law of the People's Republic of China, in guidelines established by the State Administration for Industry & Commerce, in specific measures for drug advertisements, and in standards for censorship of pharmaceutical advertisements. Most of these laws and regulations are prohibitive norms.

The regulation of medical device advertisements are found in the Advertisements Law, in Measures for Administration of Medical Device Advertising, in Criteria for the Examination and Publication of Medical Apparatus Advertisements, and in Measures for the Examination of Medical Apparatus Advertisements. Again, the regulations are mainly prohibitive.

The regulation for pesticide advertisements is referred to in Article 17 of the Advertisements Law, in specific measures for pesticide advertisements, and in criteria for the examination of pesticide advertisements.

Food advertisements make up a very large proportion of China's ad inventory. With the growing number of food advertisements, there are many untrue, inaccurate, deceptive, and misleading advertisements emerging. Therefore, for the purpose of strengthening the supervision of food advertisement, SAIC issued the Provisional Rules on Food Advertising (PRFA). The management scope of the provisions includes ordinary food advertising, health food advertising, new resources food advertising, and special nutrition food advertising.

Article 18 in the Advertisements Law states that advertisements for tobacco are prohibited in the broadcast media, in films, on television, and in newspapers or periodicals. It is illegal to post tobacco advertisements in any waiting rooms, cinemas, theaters, meeting halls, sports sites, gyms, and other public places. An advertisement for tobacco should carry the warning: "Smoking is harmful to your health." Apart from the Advertisements Law, the main regulations on tobacco advertising are the Provisional Measures for the Administration of Tobacco Advertisements issued by the SAIC. The laws governing the advertisement of cosmetics are very important because of the broad impact and great public interest in the health and beauty industry. Apart from the Advertisements Law, related regulation can be found in the Measures for the Administration of Cosmetics Advertisements issued by the SAIC.

ADVERTISING TO CHILDREN

In Section 8 of the Advertisements Law, it is stated that an advertisement should not have any content that is injurious to the physical and mental health of underage persons or handicapped persons. However, there is no clear statement as to what kind of advertising might damage the mental and physical health of juveniles. Operationally, we generally define it as "referring to the published guidelines of advertising to children" in Standards for Censorship of Advertisements issued by the SAIC. The purpose of including the handicapped in this is to guarantee their legal rights and ensure their human dignity; it is an extension of the principles and provisions relating to the protection of the disabled in the People's Republic of China Law on the Protection of Persons with Disabilities.

According to the Standards for Censorship of Advertisements, advertising to children covers two types of ads: products for children, and products featuring children in their ads. Children's advertising must benefit the mental and physical health of the child and work to cultivate high quality, moral ideas.

SPECIAL CONSIDERATIONS OF ADVERTISING REGULATION FOR PUBLIC TASTE AND CULTURAL TRADITIONS

Traditional social order in China was governed by "manner" and "custom." Max Weber believed that in ancient China, there were no real divisions between law and religion or between ethics and customs. The ambiguous line between ethical admonition and legal order led to an exceptional form of legislation; the traditional legal order was, in essence, the "law of morality"—it was dependent on the acknowledgment and obedience of the people. No matter how the world evolves, some social taboos have been passed on and preserved; violating such taboos is considered a breach of an unwritten social contract.

Unacceptable advertisements refer to "uncivilized commercial advertising behavior" (Guan Jianqiang 2008) and include all kinds of advertising with a negative effect, including false and misleading advertisements or illegal advertisements. Such ads may be unacceptable in content or in behavior. From the perspective of the norm that demands advertisements must be decent and adhere to certain standards, unacceptable advertisements clash with the socialist spiritual philosophy, public morals, and popular will. Thus, unacceptable advertisments, regardless of regulations, are ads that are inappropriate, disgraceful, unhealthy, offensive, or discriminatory.

Article 7, clause one of the Advertisements Law stipulates that ad content should align with mental and physical health, should protect consumers' legal rights, should abide by social moral and professional ethics, and should safeguard the dignity and interests of the state. Examples of advertisements with content that damages social public interests are:

1. Advertisements using the flag of the People's Republic of China, the national emblem.
2. Advertisements with content that maligns state organizations or civil workers.
3. Advertisements with content that undermines social security, individual safety, and property. This includes the implication or statements like "one China, one Taiwan" or "two Chinas" or using a map of China as background without Taiwan province as part of its territory.
4. Advertisements with content that goes against social morals; for instance, promoting sexual products through mass media is prohibited.
5. Advertisements that contain obscenities or references to superstition, horror, or violence.
6. Advertisements that portray national, racial, religious, or sexual discrimination.
7. Advertisements with content detrimental to the environment or natural resources.

RESTRICTIONS ABOUT IMPORTING FOREIGN ADVERTISEMENTS

On March 15, 1979, Shanghai Television Station broadcast the first foreign advertisement—Rado Swiss watch. This advertisement was entrusted by the Shanghai Advertisement Company and shown in English with Chinese subtitles. Although few people knew English at that time, in only three days time more than 700 people asked about the watch. Consequently, a few months later China issued a Notice on Publishing and Broadcasting by TV and Radio of Foreign Advertisements.

DIFFICULTIES WITH CHINA'S ADVERTISING SUPERVISION

Since the implementation of the Advertisements Law in 1995, enforcement has been difficult and sporadic. The law demands that ads must be authentic, legal, specific, and clear, but there is a lack of agreed-upon definitions and concrete criteria regarding the meaning of *authentic*. Article 4 of the law stipulates that "the advertisement must not make use of any false information and must not deceive and mislead consumers," but it fails to explain what *false* means in this context. The current Chinese law on comparative advertising is obscure; while there are laws against drug and medical equipment comparisons, no other products are mentioned specifically.

The initial scope of the Advertisements Law was commercial ads, either printed or broadcast. Corresponding laws for newly developing media must be formulated.

Complicating the enforcement issue is the fact that multiple agencies are involved in the administration of the process: The Administration of Industry and Commerce has supervisory responsibility; various organizations (Health Administrative Organizations, Food and Drug Supervision Bureau and Agricultural Administrative Departments) have advertising approval responsibility; and penalties are levied by the Administration of Industry and Commerce. While there is some cooperation among agencies, the number of various bodies involved makes it difficult to enforce the laws.

FREEDOM OF COMMERCIAL SPEECH VS. CORPORATE ADVERTISING RIGHTS

Article 35 of China's constitution stipulates that "citizens of the People's Republic of China enjoy freedom of speech, of the press, of assembly, of association, of procession and of demonstration." The freedom of speech is stipulated as an important part of political freedom in China; it's the basic right of every citizen. But there is no relevant law or legal interpretation about whether this should be applied in commercial activities. Technically, freedom of speech does not include commercial speech.

In China, the freedom of commercial speech is a new topic for constitutional and economic law. From the perspective of legal norms of commercial ads, there is no specific rule protecting the freedom of commercial speech (ads). Moreover, the Chinese government considers all advertising law as "an administrative law that embodies social management function of the State." The current legislation and correspondent administrative laws and rules have set strict limitations on advertisements.

AGENCIES AND ASSOCIATIONS

China Advertising Association of Commerce (CAAC). http://www.maxtie.com/en/4028801416137da5011 61d9e6bfe02bf.htm.

State Administration for Industry and Commerce (SAIC), People's Republic of China. http://www.saic.gov. cn/english/index.html. Includes all laws and regulations relating to commerce.

BIBLIOGRAPHY

Chen Liuyu and Tang Mingliang. 2009. *Legislation and Government Regulation of the Advertisement Industry.* Beijing, China: Social Science Academic Press.

Chen Peiai. 2002. *History of Chinese and Foreign Advertising.* Beijing, China: Chiba Price Press.

———. 2009. *A New History of Advertising,* Beijing, China: Higher Education Press.

Jiang Enming. 2007. *Advertising Legal System.* Nanjing, China: Nanjing University Press.

Jianqiang Guan. 2008. "Thinking of the Banned Commercials Uncivilized Behavior." *Market Modernization,* 26: 69.

Kantar Media. 2012. "Money Best Measure of Success in Key Developing Markets, but Western Consumers Happier and Less Financially Driven, Reveals New Insight from Kantar Media." Press release, June 12. http://www.kantarmedia.com/sites/default/files/press/Kantar_Media_Global_Perpsectives_press_release_final.pdf.

KPMG. 2006. "Luxury brands in China." Report, November. http://www.kpmg.de/docs/Luxury_Brands_in_China.pdf.

Liu Linqing. 2009. *Advertising Regulations and Management.* Beijing: Higher Education Press.

People's Republic of China. 1995. Advertisements Law of the People's Republic of China. Adopted at the 10th session of the standing committee of the Eighth National People's Congress on October 27, 1994, promulgated by Order No. 34 of the President of the People's Republic of China on October 27, 1994, and effective as of February 1, 1995. http://www.civillaw.com.cn/qqf/weizhang.asp?id=36630.

State Administration for Industry and Commerce (SAIC), People's Republic of China. 2009. http://www.saic.gov.cn/english/Home/.

CHAPTER 18

HONG KONG, TAIWAN, AND MACAU

LIU JING

HONG KONG

The advertising industry was officially established in Hong Kong in the 1930s, and advertising billboards appeared nearly two decades earlier. As the nation's economy took off in the late 1960s, a comprehensive advertising system formed. In Hong Kong, advertising is a rather mature industry; it has become the main income source for all types of media.

Hong Kong is a free and highly competitive society, yet it attaches great importance to regulations that underlie the development of the advertising industry. Advertising billboards are at the heart of Hong Kong's advertising industry. Bad management and chaotic arrangement of outdoor advertisements was a serious problem until the late 1990s, when Hong Kong's government issued its Instructions on Advertising Board Installation and Maintenance. This clearly stated the restrictions on the height, the construction, and maintenance of outdoor billboards. By implementing a series of security measures, the advertising billboard soon regained its vitality and became one of Hong Kong's landmarks.

Hong Kong's advertising management system combines aspects of governmental regulation with industry self-regulation. Hong Kong's advertising laws are less comprehensive than those of China. Rules typically target certain situations—for instance, there are TV Advertising Standards, Hong Kong Cigarettes and Tobacco Advertising Standards, Drug Advertising Standards, Television Regulations, Trademark Regulations, Copyright Regulations, Drugs and Poison Regulations, Regulations for Places of Public Entertainment, and Product Introduction Regulations, among others. The TV Advertising Standards are probably the most important advertising management regulations in Hong Kong; they were formulated by the Television and Entertainment Licensing Authority and stipulate that advertisements must follow the basic rules of legality, authenticity, and honesty—rules that apply to all types of ads published in Hong Kong.

There are no comprehensive and unified bodies of advertising regulation in Hong Kong. The Television and Entertainment Licensing Authority, Broadcasting Authority, Board of Film Censorship Committee, and Medical and Health Department exercise the right to regulate together. The law in Hong Kong stipulates that only drugs approved by the head of the Department of Health can be advertised on TV. The Television and Entertainment Licensing Authority is the most important overseer of advertising; however, it also manages all types of entertainment media such as TV and film.

In Hong Kong, advertising industry self-regulation is highly developed. The Association of Accredited Advertising Agencies of Hong Kong (HK4As, or 4As) is particularly notable. The Self-Regulation Guidelines drafted by HK4As is seen as the primary guide in the advertising industry and an integral part of Hong Kong's advertisement law system. Hong Kong has four main industry self-regulation organizations that focus on improving service standards and preventing unfair competition: the Association of Accredited Advertising Agencies of Hong Kong, the Hong Kong Hua Zi Advertising Agency, the Advertising Federation of Hong Kong, and the Hong Kong Advertisers Association.

The Association of Accredited Advertising Agencies of Hong Kong

The aforementioned Association of Accredited Advertising Agencies of Hong Kong (HK4As) was established in 1957. Each of its members is a well-known advertisement company. In its early years, routine work was shared by member companies. On September 1990, the Office of the Secretary was established with three employees in charge of routine work. Each year an executive committee of four to five members is selected to discuss problems and suggest resolutions. The executive committee has many working groups, including a media group, a creative group, and an interactive group. Moreover, there are groups in Beijing and Shanghai to oversee matters in the mainland.

Members of the Association of Accredited Advertising Agents of Hong Kong pay membership fees every month. The main purpose of the money is for its member to share media data. With a great professional creative team at their disposal, member companies enjoy an advantage in business negotiations. They also get a better price on the use of media research data.

HK4As is in charge of the formulation and implementation of self-regulations, the resolution of disputes, and the provision of business consultation. The organization formulates and publishes the Hong Kong Advertisement Commerce Self-Regulation Guidelines and Hong Kong 4A Business Guidelines. The objective of the guidelines is to unify industry standards, safeguard professionalism within the advertising industry, and uphold the public interest. The regulations set standards on fees, tariffs, taxes, disclosure rules, and the distribution of commissions, advertising materials, and labor charges.

HK4As provides professional training in the areas of creative, media, and client service. International conferences are held by the organization, and lectures and publications are often used by 4A to spread knowledge in the field.

Hong Kong Hua Zi Advertising Agency

Established in 1982, the Hong Kong Hua Zi Advertising Agency is a professional self-regulation organization comprised of more than 30 member companies whose target is mainly the press media.

Advertising Federation of Hong Kong

Most of the members of the Advertising Federation of Hong Kong have business in mainland China (China Advertisement Cooperation and XinHua Advertisement Cooperation, for example). The federation is a professional organization for advertisement companies. There is no limit on the number of members allowed to join.

The Hong Kong Advertisers Association

The Hong Kong Advertisers Association is an organization for advertisers whose members include subsidiaries of multinational companies like CITICORP, Pacific Bank, Philips Globe, and Kodak. The main task of the association is to protect the interest of its members.

Moreover, consumers' inspection toward advertisement is one of the main tasks of Hong Kong's community inspection on advertisement. Established on April 1974, the Hong Kong Consumer Council has long been empowering consumers through dissemination illegal trading behavior and deceiving advertisement. The council also safeguards consumers' interest through providing information in how to choose products.

TAIWAN

Japanese colonial rule of the Southeast Asian islands known collectively as Taiwan ended in 1945, and the first signs of the advertising industry began to appear in Taiwan in the 1950s. In 1960, Taiwan took part in the Second Asian Advertising Conference held in Japan. Around the same time, the Orient Advertising Agency was founded. In 1961, the first comprehensive advertising agency, Taiwan Advertisement Corporation, was established, marking a serious step in the development of the nation's fledgling advertising sector. As Taiwan's economy continues to expand, the growth of its advertising industry maintains a strong momentum. By the end of 1990s, advertising in Taiwan was thriving, with more than 60 well-known agencies each employing about 100 creative professionals. Currently, all the large-scale corporations in the industry operate in the capital city of Taipei.

Taiwan advertising regulation management combines governmental inspection with industry self-regulation. The combined management offers a platform of stability and rapid development.

Advertising Administrative Management of Taiwan plays a leading role in Taiwan's advertising management system. There is no unified advertising regulation body in Taiwan; rather, the advertisement of food and drugs is overseen by the Department of Health Administration, which also approves ad content. Real state advertisements are overseen by the Construction Committee, media advertisement by the Press Bureau, and TV advertisement regulation is carried out in accordance with the prior censorship system.

Taiwan lacks unified laws and rules for advertising activities, but industries have their own regulations—TV Broadcasting Rules, Food Sanitation Management Laws, Cosmetic Sanitation Management Rules, and Outdoor Objects Management among them. Unfair competition is prohibited in Taiwan to safeguard fair competition, protect the interest of consumers, and forbid any misleading and deceptive advertisements.

Taiwan's Advertisements Law has formulated strict stipulations on the advertisement of drugs, alcohols, food and products of consumers' health. Rules about drug advertising are listed in the Taiwan Pharmaceutical Affairs Act and Taiwan Medical Law. Alcohol advertisers cannot use underage actors in their ads, and all alcohol advertisements must include a clearly stated message that alcohol-containing products are for adults only. Deceptive, indecent, and misleading advertisements are prohibited.

There are stipulations targeting advertisement publishers. In 1976, the TV Broadcasting Law came into effect. On December the same year, Radio and Television Act Enforcement Rules were launched, Management Rules on Radio and Television Program Supply Business and Television Advertisement Production Standard were drafted. Detailed stipulations were made in setting up procedures of radio and TV media, approval procedures of radio and TV advertisements, performance manners of advertisement content, broadcasting time and means, broadcasting intensity, qualifications of advertising media. Among them, the TV Broadcasting Law made comprehensive rules at radio and TV advertisement; Television Advertisement Production Standards systematized TV advertisements, from the basic principles of advertising, social responsible to norms and standards of comparative advertisement.

Advertising industry self-regulation in Taiwan lies with organizations such as the Advertisers

Guild, Taipei Advertisement Agency Guild, and all kinds of professional media associations. Advertisers, advertisement operators, advertisement publishers, and self-regulatory bodies formed by various institutions work together to formulate rules that help standardize industry regulations. The principles of self-regulation related to the advertising industry are embodied in the Advertiser Self-Discipline Rules, Ethics in Press, Ethics in Radio Broadcasting, Ethics in TV, Regulations on News Industry, and Agreements in Practicing Business for Members.

MACAU

Macau was originally colonized by the Portuguese in the sixteenth century. On December 20, 1999, sovereignty was returned to the People's Republic of China (PRC). Macau is now one of two special administrative regions (the other being Hong Kong) of the PRC. According to the Joint Declaration of the Government of the People's Republic of China and the Government of the Portuguese Republic on the question of Macau, China has declared that it will allow Macau a "high degree of autonomy," which will "remain unchanged for 50 years" (Macao Special Administration Region, 1999).

Tourism, gambling, and hospitality services are the main economic pillars in Macau; hence, advertising centers mainly on these three industries. Because these entertainment industries are so large, public event planning has become their main service.

Promoting awareness of the obligations of citizens and issuing government orders are usually carried out through advertisements. Foreign tourists became the principal target of the ads. There are two radio stations and TV stations respectively in Macau. Inadequate electronic media development in Macau makes printed advertisement the leading publishing method, accounting for over 85 percent of the total business.

Advertising is mostly regulated by Law No. 7/89/M, the General Regime of Advertising Activities. The law specifically prohibits misleading advertising and hidden or fraudulent messages. A license must be obtained from the Macau government to publish advertising, and "certain products or services, such as vehicles, medicine, real estate and travel, shall also . . . comply with special regulations" (HKEx News 2011). There are also strict regulations in place for gambling advertisements; for example, the gaming industry cannot advertise gamblers' winnings. Tobacco and alcohol ads are also tightly regulated, or banned from certain media. However, enforcement of these laws is inconsistent.

The advertising industry in Macau is in its infancy. It faces stiff competition from advertising companies in Hong Kong and other cities. With the development of the economy and the continued help of government policies, increasing cooperation between Macau and mainland China is likely, as is the development of the advertising industry for both sides.

AGENCIES AND ASSOCIATIONS

Association of Accredited Advertising Agencies of Hong Kong (HK4As). http://www.aaaa.com.hk/en/index.php.
The Association of Advertising Agents of Macau. http://www.aaam.org.mo/.
The Hong Kong Advertisers Association. http://www.hk2a.com/nne02.htm.
Taiwan Advertisers' Association. http://www.advertisers.org.tw/e_index.php.

BIBLIOGRAPHY

BBC News. 2012. "Macau profile." December 1. http://www.bbc.co.uk/news/world-asia-pacific-16599919.
Central Intelligence Agency. 2012. "Macau." *The World Factbook*, December 5.

Closer Economic Partnership Arrangement (CEPA). 2008. "Advertising Services." Macao Special Adminis-tration Region. http://www.cepa.gov.mo/cepaweb/front/eng/itemII_1_3.htm#05.

HKEx News. 2011. Applicable Laws and Regulations in Hong Kong, Macau and China. Draft, November 25. http://www.hkexnews.hk/reports/prelist/Documents/EWPOTOHL-20111125–10.pdf.

Lages, A. 2010. "What does the advertising law say?" *Macau Daily Times*, April 29. http://www.macaudai-lytimes.com.mo/macau/11710-What-does-the-Advertising-Law-say.html.

Macao Special Administration Region. 1999. Joint Declaration of the Government of the People's Republic of China and the Government of the Republic of Portugal on the Question of Macao. Macau: Government Printing Bureau. http://bo.io.gov.mo/bo/i/88/23/dc/en/.

Macau News. 2012. "Forum speaker says gaming ads in Macau are 'crossing the line.'" August 5. http://www.macaunews.com.mo/content/view/1731/13/lang,english/.

Portal do Governo da RAE de Macau. 2012a. "Economy." Fact sheet, June. http://www.gcs.gov.mo/files/factsheet/Economy_EN.pdf.

———. 2012b. "Tourism." Fact sheet, June. http://www.gcs.gov.mo/files/factsheet/Tourismo_EN.pdf.

Tobacco Control Laws. 2012. "Macau (China): Advertising, Promotion & Sponsorship." Fact sheet, August 15. http://www.tobaccocontrollaws.org/legislation/factsheet/aps/macau-%28china%29.

Quintã, Vítor. 2011. "Casino jackpot publicity 'misleading': experts." *Macau Daily Times*, January 18. http://www.macaudailytimes.com.mo/macau/21312-Casino-jackpot-publicity-misleading-experts.html.

CHAPTER 19

THE REPUBLIC OF KOREA

SOONTAE AN

The Republic of Korea, commonly known as South Korea, is a presidential republic with just over 50 million citizens, about 81 percent of whom reside in urban areas (UNICEF 2012). Population density is very high, with a total area of 38,023 square miles (slightly larger than the state of Indiana), but the annual population growth rate is only 0.23 percent (U.S. Department of State 2012), showing one of the lowest birthrates worldwide (CIA 2012). The gross domestic product (purchasing power parity) of South Korea is $1.554 trillion (2011 est.), making it 13th in the world (CIA 2012).

In the last half of the twentieth century, Korea's economy underwent a profound transformation, from being devastated by the Korean War in the 1950s to becoming the 15th largest economy in the world (U.S. Department of State 2012). The country is now a member of the United Nations, the World Trade Organization, the Organization for Economic Co-operation and Development, and G-20 major economies. Its legal system is a hybrid of European civil law and English common law, with a political system based on checks and balances among the presidential, parliamentary, and judiciary branches. The judicial branch is composed of a supreme court, appellate courts, local courts, and the constitutional court. The constitutional court was established in 1988 to adjudicate on the constitutionality of statutes (Constitutional Court of Korea 2012). The constitutional court has recently rendered several key decisions affecting advertising practices in South Korea.

South Korea's media environment includes a wide range of platforms, such as terrestrial TV and radio, cable TV, satellite TV, Digital Multimedia Broadcasting (DMB), and Internet Protocol-Based Television (IPTV). Terrestrial TV is still the most popular medium, with an average viewing time of about 163 minutes a day per person, followed by 104 minutes of Internet, 100 minutes of satellite TV, 90 minutes of cable TV, 79 minutes of radio, 74 minutes of IPTV, 31 minutes of DMB, and 30 minutes of newspapers (Kobaco 2010). With regard to its Internet infrastructure and usage, the country has been often labeled as "the most wired country," the "global digital test bed," and the "IT powerhouse" (Ok 2011, p. 320). The high urban density of South Korea is a key element in how the country became so wired in such a short time, among other economic and social factors (Ok 2011). With its major export products, such as semiconductors, wireless telecommunication devices, and computers, the IT industry is a core business sector (U.S. Department of State 2012).

In 2010, advertising expenditures of the four major media (terrestrial TV, radio, newspapers, and magazine) amounted to about 3.5 billion dollars; that of cable, online, and mobile media was about 2 billion dollars; and that of outdoor advertising was about 1.5 billion dollars (Oh 2011). The share of terrestrial TV advertising spending accounted for 38 percent of all advertising spending in 2002, but trended down to 26 percent in 2007, indicating increasing shares of cable TV, Internet, and DMB (Kobaco 2010). For example, the average rating of terrestrial TV in 2000 was 12.29 percent, which fell to 7.9 percent in 2006, while ratings of cable TV changed from .19 percent in

2000 to 3.2 percent in 2006 (Kobaco 2010). In 2011, the terrestrial TV advertising expenditure was about 2.5 billion dollars (Kobaco 2012).

When it comes to broadcast advertisers, telecommunications companies such as SK Telecom and KT are the top two advertisers, followed by multinational companies such as Samsung Electronics, Hyundai Motors, and LG Electronics. Cheil Communications, of Samsung Corp., is the top advertising agency for broadcast advertising, followed by Innocean of Hyundai Motors (Kobaco 2010). Other top agencies in Korea are also affiliated with Korean conglomerates such as HS Ad (LG), Daehong Communications (Lotte), and Oricom (Doosan). Those agencies handle the majority of their holding companies' accounts. In addition, more than 20 international advertising agencies operate in South Korea, such as TBWA Korea, BBDO Korea, Diamond Ogilvy, and JWT Adventure.

HISTORY OF ADVERTISING REGULATION

Until the constitutional court ruled preemptive censorship by the Korean Advertising Review Board (KARB) to be unconstitutional in 2008, broadcast advertising in South Korea had long been reviewed prior to broadcast. The landmark 2008 decision was viewed as a turning point that broadened constitutional protection of advertising as a form of expression in South Korea.

The earliest form of advertising regulation in South Korea traces back to the 1960s. The Korea Broadcasting Ethics Commission (KBEC), founded in 1962, evaluated broadcast ads, as authorized by the Broadcasting Act of 1964. In 1966, the Korea Broadcasters Association (KBA), a civilian organization, was formed and launched an industry-initiated review of advertising prior to broadcasting.

Moving into the 1970s, the KBEC began prior review of all broadcast advertising according to the Broadcasting Ethics Codes (Article 7, clauses 74 through 81), strengthening the regulation of advertising content. Although the KBEC was a self-regulatory body, it had law-enforcement powers, such as issuing consent decrees and cease-and-desist orders to broadcast stations. This type of review of broadcast advertising, carried out in many different forms over the years, continued until 2008.

In the 1980s, major statutes on advertising regulations were developed with the formation of two key regulatory bodies: the Korea Broadcasting Commission (KBC) and the Korea Broadcast Advertising Corporation (Kobaco). The KBC, which later became the Korea Communications Commission (KCC), was established in 1981 as a government administrative body. Its principal mission was to promote public responsibility, impartiality, and the public interest of broadcasting. The Kobaco was also created in 1981 to centrally manage all broadcast advertising sales. While acting as an intermediary between the advertisers and the broadcast stations, the Kobaco served as an exclusive sales agent that set ad rates and screened all advertising prior to broadcast. Because only those broadcast ads pre-reviewed by the Kobaco could be aired, it owned the exclusive right to preemptive censorship.

The Kobaco has showcased South Korea's unique advertising market infrastructure. Its key mission was identified as minimizing the commercialization of broadcast media. One of its main goals was aimed at financing small local broadcasters and religious broadcasters, who were more vulnerable to the free-market system of advertising sales. It states "the prime objective of broadcast advertising sales is to stably provide a revenue source to broadcasting companies so that broadcasting companies can produce programs and prepare for the future without any financial worries or external interventions" (Kobaco 2012). Another goal identified by the Kobaco is to "give back the profits it has made from broadcast advertising through social contribution activities, media promotion projects, and culture and arts projects" (Kobaco 2010). That said, the Kobaco produces and manages the broadcasting of public service advertising. Since 1981, with its first public service advertising, "Creating an affluent tomorrow through savings," the Kobaco has addressed a wide range of social issues ranging from the environment to families. However, despite its mission of protecting quality programming and promoting public interests, its presence has been vigorously debated.

In the changing political climate of the 1990s, the Korea Broadcasting Commission (KBC) took over prior review of all broadcast advertising from the Kobaco. This period is considered to be the strongest governmental control of advertising in South Korea's history (Cho 2002). With increasing criticism about government involvement in advertising regulation, the Korea Advertising Review Board (KARB), a civilian self-regulatory body, was established in 1991. The creation was sponsored by eight advertising industry associations, including the Korea Advertisers Association (KAA) and the Korea Association of Advertising Agencies (KAAA). Its mission is stated as "promoting advertising's independence and credibility" (KARB 2010).

In the 2000s, prior review of advertising continued, but the oversight moved to the civilian organization, the KARB. The government entrusted the review of all broadcast advertising to this self-regulatory body in 2000. The KARB functioned as a clearinghouse for broadcast advertising and monitored print advertisements after they were published. Although the KARB is an independent civilian organization, its prior review of broadcast advertising followed the rules set forth in the Broadcasting Act. Practitioners and scholars criticized the fact that, although the reviewing entity was now a civilian organization, the basic nature of prior review and potential preemptive censorship by the government had not changed. After three constitutional challenges, on June 26, 2008, the constitutional court finally sided with the advertising industry and declared the preemptive censorship of broadcast advertising as unconstitutional.

Upon the constitutional court's decision in 2008, the KARB stopped its prior review of broadcast ads immediately. At the same time, each broadcasting station that had relied on the KARB's ad screening system started to operate its own preclearance system. To ease the broadcasters' burden of screening all the ads and remove redundancy among separate broadcasters, the Korean Broadcasters Association (KBA) formed an ad review committee to serve terrestrial broadcasters on November 3, 2008.

The constitutional court declared another critical change in December 2008. It ruled the role of the Kobaco, as an exclusive advertising sales agent, as unconstitutional. To purchase airtime, advertising agencies representing advertisers went through the Kobaco. However, this three-decade-long government-controlled advertising sales process was suddenly no longer allowed, leading to a dramatic change in advertising sales in South Korea. As of now, the government and the industry are still working to create new media representative systems that will replace the Kobaco. Although the major networks praised the decision from the constitutional court, small private broadcasters, such as religious networks, have been strongly against the ruling on the grounds that their existence will be critically threatened by the abolishment of the government-controlled advertising sales system in favor of a free-market system.

COMMERCIAL SPEECH

As confirmed by the Constitutional Court of Korea in 2008, advertising is considered to be a form of protected speech under Article 21 of the constitution. In 1998, the constitutional court first classified advertising as a type of expression by stating that "advertisements also deliver ideas, knowledge, and information to the general public, which falls within the scope of freedom of press" (헌재 1998.2.27. 선고 96 헌바2) [Constitutional Court, 96

Hun-Ba 2, February 27, 1998]. The court said that advertising provides consumers a means by which to seek out new lifestyles and values, leading to the formation of a new culture (헌재 2002.12.18. 선고 2000헌마 764) [Constitutional Court, 2000 Hun-Ma 764, December 18, 2002], acknowledging the value of the free flow of commercial information in assisting the public's resource allocation. The court viewed advertising not only as a type of marketing communication to promote the interests of corporations, but also as an indispensible way to provide information to consumers.

However, the level of constitutional protection commercial advertising is afforded is narrower than other protected speech (헌재 2002.12.18.선고 2000헌마 764) [Constitutional Court, 2000 Hun-Ma 764, December 18, 2002]. The court made it clear that commercial advertising is under the constitutional scope of freedom of expression, but different from ideas or knowledge about political or civic matters (헌재 2005. 10.27. 선고, 2003헌가3) [Constitutional Court, 2003 Hun-Ka 3, October 27, 2005]. The rationale for the restricted level of constitutional protection was that its influence on personality manifestation and extension of individuality is not as great as other political expressions (헌법재판소 2005. 10.27. 선고, 2003헌가3) [Constitutional Court, 2003 Hun-Ka 3, October 27, 2005].

Given the constitutional court's stand on advertising, the long-continued prior review of broadcast advertising has often been criticized as a form of censorship. Many scholars argued that the prior review of broadcast advertising infringed on constitutional rights and that standard on the deliberations were ambiguous and overextended (Jang 2007; Lee 1997; Seo 1995). Even after the government entrusted a civilian organization, the KARB, as the review entity, scholars and practitioners pointed out that the prior review was still a form of administrative governmental control with a legal-enforcement power that was based on the Broadcasting Act of 1964 (Cho 2002; Chung 2004).

In fact, there were several constitutional challenges by various entities from 1996 to 2008. In 2004, for example, four advertising industry organizations—the Korea Federation of Advertising Associations (KFAA), the Korea Advertisers Association (KAA), the Korea Association of Advertising Agencies (KAAA) and the Korea Commercial Film Maker Union (KCU)—brought the case regarding prior review of broadcasting ads to the constitutional court, but without success.

Then, in 2008, the landmark case began with a businessman who wanted to place his commercial on local television. When the commercial was declined because it did not go through the prior review process, he challenged the related broadcasting laws as a violation of his freedom of expression. The problem at hand was broadcasting laws such as the Broadcasting Act of 1964 and its regulations on broadcast deliberations. Section 32–2 of the act stated that "(2) Notwithstanding the provisions of paragraph (1), the Korea Communications Standards Commission may deliberate on the contents of a commercial broadcast prescribed by Presidential Decree before it is broadcast, and deliberate on and pass a resolution as to whether it may be broadcast," followed by 32–3, "A broadcasting business operator shall not broadcast differently from the contents of the deliberation and resolution of the Korea Communications Standards Commission with respect to the commercial broadcast under paragraph (2), or broadcast a commercial broadcast which has not undergone a deliberation and resolution." More specifically, Regulations Concerning Deliberation on Broadcast Advertising, Article 2 (Scope of Deliberation), stated that broadcasters shall not air broadcast advertising that has not been previously reviewed.

The court, citing the constitution, Article 21–1 on freedom of speech and the press, reiterated that advertising is within the scope of constitutional protection because it delivers ideas, knowledge, and information to the general public. Although the prior review was handled by an independent civilian organization, it was entrusted to the government-sanctioned Korea Communications Commission (KCC), thus violating the tenets of free speech. The court struck down the related broadcasting laws as unconstitutional (헌재 2008.6.26. 선고 2005 헌가 506) [Constitutional Court, 2005 Hun-Ka 506, June 26, 2008], critically affecting advertising practices in South Korea since then.

GOVERNMENT REGULATION

The Korea Communications Standards Commission (KCSC) and the Korea Fair Trade Commission (KFTC) are the two major government entities that regulate advertising practices in South Korea. First, the KFTC, which was established in 1981, is a ministerial-level central administrative organization under the authority of the prime minister. The KFTC's primary role is to develop and administer competition policies and handle antitrust cases. It is comprised of nine commissioners, and the chairman and the vice-chairman are recommended by the prime minister and appointed by the president. The commissioners' term of office is three years.

One of the most important tasks of the KFTC is to protect consumers from false and misleading labeling or advertisements. It enacted the Fair Labeling and Advertising Act in 1999 to assist in this process. The act was most recently revised in 2008, stating its purpose to "prevent unfair labeling and advertising of products and services likely to deceive or mislead consumers and to facilitate the provision of correct and useful information to consumers so as to establish fairness in trade and protect consumers" (Fair Labeling and Advertising Act, Article 1). In 2007, the KFTC became the sole authority on consumer issues as it took over the jurisdiction of the Framework Act on Consumers from the Ministry of Finance and Economy. It also restructured the Korea Consumer Agency (KCA) as an organization operating within the KFTC.

The KCA is a government organization that was established in 1987 based on the Consumer Protection Act, which, since 2007, has operated under the umbrella of KFTC. Its role is to protect consumer rights and interests, to promote rational consumption habits, and to contribute to the sound development of the nation's economy. Its main functions include: conducting tests and investigations on the standards, quality, and safety of products and services; handling consumer-related matters; and investigating and deliberating consumer protection laws and regulations as requested by central and local governments.

The KCA's Consumer Counseling Team provides counseling and handles complaints. Consumer redress is provided in accordance with the Compensation Criteria for Consumers' Damages. If the parties fail to reach an agreement, the case is referred to the Consumer Dispute Settlement Commission (CDSC) for a mediation decision. The CDSC has quasi-judicial power. The CDSC consists of 30 experts in the fields of law, medicine, automobiles, insurance, and product liability, and representatives of consumer and business organizations, all of whom are appointed by the minister of finance and economy on the recommendation of the KCA president. If one or both parties do not accept the CDSC decision, civil suits can be filed. The KCA can assist consumers in filing civil suits through the Legal Assistance Group. The Legal Assistance Group is comprised of 20 incumbent attorneys from metropolitan and rural areas.

The Korea Communications Standards Commission (KCSC), an independent statutory organization, reviews broadcast content, including broadcast ads. The KCSC was established in 2008 under the Act on the Establishment and Operation of the Korea Communications Commission (KCC). The KCSC consists of nine members appointed by the president, three members commissioned upon recommendation by the speaker of the National Assembly, and three members commissioned upon recommendation by a competent standing committee of the National Assembly. The KCSC monitors and receives complaints from the public.

The Korea Communications Commission (KCC), the government organization in charge of all communications policies and regulation, was established in 2008 by consolidating the former Ministry of Information and Communication (MIC) and the Korean Broadcasting Commission (KBC). The newly established KCC, under the office of the president, manages broadcasting and communications, promotes the convergence process between broadcasting and telecommunications, and administers government regulations.

The KCC developed Regulations Concerning Deliberation on Broadcast Advertising. These regulations promote public responsibility of broadcast advertising, which has been the key advertising code for reviewing advertising content.

SELF-REGULATION

The Korea Advertising Review Board (KARB) was established in 1993 as a civilian organization. Seven committee members were responsible for conducting the prior review of advertising at that time. The committee reviewed submitted cases twice a week, categorizing cases as allowed for broadcast, conditionally allowed, and not allowed. Those conditionally allowed for broadcast were to be modified, or additional supporting information was to be provided. Those parties who received the decision of "not allowed" were able to appeal once. Committee members consisted of professors, lawyers, and advertising industry executives. The KARB reviewed (1) ads for terrestrial broadcasters, (2) ads for cable broadcasters, satellite broadcasters, and outdoor, and (3) ads for print media. Unlike the first two categories, print ads were reviewed after they were published. Until 2008, when the constitutional court decided prior review by the KARB was unconstitutional, it had reviewed an average of about 40,000 TV and radio ads yearly, ranging from 35,008 in 2002 to 48,623 in 2005, as Table 19.1 shows.

For example, in 2006, 22,156 television commercials (57.3 percent) were allowed for broadcast; 16,476 (42.6 percent) were conditionally allowed; and nine (.02 percent) were not allowed. In the case of radio, there were 2,438 (51.5 percent) allowed; 2,387 (49.4 percent) conditionally allowed; and eight (.16 percent) not allowed. From 2002 to 2006, the rate for allowed broadcasts ranged from 48.5 percent (2002) to 56.6 percent (2006). Similar proportions of broadcast ads were determined to be conditionally allowed; the rate for conditionally allowed ads was between 51.4 percent (2002) and 43.5 percent (2006). The rate for not allowed was .16 percent in 2002, .10 percent in 2003, .03 percent in 2004, .05 percent in 2005, and .04 percent in 2006.

Details of the review activity in 2003 indicate that lack of verification and the use of a foreign language were the top two reasons for not allowing ads to be broadcast as received (Chung 2004). That is, the biggest reason for conditionally allowed broadcasts was the need for further verification of data or claims (5,826 or 20.4 percent for TV; 1,585 or 33.4 percent for radio) in 2003, except the "other" category (10,129 or 35.4 percent for TV; 1,086 or 22.9 percent for radio). The second largest category was the use of unnecessary foreign language (4,115 or 14.4 percent for TV; 615 or 13 percent for radio). The Regulations Concerning Deliberation on Broadcast Advertising specifically state that broadcast ads should not use unnecessary foreign language, except on channels broadcast in languages other than Korean (Article 21). The next largest category was misleading expression (2,216 or 7.7 percent for TV; 776 or 16.4 percent for radio).

In the analysis of 2003 cases (Chung 2004), examples of cases decided as "not allowed" fell into (1) foods or medicines with misleading claims (16 or 39 percent for TV; none for radio); (2) untruthful or misleading contents (11 or 26.8 percent for TV; none for radio); and (3) unfair comparison (2 or 49 percent for TV; none for radio). Most notably, the cases of foods or medicines with misleading claims increased from 4 percent in 2001 to 28 percent in 2002 and again to 34.1 percent in 2003 (Chung 2004).

Table 19.1

Prior Reviews of Broadcast Ads by KARB, 2002–2006

	Broadcast allowed	Conditionally allowed	Broadcast not allowed	Total
2002				
TV	14,005	14,830	40	28,875
Radio	2,967	3,149	17	6,133
Total	16,972	17,979	57	35,008
2003				
TV	18,666	15,967	35	34,668
Radio	3,582	2,868	6	6,456
Total	22,248	18,835	41	41,124
2004				
TV	20,415	17,963	12	38,390
Radio	3,159	3,307	2	6,468
Total	23,574	21,270	14	44,858
2005				
TV	23,906	18,428	24	42,358
Radio	3,531	2,734	0	6,265
Total	27,437	21,162	24	48,623
2006				
TV	22,156	16,476	9	38,641
Radio	2,438	2,387	8	4,833
Total	24,594	18,863	17	43,474

Source: Korea Advertising Review Board (KARB), www.kobaco.co.kr/eng/index.asp.

The second division of the KARB was concerned with reviewing cable television, satellite broadcasters, and outdoor ads. Like terrestrial broadcasters, ads were categorized into three groups: allowed, conditionally allowed, or not allowed. The third division of the KARB handled ads for print media. They were reviewed after being published. The committee categorized cases into those warranting caution, warning, modification, discontinuation, and corrective advertising. The compliance rate was 97.1 percent in 2000, 96.1 percent in 2001, 97.6 percent in 2002, and 88.8 percent in 2003 (Chung 2004).

The KARB reviewed advertising content according to the Regulations Concerning Deliberation on Broadcast Advertising. Although the KARB is a civilian organization, a key issue was that its review guidelines were based on legislation enacted by the Korea Communications Commission (KCC). However, since the 2008 constitutional court decision, the KARB only reviews advertisements before broadcasting when requested to do so by the advertisers. It also monitors and receives complaints about print advertisements from the public.

Table 19.2

Prior Reviews of Broadcast Ads by KBA, January–September 2011

	Allowed	Review Pending	Not allowed	Total
January 2011	2,339	108	0	2,447
February 2011	1,905	133	0	2,038
March 2011	2,715	158	0	2,873
April 2011	2,944	171	0	3,115
May 2011	2,922	125	0	3,047
June 2011	2,698	237	0	2,935
July 2011	2,393	124	0	2,517
August 2011	2,710	196	0	2,905
September 2011	2,852	245	0	3,097

Source: Korean Broadcasters Association (KBA), http://www.kba.or.kr/.

Since the KARB stopped its prior review of broadcast ads in 2008, the Korean Broadcasters Association (KBA) has conducted its own advertising reviews for preclearance of broadcast ads. It developed an electronic commercial review system (CmReview) through which cases can be submitted and reviewed in a timely manner. The review board at the KBA is composed of five members—three members come from terrestrial TV stations, one member from the KBA itself, and one from a pool of industry experts. The KBA's prior review of ad contents results in (1) broadcast allowed, (2) conditionally allowed, or (3) not allowed. Conditionally allowed ads are required to substantiate claims or modify contents before broadcast.

Table 19.2 shows the most recent activity of the KBA in 2011. The rate for allowed hovered around 95 percent, with no ads determined to be not allowed. The rate ranged from 96.59 percent in January 2011 to 91.9 percent in June 2011. For cable TV advertising, the Korea Cable Television and Telecommunication Association (KCTA) provides prior review of advertising via its five-member review committee, who are industry experts and legal professionals.

In addition to self-regulation by the media industry, major industries conduct their own self-regulation of ads. Advertising for medical services are reviewed by the Korean Medical Association (KMA); advertising for medical devices by the Korea Medical Devices Industry Association (KMDIA); advertising for medical and pharmaceutical products by the Korea Pharmaceutical Manufacturers Association (KPMA); advertising for health supplement products by the Korea Health Supplement Association (KHSA); advertising for cosmetic products by the Korea Cosmetic Association (KCA); advertising for banking and financial services by the Korea Financial Investment Association (KFIA); and alcohol advertising by the Korea Alcohol and Liquor Industry Association (KALIA).

ADVERTISING CODES

About 180 laws governing advertising exist in South Korea, which is an indication that there is currently no unified advertising regulatory system (Lee and Kim 2001). For example, in cases of misleading and deceptive advertising, various laws such as the Broadcasting Act, the Food Sanitary Act, and the Pharmacy Act can apply. Among them, key statutes most relevant to advertising regulation are the Monopoly Regulation and Fair Trade Act enacted in 1981 and the Fair Labeling and Advertising Act enacted in 1998.

In the Broadcasting Act of 1964, revised in 2008, Article 5 emphasizes the public responsibility of broadcasting by stating that:

> 1) A broadcast shall respect the dignity and value of human beings as well as the fundamental democratic order; 2) a broadcast shall contribute to the unity of the people to a harmonious development of the State and a democratic formation of the public opinion, and shall not promote any discord among regions, generations, classes, and sexes; 3) a broadcast shall not injure others' reputation or infringe on others' rights; 4) a broadcast shall not promote crimes, immoral conducts, or a speculative spirit; 5) a broadcast shall not promote lewdness, decadence, or violence which has a negative influence on a sound family life and on a guidance of children and juveniles. (Broadcast Act 2008)

Using these principles for broadcast contents, the KCC developed Regulations Concerning Deliberation on Broadcast Advertising, which includes a section on "Level of Morality" covering issues such as morality, respect for life, and maintaining dignity. Those articles require advertisements to respect cultural traditions, national symbols, and the public's pride. Accordingly, Regulations Concerning Deliberation on Broadcast Advertising (Article 4) specifically state that broadcast ads shall not contain expressions (1) making light of human dignity or life, (2) instilling violence, crime, or antisocial behavior, (3) inciting too much fear or hatred, (4) exposing too much of the body or featuring obscene, lewd materials, (5) ridiculing or parodying physical handicaps or weaknesses, (6) promoting overly vulgar contents or damaging public morals, or (7) belittling a specific gender or causing a sense of sexual shame.

Article 22, which specifically refers to the language used in commercials, is also worth noting. In principle, broadcast ads should use standard Korean, abiding by orthography. Slang, argot, or coinage of vulgar words should not be used. Also, unnecessary use of foreign language should not be used, except in the case of brand names, brand slogans, corporation names, or corporate mottos. Channels broadcast in foreign languages other than Korean are an exception.

In addition to prohibited expressions, some objects are not allowed in broadcast ads. Article 9 of the Regulations Concerning Deliberation on Broadcast Advertising states that (1) broadcast advertising shall not disrespect or use inappropriately a national flag, anthem, or cultural relics, and (2) broadcast advertising shall not harm the dignity and pride of the nation. With a total of 47 specific articles, Regulations Concerning Deliberation on Broadcast Advertising cover a wide range of issues from alcohol and cosmetics to real estate advertising.

SPECIAL TYPES OF ADVERTISING

Advertising for Children

Advertising targeting children and adolescents is regulated by the Adolescent Protection Act, enacted in 1997, and the Broadcasting Act of 1964. Children are defined as persons under 13, while adolescents are persons under 19.

First, the Broadcasting Act Article 5–5 states that "a broadcast shall not promote lewdness, decadence, or violence which has a negative influence on a sound family life and on the guidance of children and juveniles." Article 33–2-3 specifically points out deliberations on matters concerning the protection of children and juveniles and sound character building. Furthermore, Article 33–3 stipulates that "a broadcasting business operator shall classify and rate the broadcast programs in light of the degree of harmfulness of a broadcast program's violent nature and lewdness, etc., and the age of the viewers, and indicate it during the broadcast." Finally, Broadcasting Act Article 73 states that "a broadcasting business operator shall clearly separate commercial broadcasts from the broadcast programs so as to avoid any confusion." For commercial broadcasts during programs that are directed toward children or juveniles, they must inscribe captions clarifying them as "commercials" so that they may distinguish broadcast programs from commercial broadcasts.

Article 23 in Regulations Concerning Deliberation on Broadcast Advertising covers specific issues on broadcast advertising targeting children and adolescents. It states that:

1. broadcast ads shall not harm children and adolescents' character, emotion, and values,
2. broadcast ads shall not contain any of the following:
    a. messages delivered by children about the advertised product's features or promotional messages, and songs;
    b. suggestions that the possession of the advertised product will change children's abilities and behaviors;
    c. suggestions that without the advertised product, children can be an object of ridicule or feel inferior;
    d. messages urging children to purchase the advertised product or to pester their parents to purchase it;
    e. messages that incite gambling;
    f. messages that place children in danger or encourage them to partake in risky behavior;
    g. messages that promote an unhealthy diet in children.

Article 23–3 continues as:

3. broadcast ads on toys, game controls or any other products attracting children's interest shall not use the following methods, given children's limited judgment and experience:
    a. expressions that make the size and proportion of the advertised product look bigger than actual size;
    b. expressions that are ambiguous as to whether a toy operates mechanically or manually;
    c. expressions or sounds that confuse the toy with the actual object.

Finally, Article 23–4 states that broadcast ads targeting children shall not emphasize ancillary products or prizes beyond the advertised product.

In striving to help children and youth form good character, the relevant laws in South Korea stipulate that advertisements shall not use language or images that might be harmful to the character, emotion, or values of children or juveniles. The country's Youth Protection Law poses expansive restrictions on advertisements deemed to be "media materials harmful to juveniles," so that children and youth will not gain access to such materials. For instance, the time between 1:00 P.M. and 10:00 P.M. and, in the case of holidays and school breaks, 10:00 A.M. to 10:00 P.M. are designated as the "Juvenile Viewing Time Zone," during which media materials deemed harmful to children are prohibited from being broadcast.

Broadcast Advertising Prohibited

The following products or services are not allowed to be advertised through broadcast media according to the Regulations Concerning Deliberation on Broadcast Advertising: (1) bars and taverns in relation to the Food Sanitary Act, (2) private investigators or detectives, (3) businesses arranging marriages or relationships, (4) fortune-telling, psychic readings, astrology, or any other superstitious materials, (5) firearms (real or toy), (6) gambling or similar speculative behaviors, (7) tobacco or smoking-related ads, (8) baby formula, baby bottles, or pacifiers, (9) obscene materials or performances, including any obscene audio/video/text information through telecommunication, (10) financial business without a license according to finance laws, (11) massage treatment services, (12) alcohol of level 17 or higher, and (13) spring waters for terrestrial TV ads.

CONCLUSION

Advertising regulation in South Korea demonstrates a unique regulatory environment and continued change as political and economic climates shift. One of the key characteristics is that broadcast advertising in South Korea has long been prior reviewed, raising the issue of censorship, until the constitutional court ruled the prior review system unconstitutional in 2008. The practice of prior review is now handled by self-regulated organizations within the media industry; the KBA for terrestrial TV ads, and the KCTA for cable ads, for example. Many professional associations continue to review their own industry's broadcast ads prior to broadcast. The advertising industry is currently in the process of developing a more efficient and unified advertising review system to handle the preclearance of broadcast ads.

With the long history of preclearance of broadcast ads, having a government-sanctioned agency as an exclusive sales agent for all broadcast ads had been another characteristic unique to South Korea. Since the constitutional court decided the Kobaco's role of advertising sales agent was unconstitutional in 2008, the country is still debating about ways to deal with the change in the dynamic of advertising sales in South Korea.

There are many restrictions in terms of products and the ways they can be advertised. Several noticeable products with restrictions include spring water for terrestrial TV, baby formula, and pacifiers, whereas gambling, alcohol, and tobacco advertising are prohibited on broadcast media, similar to many other countries. Those restrictions are by-products of South Korea's emphasis on morality and values. As such, inappropriate use of cultural relics and harming the dignity and pride of the nation is explicitly prohibited. While advertising is considered to be a type of speech and expression within the realm of the South Korean constitution, it is subject to many restrictions that reflect the country's strong respect for tradition and cultural values.

BIBLIOGRAPHY

Broadcast Act of 2008. http://www.moleg.go.kr/english/korLawEng?pstSeq=47560.
Central Intelligence Agency (CIA). 2012. "East & Southeast Asia: Korea, South." *The World Factbook.* https://www.cia.gov/library/publications/the-world-factbook/geos/ks.html.
Cho, Byunglyang. 2002. "A Study on the Change of Korea Broadcasting Advertising Regulation Code." *The Korean Journal of Advertising,* 13(2), 75–91.
Chung, Geehyun. 2004. "The Present Situations and Issues of Korea Advertising Review System." *The Korean Journal of Advertising and Public Relations,* 6(3), 164–95.
Constitutional Court of Korea. 2012. "Introduction: About the Court." http://english.ccourt.go.kr/.
Jang, Hosoon. 2007. "A Study on the Constitutionality of the Prior Review Rules on Broadcast Commercials." *The Korean Journal of Communication and Information Studies,* 39, 69–101.

Kobaco. 2010. *2010 Media & Consumer Report MCR*. Seoul: Korea Broadcast Advertising Corporation.

———. 2012. *2011 Broadcast Advertising Market Closing Accounts Report*. January 11. http://www.kobaco. co.kr/kobaco/kobaconews/cyberprnews_read.asp?reports_no=382&Cnt=285&page=1&key=&field=&title =&content=&writer=.

Korea Accreditation Board (KAB). 2011. "Prior Reviews of Broadcast Ads by KAB." http://www.kba.or.kr/.

Korea Advertising Review Board (KARB). 2010. "Prior Reviews of Broadcast Ads by KARB." http://www. karb.or.kr/data/data02_01.asp.

Korea Communications Commission (KCC). 2008. "Enforcement Decree of the Broadcasting Act." Seoul: Korea Communications Commission. http://www.kcc.go.kr/user.do?page=P02030100&dc=K02030100.

———. 방송광고 판매제도 변화가 지역방송 경영에 미치는 영향, Seoul: Korea Communications Commission.

Korea Fair Trade Commission (KFTC). 1999. "Fair Labeling and Advertising Act." Enacted by Law No. 5814, February 5. http://www.google.co.kr/url?sa=t&rct=j&q=FAIR+LABELING+AND+ADERTISING+ACT &source=web&cd=1&ved=0CDsQFjAA&url=http%3A%2F%2Fftc.go.kr%2Fdata%2Fhwp%2FG00014. doc&ei=O_1VTveKc3HmQX9hoTdCQ&usg=AFQjCNH3-qVyyyn1ZuJnecRRIcB5Cd03RQ&cad=rjt.

Lee, Chongmin, and Jisun Kim. 2001. "Problems under 'monopoly regulation and fair trade act' and improvements under 'fair labeling and advertising act': Based upon the regulations of misleading and exaggerating advertising." *The Korean Journal of Advertising*, 12(4), 207–229.

Lee, Koohyun. 1997. 광고와 표현의 자유에 관한 연구. Kobaco (광고연구), 35, 95–124.

Oh, Jaehyun. 2011. 지난해 광고산업 첫 10조원 돌파. Maeil Business News on the Web, December 7. http://news.mk.co.kr/newsRead.php?year=2011&no=790410.

Ok, Hyeryoung. 2011. "New Media Practices in Korea." *International Journal of Communication*, 5, 320–340.

The Republic of Korea. 2008. "Enforcement Decree of the Broadcasting Act." December 31. http://www. kcc.go.kr/download.do?fileNm=broadcasting_act_02.pdf.

Seo, Beomseok. 1995. 방송광고 심의제도 개선에 관한 연구. Kobaco (광고연구), 26, 121–151.

U.S. Department of State. 2012. "U.S. Relations with South Korea." Fact sheet, December 17. http://www. state.gov/r/pa/ei/bgn/2800.htm.

UNICEF. 2003. "At a glance: Korea, Republic of." June 2. http://www.unicef.org/infobycountry/repkorea_statistics.html#46.

CHAPTER 20

JAPAN

MARIKO MORIMOTO

OVERVIEW OF COUNTRY

Japan is located in northeastern Asia between the Pacific Ocean and the Sea of Japan. The area of Japan is 377,873 square kilometers, slightly smaller than the size of California; the country consists of four major islands and over 4,000 smaller islands (Japan National Tourism Organization 2011). The population is approximately 127 million with the majority (about 99 percent) being Japanese in terms of ethnicity (U.S. Department of State 2011).

Japan is a constitutional monarchy with a parliamentary government (U.S. Department of State 2011); however, the emperor does not hold political power and is considered a ceremonial figure. The prime minister, chosen from the elected representatives of the National Diet, holds the majority of power, while the sovereignty lies with the Japanese citizens (National Diet Library 2011).

The Japanese media market is characterized by heavy consumption of newspapers and television compared to the global standard (Open Source Center 2009). There are approximately 120 daily newspapers in Japan (Gatzen 2001), with an average subscription rate of 0.98 per household in 2007 (Open Source Center 2009). There are five national daily newspapers in Japan: *Yomiuri Shimbun* (the largest), *Asahi Shimbun*, *Mainichi Shimbun*, *Nihon Keizai Shimbun* (better known as *Nikkei*), and *Sankei Shimbun*. Home delivery is the main distribution method, and many subscribers receive both morning and evening editions (Open Source Center 2009).

In the television industry, Japan has one public broadcaster (Nippon Hoso Kyokai, NHK) that owns two stations (general and educational), and the revenue is mainly composed of subscription fees (Gatzen 2001). Five major commercial broadcasters (TV Asahi, Fuji TV, Tokyo Broadcasting Systems [TBS], Nihon TV [NTV], and TV Tokyo) exist in Japan; cross-ownership (e.g., TV stations and newspapers) is common (Gatzen 2001).

Japanese radio, similar to television, has both public (NHK) and commercial broadcasters. In terms of content, while AM programming offers both entertainment and news, FM programming mainly offers music and entertainment. There are 338 AM stations and 275 FM stations, and these stations broadcast mostly in Japanese (Open Source Center 2009).

Magazines are still considered a large medium in terms of circulation numbers: 2.48 billion monthlies and 1.63 billion weeklies were published in 2006 (Open Source Center 2009). However, readership has been declining in the past decade. Meanwhile, digital media have risen as one of the key information sources in Japan; cell phones, in particular, play an important role. Recent research, such as Net Asia's 2008 study, reveals that approximately 60 percent of respondents access mobile news sites while only 48 percent of respondents read online magazines using computers (Open Source Center 2009).

Advertising revenues have also shifted from traditional to online media. Total advertising expenditures in 2010 was 5,842.7 billion yen, a decrease of 1.3 percent from the previous year (Dentsu 2011). Overall, print media experienced a decline in advertising revenues (1.9 percent decrease from 2009) while Internet media enjoyed a 10.8 percent increase in advertising revenues in 2010 (Dentsu 2011). The declining trend in advertising expenditures in Japan reflects a slow recovery of its economy. However, a positive sign of recovery is shown in the small 1.8 percent increase in gross domestic product (GDP) in 2010, the first increase in three years (Dentsu 2011).

HISTORICAL BACKGROUND

Pre–World War II Period: The Era of Governmental Censorship

The history of advertising/media-related regulation in Japan dates back to the period of Meiji Restoration in the nineteenth century. The main purpose of this early form of advertising and media-related law in Japan was censorship in order to establish the authority of the new imperial government after the overthrow of the Tokugawa government. The newly established Japanese government introduced the newspaper law in 1869 to censor editorial content, including advertising to prohibit publication of criticism against the imperial government (Okada and Yanase 2006). Subsequently, when the Constitution of the Empire of Japan (also known as the Meiji Constitution) was enacted in 1890, article 29 provided limited freedom of speech, assembly, and association to the citizens. Out of this article, the government issued the Peace Preservation Law in 1925, which was to restrict the Freedom and People's Rights Movement. In particular, this imperial ordinance restricted distribution of posters and flyers featuring speech that was supportive of socialism, communism, and anarchism (Okada and Yanase 2006; Tamura 2010). Coupled with the law that granted the police specific authority to control and regulate socialistic, communistic, and/or anarchistic speech in newspaper and magazine ads (Okada and Yanase 2006), this regulation played a significant role in media censorship in the pre-WWII era. As Japan was heading toward WWII, the National Mobilization Law was passed to prepare for the upcoming war. This legislation further strengthened the ability of the government to censor and prohibit "inappropriate" materials (as deemed by the governmental standard) from publication in media, including advertising.

Regulation for Consumer Protection Prior to 1945

The first regulation that focuses on business conduct and consumer protection in modern Japan is the Civil Law. Enacted in 1898, this law allowed consumers to demand compensation from advertisers if they were misled and/or deceived by their advertising claims (Suzuki 2004). This civil law also protected consumers from fraud, and had the ability to invalidate any legal actions related to fraud. Another notable pre–World War II business regulation that had some impact on advertising was the Unlawful Competition Prevention Law of 1934. The law allowed businesses to request monetary compensation when advertising claims were incorrect and/or misleading about product qualities and quantities, and such claims hurt profits of the business (Suzuki 2004). While these regulations provided some protections for consumers from unlawful and deceptive advertising claims, it was after World War II that the Japanese government began to see the need for more structured regulations for consumer protection.

Post–World War II to Present

Calling for More Consumer Protection

After the Japanese defeat in WWII, several laws indirectly related to advertising were modified. It is notable that the trend in advertising-related regulations in Japan shifted its focus from censorship to consumer protection. For instance, the revision of the Pharmaceutical Affairs Act in 1948 was made to prohibit any exaggerated claims concerning drugs, cosmetics, and medical equipment in advertising. In 1950, the Unfair Competition Prevention Act was amended, and the revision stated that any misleading or incorrect notations of product origins, ingredients, qualities, and quantities in advertising would be subjected to penalties (Suzuki 2004).

In the 1960s, Japan experienced a major consumer movement due to the increase of incidents associated with deception in advertising claims, which resulted in the Consumer Protection Basic Act enacted in 1968. This was the first official consumer protection act introduced in Asia that specified consumers' rights, and it is regarded as the constitution for consumer policies in Japan (Okada and Yanase 2006). Following this trend, self-regulation by the advertising industry in Japan became more active, and in 1974, the Japan Advertising Review Organization (JARO) was formed (JARO 2010a).

The Internet Age

As Internet technology has become widely available for both consumers and advertisers, the need for laws applicable to Internet advertising has also arisen. Particularly in the past decade, a wide range of laws concerning e-commerce appeared in Japan. One of the laws that greatly influenced consumer protection is the Act on the Protection of Personal Information, which was promulgated in 2003 and enforced in 2005 (Cabinet Office, The Government of Japan 2010). It was introduced to protect consumers' personal information from financial institutions and marketers in general by restricting the transfer of such personal information to the third party without permission from consumers. In addition, other laws that had been initially applied to conventional advertising media have been expanded and modified to apply to Internet advertising. Such examples include, but are not limited to, copyright and trademark regulations, electronic signature law, and unsolicited commercial e-mail prevention law (Okada 2003). However, due to the high rate of changes and advancements in digital technology, it is expected that more modifications, adaptations, and revisions of existing business regulations will take place in the future.

CURRENT GOVERNMENT REGULATION

Government Agencies

Several key government agencies exist in Japan that directly or indirectly oversee advertising-related regulations. Among them, the Consumer Affairs Agency and the Japan Fair Trade Commission play a major role in the enforcement of advertising-related laws.

Consumer Affairs Agency

Established in 2009, the Consumer Affairs Agency (CAA) is a division of the Cabinet Office and has legal authority on consumer-related issues including product labeling, safety, and trade; its primary goal is consumer protection (CAA 2010). The original purpose of the CAA was to fill the niches between each ministry's responsibilities, as well as to centralize the authority in one agency specialized in consumer affairs. This new agency also has the power to plan new consumer protection policies, and it handles any consumer problems that cannot be governed or regulated by other ministries.

CAA works closely with other government ministries and offices such as the Ministry of Economy, Trade, and Industry (on product labeling associated with household items), Food Safety Commission (concerning Food Safety Basic Law), Ministry of Internal Affairs and Communication (concerning the Act on Regulation of Transmission of Specific Electronic Mail), and Ministry of Agriculture, Forestry and Fisheries (on Japan Agricultural Standard Act [JAS Act]).

Specifically, CAA is responsible for the following three acts on product labeling: (1) the Law for Preventing Unjustifiable Extra or Unspecified Benefit and Misleading Representations, which regulates representations made in advertising claims to protect fair competition and consumer benefits; (2) the JAS Act, which regulates food product labels; and (3) the Food Sanitation Act (CAA 2010). In addition to these labeling-related acts, CAA also handles trade and safety issues in relation to consumer affairs. Because the organization is still in the development stage, it is expected that the range of its responsibilities and roles will increase in the future.

Japan Fair Trade Commission

Japan Fair Trade Commission (JFTC), established in 1947, is very similar to that of the United States in many regards. JFTC's main responsibility is to enforce and facilitate fair market competition (JFTC 2013). JFTC oversees business conduct based on three fundamental acts: the Antimonopoly Act, the Subcontract Act, and the Premiums and Representation Acts. The commission consists of five members, including a chairperson and four commissioners who are appointed by the prime minister based on the consent of the Diet. It is independent from other administrative organizations and has the authority (1) to give cease-and-desist orders for any illegal acts prohibiting fair competition, and (2) to surcharge payment orders for price curtails (JFTC 2013). JFTC handled a total of 180 cases in 2011. Among these cases, JFTC issued cease-and-desist orders in 22 cases and warnings in 2 cases; in particular, of 22 cease-and-desist orders, 5 cases were identified as a violation of the unfair trade practices (JFTC 2013).

Regarding advertising, JFTC has recently been given more authoritative power on regulating product/service labeling for consumers' benefit, as well as claims made without proper substantiation (Okada and Yanase 2006). In addition to regulating incorrect and/or misleading contents of advertising claims, JFTC requires advertisers to make their claims clear and easy to understand for general consumers. The examples of specific JFTC guidelines for clear advertising claims include (but are not limited to) (1) repeating important claims for purchase; (2) plainly stating information on additional charges and conditions; and (3) using advertising layouts that can be easily followed by consumers (Okada and Yanase 2006).

Ministries

Additionally, some regulations are enforced by specific ministries. For example, the Ministry of Internal Affairs and Communication handles intellectual property (trademark, Internet advertising, etc.), and the Ministry of Justice is responsible for Commercial Law, the Constitution, and Civil Law concerning product liability. Health-related advertising claims are also regulated by the Ministry of Health, Labor, and Welfare based on the Pharmaceutical Affairs Act and Health

Promotion Act (Functional Foods & Nutraceuticals 2005). In addition, food advertising is regulated by the Ministry of Agriculture, Forestry, and Fisheries. Also, the Ministry of Economy, Trade, and Industry (METI) oversees the Japan Patent Office, direct marketing practices, and unsolicited commercial e-mail practices (Mutel 2002).

The Six Advertising Laws

There are over 200 laws relevant to advertising in Japan. Among them, Okada (1996) identified major laws in Japan concerning advertising and dubbed them the "Six Advertising Laws":

1. Consumer Protection Basic Act
2. Civil Law
3. Unfair Competition Prevention Act
4. Act Against Unjustifiable Premiums and Misleading Representations
5. Copyright Law
6. Trademark Law

Consumer Protection Basic Act

The Consumer Protection Basic Act was introduced in 1968 as the first regulation concerning consumer protection in Asia and was revised in 2004 (Okada and Yanase 2006). The revision was made to help consumers make rational purchase decisions based on accurate product information provided by marketers, leading to the independence of consumers and to fair and equal relationships between consumers and marketers. With this principle, the act provides the directions for: (1) consumers' rights and safety, including remedies for damages due to any unlawful and deceptive advertising claims; (2) consumer education; (3) responsibilities for marketers; and (4) consumer organizations (Okada and Yanase 2006). The revision also specifies that advertising claims are subject to this regulation.

The Consumer Protection Basic Act has two approaches to advertising regulation. First, the law requires business entities to include material information necessary for purchase decisions in advertising claims. This element of the law is often applied in conjunction with laws for consumers' safety (e.g., Food Sanitation Act) and laws for product quality control (e.g., JAS Act). Manufacturers and service providers are also prohibited from making deceptive claims that may mislead consumers' purchase decisions (Yabe 2009a). This approach is often used to regulate advertising claims in conjunction with the Act Against Unjustifiable Premiums and Misleading Representations. Overall, this law serves as the guiding principle to ensure the welfare, benefits, and safety of consumers and protect them from unlawful and deceptive actions and claims from marketers.

Civil Law

Considered indispensable to protect citizens' rights, the Civil Law in Japan can be extended to a variety of promotional activities such as advertising and publicity. Products Liability Law and Business Law are special acts under the Civil Law (Okada and Yanase 2006).

While the Civil Law is related to a wide range of acts and laws concerning advertising, it only uses the word *advertising* in its section on contests in advertising claims (Yabe 2009a). Other related laws in the context of advertising executions include the Unfair Competition Prevention Act and the Copyright Law (discussed in the following sections).

Unfair Competition Prevention Act

Together with the Antimonopoly Act, the Unfair Competition Prevention Act regulates deceptive advertising claims that may hinder fair competition in the marketplace (Yabe 2009a). Okada and Yanase (2006) point out that this law focuses more on maintaining fair competition among businesses while the Antimonopoly Act and the Act Against Unjustifiable Premiums and Misleading Representations (discussed in the following section) are more for protecting consumers' benefits. The Unfair Competition Prevention Act's approach is very similar to the original intent of the Federal Trade Commission in the United States. The act is also responsible for regulating the use of copyrighted and/or trademarked materials in advertising, particularly with regard to comparative advertising (Okada and Yanase 2006).

Under the jurisdiction of the Ministry of Economy, Trade, and Industry (METI 2010), the act defines unfair competition as when businesses use trademarked/copyrighted materials (held by others) to sell or promote products and services without authorization and sell imitated products.

Act Against Unjustifiable Premiums and Misleading Representations

The Act Against Unjustifiable Premiums and Misleading Representations was introduced to supplement the Antimonopoly Act (Okada and Yanase 2006). Because it regulates deceptive and/or misleading advertising claims and exaggerated giveaways designed to induce purchase, it is quite relevant to advertising's creative executions.

While this law is under the jurisdiction of the Consumer Affair Agency (CAA), it is actually the Japan Fair Trade Commission (JFTC) that conducts investigations of applicable cases (Yabe 2009a). Also, the JFTC has the authority to issue cease-and-desist orders to violators and requires guilty advertisers to run corrective advertising, which is very similar to the authoritative power exercised by the FTC in the United States. The law also requires the violators to report to the JFTC on corrective advertising executions (Okada and Yanase 2006).

Copyright Law

Copyright Law plays a critical role in regulating intellectual properties. In advertising, the law can be applied to the use of copyrighted materials, including visual and audio materials. However, because the law was not established to specifically regulate expressions in ads and was not introduced with Internet technology in mind, applying the law to advertising can be difficult (Okada and Yanase 2006).

Trademark Law

Trademarks are defined as words, diagrams, and marks, as well as combinations of these elements, that manufacturers use to represent their products/services (Yamaguchi 2009). This regulation protects the trademark holders' benefits and interests by protecting trademarks from unlawful use. Trademark Law is a part of Industrial Property Law; however, it is somewhat different from other subcomponents of Industrial Property Law (such as Patent Law, Utility Mobile Law, and Design Law). While other industrial property laws protect a person's creativity and the products of that creativity, Trademark Law provides its holders with exclusive rights to use trademarks for business and sales efforts (Yamaguchi 2009). The initial and original intent of Trademark Law is to protect the trust value of trademarks.

Trademark infringement occurs when a trademark is used by nontrademark holders with no limit. A trademark must be registered with the Japan Patent Office (a division of the Ministry of Economy, Trade, and Industry) to receive protection from unlawful usage (Japan Patent Office 2010). It is important to note that trademark registration notations such as ® and ™ are based on the U.S. Trademark Law, and therefore, they are not technically Japanese notations. If companies use these notations to export products to the United States without the approval from the U.S. Patent and Trademark Office (USPTO), such usage may be regarded as trademark infringement by the USPTO. Also, if trademark protection is required for international business, it is necessary to apply for international trademark registration based on the Protocol Relating to the Madrid Agreement Concerning the International Registration of Marks, or else, legal protection is limited to within Japan (Japan Patent Office 2010).

INDUSTRY ASSOCIATIONS AND SELF-REGULATION

The role that advertising industry associations play should not be ignored in the efforts to regulate advertising. In a sense, Japanese advertising regulation is a hybrid system where industry associations take the initiative to self-regulate their advertising activities. Several notable industry organizations exist in Japan, and these organizations aim to clarify the role of advertising in Japanese society while earning consumers' trust by regulating deceptive and false advertising (Adlegal 2010).

Japan Advertisers Association (JAA)

Japan Advertisers Association (JAA) was established in 1957 to improve the quality of advertisers' activities based on the belief that advertisers earn trust from consumers by communicating the truth (JAA 2010). The organization has the membership of 300 companies, and its board of directors consists of advertising and public relations professionals from major corporations in the field. JAA is engaged in several areas of activity ranging from conducting research to organizing seminars and advocating the code of ethics among advertisers (JAA 2010). The original code of ethics was created in 1960 to accommodate increasing complaints from consumers and businesses; in 1993, the code was further improved by officially addressing the principles of ethical advertising and the guidance for actual conduct (for the actual code of ethics, refer to http://www.jaa.or.jp/jaa_eng/orga2.html). It is also the continuous effort of JAA for self-regulation that eventually led to the founding of the Japan Advertising Review Organization (JARO) (Okada and Yanase 2006).

Japan Advertising Agencies Association (JAAA)

Japan Advertising Agencies Association (JAAA) was founded by advertising agencies in 1955 to facilitate quality advertising (JAAA 2010). The board members are elected from the participating agencies, and the association is engaged in a variety of activities, including research, promotion of its code of ethics, and collaboration with other organizations (both government and industry organizations) for activities to improve advertising conduct (JAAA 2010). Like JAA, the organization has its own code of ethics. Specifically, their code of ethics provides guidelines for ethical and creative advertising (for the actual code, refer to http://www.jaaa.ne.jp/introduction/5.html). Okada and Yanase (2006) point out that because advertising agencies specialize in creating advertisements, all employees in agencies are considered specialists; for Japanese advertisers, though, advertising is not necessarily the key component of their business activities. Monitoring the compliance of advertising activities is complex, so it can be difficult for in-house advertising/marketing personnel to become heavily involved and knowledgeable in the field due to their other job responsibilities. Thus, the creative teams in Japan's advertising agencies, as advertising professionals, are expected to play a key role in reinforcing ethical advertising activities (Okada and Yanase 2006).

Japan Advertising Review Organization (JARO)

Japan Advertising Review Organization (JARO) was established in 1974 to foster good quality advertising. The organization consists of members from advertising agencies, media, and advertisers, and their goal is to investigate advertising claims that consumers and businesses report as deceptive and/or misleading (JARO 2010a). If JARO finds potentially misleading/deceptive advertisements, the organization officially instructs the responsible advertiser to correct the ads. JARO also provides advertisers advice on advertisement claims prior to the execution of a campaign. In 2008, JARO (2010b) handled 5,794 cases, of which 312 were about advertisement complaints, and 5,481 dealt with precampaign advice. These statistics illustrate that JARO has been successful in meeting its goal of preventing false and/or deceptive advertising by providing proper guidance to advertisers and agencies.

Self-Regulation Efforts by Media Organizations

Media organizations in Japan also have their own code of ethics concerning advertising placement. The Japan Newspaper Publishers & Editors Association (NSK) has its own standards for advertising placement in Japanese newspapers, specifying 21 criteria for advertisements (NSK 2010). In addition to these criteria, each newspaper publisher in Japan sets its own advertising guidelines (Okada and Yanase 2006).

For magazine advertising, the Japan Magazine Advertising Association (JMAA) has published a guidebook about regulations and issues related to acceptance and publication of advertisements in magazines (JMAA 2010).

With regard to broadcast media, the National Association of Commercial Broadcasters in Japan (NAB) regularly revises and updates its broadcasting standards (usually every five years). Particularly, NAB has set the guidelines for TV commercials targeted toward children (NAB 2010; revised in 2009), and advertisements on health-related products and financial services (Okada and Yanase 2006) to meet its goal for better broadcasting. In addition, the All Japan Radio & Television Commercial Confederation (ACC), an organization that works closely with JAA, JAAA, and NAB, has a copyright committee to accommodate trends in digital media (ACC 2010).

RESOLUTIONS AND SANCTIONS

Roles of Governmental Organizations

JFTC and CAA can be listed as the key players who handle complaints regarding advertising, provide resolutions, and impose sanctions. As a part of the Cabinet Office, these government organizations can officially enforce sanctions on violators. As noted earlier in this chapter, the JFTC has the authority to issue cease-and-desist orders to those advertisers who violate the Act Against Unjustifiable Premiums and Misleading Representations.

Meanwhile, the newly established CAA is in the position of enforcing legal sanctions based on several laws due to its role as an overseer of consumer safety. Although no statistics about CAA's activities are available at this point, the number of cases that this agency will handle concerning consumers' injuries due to advertising claims is expected to be large. For example, regarding violations of the Act Against Unjustifiable Premiums and Misleading Representations, the CAA, as well as local governments, can issue cease-and-desist orders (like the JFTC) and corrective advertising orders (Yokota 2009). Usually, such corrective ads are placed in local newspapers. Another notable function of CAA is its involvement with food safety and consumer protection. The CAA makes special efforts to oversee food advertising based on the Food Sanitation Act, and if advertisers make deceptive and/or exaggerated claims that can endanger public health, it can advise local governments to strip business approvals from the guilty advertisers, or to temporary suspend such approval (Obata 2009a).

In addition, some of the Six Advertising Laws (Okada 2003) also specify sanctions for violations. For instance, the Trademark Law allows one company to sue another for the damage due to the incorrect and/or deceptive use of trademarks (Yamaguchi 2009). The law also provides trademark owners with the right to request others to stop using their trademark if the trademark is misused. Moreover, if the trademark owner's benefit is damaged by such misuse, the owner can demand compensation for damages (Yamaguchi 2009). Overall, common sanctions in Japan are cease-and-desist orders and warnings. However, businesses frequently seek resolutions at the civil lawsuit level.

Resolutions by Industrial Organizations

As a key representative of the advertising industry in Japan, the Japan Advertising Review Organization (JARO) takes the initiative in facilitating better advertising practices. Upon the receipt of complaints from consumers or businesses, JARO analyzes the ad in question and requests the advertiser to respond to complaints/concerns (JARO 2010b). If an agreement cannot be made between advertisers and consumers/other businesses, JARO sends the case to the review board. The review board consists of scholars and attorneys who do not have direct connections with advertising businesses, and they make the decision and notify JARO and related organizations such as JAA and JAAA (Ichikawa 2009). Because the decision by the review board will be sent not only to the responsible advertiser but also to other influential advertising organizations, this review process is believed to serve as a form of self-regulation.

SPECIFIC REGULATIONS FOR ADVERTISING CONCERNING CHILDREN AND HEALTH

Advertising to Children

Unlike the Federal Trade Commission in the United States, which has specific rules covering advertising targeted toward vulnerable groups including children (Fueroghne 2007), there is no regulation tailored exclusively to children's advertising in Japan. At this point, ethical conduct depends on self-regulation. For example, the creative code of the Japan Advertising Agency Association (JAAA) mentions that advertising should not prevent the sound growth of children (2010). In addition, the National Association of Commercial Broadcasters in Japan (NAB) has an amendment on ethical guidelines for TV commercials targeting children, and encourages broadcasters not to air TV commercials that (1) violate social ethics; (2) feature dangerous actions children may imitate; (3) children may fear; (4) justify violence and antisocial movements; or (5) deal inappropriately with household matters (NAB 2010).

Advertising Medical and Health-Related Products

Advertising for health-related products/services is regulated according to the Pharmaceutical Affairs Act. The act oversees advertising for three product categories: 1) medicines; 2) quasi-drugs, which have weaker effects on human bodies compared to medicines; and 3) cosmetics that consumers apply to enhance their appearance (Yabe 2009b). The act prohibits advertising preapproved medicines; the use of exaggerated claims of medicines, quasi-drugs, and cosmetics in ads; and the use of testimonials by medical professionals (Yabe 2009b). Violators are subject to imprisonment for less than two years or fines less than ¥2,000,000. The Health Promotion Act also prohibits claims clearly intended to mislead consumers (Functional Foods & Nutraceuticals 2005). This law mainly handles advertising claims related to nutrition, and the Consumer Affairs Agency (CAA) has the authority to issue a warning to the violator (Yabe 2009c).

Tobacco and Alcohol Advertising

The advertising of tobacco products in Japan is regulated by the Tobacco Business Act, and the law requires advertisers to include a statement that indicates consumption of tobacco products may cause health hazards (Iju 2009). As of 2010, tobacco advertising was not prohibited in Japan, but regulations are expected to be tightened to accommodate the direction of the World Health Organization (WHO) (Hashimoto 2010). Similarly, responding to this trend, the Tobacco Institute of Japan has introduced self-regulation to remove commercials for all tobacco brands from TV and radio (Shimamura 2000).

As for alcohol advertising, it is required to include a statement indicating that the sale of alcohol is prohibited unless the age of the purchaser is confirmed to be 20 or older (Yabe 2009d). While the future of alcohol advertising is likely to head toward more strict regulation, at the moment, the industry takes initiatives to regulate alcohol advertising, particularly toward underage individuals. In addition, the Japan Spirits & Liquor Makers Association (2010) states that advertisers should not place their alcohol product ads in public transportation (including stations and stops) or within a radius of 100 meters from elementary, middle, and high schools.

CONSUMERISM IN JAPAN AND ITS EFFECTS ON ADVERTISING REGULATION

In the past couple of decades, Japan has been leaning toward deregulation in many areas of advertising. It is a reflection of consumers' expectations toward the role of advertising. Japanese homemakers, who are often the primary purchase decision makers in their households, tend to rely on TV commercials for purchase decisions for relatively low-priced products; for more expensive items, they prefer newspaper ad inserts as a source of information (Sakurai 1995). It is also reported that Japanese consumers who are not confident in selecting high-quality products tend to rely on advertising to assist in the decision-making process, and consumers expect advertising to provide accurate information on product features, quality, and price (Sakurai 1995).

In response to such consumer expectations, several major changes have been made in advertising-related regulations in the past decade to better serve consumers. One such example is the deregulation of comparative advertising. Though not a common advertising tactic in Japan, comparative advertising was officially permitted based on the idea that it provides more options for consumers and facilitates competition among advertisers (Shimamura 2000). Another area that benefits from deregulation is legal services. Since 2000, attorneys have been able to advertise their services in both traditional and nontraditional media. However, comparative advertising is prohibited for advertising legal services and medical professional services (Shimamura 2000).

On the other hand, consumers' concerns about advertising have also called for greater regulation in other areas. Skepticism toward advertising related to deceptive ad claims—especially on food product labels—still remains a strong consumer concern. For instance, in 2008, Senba Kitcho, a high-end authentic Japanese restaurant, was accused of deceptive labeling of their products (e.g., camouflaging expiration dates of processed food products, purposely mislabeling origins of ingredients, etc.). Several manufacturers of confectionaries were accused of similarly misleading labeling (e.g., Akafuku Mochi, Japanese-style rice cakes; and Shiroi Koibito chocolate-coated cookies). These incidents and resulting consumers' concerns led the Japanese government to establish the Consumer Affairs Agency (CAA), allowing the agency to oversee and work closely with responsible ministries and protect consumers' safety.

Another area of advertising with increased regulation is digital (Internet) advertising. The growing popularity of e-commerce has resulted in an introduction of a wide range of regulations concerning Internet media. Japan's Federal Trade Commission (JFTC) has issued guidelines on labeling and advertising claims on the Internet to encourage fair competition and business transactions between marketers and consumers (Obata 2009b). The Act on the Protection of Personal Information was established in 2003 (came into effect in 2005) for consumer online privacy protection, prohibiting the sale of consumer information to any third party without permission (Yanase and Okada 2003). In addition, the Act on the Regulation of Transmission of Specific Electronic Mail was amended in 2008, prohibiting advertisers from sending unsolicited commercial e-mail messages to consumers without prior permission (or opt-in) (Ministry of Internal Affairs and Communication 2010). These are just a few examples of many emerging Internet-related regulations; as the use of the Internet for advertising becomes more and more diverse, it is expected that this area of advertising regulation will be further strengthened.

SHORTCOMINGS IN ADVERTISING REGULATIONS IN JAPAN

While Japan has come a long way in establishing a solid regulation system for advertising to protect consumers' rights and safety, some shortcomings have arisen with the diffusion of Internet media as advertising outlets. Although more regulations are emerging regarding Internet advertising, this segment is not as established as the more traditional media outlets. Unlike broadcasting media, the Internet is not subject to the Television Broadcast Act and/or the Radio Act (Yanase and Okada 2003). Due to the Japanese Constitution and the Telecommunication Business Act that prohibit censorship and protect communicators' privacy, some laws cannot be applied to advertising content delivered via the Internet. It is hoped that such legal loopholes will be reduced as more telecommunication laws are adjusted to regulate Internet media; currently, however, this remains a matter of concern for consumer protection in Japan.

Interactivity, one of the notable characteristics of the Internet, further complicates issues of advertising regulation: It is possible for consumers to purchase an item immediately after they see online ads for products or services. Yanase and Okada (2003) argue that—traditionally speaking—advertising did not necessarily establish a legal relationship (i.e., purchase or contract) between businesses and consumers, but that argument might not hold up in the digital age. As a result, online advertising may fall under a category of laws concerning business contracts. This trend could very well affect legal judgments in determining the extent to which online ads can be considered business contracts; thus, it becomes extremely difficult to figure out the degree of applicability of related business laws to online advertising activities.

The Internet has also blurred the boundaries across nations, opening the door to globalization. Yanase and Okada (2003) point out that it is possible for Japanese standards and advertising practices to be considered invalid and/or unlawful in other countries—a fact that might expose Japanese marketers to lawsuits and/or penalties. Of course, the opposite case is possible for international and/or non-Japanese advertisers when they conduct advertising campaigns in Japan. It is essential to specify the clear boundaries of legal responsibilities by the government to better protect consumer welfare.

Although it should not be considered a major shortcoming, the effectiveness of the newly created Consumer Affairs Agency (CAA) in terms of its role as a key organization for consumer protection is not yet known. The agency will work with ministries to regulate business conduct, including advertising activities, to protect consumer safety. However, it is unknown how effectively and efficiently this agency collaborates and coordinates with other ministries at this point. It is expected that this concern will be reduced once the agency's operation, as well as the procedure for regulation, is well established.

EVALUATIONS AND CONCLUSION

Despite some potential concerns, overall, advertising-related regulations in Japan can be regarded as sufficient and effective. In general, Japan has three layers of regulation for advertising. The first layer is industry regulation, which is expected to serve as a discouragement for deceptive and/or false advertising through self-monitoring. The principles of advertising ethics operate at this level. The second layer involves administrative guidelines issued by government agencies such as CAA and ministries to protect consumers. This group of regulations forms the core of advertising regulations in Japan (Yabe 2009a), and is viewed as the practical manual for advertisers to follow (Okada and Yanase 2006). Actual legal prosecutions are meant to punish the wrongdoings of advertisers, but such procedures require plaintiffs to specify *individuals* who committed illegal advertising practices (Yabe 2009a). Hence, it is extremely difficult to apply such laws to large corporations, since it is often difficult to specify a responsible individual under the Unfair Competition Prevention Act. As a result, the third layer of Japanese advertising regulations—laws to protect fair competition and consumer rights—does not function in reality. This phenomenon makes the role of the administrative guidelines critical in advertising regulations to a great extent.

Responding to the need, the Japanese government has recently established the Consumer Affairs Agency (CAA). This movement toward more consumer protection should be regarded highly in terms of advertising regulations. The agency is expected to fill the niche where ministries do not oversee in terms of advertising conduct, while enforcing the administrative power by working along with each ministry to maximize consumer welfare and safety. Because the agency is an extension of the Cabinet Office, it is also expected that the agency will respond to consumers' concerns in a prompt manner and/or request (and urge) related ministries to instruct responsible advertisers appropriately. In this regard, the agency holds a key to the future of advertising regulation in Japan.

BIBLIOGRAPHY

Adlegal. 2010. "Regulations for TV Commercials." http://www.cm-kousa.jp/category/1207226.html (accessed February 27, 2010).

All Japan Radio and Television Commercial Confederation. 2010. "ACC Activities." http://www.acc-cm.or.jp/acc/06iinkai.html (accessed March 1, 2010).

Cabinet Office, Government of Japan. 2010. "Act on the Protection of Personal Information." Consumer Information Protection. http://www.caa.go.jp/seikatsu/kojin/foreign/act.pdf (accessed January 23, 2010).

Consumer Affairs Agency, Government of Japan. 2010. "Consumer Affairs Agency." http://www.caa.go.jp/en/index.html (accessed January 24, 2010).

Dentsu. 2011. *Advertising Expenditures in Japan.* http://www.dentsu.com/books/pdf/expenditures_2010.pdf (accessed October 1, 2011).

Fueroghne, Dean K. 2007. *Law and Advertising.* Pasadena, CA: Yellow Cat Press.

Functional Foods & Nutraceuticals. 2005. "Global Dispatches Japan: Nothing Sells Like Television." May, 26–30.

Gatzen, Barbara. 2001. "Media and Communication in Japan." *Electronic Journal of Contemporary Japanese Studies,* April 17. http://www.japanesestudies.org.uk/discussionpapers/Gatzen.html (accessed October 1, 2011).

Hashimoto, Satoshi. 2010. "WHO Advises to Restrict Tobacco and Alcohol Advertising." *Asahi Shinbun,* January 18. http://www.asahi.com/business/update/0118/TKY201001170292.html (accessed March 12, 2010).

Ichikawa, Takashi. 2009. "The Role of Japan's Advertising Review Organization." In *Koukoku Hyoji Kisei Hou,* ed. Hiroshi Iju and Jotaro Yabe. Tokyo: Seirin Shoin, 623–630.

Iju, Hiroshi. 2009. "Advertising Regulations for Non-Deceptive Claims." In *Koukoku Hyoji Kisei Hou,* ed. Hiroshi Iju and Jotaro Yabe. Tokyo: Seirin Shoin, 39–41.

Iju, Hiroshi, and Jotaro Yabe, eds. 2009. *Koukoku Hyoji Kisei Hou (Advertising Claim Regulations).* Tokyo: Seirin Shoin.

Japan Advertisers Association. 2010. "Welcome to JAA." http://www.jaa.or.jp/jaa_web/index.html (accessed February 27, 2010).

Japan Advertising Agencies Association. 2010. "Introduction of JAAA." http://www.jaaa.ne.jp/introduction/0.html (accessed February 27, 2010).

Japan Advertising Review Organization. 2010a. "JARO's Establishment and Its 30 Years of History." http://www.jaro.or.jp/a30/pdf/2seturitu.pdf (accessed January 23, 2010).

———. 2010b. *JARO Report 2008.* http://www.jaro.or.jp/nsod.html/toukei20(release_ver).pdf (accessed February 28, 2010).

Japan Fair Trade Commission. 2013. "Annual Report of FY 2011." http://www.jftc.go.jp/en/about_jftc/annual_reports/index.files/130116_Annual_Report_FY2011.pdf (accessed April 2, 2013).

Japan Magazine Advertising Association (JMAA). 2010. "About JMAA." http://www.zakko.or.jp/jpn/outline/index.html (accessed February 28, 2010).

Japan National Tourism Association. 2011. "Japan Overview." http://www.jnto.go.jp/eng/arrange/essential/overview/index.html (accessed October 1, 2011).

Japan Newspaper Publishers & Editors Association (NSK). 2010. "Code of Ethics for Advertisements in Newspapers." http://www.pressnet.or.jp/ (accessed February 28, 2010).

Japan Patent Office. 2010. "About Trademark." http://www.jpo.go.jp/index/shohyo.html (accessed February 21, 2010).

Japan Spirits & Liquor Makers Association. 2010. "Code of Ethics." http://www.yoshu.or.jp/statistics_legal/legal/independence.html (accessed March 12, 2010).

Ministry of Economy, Trade, and Industry (METI). 2010. "Unfair Competitive Prevention Act." http://www.meti.go.jp/policy/economy/chizai/chiteki/unfair-competition.html#19 (accessed February 14, 2010).

Ministry of Internal Affairs and Communication. 2010. "The Guideline for the Act on Regulation of Transmission of Specific Electronic Mail." http://www.soumu.go.jp/main_sosiki/joho_tsusin/d_syohi/m_mail.html#ordinance (accessed March 27, 2010).

Mutel, Glen. 2002. "Japan Revises Law to Stem Flow of Unsolicited E-mails." *Precision Marketing,* 14(14), 9.

National Association of Commercial Broadcasters in Japan. 2010. "Broadcasting Ethics." http://nab.or.jp/index.php?%CA%FC%C1%F7%c.e.%D1%CD%FD (accessed March 1, 2010).

National Diet Library. 2011. "The Birth of the Constitution of Japan." http://www.ndl.go.jp/constitution/e/etc/c01.html (accessed October 1, 2011).

Obata, Tokuhiko. 2009a. "Advertising Regulation Based on the Food Sanitation Act." In *Koukoku Hyoji Kisei Hou,* ed. Hiroshi Iju and Jotaro Yabe. Tokyo: Seirin Shoin, 173–179.

———. 2009b. "Unfair Labeling and Claims in E-Commerce." In *Koukoku Hyoji Kisei Hou,* ed. Hiroshi Iju and Jotaro Yabe. Tokyo: Seirin Shoin, 449–453.

Okada, Yonezo. 2003. *Digital Jidai No Kokoku Hoki (Advertising Laws in the Digital Age).* Tokyo: Nikkei Koukoku Kenkyusho.

———. 1996. *Wakariyasui Kokoku Roppo (Six Advertising Laws).* Tokyo: Nikkan Kogyo Shinbunsha.

Okada, Yonezo, and Kazuo Yanase. 2006. *Koukoku Hoki (Advertising Law & Ethics).* Tokyo: Shojihomu.

Open Source Center. 2009. "Japan—Media Environment Open; State Looms Large." Media guide, August 18. http://www.fas.org/irp/dni/osc/japan-media.pdf (accessed October 1, 2011).

Sakurai, Kuniro. 1995. *Kokoku No Houteki Imi (The Legal Meaning of Advertising: Economic Effects of Advertising and Consumer Protection).* Tokyo: Keiso Shobo.

Shimamura, Kazue. 2000. "Japanese Trends of Advertising Regulation and the Factors Affecting Them." *The Waseda Commercial Review,* 385 (June), 195–213.

Suzuki, Miyuki. 2004. "The Development of Advertising Regulation." *History of Japan Advertising Regulation Organization (JARO): The 30th Anniversary.* http://www.jaro.or.jp/a30/pdf/1–2.pdf (accessed January 10, 2010).

Tamura, Yuzuru. 2010. "The Peace Preservation Law." http://www.cc.matsuyama-u.ac.jp/~tamura/tiannijihou.htm (accessed January 9, 2010).

U.S. Department of State. 2011. "Background Note: Japan." Bureau of Public Affairs: Electronic Information and Publication. http://www.state.gov/r/pa/ei/bgn/4142.htm (accessed October 1, 2011).

Yabe, Jotaro. 2009a. "Regulation of Advertising Claims Based on the Antimonopoly Act." In *Koukoku Hyoji Kisei Hou,* ed. Hiroshi Iju and Jotaro Yabe. Tokyo: Seirin Shoin, 140–149.

———. 2009b. "Regulations of Medical and Beauty Product Labeling." In *Koukoku Hyoji Kisei Hou,* ed. Hiroshi Iju and Jotaro Yabe. Tokyo: Seirin Shoin, 202–212.

———. 2009c. "The Consumer Affairs Agency and Its Establishment." In *Koukoku Hyoji Kisei Hou,* ed. Hiroshi Iju and Jotaro Yabe. Tokyo: Seirin Shoin, 150–158.

———. 2009d. "Regulation of Alcohol Labeling." In *Koukoku Hyoji Kisei Hou,* ed. Hiroshi Iju and Jotaro Yabe. Tokyo: Seirin Shoin, 184–201.

Yamaguchi, Isamu. 2009. "Regulations Based on Trademark Law." In *Koukoku Hyoji Kisei Hou,* ed. Hiroshi Iju and Jotaro Yabe. Tokyo: Seirin Shoin, 339–346.

Yanase, Kazuo, and Okada Yonezo. 2003. *Advertising Laws in the Digital Age.* Tokyo: Nikkei Advertising Research Institute.

Yokota, Naokazu. 2009. "Sanctions for Violations of the Act Against Unjustifiable Premiums and Misleading Representations." In *Koukoku Hyoji Kisei Hou,* ed. Hiroshi Iju and Jotaro Yabe. Tokyo: Seirin Shoin, 104–109.

PART VI

GLOBAL ADVERTISING REGULATION

CHAPTER 21

CONCLUSION

Advertising Regulation Worldwide

Regulation of advertising is influenced by a country's culture, economy, and various political and societal factors. Accordingly, the chapters in the book present the history and overview of advertising regulation in a country-specific way. This chapter is aimed at pointing out some noticeable features of advertising regulatory systems throughout the world. Similarities and differences across countries can be seen in areas such as methods of regulation, restrictions on specific types of ads, and areas of regulatory emphasis.

Differences can be found in the ways advertising's constitutional status is recognized and the degree to which restrictions against other interests are sanctioned, but the notion of advertising as a type of expression is universally accepted and recognized. In the United States, the Supreme Court case of the *New York Times Co. v. Sullivan* (1964) recognized that an advertisement with commentary concerning a public figure could be run in a newspaper as long as the writer believed that the statements were true and that there was no actual malice. Such an advertisement would not be considered libelous or defamatory. While this particular ruling did not apply to other kinds of advertising, later judgments established the fact that commercial speech was protected by the First Amendment of the Bill of Rights, which historically protected only noncommercial speech. It states that "Congress shall make no law . . . abridging the freedom of speech." The historic *Central Hudson* case set guidelines in determining whether restrictions to advertising practices are justified. Under the *Central Hudson* test, advertising should not be misleading or illegal; the government should have a substantial interest; the regulation should directly advance the government's interest; and the regulation should not be more extensive than necessary.

Similarly, in Canada, Section 2(b) of the Charter of Rights and Freedoms provides that "everyone has the following fundamental freedoms: . . . (b) freedom of thought, belief, opinion and expression, including freedom of the press and other media of communication." To determine the applicability of advertising in the protected expression, the Canadian Supreme Court has provided guidelines, the so-called Oakes test, where the Court first decides whether the speech in question was attempting to convey a meaning. Then, two key questions follow: whether the objective the restriction is designed to achieve is of sufficient importance to warrant overriding the constitutionally protected speech, and whether the measures to achieve the objective are proportional to the objective.

Compared to the specific guidelines and substantial Supreme Court cases in the United States and Canada, courts in Europe have provided a less conceptual argument on commercial speech doctrine. Article 10 of the European Convention on Human Rights decrees freedom of expression, and the European Courts have held that Article 10 does apply to purely commercial advertising. However, in practice, the courts in Europe have been more willing to defer to governmental regulations. Therefore, legal challenges to governments' infringements on commercial speech based on

Article 10 of the convention have been relatively rare. For example, in Sweden, specific directives are not found, although advertising is recognized as a type of expression.

In fact, advertising is highly regulated in European countries such as France. The first article in France's Freedom of Communication Law grants great discretionary power to the government, stating: "Audio-visual communication is free. The exercise of this freedom may be limited only, to the extent required, on the one hand, for the respect of human dignity, the freedom and property of other people, the pluralistic nature of the expression of ideas and opinions and, on the other hand, for the safeguarding of law and order, for national-defense and public-service reasons, for technical reasons inherent to the means of communications, as well as for the need to develop a national audio-visual production industry." Specific mentions of other interests such as human dignity and national defense are noteworthy, as opposed to the more abstract statement of the U.S. and Canadian constitutions. Indeed, until 1968 in France, commercials were not allowed on television and television channels were entirely owned by the government. More recently, in 2003, large-scale retailers were allowed to start advertising on television. Since 1990, a complete ban of political advertising, regardless of medium, has been in place during the months preceding an election in France.

As the Freedom of Communication Law in France elucidates, advertising is subject to many government regulations. Advertising is primarily regulated by the country's government entity responsible for overseeing anticompetitive business practices. The Federal Trade Commission in the United States, the Competition Bureau in Canada, the Japan Federal Trade Commission, the Korea Fair Trade Commission, the Australian Competition and Consumer Commission, the National Consumer Service (SERNAC) in Chile, and the Office of Fair Trade in the UK are examples of such government agencies.

Those agencies have the authority to take many types of actions, such as cease-and-desist orders, warnings, fines, and corrective advertising. For example, in 2010, the Japan Federal Trade Commission handled a total of 612 cases; cease-and-desist orders were issued for 52 and 9 warnings were given. The Federal Trade Commission in the United States ordered Exxon to run corrective advertising in 1997 to inform consumers that regular gasoline is the right fuel for most cars, not the more expensive premium-grade, as they advertised. In 2011, the Australian Competition and Consumer Commission ordered a fine of $5.2 million for Optus broadband advertising deemed to be misleading and deceptive. In Sweden, under the Marketing Act, there is a separate clause called a Market Disruption Charge, which can be levied for deceptive and/or misleading ads. In Peru, the Audit Commission of Unfair Competition dealt with 243 cases in 2006, 260 cases in 2007, and 216 cases in 2008.

Depending on the nature and type of advertising, many different specialized government agencies oversee its regulation. For example, in Japan, while the Japan Fair Trade Commission has the primary oversight of advertising regulation in general, the Ministry of Internal Affairs and Communications is involved with trademark and Internet advertising; the Ministry of Agriculture, Forestry, and Fisheries deals with food advertising; the Ministry of Health, Labor, and Welfare takes on health-related advertising claims; and the Ministry of Economy, Trade, and Industry oversees advertising related to patents and direct marketing. Often, these agencies act autonomously in evaluating and imposing penalties for violations within their area of specialty. For example, in the United States, the Food and Drug Administration, which has authority over the labeling and advertising of packed foods, cosmetics, and drug products, ordered Bayer to run $20 million in corrective advertising for its deceptive and false advertising claims for the prescription birth control pill Yaz in 2009.

In most countries, broadcast advertising is overseen by the government entity possessing the power to enforce licensing and fine broadcasting stations. The Federal Communications Commission in the United States, the Canadian Radio-Television Commission, the Australian Communications and Media Authority, and the Korea Communications Standards Commission are a few examples of such agencies. These agencies provide various codes to regulate the contents of broadcast advertising, and compliance is generally required for the renewal of a station's broadcasting license. For example, in Canada, the Canadian Radio-Television Commission enforces the Codes for Broadcast Advertising of Alcoholic Beverages and Codes for Broadcast Advertising to Children. In the UK, Ofcom regulates television, radio, telecommunications, and wireless services, requiring all television broadcasters to comply with the Television Advertising Standards Code in any advertising they transmit. Even after Ofcom transferred its responsibility to the Advertising Standards Authority in 2004, it still retains ultimate responsibility for all television advertising standards.

Similarly, the Australian Communications and Media Authority deals with broadcast advertising issues, such as the placement of advertisements, the amount of nonprogram material per hour, the loudness of the advertisements, and the disclosure of any commercial agreements such as the endorsement of products in programs. Policies and principles of those government agencies reveal country-specific orientations. For instance, in Chile, the National Television Council (Consejo Nacional de Televisión, CNTV) emphasizes the moral and cultural values characteristic of the country, the dignity of individuals, families, pluralism, democracy, peace, protection of the environment, and the spiritual and intellectual formation of children and youth within the "Chilean value" setting. The Korea Communications Standards Commission reviews the contents of broadcast ads and has a section in its guidelines specifically pertaining to "Level of Morality" issues such as respect for life and maintenance of dignity, among others. Additionally, broadcast advertising in South Korea is forbidden from disrespecting or inappropriately using a national flag, anthem, or cultural relic, in order to respect the dignity and pride of the nation.

In many countries, self-regulation is another important factor in advertising regulation. Self-regulatory agencies review claims submitted by consumers and various organizations, monitor advertising contents, and sometimes provide copy advice prior to the publication of ads. Examples include the Japan Advertising Review Organization, the National Advertising Division in the United States, the Autorregulación de la Comunicación Comercial (AACC) in Spain, the Advertising Standards Bureau in Australia, the Advertising Standards Authority in the UK, Advertising Standards Canada, the National Council for Advertising Self-Regulation (Consejo Nacional de Autorregulación Publicitaria, CONAR) in Chile, the Advertising Self-Regulation Council (Consejo de Autorregulación Publicitaria, CONARP) in Argentina, Advertising Self-Regulation Council (Consejo de Autorregulación Publicitaria, CONAR) in Peru, the National Council of Self-Regulation and Advertising Ethics (CONAR) in Mexico, the National Commission of Advertising Self-Regulation (CONARP) in Columbia, and the Autorité de la Régulation Professionnelle de la Publicité (ARPP) in France.

The amount of cases handled by each self-regulatory system varies by country. For instance, the Japan Advertising Review Organization, which was established in 1974, handled 5,794 cases in 2008, of which 312 were advertisement complaints; 5,481 dealt with pre-campaign advice. In Canada, the total number of cases received by Advertising Standards Canada ranged from 1,040 in 2006 to 1,228 in 2009. In Chile, 765 cases were admitted to CONAR between 1987 and 2009, about 30 cases per year. NAD in the United States handled 176 cases in 2007, 179 cases in 2008, 116 in 2009, and 145 in 2010. In France, the Advertising Deontology Jury (JDP) received 502 complaints in 2009.

Some countries have established dual or multiple complaint systems for their self-regulation body. In Australia, the Advertising Standards Bureau has two boards: the Advertising Standards Board for consumer complaints and the Advertising Claims Board for competitor complaints. The Advertising Claims Board adjudicates complaints between competitors on a user-pays basis. While the ACB deliberates on matters of truth, accuracy, and questions of law, the Advertising Standards Board deliberates on issues of health and safety, the use of language, the discriminatory portrayal of people, the protection of children, and the portrayal of violence, sex, sexuality, and nudity (all on a cost-free basis).

Canada's self-regulation also provides diverging avenues for different types of complaints. Advertising Standards Canada is the self-regulatory body that consists of representatives from advertisers, advertising agencies, media organizations, and the public. However, along with consumer complaints, ASC also offers a separate procedure to resolve disputes between advertisers. As a fee-based service, the Trade Dispute Procedure handles competitive disputes. Furthermore, complaints about advertising from special-interest groups are administered under ASC's Special Interest Group Complaint Procedure.

The National Advertising Division in the United States does not have duality of complaints for consumers and competitors, but in 2004 it added the Electronic Retailing Self-Regulation Program (ERSP) to provide an expeditious review of matters regarding direct-response advertising. Any commercial messages in any electronic medium—e.g., 1–800 numbers, email, or websites—are referred as "electronic retailing." Data shows that 60 cases were handled in 2007; 41 cases in 2008; 43 cases in 2009; and 39 cases in 2010. There were one to three cases each year referred on to government agencies.

Sweden represents an advertising regulatory system that employs both an Advertising Ombudsman and a Market Court, which hears unresolved cases that the ombudsman cannot mediate. The Market Court is the highest court of appeals for cases involving competition. In 2009, the Advertising Ombudsman received 400 complaints, resulting in 298 referred cases. All but 14 were resolved at this level, while remaining cases were forwarded to other relevant agencies for further reviews. The Market Court handled just under 100 cases each year from 2001 and 2009, with a maximum of 97 in 2001 and a minimum of 82 in 2008.

In many countries, advertisers can seek self-regulatory systems for copy advice prior to publication of ads. In Spain, the Autorregulación de la Comunicación Comercial (AACC) is a free service for consumers, consumer associations, and public authorities. From 1996 to 2010, 2,373 cases, on average about 170 cases per year, were handled. During the same period, 45,160 copy-advice requests were made. The copy-advice service consists of a technical opinion and/or advice on the legal and ethical correctness of a specific advertisement. It is a free service for AACC members, but nonmembers have to pay a fee to utilize the service. In France, Autorité de la Régulation Professionnelle de la Publicité (ARPP) is the major self-regulation body that provides copy advice. It normally offers a return time of 48 hours. In 2009, more than 15,000 advertisers requested copy advice and ARPP delivered within the allotted time.

In some countries, preclearance of broadcast advertising or special types of ads is mandatory. In France, all television commercials must be precleared by ARPP. It granted more than 20,000 television preclearances in 2009. A similar situation is found in Korea. Preclearance of all broadcast advertising is required, and corresponding media industry professionals provide the prior review of all ads. The Korea Broadcasters Association reviews terrestrial ads, while the Korea Cable Television and Telecommunication Association screens all cable ads. For example, in 2011, the Korea Broadcasters Association reviewed between 2,000 and 3,000 commercials every month, rendering decisions of "allowed," "not allowed," and "pending." Those advertisers whose ads fell into the "pending" decision were instructed to modify the contents of said ads in order for them to be aired.

In Canada, every broadcast advertisement directed to children must be precleared. The Canadian Association of Broadcasters developed the Broadcast Code for Advertising to Children. Broadcasters in Canada, except for Quebec, have agreed to adhere to the code as a Canadian Radio-Television Commission's condition of licensure. All children's commercials must be approved by the Children's Clearance Committee and carry a valid ASC approval number. The Children's Clearance Committee consists of industry and public representatives.

In fact, advertising targeting children receives close scrutiny in many countries. In Sweden, there is a special ombudsperson for advertising issues relating to children and to young people. Section 4 of the Swedish Marketing Act forbids advertising to children under the age of 12. In Australia, special provisions for the amount and content of advertisements directed toward children are outlined in the Children's Television Standards.

In particular, many countries have recently strengthened regulation of food and beverage advertising to children. ARPP in France specifically outlines that "advertising must not create risks for the public or for a category of the population—particularly, the most vulnerable ones such as children." In January 2010, ARPP issued a recommendation on "Eating Habits" for food ads, which, for example, cannot show unbalanced diets or people snacking between meals. Denmark also has very specific regulations regarding children's advertising, stating that it must not exploit the natural credulity of children and cannot contain any information that could harm a child.

In 2009 in Spain, an agreement was signed between television channels, the Spanish Agency of Food Security and Nutrition, and the AACC, where the television stations committed to collaborate in the application of the code of self-regulation on food advertising aimed to children under 12 years of age. The AACC has signed more than 14 codes with different professional associations, among them the Code for Children's Advertising, signed with the Spanish Association of Toy Manufacturers. In Portugal, specific limitations regarding advertising for children are set in the codes for advertising food and beverages to children. Starting from the general rule that advertising for food and beverages should not be deceptive about potential benefits that such products may induce, it states that a sedentary lifestyle cannot be instigated, approved, or advertised; that advertisers should not make direct appeals to children so as to persuade adults to acquire advertised goods; and that they should not suggest physical or other advantages that may be achieved with the acquisition of the good or service.

Such specific limitations are also found in South Korea. Broadcast advertising targeting children and adolescents may not contain expressions that the possession of the advertised product will change children's abilities and behaviors; expressions that without the advertised product, children can be an object of ridicule or feel inferior; and expressions urging children to purchase the advertised product or to pester their parents to purchase it. In Mexico, advertising should not suggest that the possession or use of certain product would provide a physical, social, or psychological advantage or disadvantage, and advertisements must not undermine parental authority, judgment, or preferences. Furthermore, advertising for alcoholic beverages may not include actors or models under the age of 25, and for tobacco may not include actors or models under the age of 18.

It is interesting to see that advertising of certain products is explicitly prohibited, especially on broadcast media. In France, the cinema sector cannot advertise except on channels dedicated to movies. In South Korea, ads for spring waters, baby formula, and pacifiers are prohibited on television channels. Tobacco and alcohol ads are prohibited in most countries on terrestrial TV. In the UK and Australia, no tobacco ads are allowed in any medium. Direct-to-consumer prescription drug advertising is prohibited in all countries except in the United States and New Zealand.

In terms of language, many restrictions can be observed. In France, the 1994 Toubon Law requires that all expressions not belonging to the French language be translated, except trademarks and advertising slogans. Similarly, in Peru, information in ads is required to be truthful, fair, easily understood, appropriate, timely and easily accessible, and in Spanish. In Portugal, advertisements must use the Portuguese language, and foreign words can be applied only exceptionally. Similarly, in South Korea, unnecessary use of foreign language is not allowed, except for brand names, slogans, corporation names, and mottos.

As advertising evolves in ever-changing media environments, countries are continuously encountering new regulatory issues. Recently, privacy issues related to the collection of purchasing and browsing data have been the subject of heated debate. Government bodies such as the FTC in United States are trying to come up with workable solutions, while self-regulation is also becoming more commonplace in the industry. The U.S. Network Advertising Initiative (NAI), composed of leading Internet advertising networks, developed a set of principles to provide consumers with ways to control the privacy of information by offering the choice to "opt out" of behavioral target marketing. Such examples showcase the efficiency of self-regulation for advertising practices, ultimately serving the interest of the industry in utilizing new technology as an advertising tool, while simultaneously contributing to the protection of consumer privacy.

Looking at the countries specifically, one can see several similarities. Almost all of the countries studied have some form of democratic government. In the European countries, Spain, Denmark, the UK, and Sweden all have a constitutional monarchy, but all have self-regulation, as well, with the power to identify and sanction advertisers and managers who violate the regulations set for advertising. The European advertising regulations are in accord with the International Chamber of Commerce and the European Advertising Standards Alliance. Many of the regulations have been modified to align with these bodies.

China, Hong Kong, and Macau are exceptions to the democratic government similarities as they are to specific tenets of free speech.

Across the various countries, one can see differences in the balance between self-regulation or industry regulation on the one hand and governmental regulations backed by law and the court systems on the other. A good example of this dichotomy is the contrast between Australia, where self-regulation handles the greater majority of complaints, and China, where the regulation is government controlled.

Regulation is determined by history, culture, business climate, and other aspects particular to each country. Its power also varies by country along with the importance of industry and the public in its development.

THE CONSOLIDATED INTERNATIONAL CHAMBER OF COMMERCE (ICC) CODE

INTERPRETATION

The Consolidated ICC Code is to be interpreted in the spirit as well as to the letter. It applies to marketing communications in their entirety, including all words and numbers (spoken and written), visual treatments, music and sound effects, and material originating from other sources.

GENERAL PROVISIONS

Article 1—Basic principles

All marketing communications should be legal, decent, honest and truthful.

All marketing communications should be prepared with a due sense of social and professional responsibility and should conform to the principles of fair competition, as generally accepted in business.

No communication should be such as to impair public confidence in marketing.

Article 2—Decency

Marketing communications should not contain statements or audio or visual treatments which offend standards of decency currently prevailing in the country and culture concerned.

Article 3—Honesty

Marketing communications should be so framed as not to abuse the trust of consumers or exploit their lack of experience or knowledge.

Relevant factors likely to affect consumers' decisions should be communicated in such a way and at such a time that consumers can take them into account.

Article 4—Social responsibility

Marketing communications should respect human dignity and should not incite or condone any form of discrimination, including that based upon race, national origin, religion, gender, age, disability or sexual orientation.

Marketing communications should not without justifiable reason play on fear or exploit misfortune or suffering.

Marketing communications should not appear to condone or incite violent, unlawful or anti-social behaviour.

Marketing communications should not play on superstition.

Article 5—Truthfulness

Marketing communications should be truthful and not misleading.

Marketing communications should not contain any statement, claim or audio or visual treatment which, directly or by implication, omission, ambiguity or exaggeration, is likely to mislead the consumer, in particular, but not exclusively, with regard to:

- characteristics of the product which are material, i.e. likely to influence the consumer's choice, such as: nature, composition, method and date of manufacture, range of use, efficiency and performance, quantity, commercial or geographical origin or environmental impact;
- the value of the product and the total price to be paid by the consumer;
- terms for delivery, exchange, return, repair and maintenance;
- terms of guarantee;
- copyright and industrial property rights such as patents, trade marks, designs and models and trade names;
- compliance with standards;
- official recognition or approval, awards such as medals, prizes and diplomas;
- the extent of benefits for charitable causes.

Article 6—Use of technical/scientific data and terminology

Marketing communications should not

- misuse technical data, e.g. research results or quotations from technical and scientific publications;
- present statistics in such a way as to exaggerate the validity of a product claim;
- use scientific terminology or vocabulary in such a way as falsely to suggest that a product claim has scientific validity.

Article 7—Use of "free" and "guarantee"

The term "free," e.g. "free gift" or "free offer," should be used only

- where the offer involves no obligation whatsoever; or
- where the only obligation is to pay shipping and handling charges which should not exceed the cost estimated to be incurred by the marketer, or
- in conjunction with the purchase of another product, provided the price of that product has not been increased to cover all or part of the cost of the offer.

Marketing communications should not state or imply that a "guarantee," "warranty" or other expression having substantially the same meaning, offers the consumer rights additional to those provided by law when it does not.

The terms of any guarantee or warranty, including the name and address of the guarantor, should be easily available to the consumer and limitations on consumer rights or remedies, where permitted by law, should be clear and conspicuous.

Article 8–Substantiation

Descriptions, claims or illustrations relating to verifiable facts in marketing communications should be capable of substantiation. Such substantiation should be available so that evidence can be produced without delay and upon request to the self-regulatory organisations responsible for the implementation of the Code.

Article 9—Identification

Marketing communications should be clearly distinguishable as such, whatever their form and whatever the medium used.

When an advertisement appears in a medium containing news or editorial matter, it should be so presented that it is readily recognisable as an advertisement and the identity of the advertiser should be apparent (see also article 10).

Marketing communications should not misrepresent their true commercial purpose. Hence a communication promoting the sale of a product should not be disguised as for example market research, consumer surveys, user-generated content, private blogs or independent reviews.

Article 10—Identity

The identity of the marketer should be apparent.

Marketing communications should, where appropriate, include contact information to enable the consumer to get in touch with the marketer without difficulty.

The above does not apply to communications with the sole purpose of attracting attention to communication activities to follow (e.g. so-called "teaser advertisements").

Article 11—Comparisons

Marketing communications containing comparisons should be so designed that the comparison is not likely to mislead, and should comply with the principles of fair competition. Points of comparison should be based on facts which can be substantiated and should not be unfairly selected.

Article 12—Denigration

Marketing communications should not denigrate any person or group of persons, firm, organisation, industrial or commercial activity, profession or product, or seek to bring it or them into public contempt or ridicule.

Article 13—Testimonials

Marketing communications should not contain or refer to any testimonial, endorsement or supportive documentation unless it is genuine, verifiable and relevant.

Testimonials or endorsements which have become obsolete or misleading through passage of time should not be used.

Article 14—Portrayal or imitation of persons and references to personal property

Marketing communications should not portray or refer to any persons, whether in a private or a public capacity, unless prior permission has been obtained; nor should marketing communications without prior permission depict or refer to any person's property in a way likely to convey the impression of a personal endorsement of the product or organisation involved.

Article 15—Exploitation of goodwill

Marketing communications should not make unjustifiable use of the name, initials, logo and/or trademarks of another firm, company or institution.

Marketing communications should not in any way take undue advantage of another firm's, individual's or institution's goodwill in its name, brands or other intellectual property, or take advantage of the goodwill earned by other marketing campaigns without prior consent.

Article 16—Imitation

Marketing communications should not imitate those of another marketer in any way likely to mislead or confuse the consumer, for example through the general layout, text, slogan, visual treatment, music or sound effects.

Where a marketer has established a distinctive marketing communications campaign in one or more countries, other marketers should not imitate that campaign in other countries where the marketer who originated the campaign may operate, thereby preventing the extension of the campaign to those countries within a reasonable period of time.

Article 17—Safety and health

Marketing communications should not, without justification on educational or social grounds, contain any visual portrayal or any description of potentially dangerous practices, or situations which show a disregard for safety or health, as defined by local national standards.

Instructions for use should include appropriate safety warnings and, where necessary, disclaimers.

Children should be shown to be under adult supervision whenever a product or an activity involves a safety risk.

Information provided with the product should include proper directions for use and full instructions covering health and safety aspects whenever necessary.

Such health and safety warnings should be made clear by the use of pictures, text or a combination of both.

Article 18—Children and young people

Special care should be taken in marketing communications directed to or featuring children or young people. The following provisions apply to marketing communications addressed to children and young people as defined in national laws and regulations relevant to such communications.

- Such communications should not undermine positive social behaviour, lifestyles and attitudes;
- Products unsuitable for children or young people should not be advertised in media targeted to them, and advertisements directed to children or young people should not be inserted in media where the editorial matter is unsuitable for them.

Material unsuitable for children should be clearly identified as such.

For rules on data protection relating specifically to children's personal information see article 19.

<u>*Inexperience and credulity*</u>

Marketing communications should not exploit inexperience or credulity, with particular regard to the following areas:

1. When demonstrating a product's performance and use, marketing communications should not

   - minimise the degree of skill or understate the age level generally required to assemble or operate products;
   - exaggerate the true size, value, nature, durability and performance of the product;
   - fail to disclose information about the need for additional purchases, such as accessories, or individual items in a collection or series, required to produce the result shown or described.

2. While the use of fantasy is appropriate for younger as well as older children, it should not make it difficult for them to distinguish between reality and fantasy.
3. Marketing communications directed to children should be clearly distinguishable to them as such.

Avoidance of harm

Marketing communications should not contain any statement or visual treatment that could have the effect of harming children or young people mentally, morally or physically. Children and young people should not be portrayed in unsafe situations or engaging in actions harmful to themselves or others, or be encouraged to engage in potentially hazardous activities or behaviour.

Social values

Marketing communications should not suggest that possession or use of the promoted product will give a child or young person physical, psychological or social advantages over other children or young people, or that not possessing the product will have the opposite effect.

Marketing communications should not undermine the authority, responsibility, judgment or tastes of parents, having regard to relevant social and cultural values.

Marketing communications should not include any direct appeal to children and young people to persuade their parents or other adults to buy products for them.

Prices should not be presented in such a way as to lead children and young people to an unrealistic perception of the cost or value of the product, for example by minimising them. Marketing communications should not imply that the product being promoted is immediately within the reach of every family budget.

Marketing communications which invite children and young people to contact the marketer should encourage them to obtain the permission of a parent or other appropriate adult if any cost, including that of a communication, is involved.

For other specific rules on marketing communications with regard to children:

- in the digital interactive media see chapter D, article D5;
- within the context of food and non-alcoholic beverages see the ICC Framework for responsible food and beverage marketing communication.

Article 19—Data protection and privacy

When collecting personal data from individuals, care should be taken to respect and protect their privacy by complying with relevant rules and regulations.

Collection of data and notice

When personal information is collected from consumers, it is essential to ensure that the individuals concerned are aware of the purpose of the collection and of any intention to transfer the data to a third party for that third party's marketing purposes. (Third parties do not include agents or others who provide technical or operational support to the marketer and who do not use or disclose personal information for any other purpose.) It is best to inform the individual at the time of collection; when it is not possible to do so this should be done as soon as possible thereafter.

Use of data

Personal data collected in accordance with this code should be

- collected for specified and legitimate purposes and not used in any manner incompatible with those purposes;
- adequate, relevant and not excessive in relation to the purpose for which they are collected and/or further processed;
- accurate and kept up to date;
- preserved for no longer than is required for the purpose for which the data were collected or further processed.

Security of processing

Adequate security measures should be in place, having regard to the sensitivity of the information, in order to prevent unauthorised access to, or disclosure of, the personal data.

If the information is transferred to third parties, it should be established that they employ at least an equivalent level of security measures.

Children's personal information

When personal information is collected from individuals known or reasonably believed to be children 12 and younger, guidance should be provided to parents or legal guardians about protecting children's privacy if feasible.

Children should be encouraged to obtain a parent's or other appropriate adult's permission before providing information via digital interactive media, and reasonable steps should be taken to check that such permission has been given.

Only as much personal information should be collected as is necessary to enable the child to engage in the featured activity.

Data collected from children should not be used to address marketing communications to the children's parents or other family members without the consent of the parent.

Identifiable personal information about individuals known to be children should only be disclosed to third parties after obtaining consent from a parent or legal guardian or where disclosure is authorised by law. (Third parties do not include agents or others who provide technical or operational support to the marketer and who do not use or disclose children's personal information for any other purpose.)

Additional rules specific to marketing communications to children using digital interactive media can be found in chapter D, article D5.

Privacy policy

Those who collect data in connection with marketing communication activities should have a privacy policy, the terms of which should be readily available to consumers, and should provide a clear statement if any collection or processing of data is taking place, whether it is self-evident or not.

In jurisdictions where no privacy legislation currently exists, it is recommended that privacy principles such as those of the ICC Privacy Toolkit (available from ICC website) are adopted and implemented.

Rights of the consumer

Appropriate measures should be taken to ensure that consumers understand and exercise their rights

- to opt out of marketing lists including the right to sign on to general preference (services);
- to require that their data are not made available to third parties for their marketing purposes; and
- to rectify incorrect data which are held about them.

Where a consumer has expressed a wish not to receive marketing communications using a specific medium, whether via a preference service or by other means, this wish should be respected. Additional rules specific to the use of the digital interactive media and consumer rights are to be found in chapter D.

Cross-border transactions

Particular care should be taken to maintain the data protection rights of the consumer when personal data are transferred from the country in which they are collected to another country.

When data processing is conducted in another country, all reasonable steps should be taken to ensure that adequate security measures are in place and that the data protection principles set out in this code are respected. The use of the ICC model clauses covering agreements between the originator of the marketing list and the processor or user in another country is recommended (available from ICC website).

Article 20—Transparency on cost of communication

Where the cost to consumers of accessing a message or communicating with the marketer is higher than the standard cost of postage or telecommunications, e.g. "premium rate" for an online message, connection or telephone number, this cost should be made clear to consumers, expressed either as "cost per minute" or as "cost per message."

When this information is provided on-line, consumers should be clearly informed at the time when they are about to access the message or online service, and be allowed a reasonable period of time to disconnect without incurring the charge.

Where a communication involves such a cost, the consumer should not be kept waiting for an unreasonably long time in order to achieve the purpose of the communication and calls should not be charged until the consumer can begin to fulfil that purpose.

Article 21—Unsolicited products and undisclosed costs

Marketing communications associated with the practice of sending unsolicited products to consumers who are then asked for payment (inertia selling), including statements or suggestions that recipients are required to accept and pay for such products, should be avoided.

Marketing communications which solicit a response constituting an order for which payment will be required (e.g. an entry in a publication) should make this unambiguously clear.

Marketing communications soliciting orders should not be presented in a form which might be mistaken for an invoice, or otherwise falsely suggest that payment is due.

For specific rules on unsolicited individually addressed digital marketing communications, see chapter D, article D4.

Article 22—Environmental behaviour

Marketing communications should not appear to condone or encourage actions which contravene the law, self-regulatory codes or generally accepted standards of environmentally responsible behaviour.

They should respect the principles set out in chapter E, Environmental Claims in Marketing Communications.

Article 23—Responsibility

These general rules on responsibility apply to all forms of marketing communications. Rules on responsibility with special relevance to certain activities or media can be found in the chapters devoted to those activities and media.

Responsibility for the observance of the rules of conduct laid down in the Code rests with the marketer whose products are the subject of the marketing communications, with the communications practitioner or agency, and with the publisher, media owner or contractor.

Marketers have overall responsibility for the marketing communications of their products.

Agencies or other practitioners should exercise due care and diligence in the preparation of marketing communications and should operate in such a way as to enable marketers to fulfil their responsibilities.

Publishers, media owners or contractors, who publish, transmit, deliver or distribute marketing communications, should exercise due care in the acceptance of them and their presentation to the public.

Individuals employed by a firm, company or institution falling into any of the above categories and who take part in the planning, creation, publication or transmission of a marketing communication are responsible, to an extent commensurate with their respective positions, for ensuring that the rules of the Code are observed and should act accordingly.

The Code applies to the marketing communication in its entire content and form, including testimonials and statements, and audio or visual material originating from other sources. The fact that the content or form of a marketing communication may originate wholly or in part from other sources does not justify non-observance of the Code rules.

Article 24—Effect of subsequent redress for contravention

Subsequent correction and/or appropriate redress for a contravention of the Code, by the party responsible, is desirable but does not excuse the contravention.

Article 25—Implementation

The Code and the principles enshrined in it, should be adopted and implemented, nationally and internationally, by the relevant local, national or regional self-regulatory bodies. The Code should also be applied, where appropriate, by all organisations, companies and individuals involved and at all stages in the marketing communication process.

Marketers, communications practitioners or advertising agencies, publishers, media owners and contractors should be familiar with the Code and with other relevant local self-regulatory guidelines on advertising and other marketing communications, and should familiarise themselves with decisions taken by the appropriate self-regulatory body.

They should ensure an appropriate means exists for consumers to make a complaint and that consumers can readily be aware of it and use it easily.

Further details regarding implementation of the Code by companies and other bodies can be found in the Implementation Guide for the ICC Marketing Codes.

Requests for interpretation of the principles contained in this code may be submitted to the ICC Code Interpretation Panel.

Article 26—Respect for self-regulatory decisions

No marketer, communications practitioner or advertising agency, publisher, media owner or contractor should be party to the publication or distribution of an advertisement or other marketing communication which has been found unacceptable by the relevant self-regulatory body.

All parties are encouraged to include in their contracts and other agreements pertaining to advertising and other marketing communication, a statement committing the signatories to adhere to the applicable self-regulatory rules and to respect decisions and rulings made by the appropriate self-regulatory body.

Where no effective self-regulatory codes and arrangements are in place in a particular country, all parties are encouraged to include in their contracts and other agreements pertaining to advertising and marketing communication a statement committing the signatories to respect the current Consolidated ICC Code.

Source: International Chamber of Commerce (ICC), CodesCentre™ for advertising & marketing, www.codescentre.com/index.php/icc-code.

Appendix B

THE EUROPEAN ADVERTISING STANDARDS ALLIANCE (EASA)

The European Advertising Standards Alliance (EASA) was formed in 1992, bringing together groups from European countries that had met on an ad hoc basis to discuss self-regulation processes generally and cross-border advertisement problems specifically.

In 1997, industry professionals agreed to support the EASA mission to promote the value of self-regulation. A restructuring in 2002 brought the national self-regulatory members and the industry advertisers, agencies, and media into a partnership with EASA, thus making it a single voice speaking for advertising best practices as well as a forum for bringing complaints forward.

Mid-2004, a Self-Regulatory Charter was agreed upon. Some of the tenets of the charter were to develop codes for behavior based upon the International Chamber of Commerce Codes (ICC). The EASA Codes included promulgation of best practices, handling of complaints, and the involvement of nongovernmental persons in the adjudication process.

According to EASA, it "promotes high ethical standards in commercial communication by means of effective self-regulation while being mindful of national differences of culture, legal and commercial practice." It also states that both consumers and the industry are protected by its work.

EASA is a nonprofit entity. It speaks for the value of self-regulation throughout Europe. Beyond the promulgation of best practices, EASA handles complaints that cross national borders. EASA provides information on how to follow a complaint within a country to organizations that are members of EASA and also provides guidelines to facilitate the handling of a complaint.

As to sanctions, EASA urges resolution of a complaint as quickly as possible. Various means of enforcing self-regulatory organization guidelines are suggested. These may include adverse publicity by publishing decisions and media refusal to take misleading advertising. When these practices are not sufficient, EASA encourages the use of more formal action through the designated statutory bodies of the country involved.

There were 21 cross-border complaints from 2006 through 2011. Typically, EASA will direct the complaint to the valid self-regulation organization for the country involved.

For additional information on EASA practices and the provisions of its two charters, one may search the website: http://www.easa-alliance.org.

INDEX

Page numbers in *italics* indicate illustrations

A

ABOUT THE EDITORS
AND THE CONTRIBUTORS

Soontae An is Associate Vice President of International Affairs and Associate Professor in the Division of Media Studies at Ewha Womens University in Seoul, Korea. She is editor of *Korean Health Communication Research*. Her research centers on various advertising issues such as pharmaceutical advertising, commercial speech, and food advertising targeting children. She is cohost of a weekly televised ombudsman program on SBS, a major television network in Korea.

Jean J. Boddewyn is Emeritus Professor of International Business at the Baruch College of the City University of New York. He was editor of *International Studies of Management and Organization* for many years.

Paulo Faustino is a Media Policies, Economics, Management and Marketing Professor at Porto University in Portugal. He has coedited several books, the latest being *The Media as a Driver of the Information Society.*

Maria-Elena Gronemeyer is a professor at the School of Communications in the Pontificia Universidad Católica de Chile in Santiago. Her research areas include ethics and regulation.

Gayle Kerr is an associate professor in advertising and IMC in the School of Advertising, Marketing and Public Relations, Queensland University of Technology, Australia. Her areas of research include advertising ethics and self-regulation, management, and strategic research.

Liu Jing is a professor in the Department of Advertising, Academy of Art Design at North China University of Technology in Beijing, China. Her research work centers on management and marketing.

Mercedes Medina is an associate professor at the University of Navarra in Pamplona, Spain. Her research focuses on media companies and market analysis in Europe and Latin America.

Mariko Morimoto is an associate professor of marketing at the Faculty of Liberal Arts, Sophia University in Tokyo, Japan. Her work centers on cross-cultural advertising, integrated marketing communication, and consumers' privacy concerns on the Internet.

Luísa Ribeiro is on the economics faculty of the University of Porto in Portugal. She worked in industry for several years and is currently studying for a PhD.

Dan Shaver is the immediate past director of the Media Management and Transformation Centre in the Jönköping International School of Business in Jönköping, Sweden. He is currently affiliated with Elon University in North Carolina. He is also coeditor of the *International Journal on Media Management.*

Jean-Pierre Teyssier is the immediate past president of the French Advertising Standards Authority, having served in that role from 1999 to 2010. He is a lecturer at Sciences Po in Paris, France, and Professor at the Superior School of Advertising in Paris.

Dr. Mary Alice Shaver (1938–2012) earned her bachelor's degree in 1959 from St. Mary-of-the-Woods College in Indiana, her MS in 1973 from the University of Illinois, and her PhD in 1984 from Indiana University. She taught at the University of North Carolina at Chapel Hill, Florida International University in Miami, and Queens College in Charlotte. Her research focused on advertising, advertising management, competition for advertising among media, and media management.

She served as president of the Association for Education in Journalism and Mass Communication and as president of the American Academy of Advertising. She was the author of *Make the Sale! Selling Media with Marketing* as well as dozens of journal articles and conference presentations.

Dr. Shaver left UNC-CH to become chair of the Department of Advertising in the College of Communication Arts at Michigan State University. From there, she went to the University of Central Florida in Orlando to become director of the Nicholson School of Communication. She concluded her career as the Hamrin Professor of Media Management in the Media Management and Transformation Center of the Jönköping International School of Business in Jönköping, Sweden.